Wilfrid Harrington is extremely well-known both in Ireland and in the US where his works have been published by Helicon, Paulist Newman and Alba House. His major work is *The Bible: Record of Revelation*, the French edition of which was published by Editions du Seuil.

# THE PATH OF BIBLICAL THEOLOGY

Other works by Wilfrid Harrington

*Record of the Fulfillment. The New Testament*, Chicago/London 1967.
*Vatican II on Revelation* (Harrington/Walsh) Dublin 1967.
*The Gospel According to St Luke: A Commentary*, New York/London 1967.
*The Promise to Love. A Scriptural View of Marriage*, New York/London 1968.
*The Apocalypse of St John. A Commentary/Understanding the Apocalypse*, London/New York 1969.
*Nouvelle Introduction à la Bible*, Paris 1971.

Wilfrid J. Harrington OP

# THE
# PATH OF BIBLICAL
# THEOLOGY

Gill and Macmillan

First published in 1973

Gill and Macmillan Limited
2 Belvedere Place
Dublin 1
and in London through association with the
Macmillan
Group of Publishing Companies

*Nihil obstat:* Liam Walsh OP
            Benedict Hegarty OP
*Imprimi potest:* Flannan Hynes OP, Provisional. 19 March 1972.

*Nihil obstat:* Eduardus Gallen, Censor Theol. Deput.

*Imprimi potest:* Dermitius, Archiep. Dublinen. Hiberniae Primas. Dublini
die 14a Novembris, anno 1972.

The *Nihil obstat* and the *Imprimi potest* are a declaration that a book on
publication is considered to be free from doctrinal or moral error. This declaration does not imply approval of or agreement with the contents, opinions
or statements expressed.

7171 0581 4

Jacket designed by Hilliard Hayden

Printing history: 5 4 3 2 1

Printed and bound in the Republic of Ireland by the
Book Printing Division of Smurfit Print and Packaging Ltd.
Dublin

# Contents

CHAPTER IV

# ABBREVIATIONS

| | |
|---|---|
| BibTB | *Biblical Theology Bulletin* |
| CBQ | *Catholic Biblical Quarterly* |
| ETL | *Ephemerides Theologicae Lovanienses* |
| ExposTimes | *Expository Times* |
| JBL | *Journal of Biblical Literature* |
| NRT | *Nouvelle Revue Théologique* |
| RB | *Revue Biblique* |
| RSPT | *Revue de Sciences Philosophiques et Théologiques* |
| RSR | *Recherches de Science Religieuse* |
| RT | *Revue Thomiste* |
| ZATWiss | *Zeitschrift für die Alttestamentliche Wissenschaft* |
| NovTest | *Novum Testamentum* |

# Preface

VATICAN II has described Scripture as the 'foundation' and
the study of Scripture as the 'soul' of theology—the implication is that systematic theology should build on the foundation of biblical theology and be enlightened by it. It has
become all the more important, then, to discover what
biblical theology really is. Scriptural scholars are agreed that
we must begin with the theological views of the biblical
writers themselves; and since a pluralism of theological
views and ideas is a feature of the Bible, we find 'theologies'
within the Bible itself. Some would be satisfied with presenting these theologies as so many facets of God's revelation.
Others, however, argue that theology, in a proper sense,
demands a synthesis; hence biblical *theology* must be a
synthesis of biblical *theologies*. But the Bible does not easily
lend itself to systematisation. It may be that the extreme
difficulty of shaping any acceptable synthesis—one which
would not do violence to the distinctive categories and
dynamic character of the Bible—is a discouraging factor. A
synthesis is desirable, but some doubt that a satisfactory
synthesis is feasible.

With a view to making some contribution towards a
clarification of the situation, I have written this book. In it
I survey the work done, respectively, in the theology of the
Old Testament, the theology of the New Testament, and
the theology of the Bible as a whole. I have not been content
to trace the path of biblical theology; I have, besides, offered
lengthy summaries of the outstanding works in these areas.
In this way it is hoped, indeed intended, that the book will
be useful not only to the biblical student, but also to the
student of dogmatic theology who could not himself reason-

ably be expected to familiarise himself at first hand with the many *Theologies* of both Testaments. In the fourth part of the book I look to the theorists, to those who have expressed views as to what biblical theology really is, or what it ought to be. And then I have moved to the vital question of the place of biblical theology in the wider area of theology in general—in particular, the relation of biblical theology to Roman Catholic dogmatic theology. The book is meant to depict the method, the scope and the range of biblical theology. It is also a call for a practical recognition of the place of biblical theology: the foundation of all theology, the living soul of theological study and development.

Not for the first time I gladly acknowledge my indebtedness to my friends: Michael Glazier who encouraged me to undertake this work in the first place—without his persuasion I am sure that I never would have begun this project; and Penny Livermore whose painstaking and invaluable help has added a needed quality and dimension to the book.

Wilfrid Harrington

# Introduction

How does one approach an 'introduction' to a work that is itself largely a compendium of Introductions? For our answer we turn to the Scriptures themselves and to a text which seems, at first glance, to be the most burdensome, belaboured with words, and uninviting passage in the Bible: Psalm 119. Yes, this mechanical alphabetical psalm, the longest and most structured in the psalter, we shall take as an outline in our preview of the work to follow. For, working through this psalm (a process similar to that of working through the sometimes ponderous subject of biblical theology), one unearths certain treasure verses describing God's *word*. And since his word is the ultimate concern of biblical theology and of this study, we shall select some of these verses to offer a glimpse into the treasures contained in the books we shall be discussing. Whether it be in the psalm or in our theologies, we can but spot certain high-lights—some of which may seem needless but follow from the scope of this work. All, however, are drawn together by that living word.

## The Purpose of Biblical Theology

*Remember your word to your servant, in which you have given me hope. This is my comfort in my affliction—that your promise gives me life* (Ps. 119:49f.).

Somehow, with this call upon God to 'remember' his people with the word in which they have found life and hope, we are reminded of the whole purpose of biblical theology—as of the Bible: to bear witness to God. It is a witness not so much of or to the words themselves, but to the *reality* behind the words; this is why the deeper reaches of Scripture, perceived really only by the eyes of faith, belong to the field of biblical theology. This theology bears the character of witness because it is 'confessional', a theology of recital in which the men and women of the Bible confess their faith in God's redemptive acts. The Bible's authority can be seen as something personal in which the witness borne by the Holy Spirit is matched and understood by that in the believer's own spirit. As the record of the original witness borne to Jesus in the apostolic age, there must be continuous recourse to the Bible as a source. God's 'word to his servant' is his guarantee of the first beginnings found in Scripture, and all subsequent trends return to this sure pledge.

Yes, God's 'word'—as Scripture, as promise, as the Word himself—has meaning, really, only as a gateway to himself as the *living* God. Here, at the outset, we would do well to state a thought we shall often repeat explicitly and conclude silently in our hearts: 'though we speak much, we cannot reach the end, and the sum of all our words is: He is the all' (*Sirach* 43 : 27). Out of the classic division of biblical theology into theology, soteriology and anthropology, the theologian must bring out the 'one thing needful': the *living* God and his revelation to *persons*. Though he is beyond all plans and systems in theology, he is the centre of all of them; the very term 'theo-logy' implies both the presence and living action of God. It is the nature of this Yahweh which lends to Israel's religion its emphasis on the heart, and his one signature is threaded throughout both Testaments to create the unity of the Bible. Stated differently, since all books of the Bible are inspired by this same living God, they *must* be unified by God's own plan. It is the theologian's task to deepen our faith in this plan by unveiling this unity. Well was the child of the Isaian prophecy, and its fulfilment, called *Immanu-el* —God-with-us—for the whole Bible but testifies to this God living in our midst, as expressed most perfectly in Jesus' 'fare-well' blessing: 'Lo, I am with you always . . .' (*Matt.* 28 : 20). Through contact with the person and work of Jesus, the disciples grasped his identity far more perfectly than any dogma could define: they simply felt themselves to be in the presence of the living God himself. The Bible—and hence, biblical theology—is one whole because of God's fidelity to his promise to Israel, progressively revealing himself until his full disclosure in Jesus.

And so, God has given the psalmist, and all of us, *hope* in his word—in this Book, in himself, in his Son—and life through his promise. This leads us to consider one important theme which we shall find recurring differently in the works we shall be studying: the concept of 'promise' and 'fulfilment' as an interpretation for the words and events in both Testaments, as well as the relationship between them. The whole of salvation history can be seen as an unceasing movement of promise and fulfilment, or prophecy and accomplishment. The Old Testament is simply a 'veil' of provisional structures in which Jesus is present as an object of faith until he himself comes to remove that veil. We shall see how the 'promise-fulfilment' method for biblical theology is valid—provided we realise that not a method, but a fact unites the Testaments: the advent of Jesus is that fact, and he opens hearts to understand a meaning which the earlier words already had on their own. He is the fulfilment of all 'promises'. But, 'fulfilment' is simply the wholeness of what was already in part. It is the flowering of what was already in seed and tender shoot.

The psalmist has called upon God to 'remember' his words even as all biblical writings can be seen as God's people 'remembering' what God has done on their behalf. This leads us to another important approach in biblical theology: that which considers history, or events, as revelation. The events in Israel's history point to a manifest working of divine Providence, of the living God. Because *we* continue to participate in those events, the continuing life of the Church is the most conducive milieu for pursuing biblical theology. The entire Bible can be seen as the Church's documentary history concerning Jesus and his gospel. God makes himself known by the events where his action becomes tangible, not by mystical contemplation. Scripture gives authentic expression to God's word as it has been historically transmitted through those events and been perfectly realised in the living Word, Jesus. This is why the basis of biblical theology must be Christian: the apostolic Church grasped that God's turning to mankind throughout history had found its ultimate expression in Jesus, and the Scriptures objectify this in permanent, verbal form. This was the faith of the primitive Church—whose conviction, hence whose Scripture, must serve as a standard for the present Church. Indeed, it is through reflective faith and believing interpretation that the events throughout Israel's history—and the Christ-event—came to light. Yes, biblical theology must keep us mindful of God's actions in *history*, in real life as it is lived in community; dealing with history, it must consider both facts and interpretation, a faith both lived and proclaimed.

In comparing biblical and dogmatic theology, a comparison we shall eventually reach in this work, it could be felt that, because biblical theology must find its starting point in the events and words of the actual text, it is more restricted and confined than other branches of theology. But, just the opposite is the case. For, while the eyes of the mind and its historical-critical methods welcome the 'earthen vessel', the concrete structure of the 'letter' provided by the actual events, institutions and words in the biblical text, the heart sees through this with the eyes of faith to the treasure of the 'spirit' within the letter (cf. *2 Cor.* 4:7). It is indeed a life-giving spirit, as the biblical theologian discovers—and as our psalmist, too, has found in that God's promise gives him life. As we shall see, it is the indestructibility of *life* with God which is the sustained note throughout the Bible and the conviction sustaining our authors. It is faith's 'nevertheless' (cf. *Ps.* 73:23) that, even as God is with us, so too—come what may—are we with him. This, for us, is life. The fruit of biblical theology is to deepen our conviction: 'As for me, it is good to be near God. I have made my place of shelter in Yahweh' (*Ps.* 73:28).

## The Fruits of Biblical Theology

*How sweet are your words to my taste, sweeter than honey to my mouth!* (*Ps.* 119:103).

If the psalmist has found comfort and life in God's word, he has known, too, the sweetness of that word—the joys of personal meditation on the words of Scripture and personal

communion with their author. And so too, lest we feel over-
laden by the solemnity of our subject, it is good for us to
pause and consider some of the 'joys' in the study of biblical
theology, some of the fruits which can be 'sweet to our taste'.
We shall come to see how frequently our theologians point
out the consistent biblical attitude of the *goodness* of life on
earth, the wholeness of God's gifts to man—the fruits of
earth and sky, the works of his hands. We shall see how this
goodness of human life and created things reaches its epitome
when material things become vehicles for spiritual truths—
the biblical basis for our sacraments. As we trace salvation
history, we shall hear the Good News unfolding—from the
Old Testament's hailing of a messenger to come, 'How
beautiful upon the mountains are the feet of him who brings
glad tidings!' (*Is.* 52:7), to the coming of *the* messenger
himself, whose birth was the occasion for 'glad tidings of
great joy' (*Luke* 2:10). There is indeed Good News for
us, the gospel, in coming to see how God, who has spoken to
his people in the old covenant as a Father to his child or a
Lord to his servants and handmaids, gives us then the new,
intimate communion with himself through his Son. We shall
share in the abiding sense of wonder, of expectation, which
flows through both Testaments, the continual new beginnings and fresh starts as old material is reinterpreted in the
light of new events. We shall share in biblical man's sense
of freedom on hearing God's assurance, 'remember not the
former things' (*Is.* 43:18), strengthened by Jesus' refrain,
'Truly, *I* say to you . . .'. And, through the careful investigations of our theologians, we shall be helped in our own
reading of the Bible to find its peculiar plenitude, a fullness
whose real richness lies in what is unsaid!

And then, there is one particular recurrent subject in all
our theologies which is itself joy, as we have seen in Jesus'
parable of the man who went and sold his all to obtain this
treasure: the kingdom—this quiet, yet dynamic, reality
which embraces the goods of both this age and the age to
come. It is, indeed, preserved by strife and suffering in this
life—the cross. But it reaches triumphal fulfilment in life
hereafter—a life in the kingdom which is brought here and
now in Jesus. And perhaps the clearest sign that we share in

this kingdom is that given at the Last Supper. The *certainty* that God will live with his people and they with him is the golden thread of the kingdom woven throughout the entire Bible. It is this which lifts man beyond a treadmill existence of futile repetition and gives him the freedom of the children of God. Yes, if biblical theology can provide even a glimpse into this marvellous reality of God's 'kingdom come', then its taste—its task—will indeed be sweet.

But, if we were to measure, surely *the* most refreshing fruit of reading the Bible is a deeper knowledge and love of God himself. Biblical theology can foster this by its consistent care to point out the nature, the attributes, the personhood of this our God. Although he defies merely human terms and categories, the 'justice', 'mercy', 'holiness', and above all the tender 'loving-kindness'—*hesed*—of this God are brought out clearly again and again through the theologians' study of the usage of these descriptions of God in the Old Testament. In the New Testament, there is a similar consideration of the different names given to Jesus—a topic which holds many interesting discoveries for the reader. We shall be led over and over to realise God's inexhaustible goodness, his love in Jesus from which nothing can separate us. The Christian can grasp the meaning of the Old Testament really only because he himself has been grasped by Jesus. Before, the Hebrew man heard, 'I am the Lord your God'; now, the Christian man speaks, and confesses, 'My Lord and my God!' (*John* 20:28).

## Guiding Principles in Biblical Theology

*Forever, O Lord, your word is firmly fixed in the heavens* (*Ps.* 119:89).

God's word is fixed and unchanging forever, unchanging as his providence and his marvellous purposefulness which flow throughout the pages of the Bible. This leads us to outline our theologians' own purposefulness in considering certain 'fixed' elements in biblical theology. We turn first— not only in respect, but also in recognition of its great value —to Vatican II's document on revelation, *Dei Verbum.*

Here, the study of Scripture is termed the 'soul of theology'
—a theology which must rely on the written word as well
as on sacred tradition, and which is built upon and strengthened by the foundation of Scripture. Contemporary man will
put new questions to the word of God; the biblical theologian must offer new answers by turning again to that word
and discerning new shades of meaning in its 'fixed' truth.

We shall be considering various approaches to the study
of biblical theology: the 'structural' or 'cross-sectioned',
'diachronic', 'lexicographic' and the method of 'biblical
themes'. And, we shall discern how the different authors
would group the books of the Bible, and in particular the
writings of the New Testament—what weight they give to
their individual messages and how they relate them to the
whole. We shall, at times, comment ourselves with personal
viewpoints—generally making clear that it is not 'either-or'
or 'black-and-white' in relation to these methods, but a combination of many. God's word *is* 'fixed'; and, indeed, with
him, the Father of Lights, there is 'no change or shadow of
variation' (*Jas.* 1 : 17). But, there are many ways of *receiving*
his word—as many as his 'every good and every perfect gift'
which comes down from 'above' where his word is fixed. One
thing is clear—a requirement for the theologian almost as
unchanging as the word: he must himself have worked
through the Bible and come to understand it as God's own
voice—come to know that word, and that God, as intimate
friends.

Something further emerges which is a consistent factor
noted by biblical theologians: biblical theology can never
really be a rounded 'system' containing all the fine points
of dogmatic theology, and never can it be really complete.
This is because neither the Old Testament nor the New
Testament—nor the individual writings within them—claim
to present any such system of doctrine. The living, vibrant
word cannot be forced into a straitjacket of scholastic terminology. The Bible reflects man's *experience* of God, and
there will always lie a gap between this and trying to communicate it in oral or written form. Taken as the gospel
itself, New Testament theology cannot but be more than
theory or system; it is a call to hearts. It is impossible to

'theorise' about the whole great mystery of God's plan for our redemption!

Another common concern is with the definition of the 'literal' versus the 'fuller' senses of Scripture. We shall see how man has devised as many different approaches to this as he has found shades in that fuller sense itself! But, we shall also see that these 'secondary senses' come down to the fact that the whole Bible has a meaning, in God's intent, beyond that of any single passage. The exegete's understanding draws them out. A further common feature of our theologies is an interest in the biblical language and idiom, necessary to bring out the religious significance in biblical typology. The old Hebrew idiom was necessary for the proclamation of Jesus as the *Messiah* of Israel; understanding his own language and style is an essential aspect of New Testament studies. And the only vehicle possible to translate authentically the divine message of salvation is the 'symbolic' language of the Bible.

As for the various opinions on the scope of biblical theology, they range from those who would treat the Bible in 'cross-section', to those who would see it as composed of various 'stories' of events with commentaries, to those who would find a single 'source' which has flowed into different channels. All these methods, quite realistically, consider particular texts and groupings. However, the 'perfect' biblical theology remains but an ideal beyond our limited vision. This complete work would seek out the whole of God's self-revelation in the entire canon: taking up all the divine words, a total understanding of revealed faith could be reached. Most of our authors do conclude that somehow, though at the cost of trial and error, the venture towards *one* biblical theology should be made.

It is somehow encouraging that these very limitations of our human vision should be a fixed assumption of so many of our authors. Indeed, one of the most noteworthy biblical texts on God's word points precisely to man's limited knowledge in relation to this word, fixed in the heavens as it is: 'As the heavens are higher than the earth, so are my ways higher than your ways and my thoughts than your thoughts' (*Is.* 55:9). Different theologies in the Church, as in the Bible, stem from the difference between the one truth of God's word and man's many attempts to explain it, his understanding being so imperfect. The apparent limitations in revelation come from *man*—his own contingency amidst the conditions of culture and history. Moreover, man not fully accepting himself as man cannot begin to grasp the full life of the Word who became man. Because some form of *kenōsis* is essential to any doctrine of the Incarnation, Christology (a segment of biblical theology) must find the divinity of Jesus in his *human* existence. There is a strong, solid line running through both Testaments, the line of God's will and Word. And if it does not always seem straight to us, it is because of our own imperfect understanding—our inability (as Job was so poignantly taught) to 'copy' the line of God's own secrets.

Finally, the firmly fixed nature of God's word is the fact underlying a truth brought out by all our authors, either implicitly or explicitly—a truth which we have already seen embodied in *Dei Verbum*. Simply, Scripture, as inspired by God, is the transcendent norm—the *norma non normata* or 'pure norm'—of all theology. The Church's consciousness of its faith must be historical, bound to its beginnings in the apostolic age as they are objectified in Scripture. And this norm, inviolable for *all* theological activity, is sure and valid because it is guided by the Spirit speaking in the writer and living on in the hearer.

## The Guiding Role of Biblical Theology

*Your word is a lamp to my feet, a light to my path (Ps. 119: 105).*

We turn now to preview the ways in which our works on biblical theology may help to reveal God's word as a source of light, as guidance. The psalmist has pictured it as a *lamp*. A lamp is often associated with *faith*; and faith, of course, is both the keystone and the hidden supporting beams on which our authors build their theologies, not to mention its being also the overt subject of many of their conclusions. Through *faith*, New Testament writers could find in the Old Testament one great 'prophecy'. Yahweh was recognised through faith in his having led his people through one hardship after another, and the words and deeds of the men who took him seriously provide the theological basis of the Old Testament. A faith which both fears the loss of God's hand, yet is willing to stand naked refusing all human security, is the import of the Scriptures—a faith strong enough to overcome even the 'offence' of the cross, of a man who claimed to be God's Son without being able to 'prove' it. Faith has freed man from his own inadequacy and lifted him into the otherness of God as revealed in Jesus. Indeed, theology is the science of faith: the theologian is guided by *his* faith to seek an understanding of the faith he shares with God's people. Yes, if faith is a dark path and believing a night sky, the acceptance of God's word is a lamp upon it. Biblical theology can help us to hear this word, though the acceptance remains our own personal decision—our act of faith.

One obvious way in which God's word functions as a 'guide' is through teaching: biblical theology both considers the teaching role of the Bible and functions in that role itself. We shall see the intense concern with *kerygma*, the early Church's proclamation of Jesus; and though, at times, this concern may be exaggerated, yet it points to the truth that the gospel is always proclamation, always a contemporary challenge. Springing from the apostles' preaching matured into the later writings of the New Testament, New Testament theology is guided by the supreme 'law' of the need for adaptation. What was to be taught henceforth should follow Jesus' own concern with principles—with the all-embracing rule of love—rather than with details of application. Finally, the Church's own teaching office is dependent on Scripture and can teach only what it has heard and received.

We shall feel our footsteps guided by a particularly beautiful 'light' when we discover how frequently our biblical theologians stress the eschatological aspects of biblical thought. They do this either by organising their own works with a view towards the eschatological victory, or by pointing out how the entire Bible is oriented towards this final consummation. This can be expressed in radical terms—

such as Jesus' message that God is a God-at-hand confronting each man, tearing him from security and placing him at the brink of the end. Or, it can be expressed in the manner we have mentioned: God's continually creating new beginnings, doing a 'new thing' to which man responds. For, every event in the Bible that has the character of 'fulfilment' is also a promise looking forward to its deeper fulfilment in Jesus. And he, in his own person, summed up the tension between the hour that is 'coming' and that which 'now is'—the kingdom not of this world (*John* 18:36) and the kingdom right here in our midst because he has come (cf. *Luke* 17:21). God's word, the 'lamp of faith', helps us to believe, even where we cannot see and appearances seem contrary, that Jesus *has* overcome the world (cf. *John* 16:33)—though we must wait for his final victory, as the Apocalypse so vividly teaches us. But, our feet and path need not be in darkness because he himself is that Word and that Lamp, and 'he who follows me shall not walk in darkness, but shall have the Light of Life' (*John* 8:12).

### The Relevance of Biblical Theology

*I rejoice at your word like one who finds rich bounty* (Ps. 119:162).

Having spoken already of the 'sweetness' of God's word, and hence of the biblical theology which is able to sharpen our hearing it, we are in a position to look ahead at a further cause for rejoicing which it offers: the 'rich bounty' of its great relevance to life today. The biblical theologian follows the example of the scribe 'trained for the kingdom' likened to the householder who knows how to make use of both the 'old' and the 'new' in his storeroom (*Matt.* 13:51f). Since the Bible is the book of *life*, the theologian cannot merely dissect it intellectually. He must bring to it his own contact with life in the current religious community. He himself must have seen the living God, and his work is relevant only in so far as it helps to draw man into that living presence.

Again we turn to *Dei Verbum* with its stress on the abiding values of the Old Testament—the Scripture written to offer 'encouragement, instruction, and hope' (*Rom.* 15:4). The Bible is relevant because of its sound wisdom about *human* life (whose very imperfections are turned to advantage), its lively sense of God. This concern to relate the abiding values of the Bible to modern theological problems really began, as we shall see, with the post-World War I dissatisfaction with the *religionsgeschichtlich* approach to explain Israel's religion. It became more important to *feel* whole situations, to stress the permanent rather than the accidentals. But, once again we must keep in mind the need for adaptation; because the word of God is addressed to *men* and ordered to *life*, its interpreters must make it significant to men of their own age and culture. The word is still being addressed to us, and the believer must be helped to hear it as it has meaning today. And if, as is very much the case, there is today a new awareness of the pure wellspring to be found in the Bible, this must include a willingness to accept nowadays the unattenuated, original demands of Jesus.

The Church itself has indeed found a great bounty in God's word and its interpreters, and provides, as we have seen, the best atmosphere for biblical theology. The early Christians saw the sayings of Jesus as challenges to be lived, not remarks to be memorised and shelved. But they too, as can be grasped from a study of the Sermon on the Mount, adapted them according to changing circumstances. The biblical theologian can also help the Church to avoid one of its pitfalls: an over-preoccupation with self-edifying dogmatics to the exclusion of God himself and his glory, a pursuit of ecclesiology rather than Christology. The new *qahal*—the *ekklēsia*—was founded by Jesus so that its institutions and functions (amongst which we include biblical theology) could truly be of *service* to the kingdom, rather than making it impossible for men to enter there (cf. *Matt.* 23:13). Our use of Scripture must include bringing the Bible into the Church of today, a Church which meditates further on the data which the biblical theologian draws from the text. Finally, biblical theology can help to point out the vital role of the Old Testament in the Church—how it can be guided by Israel's spiritual history.

Our subject can help us to grasp ever more deeply our

own position as God's chosen people—a 'rich bounty' indeed. If biblical theology is concerned with God's revelation through history, then the first inference of theology is election. It is not easy for the elect to maintain their faith and trust in God, and from a purely human viewpoint the teaching of Jesus does seem an 'impossible ethic'. Yet, 'nothing is impossible with God' . . . and this ethic has been moved by Jesus' love for man and realistic attitude towards conditions in this world. The very title 'Christian' embodies not only Jesus' proclamation but his person as well. We may need to ask ourselves, 'Do we really *know* this person, this Jesus?' And, instead of using him as a 'standard' for the Old Testament, should not the Old Testament be *accepted* as the period in which he had not yet come and be understood as something already there in the early Church, becoming then useful in interpreting his coming? Because the Old Testament records the experience of God's meeting with his people, it can help in guiding that people today to choose to truly live, to choose real life—which is the eternal life offered us here and now by Jesus.

## The Personal Value of Biblical Theology

*My soul melts away for sorrow. Strengthen me according to your word. You are my hiding place and my shield . . . I hope in your word. I trust in your word (Ps. 119 : 28, 81, 42).*

We have looked at the relevance of the Bible, and hence the widespread current interest in biblical studies today in the Church. But this can, and must, be carried one step further—for that Church is not an abstract institution or an empty shell, but a living fellowship, a *koinōnia,* of men and women united in Jesus. Hence, too, 'God's word' has a relevance deeper than being merely an abstract concept, an ideal norm, or even a study to be pursued by the Church as an organisation. All these uses of the Bible and biblical theology, while important in their own way, can only flow from something more vital: God's word as it is spoken, and received, in the hearts of individual persons alone before him. The Bible and biblical studies can be considered full of strength and value—yes, of relevance at all—only because men and women have been strengthened by the living Word in their own personal lives. These are the 'poor of Yahweh', the 'little ones', to whom the gospel is really addressed. These are the 'simple-hearted', the 'uneducated', the 'publicans and sinners'; these are, indeed, all of us. For in the end, we turn to the Bible, and to works on biblical theology, only because we have found there strength in times of sorrow, a 'hiding place and a shield' to give us hope, a God in whose word we can trust.

Throughout our survey of biblical theology, we shall encounter many thoughts for pondering to deepen our appreciation of this gift—whether it be through our authors' pointing out precise messages in the text itself or through their own personal fruits of contemplation. We shall expect to find a certain freedom in their individual approaches to God's word, each unique as the man who wrote it and each conditioned by his own particular background and conviction. For, each of our theologians has himself had to arrive at some answer to Jesus' ultimate question, 'And you, who do *you* say that I am?' (cf. *Mark* 8:29). This is similar to the observation we shall meet that the vital force behind Paul's message is precisely his own freedom in regard to 'Christology', his own intimate life with Jesus really defying structure, analysis, and any system of compact theology. Like Paul, each one of our authors has somehow been transformed by his own 'Damascene revelation'. And so too, at some stage of our lives, have we—or shall we be. This is why our discussions in the following pages of such terms as 'hope', 'salvation', 'faith', and 'Christian love' will not seem abstract and removed but near at hand—near as the God, and his Son, who is the 'Word very near you, in your mouth and in your heart . . .' (*Deut.* 30:14). This is why, when we study such themes as the 'paradox' of Jesus' earthly road of suffering or the 'scandal' of the cross, they shall not seem strange to us but as familiar as this very Jesus—whom we have come to know as our friend because he has become the lowly Son of man identified with every man. Yes, it is so: we turn in interest to this Bible (and its theology) because of what we ourselves have experienced in the real life it embraces. Scripture is the word of *my* God addressed to *me*.

One of the most consistent ways of expressing this personal relevance of the Bible is through the notion of 'communion' —a relationship, in various forms, between God and man (and a word which attains its full meaning in our commemoration of the Last Supper). Personal fellowship between God and man is the channel for revelation, and the Bible bears witness to the God who has entered history to seek communion with man. Indeed, the whole meaning of 'Yahweh' can be understood as, 'I am who am right there *with* you'—a God open to conversing with man 'face-to-face'. This presence of God with his own can be expressed in terms of the Old Testament 'covenant' or the New Testament 'body of Christ'; to read both Testaments is to meet real men and women, like ourselves, who know God has spoken to them. It is to experience *the* perfect communion: 'I have called you my friends' (*John* 15:15). And somehow, this companionship with God, and all the natural goods and life-wholeness it includes, are contained in the Hebrew term *shalōm*—PEACE—the true peace, the more abundant life, which Jesus came to give to his 'friends'—ourselves.

And so, seeing that God's word finds its true relevance in our own personal lives, we turn to the source of this relevance, a common message of all our theologians (a message which, if they do not preach, they at least cannot help proclaiming). This is the reality that God 'does well' with us by his word . . . for it is a saving word, a message of salvation. 'Salvation hope', and awaiting God's kingdom to fully come, was felt keenly by God's people throughout the Bible. Having known his care and experienced his power, they could not but hope for his coming to establish his domain. Jesus' whole message is an invitation to accept the salvation he brings, to trust this his word—a salvation continuing to take place as that word is proclaimed and made present today. The whole 'incarnation' is not a 'dogma', but the very kernel of salvation. Moreover, any dogma or doctrine or theological system holds sway only because it concerns a truth which God has revealed *for our salvation*. And Scripture must remain the objective guideline of this saving word. Yes, the psalmist of old thankfully exclaims, 'You have done well with your servant, according to your word!' (*Ps.* 119:65). For, by 'doing

well' with him, by saving his life in some specifically personal way, God had 'kept his word' to him. Little did the
psalmist know how perfectly God would keep that word and
save all our lives centuries later. Little did he know his own
song would be sung still more perfectly by another after him,
an old man who held the Child of all new hope in his arms:
'Lord, now let your servant depart in peace *according to your
word,* for my eyes have now seen your *salvation*' (*Luke* 2:29f.).

## The Living Heart: Jesus

*The sum of your word is truth* (*Ps.* 119: 160).

If our attempt to become acquainted with various authors
on biblical theology throughout the following pages bears no
other fruit, at least we shall take away with us one point we
shall find made again and again: the whole truth contained
in the Bible and sought by the Church, its theologies and
studies, and even by our investigations here, is contained in
this person of Christ. His teaching is not only revelation, his
words and deeds not only the material with which the later
Church has constructed a theology: he himself is the living
source of that theology.

The incarnation being at once a revealing and a veiling,
we shall find our authors asking many questions concerning
the exact role of Jesus in the Bible, as well as the place of
his message in a biblical theology. With patience, we shall
gradually sort out common features in their answers, though
naturally their approaches will be varied as their authorship.
Jesus it is who fulfils most perfectly the Old Testament's
reverence for Abraham as 'God's friend'. Jesus it is who embodies the whole saving purpose of God and has entered
history at the point where the ultimate truths about God
are to be found. It is he who unites all the different 'theologies' in the New Testament and their accompanying linguistic and literary forms. The growth of the early Church depended upon a strong recognition of his Person, the sole
foundation of the New Testament. That this personhood
should be cast under various lights throughout its pages
results simply from the marvellous, superhuman nature of
this Person. And yet, because of the wholeness of this Person

and the striking impression he made, the entire New Testament does fall into a great harmony. The different notes are but rays from a prism, as it were, the prism of different understandings, while Jesus abides ever behind as the one pure source of Light. The 'Christian ethic' is not a binding written code; it is a following of the Shepherd who is present to us and who himself provides the strength to follow where he leads, the love with which to obey his 'new commandment' (cf. *John* 13:34).

This word whose 'sum is truth' is made known to us by the 'Spirit of truth', the Comforter, he himself has given us. Hence, we shall see the frequent attention to the Holy Spirit paid by our authors. This is connected, of course, with the role of the Spirit in the whole subject of biblical inspiration and their discussion on that. The Holy Spirit completes Jesus' presence, rather than substitutes for his absence. Throughout the history of the Church, the Spirit of Jesus, 'teaching us all things', has always guided biblical interpretation just as he promised (cf. *John* 14:26). Yes, this Spirit who has spoken through the writer lives on in the hearer: the Jesus who has assured us that the Spirit would 'lead us into all the truth' (*John* 16:13) and who is himself Truth is not confined to the letter of the Book—as confirmed by the varying ways in which that truth is voiced.

Jesus may no longer be bodily present to us, but his Word is his abiding continually in our midst. This Word provides that wholeness, that flowering of God's first word to his people of which we spoke in the beginning. This Word is especially present to us in the 'breaking of the bread', the eucharistic table-fellowship by which Jesus offers to mankind, in particular the poor and the little ones, all of the pure good things of God. The simple, childlike acceptance of this gift—the eating of this Bread and the drinking of this Wine —is our best 'Introduction to Biblical Theology'. For, through this we meet most intimately the One who, gathering into himself all the manna, all the 'daily bread' of God's care for his people from the beginning, is himself the *living* Bread. We, who thirst for more and more knowledge in the field of biblical studies, meet the One who, as the living water and the wine of life, alone can satisfy all thirst. And, without faith's personal decision as to who he really is, this Jesus, all theology is but an 'empty cistern and a broken well' (cf. *Jer.* 2 : 13).

Biblical theology, all its fine points and ramifications, is really our searching through the Scriptures to find life—eternal life. Amidst all our searching, would it not be well to pause and listen to Jesus' own words to the Jews about this? 'You search the scriptures because you think that in them you have eternal life, and it is they which bear witness to me . . . Yet, you refuse to come to me, that you may have life!' (*John* 5:39f.). Yes, what are all our seekings, all our words, all our theology, and Scripture itself unless through them we come (because he draws us) to Jesus, the Life? Though our writings may have gone far afield and unearthed many a scriptural treasure, though our readings may have encompassed many words in the biblical sphere, we really have desired to go no place—and have no place to go—other than to this Word himself. 'Lord, to whom shall we go? You have the words of eternal life!' (*John* 6:68f.).

## CHAPTER I

# A Survey of the Biblical Theology of the Old Testament

WE have seen, in broadest outline, how the concept of biblical theology has developed; we have traced its phases and have noted a variety of approaches and methods. The following historical survey will enter into greater detail. The Old Testament, to a greater extent than the New Testament, has won the attention of biblical theologians. It is the object of this chapter to convey some idea of the prodigious work done in the field of Old Testament theology and to highlight the significant and the abiding achievements of almost two centuries of scholarship.

## 1. The Pioneers: Gabler to Davidson

Rationalism, with its historical approach to the Bible, favoured the establishment of biblical theology as an independent science; in this respect, too, it began to stand apart from dogmatic theology. These factors were first clearly formulated by J. F. Gabler in his inaugural lecture as professor of theology at the University of Altdorf, 30 March, 1787.[1] The title of his lecture—*Oratio de justo discrimine theologiae biblicae et dogmaticae regundisque recte utriusque finibus*—sets out his purpose: to define the boundaries between biblical theology and dogmatic theology. Biblical theology is historical in character and its purpose is to describe what the Old Testament writers thought of God and the things of God. Dogmatic theology is didactic in character: it makes a selection from the contents of the Bible and presents divine matters with the help of philosophy and in the light of ideas which emerged in the course of the development of the Church. Gabler outlined a method of procedure for the biblical theologian which comprised three stages. Firstly, using grammatical and historical principles and criteria, he must interpret the individual passages of Scripture. Then, he will compare the passages with one another, noting not only agreements but divergencies; for he will find, within the Old Testament, diverse and even contradictory statements. Finally, he must try to formulate general ideas, without distorting the biblical material and without obliterating the often notable differences in idea and viewpoint. All this does not spell opposition to systematic theology. On the contrary, biblical theology offers a firm, scientific foundation on which the dogmatic theologian will be able to build his superstructure of dogmatic theology. Gabler is the first to have shown that, while biblical theology and dogmatic theology are distinct disciplines, they are also complementary; both are necessary in building up an authentically Christian theology.

Gabler's insight is valuable and the validity of his basic views is undeniable. However, neither he nor his immediate successors were in a position to work out a satisfactory biblical theology. In the first place, the source and literary criticism of the Old Testament had not yet really begun, and so the interpretation and comparison of biblical passages must necessarily be unsatisfactory and even misleading. Then, too, the rationalistic philosophy of these authors made them incapable of grasping the specific character of Hebrew mentality; their approach to the Old Testament tended to be negatively critical rather than appreciative of its positive values.

The first biblical theology written according to Gabler's principles was the *Theology of the Old Testament* of G. L. Bauer.[2] His aim was to give an outline of the religious ideas of the ancient Hebrews. He divided his subject into two main divisions: theology and anthropology. However, two appendices on angels and demons witness to the practical difficulty he met in trying to treat Old Testament material systematically—a perennial problem. While in our eyes his rationalistic interpretation of the Old Testament is the manifest shortcoming of his work, his contemporaries criticised him for failing to write a history of Israel's religion. He met this need, to his own satisfaction, in his *Supplement to a Theology of the Old Testament*.[3] Here, already, we find a distinction between biblical theology and the history of the religion of Israel, a matter of major importance later on. In his *Biblical Dogmatics*[4] W. de Wette proposes to place himself above the dispute between rationalism and orthodoxy and present a higher synthesis of faith and religious feeling. His approach is based on Kantian philosophy; thus he is the first to link the treatment of biblical theology with a particular philosophical system.

The last work of the rationalistic period is the *Biblical Theology* of D. C. von Cölln.[5] In a reaction against de Wette's philosophical approach he maintains the historical character of the discipline. He believes that biblical theology should follow the development of biblical ideas, but in practice he is not very successful in working out his theory. His first volume, 'Biblical Theology of the Old Testament', arranges the material in two sections, Hebraism and Judaism, showing in each the evolution in religious thought from particularism towards universalism.

The next phase—one of very short duration—of the development of biblical theology in Germany is marked by the influence of Hegel. He had applied his well-known triadic theory to the historical evolution of religion and had divided the field into three sections: (1) nature religions, (2) religions of spiritual individuality (the Jewish religion is one of these), (3) absolute or universal religion (Christianity). Evidently, Hegelian presuppositions would notably colour one's understanding of the nature and growth of Old Testament religion. The first to attempt an Old Testament theology in Hegelian terms was Wilhelm Vatke.[6] A main part of his work, an account of the history of Israel's religion, owes far more to his own historical acumen and penetrating criticism than to Hegelian theory; in this respect Wellhausen acknowledges his debt to Vatke. Other attempts to write an Old Testament theology in Hegelian terms are not noteworthy; we may instance the work of Bruno Bauer[7] as a demonstration of the futility of the attempt. There was only one worthwhile result: the insight that an understanding of Hebrew religion demands a concept of historical development, one which allows for organic growth. At this point we may note a work of J. C. Hofmann[8] which examines the relationship between history and prophecy. He can declare that all history is prophecy in the sense that each period of history carries within it the germ of the period that follows. He views biblical theology from the viewpoint of the history of salvation (*Heilsgeschichte*).

Not unexpectedly, the rationalist and Hegelian approaches to biblical theology called forth a conservative reaction which, at first negatively critical, eventually produced its own works of biblical theology. The first of these was the work of J. C. F. Steudel, posthumously edited by his pupil G. F. Oehler.[9] Steudel is critical of the subjectivity of the Hegelians. Another posthumous work, by H. A. Hävernick,[10] is more rigidly conservative—at least with regard to his uncritical treatment of the sources. On the other hand, his views on the nature of Old Testament theology are stimulating. He demands a 'theological aptitude' which is the fruit of religious belief and experience and self-surrendering love. He perceived that God reveals himself not only in abstract ideas but also in a closely knit series of acts. Thus the ideas of Old Testament religion must not be treated in isolation from its history.

G. F. Oehler, in 1845, outlined the theory and method of Old Testament theology;[11] his massive *Theology of the Old Testament* was published almost thirty years later, in 1873, after his death.[12] Though conservative in his critical views, his work is stamped with Hegel's influence. And, while he held strongly for the revealed character of Old Testament religion, he maintained just as firmly that Old Testament theology is a historical discipline and insisted that the historical method was the only legitimate approach to a theology of the Old Testament. His *Theology of the Old Testament*,[13] the first such work to be translated into English, was divided into three parts: Mosaism, Prophetism (each containing an historical and a systematic section), and Wisdom. The work is of interest to-day almost solely because of its Preface, which is a revised edition of the *Prolegomena*. H. Ewald attempted to deal with the whole field of biblical doctrine[14] in a work which held up rather than fostered the genuine development of biblical theology.

A new period opens with the publication in 1878 of J. Wellhausen's *Prolegomena to the History of Israel*.[15] It seemed to sound the death knell of biblical theology and at the same time to usher in the new discipline that was to take its place, the history of the religion of Israel. A new generation had been moulded by the ideas of Hegel and Darwin; now Wellhausen had shown how the history of Israel might be presented in a form congenial to it. Indeed only now had it become possible to write a history of Israel's religion; and the dominant influence of *Religionsgeschichte* made this approach appear the only scientific one. The first work of this nature was that of A. Kayser, posthumously edited by E. Reuss.[16] The author candidly admits that his work might be more accurately described as a 'history of Israelite religion'. The same approach is made by R. Smend[17] and for some time to come biblical theology was, more and more, to assume the general form of a 'history of the religion of Israel'.

However, a few authors did still continue to deal with Old Testament theology systematically, or did so at least in part. A. Dillmann[18] rejected the Wellhausen theory. He asserted that the Christian cannot come to the Old Testament with cold objectivity; he must regard it as part of his own religion. And it is in this spirit that Old Testament theology must be written. He treated the material under three general headings: (1) the uniqueness of the religion of the Old Testament as the religion of 'holiness'; (2) a broad historical outline of Israel's religious development; (3) a systematic treatment of the religious concepts of the Old Testament under the divisions of theology, anthropology, soteriology. Two other scholars were to show that the Wellhausen reconstruction of Old Testament history was not incompatible with the methods of Old Testament theology. C. Piepenbring[19] arranged his material in a systematic order under three headings: Mosaism, Prophetism, Judaism, and discussed the principal topics of Old Testament religion under each of these heads. A much weightier achievement was that of H. Schultz[20] whose *Old Testament*

3

*Theology* ran into five editions (1869-1896); the fourth German edition was translated into English (1892). Schultz accepted wholeheartedly the revealed character of Old Testament religion, while at the same time he did give importance to its historical development. He saw the function of biblical theology as providing systematic theology with its working material and as furnishing the Church with a yardstick for measuring later theological developments. He found in the idea of the kingdom of God on earth the central and unifying principle of the whole Old Testament teaching.

Many of the German theologies of the Old Testament had been translated into English but there was little original writing in that language. The most important contribution was the posthumous work of A. B. Davidson.[21] The volume is, in fact, a collection of studies of unequal value which have been artificially arranged by an editor under the usual heads of theology, anthropology and soteriology. The fact is that Davidson had himself rejected such an arrangement. He declared that the threefold theological division was 'somewhat too abstract for a subject like ours. What we meet with in the Old Testament are two concrete subjects and their relation. The two are: Jehovah, God of Israel, on the one hand, and Israel, the people of Jehovah, on the other; and the third point, which is given in the other two, is their relation to one another. And it is obvious that the dominating or creative factor in the relation is Jehovah'.[22] When he goes on to detail the various ways in which the revelation about Israel's God was mediated to Israel—ethical and spiritual conceptions by the prophets, legislative and ritual conceptions by the priests, personal devotion to God by the psalmists, and personal reflections and questionings by the Wisdom writers—Davidson, in fact, suggests a division of the subject which, however, he did not follow up himself. Perhaps it is that Davidson is too confined by an exclusively historical point of view. Indeed, he can state: 'We do not find a theology in the Old Testament; we find a religion . . . Hence our subject really is the history of the religion of Israel.'[23]

Though, for Davidson, Old Testament theology was virtually *Religionsgeschichte*, his book, as edited, adopted the systematic treatment of the subject. It was practically the last to do so for a long time to come. No longer was it thought feasible to produce Old Testament theologies; scholars had come to feel that the only thing they could do was to write histories of the religion of Israel. Almost a quarter of a century must elapse before the biblical theology of the Old Testament will again interest scholars; but when it does it will dramatically move to the forefront of Old Testament studies.

## 2. A Revival of Interest

After the first World War the theological climate had changed. There was increasing dissatisfaction with the *religionsgeschichtlich* attempt to explain Israel's religion. There was also the realisation that historical truth was not to be obtained by a pure scientific 'objectivity'; the inner truth of history, its very core, was accessible only to those who could 'feel' themselves into a situation and become, in some sense, participants in it. Then again, it became clear that what mattered most were the permanent rather than the accidental and temporary elements in Israel's religion, and the profound relevance of these abiding values to modern theological problems. The need was felt of making evident the relation of the faith of Israel to modern theological needs.

A first sign of reviving interest in Old Testament theology was the work of E. König.[24] It was not a very promising sign, however, for König took a conservative stand against the dominant evolutionary school of interpretation, and his own evaluation of the sources ignored even what was of assured value in critical scholarship. His method was to give a survey of the history of Israel's religion and then discuss, systematically, the ideas and factors which were a part of that history. However, his reconstruction of the history is unacceptable and his systematic principles are unsatisfactory.

The real beginning of the re-emergence of Old Testament theology is marked by an article of C. Steuernagel in 1925[25] which asserted the autonomy of both biblical theology of the Old Testament and the history of Israel's religion as well as the need for both. The following year, Otto Eissfeldt stated the case in favour of the legitimacy of biblical theology.[26] His view is that the religion of the Old Testament may be treated in two distinct ways: historically in the form of *Religionsgeschichte* or, taken as God's revelation, as Old Testament theology. For him history is an object of knowledge while revelation, the communication of timeless truths, is an object of faith. He maintains that, in the interest of both, faith and knowledge should be kept strictly apart. This means 'that *Religionsgeschichte* is a completely neutral discipline in which members of different Christian confessions and even members of other religious faiths can work together in harmony. Biblical theology, on the other hand, is a purely confessional matter. While its method must be scientific, it always bears the character of witness and its findings will be valid only for those who share the theologian's point of view.'[27] Evidently, Eissfeldt's idea of Old Testament theology is that it is a theological and dogmatic approach to the Old Testament. His view is very different from another which takes biblical theology in the sense of a systematic and unifying but strictly historical approach to the religion of the Old Testament.

Walter Eichrodt, in an article published in 1929,[28] firmly upheld the traditional view of Old Testament theology and marked it off from what is the achievement of an historian. The history of the religion of Israel is a genetic understanding of Old Testament faith as it arose and developed amid the interplay of historical forces; or, to put it another way, it traces the stages in the growth of Old Testament religion. Old Testament theology, on the other hand, is a great systematic task which consists in making a cross-section through the historical process and laying bare the inner structures of the religion in its classic forms. From this the contrasts in Old Testament religion, and the inter-relationships of the different elements of that religion, will come to light.

The year 1933 opened the 'golden age' of Old Testament theology. In that year W. Eichrodt published the first volume of his monumental work[29] and E. Sellin his more modest two-volume *Theology*.[30] At this point we are content to remark that Eichrodt's complete *Theology of the Old*

*Testament* is still the most important contribution in the field; it will be dealt with at some length later in the chapter. However, for purposes of comparison, it is important to note that he divides his material into the sections God and People, God and World, God and Man, and groups these around the central idea of covenant. Sellin's volumes are meant as a manual for students. He stresses the complementary nature of Old Testament theology and the history of the religion of Israel, to such an extent indeed that he would prefer to see one discipline: Old Testament theology on a *religionsgeschichtlich* foundation. In the arrangement of his work, a long section on *Religionsgeschichte* comes before the systematic part; the latter he describes as the systematic description of the religious teaching and beliefs contained in the writings accepted as sacred by the Jewish community. However, Old Testament theology is interested in the contents of the Jewish canon only in so far as they came to completion in the New Testament. In other words, an Old Testament theology can be written by a Christian theologian only from the standpoint of the gospel. Sellin found as a central idea the holiness of God, and he arranged the material around the classical themes of God, man, judgement, and salvation.

L. Köhler[31] adopted the same scheme, but his central idea is that of God as the Lord. For him the fundamental assertion of Old Testament theology is that God is the Lord who lays down his commands and that man is meant to be his obedient servant. In Köhler's view a theology of the Old Testament is 'a synthesis of such ideas, thoughts and concepts of the Old Testament as are, or could be, theologically important.'[32] He finds difficulty in accommodating the cult, which he regards as man's mistaken attempt to save himself by his own works, and he treats of it as an appendix to the section on anthropology. His treatment of the theological ideas is based on a grammatical-historical interpretation of the text.

H. Wheeler Robinson had planned a complete treatise of Old Testament theology; unhappily, all we have are the posthumously published materials he had prepared for an introduction to the projected work.[33] Besides, two essays in an earlier volume edited by him contain his views. In one

of these[34] he points out that God had revealed himself to
Israel in a series of events which were interpreted to Israel
by Moses, and in Israel's subsequent history we find the same
blending of event and prophetic interpretation. If God thus
reveals himself in history, it is important to establish the
true course of Israel's history and the history of the religious
ideas of the Old Testament. Revelation came to Israel not
through the communication of abstract ideas but through
the interpretation of the events of Israel's history.

In his posthumous writing, which was planned as a prolegomena to his Theology of the Old Testament, his division
of the material falls into two main sections. The first has
three parts: God and Nature, God and Man, God and
History. The second section has four parts, which develop
the plan suggested by A. B. Davidson: Inspiration of the
Prophet, Revelation through the Priest, Revelation in Wisdom, Revelation in the Psalmists (a response to the revelation of God). Revelation in the Old Testament is bound
up with the history of Israel and comes through personal
fellowship between God and man. One can realise what
God is saying to us in the Bible only by learning to live in
the atmosphere of the Old Testament and of the New Testament which is its sequel. 'It seems fair to infer that, in
Wheeler Robinson's judgement, a theology of the Old
Testament cannot be written except by one who has a
personal experience of the life of faith.'[35] However, at the
end of his book he seems to hesitate as to how best the
revelation should be presented: in a series of propositions
to constitute a 'Theology of the Old Testament' or in the
form of a 'History of the Religion of Israel'. Either way, that
to be avoided is an abstract presentation which would be
remote from the living, dynamic faith of Israel.

The contribution of C. H. Dodd to the theology of the
Old Testament is more important than is perhaps generally
recognised. A considerable part of his book *The Bible Today*
deals with the Old Testament.[36] He is quite clear that the
historical element in the Bible is fundamental to it. Because
God's word is the creative factor in history, history itself
is the medium of revelation. 'The Bible is not simply an
account of a development of thought. It is also a history of

events, in which, and particularly in certain crucial events, we are invited to trace the manifest working of the divine providence. . . . The God of the Bible is a "living God". He reveals himself in the movement of events. What we are dealing with is not simply a history of revelation, but history as revelation."[37] Biblical history is made meaningful through the interpretation of events which the word of God supplies by the instrumentality of prophetic men. The same interpretation, which always rests upon an encounter with God, can be applied to our lives and will make them meaningful too —we can participate in the events. Biblical history becomes universal history through the emergence of the Church as a 'catholic' body, a genuinely universal society. This catholic Church is the final historical form of the people of God. The Church is still where history in its fullest sense is made, through the encounter of man with God. The Bible speaks to us most clearly in the context of the continuing life of the Church. This same context is the favourable atmosphere for an authentic biblical theology.

For Otto Procksch[38] Old Testament theology must be a 'theology of history.' But since God's revelatory history— the proper object of biblical theology—reaches its final fulfilment in the person of Christ, he is to be seen as the middle point of history. Hence, Procksch declares, right at the beginning, that 'all theology is Christology'[39] but he does not then work out his idea in detail in the body of his book. It needs faith to see Christ as the centre of history and to understand the significance of the revealing events; an Old Testament theologian must share the biblical faith.

Procksch is critical of *Religionsgeschichte* as it had developed; indeed, for that matter, its proper object is not revelation but only the phenomenon of religion. But because Old Testament theology is concerned with historical revelation, he proceeds to integrate *Religionsgeschichte* into the biblical-theological method as a first step. So, like Schultz and Sellin, he divides his book into two nearly equal parts: the first is devoted to an historical sketch, the other is concerned with the 'world of ideas.' This second, properly theological, part is arranged in a new division: God and World, God and the Nation, God and Man. Procksch also suggests the idea of a cross-section in the process of religious history; this should be made, in each case, where the theological idea comes most clearly to light. However, he has not really followed through his own method. It was from Procksch's lectures that Eichrodt got the idea for the main division of his own work and also the figure of the cross-section.

In the view of Otto J. Baab[40] there can be, ideally, only one theology of the Old Testament, and this will be a scientific theology. At the same time, the key to an understanding of biblical religion and history is the faith of the men of the Bible. But because the dynamic religion of Israel does not easily yield to logical treatment, it is obvious that no complete theology as such can be found in the Old Testament. Baab is content to handle his material under a number of broad headings: The Meaning of God, The Nature of Man, The Idea of Sin, Salvation in the Old Testament, The Kingdom of God, Death and the Hereafter. The Problem of Evil. In fact, this framework is essentially that of God-Man-Salvation, extended by the chapters on the kingdom, death and evil. At the end of his work he discusses the validity of Old Testament theology and briefly considers the relation of the Old Testament to the New. He takes up again the question of the unity of Old Testament theology. Since the message of the Old Testament is mediated through the human wills and personalities of its authors, a unifying principle must be sought in the area of human experience and history; the obvious principle is that of historical continuity. The theology of the Old Testament is one and independent, as distinctive as the self-conscious, continuing Israel community whose religious faith it expresses. With regard to the relationship of Old Testament theology to the New Testament, Baab has this to say: 'There can be no doubt whatsoever that a theology of the Old Testament indeed exists, and that it exists in complete independence of the New Testament. . . . To assert the independence of Old Testament theology is to insist that it is not to be treated as simply a background for the thought of the New Testament.'[41] But, at the same time, one must insist on the extraordinary importance of an understanding of Old Testament theology for the student of the New Testament and of the Christian religion; and Baab is concerned throughout for the relevance of the Old Testament to Christian theology and to Christian living in the modern world.

In his monograph[42] G. Ernest Wright maintains that biblical theology 'is *the confessional recital of the redemptive acts of God* in a particular history, because history is the chief medium of revelation.'[43] He feels that the presentation of biblical theology has been too much influenced by the systematic presentation of propositional dogmatics; in his view biblical theology is to be characterised rather by the words 'confessional recital' than by 'a system of ideas.' For him, 'biblical theology is first and foremost a theology of recital, in which biblical man confesses his faith by reciting the formative events of his history as the redemptive handiwork of God.'[44] The primary assumption of biblical theology is that history is the revelation of God; the first theological inference to be drawn from this fact is the doctrine of election. The covenant itself, by which the meaning and implications of election were concretely stated, was a real event of history which illumined the meaning of subsequent history. These three elements—(i) history as the primary sphere in which God reveals himself, (ii) the theological inference from this—God's election of a special people through whom he would accomplish his purposes, (iii) the election and its implications confirmed and clarified in the covenant—are, together, the core of Israelite faith and the unifying factor within it.

In keeping with his emphasis on theology as recital, Wright entitles the central chapters of his book: 'What God has Done'; 'What Man has Done'. While this might suggest the familiar theology-anthropology division, he goes out of his way to show that there is a world of difference between the two arrangements. In presenting the activity of God in history, typology and the *kerygma* are of great importance. The biblical material relating to man is best treated not by asking the abstract question as to what man is in himself, but rather by observing what he does in the great variety of situations which he faces in history; the biblical 'doctrine' of man is primarily a recital of what he has done together

with the inferences drawn from it. The perennial problem
of the elect is that of maintaining the faith and trust in God
which determine responsible human action before God. We
shall see that Wright has, in fact, expressed the general
viewpoint of Gerhard von Rad, though with greater modera-
tion and without the latter's historical scepticism.

N. W. Porteous, whose survey of recent works in Old
Testament theology is invaluable, has also provided an outline of the theology of the Old Testament.[45] He sees that the
object of Old Testament theology is the Old Testament itself
in so far as it is a witness to certain things which God is
believed to have done and the record of the human response
to these acts of God. But while its concern is with God, it
has, in practice, to concentrate its attention upon men, for
it is in human response that the revelation becomes visible.
The Old Testament is of such tremendous theological importance because it records the deeds and words of men who,
in varying measure, took God seriously and allowed their
faith to determine their conduct, or who, in their failure to
respond, became chastening examples of what failure involves. Since the lives of men are touched immediately by
this faith, the primary emphasis of the Old Testament is that
the God of Israel is a God who acts and reveals himself in
history. Porteous proffers a helpful clarification of this idea.
'To say that God reveals himself in history is a very different
thing, of course, from saying that history is the revelation of
God. Much in history is anything but the self-disclosure of
God. What is asserted is that God is a God whose activity
may be recognised in certain events in history by that form
of apprehension which is called faith, such faith expressing
itself not only in word but also in deed.'[46]

It is part of the theological task to demonstrate the broad
unity of life and thought which is to be found in the Old
Testament and in the Bible as a whole. But a consideration
of the varied types of literature we find in the Old Testament makes clear how complicated must be the method of a
discipline which has to handle and evaluate such material.
Porteous respects the complexity, while suggesting how the
material might be presented in a congenial manner. He
finds that the idea of community or, as he puts it, the 'ethics

of community', is a central part of Old Testament theology because the main purpose of God's self-revelation was the creation of a community which would serve and obey him. He feels that much is to be said for Eichrodt's view that the covenant is the most central theological concept in the Old Testament. As for belief in election, it expresses a conviction about the manner of Israel's origin as a people.

If we are to do justice to the Old Testament theologically we must attend to the different expressions of the community faith and life; we must, for instance, listen to both priest and prophet. At the same time, it is true to say that the characteristic Israelite conception of revelation—that God spoke to his people through specially chosen men—comes most clearly to light in Hebrew prophecy; and this realisation does not derogate from the contribution of priest and sage. Thus, for instance, in Deuteronomy, so influenced by Hosea, the theology of election, election for a purpose and for service, is worked out. Jeremiah and Ezekiel helped to make men more aware of the nature of human responsibility towards God. Second Isaiah (whom Porteous regards as the theologian *par excellence* of the Old Testament) not only stated with power and clarity the oneness and creative power of God but saw that election necessarily involves universalism. On the other hand, it was in the priestly tradition that man, made in the image and likeness of God—that is, in an intimate relationship with God, was most clearly seen to stand apart from every other creature. In the Wisdom literature we can see how religious faith reached to all, even the most trivial and mundane aspects of human life. Finally, it cannot fail to be a matter for astonishment that the very warmth of Israel's fellowship with a personal God was experienced against the background of a belief in only the vaguest form of survival after death. Hope of resurrection seems to have appeared in the midst of a desperate struggle to preserve the existence of the covenant people (*Dan.* 12:2).

Porteous looks always to the Old Testament as a record of the living faith of the historical Israelite community, and he is surely right in this. Theology may discern the Old Testament's central ideas and must recognise in it the different currents of practice and expression. There is a unity in the midst of great variety; there is development but it is not uniform and it does not proceed in straight lines—theology must take full cognisance of these factors. The primary emphasis in the Old Testament is that the God in whom Israel believes is a God who acts and reveals himself in history. Its major impact is the astonishing faith which, because it represented a response to a living God, was capable of survival and growth in the face of one calamity after another. It would seem, in short, that a theology of the Old Testament must do justice to the living, personal reality of Israel's God and of Israel's faith.

Though G. A. F. Knight[47] has entitled his work *A Christian Theology of the Old Testament*, the designation 'Christian' merely implies the presupposition that the Old Testament is nothing less than Christian Scripture and that the Old Testament, no less than the New, is the word of God. A total view of the Old Testament reveals that its central theme is the revelation of the redemptive activity of God in and through his Son, Israel—just as the New Testament reveals the activity of God through his Son Jesus. 'This *Christian Theology of the Old Testament* is consequently an attempt to discover and present the total meaning of the Old Testament. It does not attempt to analyse the progressive thought of Israel about God and about God's mighty purposes. But it does seek to discover the meaning of the Old Testament for the modern Church in the light of the Christian revelation as a whole.'[48]

Knight divides his *Theology* into four parts. Part one: God, examines what the Old Testament has to say about the person of the living God. Part two: God and Creation, studies God's attitude to his universe; this attitude is one of wrath, because both fallen angels and fallen man are now living in a state of rebellion against God's loving purpose for them. Part three: God and Israel, follows with a series of complementary 'pictures' portraying the unique relationship which has obtained throughout history between God and one particular nation of men. Part four: The Zeal of the Lord, seeks to discover what the comprehensive activity of God is *for*. Hence it traces God's plan in and through his choice of Israel and seeks to understand this zeal of his which burns for the redemption both of Israel and the world.

The Old Testament, as a book about God, offers us the self-revelation of God by means of his word. It will not be possible to systematise in any closely-knit fashion such knowledge as may be gained by listening to that revealing word, for a system will render lifeless the reality of that living experience of encounter between Israel and its God. We need to make the attempt to put ourselves alongside the people of Israel and seek to enter into their experience of meeting with their God. God is known as a personal Being because he reveals himself to hearts and minds; paradoxically, God can be known from what man, his image, thought of himself— anthropology and theology are mutually relevant studies in connection with the Old Testament. God reveals himself by his deeds—hence the central place of the great saving event of the Exodus. The Hebrews envisaged God's essential nature to be such that he could extend his being 'from heaven' to earth, and the conception that he could be represented on earth by an angel is very early. The 'angel' dimension is an example of the pictorial thinking that is the essence of the whole biblical revelation. The Spirit of God is God himself acting in accordance with his essential nature, but Spirit is pictured in a manner that is virtually parallel to the pictorial concept of the angelic activity. In short, pictorial terms which illumine the creative and redemptive activity of God, such as God's name, word, face, angel and spirit, 'represent the genius of the people of the Old Testament for presenting theology in picture language.'[49] The Old Testament does not reveal the nature of God in himself; we are given to know him in his actions as he performs his righteous will. The so-called attributes of God are not really such at all: we should look for verbs or active participles rather than active nouns. Yet we may speak of the holiness and of the glory of God: holiness seeks to represent the conception that God is the 'wholly other', and glory is the outward manifestation of Spirit. Though the Old Testament habitually uses descriptive terms of God's activity in place of abstractions, yet when he is described as Sovereign Lord, King, and Creator, he is recognised as being omnipotent, omniscient, unchanging and eternal.

The first chapters of Genesis are a theological exposition, in picture language, of the reason for the call of Israel out of Egypt at a historical moment in our flesh-and-blood world of space and time. Thus it is that the very idea of 'creation' takes on meaning and design through humanity and through God's relation to that humanity. 'The Old Testament can draw no line between the divine activity as God reveals himself in creation, and the divine activity as God reveals himself in redemption.'[50] The unique significance of man within God's creation is clear. The question we must ask, and continue to ask, is not 'how' God created man, but 'why'—for this is the theological question, and this alone is appropriate.

The story of the fall of man underlines the reality of sin; it is important to realise that the great prophets look upon sin not primarily as the breaking of the moral law but rather as a breaking off of relations with the living God. Sin is the element of *hybris* in man, it is insolence; it is a 'state' into which man has come, resulting from the activity he has already pursued; it is a power that pervades man's environment and can be 'caught' like a disease. However, sinful man remains the object of God's grace, the object of his saving purpose. On the other hand, there is the wrath of God, not an attribute but the positive attitude that God takes in response to the sin of man. God must necessarily hate evil which is the opposite of his love; yet his wrath is not, and cannot be, directed at the abstraction which we call sin, but at the sinful world of men. And his abandonment of sinful man proceeds not from himself, but from the effects of the corruption in man. Always, however, the idea that God is merciful and gracious was ineradicably embedded in the mind of Israel.

Having begun with the action of God's self-revelation, Knight now turns to the recipient and the object of that word: the people of Israel, the people of God. In the view of the Old Testament authors, God's revelation is to be sought in an amalgam of three elements: the historical event; the interpretation of that event in authentic tradition; their own participation, through faith and concern, in that past event. An examination of the interpretative thought-patterns within the Old Testament leads to the recognition of an essential unity within its literature. 'Despite its multifarious origins, the Old Testament presents us with a unity of thought such as no human mind could ever have impressed upon it.'[51] Thus, the Exodus has two significant meanings: the Exodus was an event inconceivable without the prior existence of empirical Israel and without Israel's interpretation of itself. 'The Exodus, then, was the fateful moment in God's cosmic plan when a people came to the birth and was adopted as God's Son. But it was also the moment, as Israel's interpreters conceived it, of the birth of the cosmos as well.'[52] The remainder of the third part studies six figures which sufficiently reveal the unique relationship that obtains between God and Israel: Vine, Son of God, Son of Man, Bride, Rock, and Servant.

Part four is a study of the whole of God's purpose, culminating in a series of shorter treatments of ideas which turn around the 'Day of the Lord'. The section opens on the question if it is necessary or even possible to demythologise the Old Testament. The answer lies in the potency of the images in which Israel interpreted its own *raison d'être*. The interpretation was governed by images, not concepts; and since it was the image which constrained the Hebrew mind to interpret the historical fact, the 'demythologisation' of the Old Testament is out of the question. The Old Testament reveals God's plan; the making of a covenant is God's means to attain his ends. The inner heart of the covenant bond was covenant fellowship, *hesed*—essentially God's unswerving loyalty and self-consistent trustworthiness. On the people's side only a remnant would prove faithful, Israel after the spirit. The covenant demanded a practical expression, so God used the Torah for the furtherance of his plan. The merciful God has a purpose for fallen man; in the furtherance of that plan he has chosen to make use of Israel as his kingdom of priests to the nations. We must seek to discover what it means for Israel both to hear God's call to be a living sacrifice and to consistently resist that call. The Old Testament conception of the divine plan saw it move forward in a series of 'moments' of crisis when God 'visits' his people; each visitation is a compound of judgement and mercy; each 'moment' is 'eschatological', having relevance for the End of the total plan.

The purpose of God is described by Knight in terms of five 'moments' in Israel's experience. Since there are three significant 'moments' in the life of men and women on this earth—birth, marriage, death—we ought to expect to find three similar 'moments' in the experience of God's son, Israel. And this, indeed, we do find: birth (called into being as God's son), marriage (at Sinai when Israel was wedded to its God), and death (the end of Judah in 587 B.C.). At this point we go beyond the analogy of the natural man because for Israel there are two further moments: the resurrection from the death of the Exile (*Ezek.* 37), and the fifth and final 'moment' which can be described in eschatological terms alone—'when even the ruins and the waste places (*Ezek.* 36:36) will be built and the desert will rejoice and blossom as the rose (*Is.* 35:1).'[53] This is a convenient scheme, but Knight goes on to draw a number of corollaries, some of which are extraordinary and which lead one seriously to doubt his critical judgement. He claims that the scheme seems to solve the problem of the Apocrypha: since the five 'moments' in the life of Israel, emerging clearly from the Hebrew Bible, correspond exactly with a like five 'moments' in the work of Christ, 'therefore any doctrine which we may discover in the Apocrypha that is nowhere parallelled by a similar doctrine in the full five-moment period in the story of Christ as it is revealed in the New Testament, is not likely to be an authentic element in the total Biblical revelation.'[54] This says, plainly enough, that if the Apocrypha disclose a truth about God and his purpose which does not fit in with Knight's scheme, that truth is of no moment—and not that the scheme may be wrong! Are the New Testament 'moments' so distinct?—that is a crucial question. Knight has to admit that in the case of Christ the first two moments, those of 'birth' and 'marriage', are one. While the third and fourth 'moments' (death and resurrection) in the life of Christ are self-evident, it is surely to beg the question to describe Israel's third 'moment', the Exile, as the 'Crucifixion' of Israel. And does the New Testament see the 'five moments' in the life of Christ as a necessary scheme?

When Knight goes on to consider the place of the individual within the community, he dismisses the Wisdom literature in cavalier fashion. He maintains that the Wisdom books are not the concern of biblical theology because the sages tell us what man thinks about God, whereas a theology of the Old Testament is concerned primarily with what God is saying to men. The sacrifices of the Old Law were intended to be means of grace, and Israel desperately sought after one supreme sacrificial act. No heavenly intercessor could make effective atonement in this world, the realm of matter. Only one of flesh and blood could validate the essential sacrificial principles: to be the means of full communion between God and men, to be the self-sufficient thank-offering due from man to God, and to be the instrument through whom man dare approach the living God. Israel was offered the honour of being this vital medium. *Is.* 53 is a theological interpretation of what Israel's existential experience of exile ought to have meant: God did destroy his people, did raise them up to newness of life, and did restore them to their land.

An important belief in Israel was that in the future also God will act; the Day of the Lord is an object of eschatological hope. The End so conceived is more comprehensive than any conception that a 'messiah' will appear; it is the Old Testament as a whole that is 'messianic'. The Old Testament knows nothing of a *doctrine* of life after death. This is one reason why for the Old Testament writers the life we lead on earth is meaningful in itself. God is working out his mighty plan in the only world that is; it is the same world that he must transform.

In an appendix Knight considers the relationship of Israel and the Church, a relationship at once of continuity and discontinuity, and both elements need equal emphasis. Neither the Israel of old nor the new Israel can be simply identified with Christ; both share in his *pléroma* and are fulfilled in him. The New Testament people of God is a people called by God to be the new eschatological community whose significance lies in its continuity with the Israel of old. And because of the oneness of Israel, through Christ from the Old Testament people of God to the new Testament of God, we discover that the Church too must be one. The incompleteness of the Israel that is the Jewish people

4

resides in their refusing to become 'one flesh', by faith, with
the Suffering Servant. Hence, they are no longer the *eschatological* Israel of God while, paradoxically, they are still the
people of God. 'It is at its peril that the Church in its pride
arrogates to itself alone the place and function of Israel. The
Church has been engrafted into the stock of Israel from
without by the grace of God alone. . . . The Christian approach to the Jew must therefore of necessity be the primary
and fundamental activity of the modern Church as it explores its ecumenical duties. . . . It is the continued existence
of the shadow Church alongside of the Church Catholic
which is the ever-present reminder to the latter of the meaning and significance of a high doctrine of Israel.'[55]

In relation to the Old Testament, Knight has taken his
stand as a Christian, and he maintains that a biblical theologian cannot be neutral. However, he is aware that if the
Church owed its fuller understanding of the Old Testament
to Jesus and what he had said and done, it was also the result
of the experience of continuity which meant that the Church
could regard the self-revelation of God as of a piece with his
act of self-revelation in Christ. Yet, his attitude to the Old
Testament is too much conditioned by a viewpoint which is
an uneasy compromise between allegorism and a historical
approach. When Knight sees events as moments in an imposed scheme, he has in reality virtually abandoned the stress
on historicity which is an essential part of an Old Testament
theology. At the same time, he is still so concerned with
history that he gives very little place to the Wisdom strand
in Old Testament thought. Besides, the book is so marred
by doubtful statements—either factually wrong or curiously
phrased—that one is left with a sense of disappointment.

### 3. Four Representative Old Testament Theologies

We have seen that considerable work has been done in the
field of Old Testament theology (especially when we take
into account also the contributions of *Religionsgeschichte*).
It is widely recognised that, in modern times, four scholars
have emerged as the dominant figures: Eichrodt, Vriezen,
Jacob and von Rad. This section, forming the bulk of the

chapter, will deal with their work; it has seemed to be a positive and effective way of presenting the achievement of Old Testament theology in our day.

I. WALTER EICHRODT

Walter Eichrodt first published volume I of his *Theologie des Alten Testaments* as an effort to meet the need he saw for a fresh survey of Old Testament theology. Although scholars came to accept his 'new departure' during subsequent years, the arguments and conflicting current positions in Old Testament theology made the author retain with emphasis the original layout of his work in preparing the fifth revised edition, of which volume I appeared in 1957 and volume II in 1964; the two volumes were published in English translation in 1961 and 1967 respectively.[56]

*Aim and Approach*

Eichrodt states his purpose in his first preface and repeats the same words in his later preface: '. . . to present the religion of which the records are to be found in the Old Testament as a self-contained entity exhibiting, despite ever changing historical conditions, a constant basic tendency and character.'[57] In his first chapter, 'The Problem and the Method', he says it is imperative to gain a comprehensive picture of Old Testament belief, a cross-section of Old Testament thought, and then to grasp the uniqueness of this unity in its relation to the New Testament. Rejecting both the purely historical approach and the purely dogmatic or doctrinal, he asserts again and again that Israelite religion, with little actual 'doctrine', resists systematising. All the Hebrew's knowledge of God came to him from the real, daily experience of his life, the living immediacy of faith in God, rather than from abstract theories about him. The Old Testament witnesses not to a 'self-contained dogmatic totality, but a real God becoming manifest in history.'[58] Eichrodt has undertaken to proclaim this witness and to clear the way for its fuller expression in the New Testament gospel.

His approach to the material is to follow the lines of Israel's own faith, of the Old Testament's own thought, which he has seen in the form of three basic relationships comprising the three major sections of his work: God and the people, God and the world, God and man. The whole work bears out the author's conviction that this testimony of faith can be seen legitimately only within the context of the Old Testament community. God's personal invasions of the human spirit, his activity in salvation history, can be expressed only 'in combination with the response of the people of God to the historical event sent to them.'[59] The action of this one God, with his one purpose of establishing his kingdom in this world, is the unitive fact in the whole of biblical theology, binding both Testaments together.

Eichrodt deplores the inadequacy of the 'usual theology' which would define the essence of Old Testament religion as 'the bloodless abstraction of "ethical monotheism".'[60] He dares to make the backbone of his whole work the very concept which he feels his predecessors have overlooked—the concept of God's initial covenant with Israel. He feels that this 'covenant concept' and its centrality in Israel's faith is the means by which he can illustrate the unified structure and underlying message of the Old Testament. Eichrodt's entire first section and volume, 'God and the People', is indeed centred around the covenant, its institutions in law and cult, and its 'instruments of expression' in prophecy and the priesthood.

## God and the People

The major opening chapter of Eichrodt's *Theology* deals with the covenant concept and relationship—a theme retained in the titles of every following chapter in the section and sustained implicitly throughout the whole work. For this is the pivotal point upon which the whole of the exposition turns. He emphasises that the covenant concept is simply a convenient symbol which he has chosen; it is not doctrinal, but the 'description of a living process' begun when God's free act at a particular time and place 'raised Israel to the rank of the people of God, in whom the nature and will of God are to be revealed'.[61] At the outset, he discusses the meaning of the covenant concept, its factual nature, its immediate circumstances in God's will: 'You shall be my people, and I will be your God'. The history of the covenant concept is then treated—its refashioning and development as evidenced in the early narratives of the Pentateuch, the work of the classical prophets, the deuteronomic law and writings, and on through the later prophets and the post-exilic period. Eichrodt emphasises that the determining factor is not the presence or absence of the Hebrew word for 'covenant', *berith,* but rather the manifold expressions of living faith in a communion between God and man. He points out that the covenant idea covers two main lines of thought, both pointing to a single divine activity: the legal aspect and the aspect of grace or eschatology. He compares these to the two sides of the idea of the 'kingdom of God' in the New Testament—its present reality and its future expectation. There is also a second conjunction of opposites which strikes the reader of the Old Testament: those concepts or expressions which derive from the realm of law, and those which grow from human life and man's experiencing God there. Or, expressed differently, Israel experienced both the demands of a 'jealous' God and his gracious personality.

At this point it is helpful to survey some of the specific places in which the covenant concept is echoed throughout the whole work. Of prime importance in the concept is the new understanding of the divine nature which came through Moses, one summed up in the specific name of the covenant God: Yahweh (ch. 5). The worship of *this* God marks Israel off from all other nations, and the very name 'Yahweh' denotes an active existence and the loving presence of God the Father which alone could have united the Israelites at the time of their deliverance. The covenant concept governs the Old Testament salvation-hope: the Israel which had experienced a real entry of God into history attained the bold expectation that God would consummate his sovereignty (ch. 11). The covenant laid the foundation for Israel's belief in Providence (ch. 17); it determined, in part, the hold which 'solidarity thinking' had in Israel (ch. 20). God's initial act of love in bending down, choosing Israel, and bearing his people through the wilderness 'as a man bears his son' (*Deut.* 1 : 31) determined man's personal relationship with him—in particular his love for God expressed in the keeping of the

Law (ch. 21). Finally, the covenant idea, sustained through-out the whole of Eichrodt's work, attains its most glorious note in his concluding chapter on immortality (ch. 24). Be-cause of the initial covenant experience Israel had a distinct attitude towards life which came to be more powerful, far more real, than the finality of death. The whole people had to pass through the furnace of destruction, the crisis of death during the Exile, in order to truly place their confidence in God alone beyond earthly security, and thus to truly under-stand what richness of eternal life he holds out to them because of the initial covenant act of his love.

Eichrodt treats the Covenant Statutes in two sections: the Secular Law (ch. 3) and the Cultus (ch. 4). What makes the secular law distinctive in Israel is that the *entire* law is re-ferred to God; the Decalogue demonstrated how moral pre-cepts are connected with basic religious commands. Because Yahweh is known as a living personality, moral sensibility in the secular law is deepened. The second section in the Covenant Statutes deals with the cult, which Eichrodt pre-sents in its pure, positive form as originally set forth in the Old Testament. As such it is a vital part of the Yahwistic religion, both as a means of expressing belief in a personal God and as a sacramental medium by which the divine power is mediated to men.

The book reaches a highpoint of rich, personal expression in the author's treatment of God's nature; this too is divided into two sections—divine being (ch. 6) and the divine activity (ch. 7). Israel's God is, first of all, personal—the 'definable, the distinct, the individual' rather than only a nameless 'ground of being'.[62] Secondly, God is spiritual, and thus man experiences his infinite superiority over human nature. Yet, as part of his graciousness, God has left his spirit-ual nature veiled and presented to man instead his person-hood. The living quality of Yahweh, the 'living God', rather than his 'spiritual nature', became the foundation of Old Testament faith. Finally, God is one—but conceived as such by Israel not through philosophical speculation, but through the experience of God's personal closeness to them.

The chapter on the divine activity deals with the power of God, and then with the *hesed*, the loving-kindness, of

God. The marvellous quality of *hesed* was seen not only in God's condescension, but in the 'mystery of a divine will which seeks communion with man.'[63] The 'righteousness' of God is an expression of his *hesed*: it is his loyalty which transcends all laws and standards, a 'loyalty manifested in the concrete relationships of community.'[64] Eichrodt then explores the nature of God's love, particularly as it is expressed in Hosea and Jeremiah. Yahweh's love is quite irrational and inexplicable, and yet it is the basis of the entire covenant relationship. Israel throughout its history experiences God's love as a mystery, a mystery which can be explained only by the even greater mystery of God's own personality.

It seems only fitting, in the light of Eichrodt's theories, that he should describe the personalities and leaders so familiar to us in the Old Testament as the 'Instruments of the Covenant'. These he divides into the charismatic leaders (ch. 8), which include Moses, the Seers, the Nazirites, the Judges, nabism (early prophecy), and classical prophecy; and the official leaders (ch. 9), consisting of the priesthood and the monarchy. He presents classical prophecy through its links with nabism, its distinctive character, and its religious structure. From the first, it is characterised by strong individuality and personal spiritual understanding: 'everything is molten in the fire of a personal experience with God, and emerges freshly minted.'[65] In the prophetic viewpoint, God's relationship with the world is dynamic; he confronts each individual and demands personal decision. Contrasted with the prophetic view is the priestly view, which Eichrodt develops in the next chapter. After discussing the history and structure of the priesthood, he speaks of how the priestly attitude stresses the visible forms of religion, the Law, because it is by those that God demonstrates his power over the world and keeps it in dependence upon himself. While the prophet taught a new reality which endangers the existence of the nation so that outwardly religious conduct is no longer of any value, the priest was concerned to guide an actually existent people; his moral teaching was described within the limits imposed by an earthly community, and thus concentrated on law and cultic activity.

The priestly view complemented prophetism by looking towards not only the eternity of God's sovereignty, but his control here and now as acknowledged through unified worship and practical conduct. Finally, under the 'Instruments of the Covenant', is treated the monarchy, which ultimately served to strengthen the priesthood and led to a clash with prophetism. For, although through the monarchy the work of the Spirit was seen to be constructively present in political, social and ethical fields, ultimately the Israelite monarchy strengthened the trend in all religious systems 'to develop and petrify its institutions, and to conceive of itself as a static relationship with ordinances laid down once and for all, a form of human life standardised by laws.'[66]

The final chapter of this first section deals with the Old Testament hope of salvation and perfect fulfilment or consummation of the covenant. Eichrodt concludes that the centre of all salvation expectation in Israel was the concrete entry of God into history, and thus that the hope simply underlined the fundamental character of the Old Testament concept of God's revelation. The bold, future hope of Yahweh's coming to set up his dominion over the world in a final, perfect way was matured by *religious,* not national, feeling. Israel came to hope in a divine act of restoration not because the people wished for a renewal of their nation as such, but because they knew God and had experienced his power and made trial of his claim to dominion.

## God and the World

We can treat volume II of Eichrodt's *Theology* in less detail—indeed not because it is any less important, but because it is an extension and illumination of many of the general ideas we have outlined from volume I. In a way, the second volume seems even more immediate to the reader because the covenant God is related to the world and man in such a manner that each individual feels this involvement far beyond the historical Israelite community. This section deals with God's self-manifestation (ch. 12), his cosmic powers (chs. 13, 14), cosmology and creation, with the place of man and the maintenance of the world (chs. 15, 16, 17), and finally the heavens and underworld (ch. 18). We will pause to indicate only some of the highlights.

Primary among the cosmic powers of God is the *ruah*, Spirit, of God. It is defined as the principle of life, the instrument of salvation history, and the consummating power of the new age. The Spirit is that of the living God who equips men for the joyous performance of his will; it brings comfort and help to both the nation and the individual, and the whole of life is seen as 'proceeding from the power of the Spirit, the aim of which is to actualise the will of God in all the forms of human existence.'[67] A second power of God, especially vital throughout the entirety of biblical revelation, is his *word*; the word of Yahweh is his sovereign, unambiguous will, and upon it rests the special relationship Israel knew with her God. In going on to discuss *creation* itself, Eichrodt touches upon ideas central to the whole Israelite attitude towards the Creator and his work: all is summarised as a 'marvellous purposefulness.'[68] This sensitivity proceeds from the fundamental Israelite attitude of optimism towards all created things. These ideas are carried out further in the discussion on the *place of man* in creation —his value and the components of his nature in terms of Old Testament psychology. The characteristic which is distinctly human is personhood: this governs the encounter between man and God, or man and woman, and as a person man is meant to develop his own aptitude to share in both the work and the joy of creation.

In the chapter on the 'Maintenance of the World' Eichrodt has given a beautiful résumé of the place of the miraculous in Old Testament thought. As in the New Testament, its real importance lies in strengthening faith through the experience of God's care. A final highlight which we may note is the discussion of Providence. God's guidance of every event without exception was first grasped through the nation's own history, so that Israel came to believe in God's Providence as his consistent care of day-to-day life.

*God and Man*

Eichrodt begins the final section of his *Theology* with a picture of the relationship between the individual and the

community in Israel (ch. 20). He deals with 'solidarity thinking' both in Israel and in its environment, the effects of this
mentality throughout its early history, the stamp given it
during the monarchy, and finally the reshaping of the individual's life with the political collapse and exile of the
nation. There is an abiding interplay and tension: on the
one hand, the teaching (especially in the prophets) that only
in the re-creation of the individual can God re-create his
community; and on the other hand, the fact that the community is always the mother of the individual's religious life,
for in the Old Testament faith there is no instance of a
'religious individualism' not rooted in the congregation.
Always, 'the individual experience of faith . . . ultimately
flows back into the service of the community.'[69] And yet, in
the following chapter, Eichrodt offers a beautiful presentation of man's personal relationship with God in the Old
Testament, a relationship characterised by fear of God, faith
in God, and love for him. The 'fear of God', so predominant
throughout the Bible, is a combination of awe in the face
of God's holy 'otherness' and of trustful wonder and thank-
fulness, a surrender to his will. Likewise *faith* is a venture
of personal trust, of taking a stand on the promises of God
in the face of all seemingly contradictory appearances. It
is a decision and a surrender to a hidden God who manifests
himself only in his word. This word is sometimes as dark
as the night sky which God showed to Abraham, but it is
lighted by his will even as the stars lit that silent sky and
beckoned Abraham to believe (*Gen.* 15:5-6). *Love* for God
is a transformation of the concept of fear; it proclaims
Yahweh's faithful concern for his people and is a response
to his initial act of covenant love.

The final three chapters of the work handle further points
in the individual's relationship with God: Old Testament
morality, sin and forgiveness, and immortality (ch. 22-24).
The norms of moral conduct in Israel were determined by
an essential unity: the will of one Lord. Because everything
was seen as a response to this, even the humblest act or attitude was elevated to an act of serving and worshipping him.
The goods of moral conduct were primarily those of natural
existence: many children, prosperity, long life, friendship,

peace; however, these were not goods in themselves, but rather witnesses to the Giver of all 'good things', to his favour and fellowship with the individual. This led, especially in the prophetic period, to ascribing a relative value to natural goods as compared with the religious goods of God's salvation. A man's happiness could be directed beyond any earthly enjoyment to companionship and union with God himself. To this end, the ethics of quiet obedience, humble renunciation, and suffering became included in the moral norms, as exemplified in the portrait of the 'servant of Yahweh' in Second Isaiah. Eichrodt continues by saying that all natural and spiritual goods could be combined in a great unity, a wholeness of life—expressed in Hebrew simply as 'peace', *shalōm*. The great value of life in God brought peace and joy out of every hard sorrow.

In a truly powerful closing chapter, 'The Indestructibility of the Individual's Relationship with God' (ch. 24), Eichrodt discusses immortality. In chapter 18 he had discussed the Israelite attitude towards the underworld and death—its finality, its being a deprivation of living in God's presence. But here, he goes on to show that despite this finality, Israel's attitude towards death is distinctive—distinctive because of its attitude towards *life*. Accepting life as indissolubly tied to God and his gifts, Israel at first accepted death too as simply the end of life. After the Exile, when Israel had come to trust in God alone and to understand more fully the life he offered in the covenant, there grew up the idea that death could indeed be overcome for each individual. This was expressed in two ways, the first of which was to see the conquest of death as an eschatological event in which God would reveal his glory and establish his kingdom. The second way of conceiving the conquest of death lay in what Eichrodt calls 'Faith Realism'; by direct encounter with God, through a final peace found in him alone by those who had struggled with pain and hardship or the thought of death, life itself became indestructible. The poet of *Job* is a major example of this victorious attitude emerging from sheer human helplessness. The second witness which he puts forward to Israel's conquest of death is Psalm 73. But such hopes of eternal life reach their completion only in the New

Testament, when the believer is offered that life here and now through Christ. A further look at Eichrodt will come in a later chapter when we shall consider the place of Jesus throughout his *Theology*.

## II.  THEODORE C. VRIEZEN

Theodore C. Vriezen's *Outline of Old Testament Theology*[70] is, according to its author, distinct from other theologies of the Old Testament in that it is directly related to the work and faith of the Christian theologian. The study is divided into two parts: the first deals with the place and interpretation of the Old Testament in Christianity; the second deals with the message of the Old Testament itself understood through modern scholarship and with a view towards its value in the Church. If one wished to find a single sentence summarising Vriezen's vision, perhaps one of his conclusions on eschatology could be taken and applied to his outlook on the whole message of the Old Testament: 'This message sprang from faith, and could only be assented to in faith. It came to be actualised by the author and finisher of our faith, Jesus Christ, and through him faith expects this promise to be fulfilled completely.'[71]

Vriezen considers that the essence of this faith, for both Israel and Christianity alike, lay first of all in a conception of God as the personal God who reveals himself in history, who has entered into the world as the living God and who seeks communion with man. This is the meaning of the Bible, and the unity of both Testaments can be found when this revelation of God is seen to be a continuous, historical line of development. Vriezen makes the valid point that an all-satisfactory evaluation of the Old Testament is well-nigh impossible to achieve, for 'theology has for its task the weighing against each other of the living word of God and the temporal, human element in the Old Testament.'[72] However, he adds immediately, the essential task of theology will always remain 'to test the Scriptures in the light of Jesus Christ the Lord, and to know him by the Scriptures.' Indeed, the true picture of the Old Testament message can never really be given, whether in connection with the history of Israel or with God's revelation in Jesus, not only because of our imperfect understanding, but even more because God's activity in salvation history can never be fully discerned. For, to return to Vriezen's idea of a continuous line of development, not only is that 'line' not always 'straight' but also 'there are only certain points of this line which are visible; the line itself cannot be copied by any man, because it is God's secret.'[73]

The first part of the work (Part I. Introduction) is given over to five chapters in which the author discusses questions confronting the Christian theologian and puts forward the key concepts in his own approach to Old Testament theology. The views expressed in the last of these chapters, entitled 'Basis, Task, and Method of Old Testament Theology', we shall note at a later stage; and the other main ideas of the Introduction will be studied later too. Here we shall consider only his chapter 3 which analyses the 'spiritual structure', the originality of the whole Old Testament and then of its individual writings. Vriezen acknowledges that there *are* all kinds of inward tensions and antinomies to be found in the divine message—and yet, he adds sagely, 'the truth of faith can only be expressed fully in antinomies. Divine reality is so full of life that not only a rational, but even a paradoxical judgement cannot exhaust it.'[74] Indeed, there would seem to be a paradox—and yet, a perfectly clear one—in Vriezen's next conclusion. He affirms his theme that the revelation of God cannot be confined to dogmatic, rational rules, but that such a living God 'can only be known truly by a living *faith* that comes to rest in God and accepts his guidance.'[75] But, he goes on to say, precisely because God *is* a *living* God, he is one 'whose strength and glory are always greater than our experience and faith can comprise and whose nature exceeds all our human knowledge, even the knowledge of faith.'[76] A final point in this chapter prepares the way for the next ('The Old Testament as the Word of God and its Use in the Church'): the Old Testament fundamentally teaches nothing other than what Jesus taught; he learned its meaning from the Father and, like the scribe trained for the kingdom (*Matt.* 13:52), sought but to bring forth greater new truths from its old treasure and apply them to life in himself.

*The Content of Old Testament Theology*

This second part of Vriezen's *Theology,* on the message and content of the Old Testament, really revolves around what for him underlies all biblical testimony and is the basis for Israel's conception of God: 'the reality of an immediate, spiritual communion between God, the Holy One, and man and the world.'[77] This idea of 'communion', expressed variously throughout six chapters in terms of 'relationship' or 'intercourse', finds its starting point in the biblical notion of 'knowledge' as a close relationship with someone or something; and it can be said to find its culminating point in Christ's great 'High Priestly Prayer' for union among his Father, himself and his own in *John* 17. In this very *living* relationship (which thereby is eternally changing), it can be seen again and again that the God who seeks such intimate communion with man is seen to remain at the same time the distinct, holy God—the two spiritual ideas of the 'immanent' and the 'transcendent' dominating the whole of the Old Testament. The first chapter (ch. 6) describes how Israel first received this special communion as a gift from Yahweh in the covenant, the basis for the certainty of a direct relationship between God and man. If Vriezen finds prophecy to be the strongest *revelation* of God's communion with man, he finds the covenant to be the clearest *illustration* of this communion because it 'presupposes a relationship between Yahweh and Israel which arose in history, not a natural relationship.'[78]

The next chapter, on God, describes Yahweh as being 'holy', 'living', 'one and unique', 'eternal', and the Creator and Redeemer. It covers the idea of 'election' as God's right to make decisions transcending man, emphasising the task and special responsibility involved for the chosen one. It explains the frequent anthropomorphisms in the Old Testament as witnessing to the living communion between the faithful and God, a bond compelling expression unlimited by human reason. Chapter 7 is a consideration of man—his creation, mortality and death, man and woman; the state of man as the image of God; the individual and the community; and man *vis-à-vis* nature and history. The sustained note in the Old Testament's doctrine of man is 'realistic'. It also stresses the personal responsibility and value of man, as well as the importance of beauty and the 'good things' of the earth giving joy in creation. In discussing life after death, Vriezen makes the point that the Old Testament leaves the hereafter entirely to Yahweh as the one on whom present communion is focused, and that in this particular doctrine the Old Testament 'clamours for its fulfilment by the New Testament.'[79] He discusses Israel's theocentric conception of history, its learning to recognise the hand of God amidst all the fluctuations of events.

The long chapter entitled 'The Intercourse between God and Man' depicts this 'intercourse' in terms of God's revelation, his redemption and judgment, the cult and piety. Having defined 'communion' with God, Vriezen shows the various ways in which the revelation of God can take place. Revelation through God's word, the 'focal point' of the Old Testament God-man relationship, repeatedly coming to his people, shows how Yahweh 'keeps his faith in his intercourse with his people.'[80] Vriezen believes that Old Testament revelation came first and foremost through the intermediation of the prophets, and thus that Israel's religion is fundamentally prophetic—a fact which has bearing on his interpretation of its link with the New Testament. He observes poignantly: 'if there is one thing that can convince us of the living communion between God and Israel, it is that ever renewed, struggling, purifying, and above all sanctifying activity of his servants the prophets.'[81]

'Judgement' provides a means for God's intercourse with man because it makes his presence apparent in this world and leads men back to God in a true exchange of love. The cult is a means to 'integrate' the communion between the covenant God and man. Piety, as man's answer to God's word, is in the Old Testament 'a living, personal, joyful thing, while its legalistic element makes itself felt only partially.'[82] It is characterised by exuberance and the certainty of relationship with the One who himself experiences human life: 'he who formed the eyes, does he not see?' (*Ps.* 94 : 9). Vriezen points out that neither the doctrine of the 'Fall' nor a complete doctrine of 'sin' is a predominant feature of the Old Testament simply because Judaism has never been able to concede an essentially sinful nature to man's will or to human life. And 'all through the Old Testament we find a fresh breeze of spiritual freedom, notwithstanding the awe-inspiring majesty of God.'[83]

In chapter 10, 'The Intercourse between Man and Man', or ethics, Israel's relationships in society are seen as determined by her relationship with God because of the 'strongly developed consciousness that the foundations of the moral law rest in Yahweh.'[84] Yahweh's sole will embraces the whole of life and is binding upon all circles of the community. Vriezen brings out the peculiar atmosphere of '*humanitas*' in the Old Testament and its emphasis on man's disposition. He delineates the different Old Testament ethical codes, rules of life and moral texts, and remarks that where ethical views seem to suffer 'limitations', it is because 'even the greatest treasures can only be offered in earthen vessels; those who received and reproduced them belonged to their own period.'[85] He offers a sound conclusion on the whole of Old Testament teaching, including the field of morality: it is 'directed entirely towards practical life, it is sober and simple; it does not lose itself in theory, but it is certainly also justified spiritually and psychologically because it includes the heart in its considerations.'[86]

And so, we come to the final chapter, in which the author reveals the full course of that 'golden thread' which has already periodically been glimpsed as a bond throughout his work—that of the kingdom of God, his rule both in the present and in the eschatological hopes of the future. It is here that Israel's 'assent of faith' attained its most distinctive shape. Through faith, the people discovered the universalism of God's sovereignty here and now, and through faith they attained the eschatological vision—the belief that, because God holds history in the 'hollow of his hand', he will bring that history to end in his advent as king in perfect communion between himself and mankind. This conviction came to sustain Israel as a people even amidst the gravest catastrophes; it brought a goal, a meaningful perspective, into this world. Vriezen summarises the eschatological vision in striking words:

The only reason . . . why the Biblical faith can see that a future dawn will break for the world is because it believes in God, or rather because it faithfully hopes for the *parousia* of God, for his coming. It lives in virtue of the fulfilment of its hopes; in this hope placed on God and his kingdom, it gained the victory over the myth of eternal repetition. And on account of this faith the believer lives in the world of freedom, as God's child, for God reigns as king and as such will make his dominion perfect.[87]

Assuming that the basis for all expectations of salvation is faith in Yahweh, in 'him who *is*', and that 'this security remains the basis of all further relationships, even of the most contradictory hopes',[88] Vriezen describes the various forms, both Messianic and more 'general', which the expectation took. He relates these step by step to Israel's history and then in retrospect classifies the development of the salvation idea in the Old Testament into four periods: the 'pre-eschatological' (before the classical prophets), the 'proto-eschatological' (the vision of a new people and kingdom as proclaimed from Amos to Jeremiah), the 'eschatological with reference to the near future' (the kingdom already realised, transforming *this* world, in the teaching from Second Isaiah to Ezekiel), and the 'transcendental-eschatological' (the apocalyptic vision of a *new* world and time order altogether). The eschatological vision arose in the first place because the people had to learn to rely on God as life's only sure foundation; the hopes were possible because 'Israel knew its God as the living God, who is near, who in his holiness does not abandon this world and goes on working in history.'[89] At the heart of his conclusions, Vriezen says that the greatest of the 'great things' to which God called Israel were two visions—of the Servant who gives himself for the sake of others, and of the coming of God's kingdom. Both find their completion in Jesus—the first in his person and mission, the second in the reign of New Life, still awaiting its final completion, which his coming has brought to all of us.

III. EDMOND JACOB

The year 1955 saw the publication, by Edmond Jacob, professor at Strasbourg, of his *Théologie de l'Ancien Testa-*

5

*ment*; it appeared in English translation in 1958.[90] In an
Introduction, far less extensive than that of Vriezen, Jacob
gives an outline of the history of Old Testament theology,
goes on to consider the place of theology in relation to other
branches of Old Testament study, and, in conclusion, notes
the place of Old Testament theology in relation to other
theological studies. These are matters that will be taken up
in a later chapter; for the moment it is sufficient to indicate
his understanding of the scope and purpose of the subject.

In his opening sentence Jacob declares that the theology
of the Old Testament may be defined as 'the systematic
account of the specific religious ideas which can be found
throughout the Old Testament and which form its profound
unity.'[91] At the same time, as a Christian discipline, it must
be concerned with the fulfilment of Old Testament history
in Christ; indeed it is possible to speak of a theology of the
Old Testament only in so far as it is based on the principle
of the unity of the two Testaments. Jacob maintains that
there is room for both the history of Israel's religion and the
theology of the Old Testament; indeed, the latter is a historically orientated discipline which makes full use of scientific research. In his view, piety, religious institutions and
ethics are not part of Old Testament theology's specific
domain. Instead, two closely connected themes are seen to
be central: the themes of the *presence* and the *action* of
God. In other words, Old Testament *theo-logy*, true to its
name, deals only with God and his relationship with man
and the world. Consequently, Jacob arranges his work in
three parts: I. Characteristic aspects of the God of the Old
Testament; II. The action of God according to the Old
Testament; III. Opposition to the final triumph of God's
work.

## The God of the Old Testament

For Israel, the reality of God was evident beyond all
demonstration; the affirmation of God's sovereignty gives
force and unity to the Old Testament. This ever-present
deity could only be envisaged as a person, as a living God;
faith in him attained its best expression in anthropomorphic
language. Following on Israelite belief that a person is con-

centrated in his name, the names of God have a special importance. The origin of the name Yahweh is to be found in the root *hawah*; but it must be remembered that in Israelite thought, existence is a concept of relation—that is, it is only real in connection with another existence: God is he who is *with* someone. Hence, Yahweh primarily conveyed the idea of presence, and 'the priority of presence over existence gives a new and unexpected aspect to all the interventions of Yahweh.'[92] God revealed himself as the jealous God, infinitely superior in power to other gods and claiming the undivided allegiance of his people; one can speak of the practical monotheism of Moses. Angelic powers are best regarded as imperfect sketches of a theology of communication between God and man. The police function of Satan in the earlier tradition—discovering and reporting on the infidelities of men—leads him to be the adversary *par excellence* and, eventually, to his role as head of the army of demons opposed to the heavenly army of Yahweh.

In theological reflection on the manifestations of God, Israel had to consider three principles: a) God is invisible and therefore essentially spiritual; b) God is present, dwelling in the midst of his people; c) God is unique. These three principles were not always easy to reconcile and, at best, Old Testament attempts could only be approaches to the biblical solution of the divine presence, that of God become man in Jesus Christ. Of the more important of these attempts we may say that the function of 'the angel of Yahweh' is comparable to that of a prophet who, though identifying himself for the time being with the one who sent him, nevertheless remains a fundamentally distinct personality, while the function of the expression 'the face of God' is to show forth his presence without reservation. The glory (*kabod*) of God is always intended to be seen. It is very clearly linked with the Temple, the place of God's presence; and the eschatological significance of the *kabod* of Yahweh is particularly evident in Second Isaiah. Yahweh can act by his *name* in as comprehensive a fashion as by angel or glory. The name, which expresses the essential nature of a being, manifests the totality of the divine presence. With Deuteronomy a tendency began to make the name of Yahweh an hypostasis.

The rest of Part I is taken up with a discussion of the outstanding attributes of God. 'From the phenomenological point of view, holiness is a supernatural and mysterious force which confers a special quality upon particular persons and things. This definition best gives the idea of what the Old Testament understands by the term holiness.'[93] Holiness is not one divine quality among others, for it expresses what is characteristic of God and corresponds precisely to his deity. Yahweh is the holy one *par excellence*, but the concept of holiness exists independently of him. The essential aspect of holiness is that of power, a power which communicates itself in order to bestow life. In face of the revelation of holiness man feels his nothingness; his reaction is fear. In the Old Testament holiness receives its particular orientation from its relationship with the God of the covenant; the link appears in its full paradox in Isaiah's 'the holy one of Israel'. Righteousness is conformity to a norm; it is always a concept of relationship fashioned upon everyday dealings between two people. It is an action more than a state: a person is righteous because he acts justly; he does not act justly because he is righteous. The righteousness of God cannot be separated from the figure of God the judge; his judgements always conform to the rule—they are right. God's righteousness is exercised simultaneously in favour of the righteous and for the punishment of the wicked. The idea of grace and deliverance never ceased to underlie the concept of righteousness, looked at in the light of election and covenant; indeed, righteousness as the free and saving favour of God has many echoes in the Old Testament. 'The use of the term *hesed* for human relationships shows clearly that the meaning of benevolence and mercy is secondary to that of solidarity or simply of loyalty.'[94] The *hesed* of God is revealed in and through the covenant; it is less a quality of God than a proof which he intends to give; *hesed* represents the permanent element which allows Yahweh to be always faithful to himself. In the prophets the *hesed* of human relations is conceived after the pattern of the divine *hesed*; and so, the imitation of God is seen as the mainspring of all the religion and ethics of the Old Testament. We see again that the Old Testament 'is interested less in the nature of God than in his work, less in his existence than in his presence.'[95] The covenant of God with his people can be defined only in terms of the mystery of election and the origin of election is found in God's love. The frequency of the figure of marriage to describe the relationship of God with his people underlines the connection between love and *hesed*. The love of God in the Old Testament may be defined as grace and as education; the prophets and most distinctly Deuteronomy stress the role of the law as the most efficacious means of education and of assuring the permanence of the election. At the same time, the Israelite really believed in the wrath of Yahweh; transgression of the covenant was the cause of wrath. The prophets tended to present the history of Israel as a series of manifestations of Yahweh's wrath. For the sages, God's wisdom embraced the universality of his knowledge and the omnipotence of his deeds. The stress was laid more on active than on theoretical wisdom: God's wisdom shines in his works. So too, the wisdom movement affirmed the universality of God in opposition to the restrictions which covenant law tended to introduce.

*The Action of God According to the Old Testament*
Jacob first considers the instruments of God's action, the Spirit and the Word. 'The goal of divine action is to maintain and to create life; to achieve this aim Yahweh chiefly avails himself of two means which we encounter in varying intensities in all the realm of his manifestation: the Spirit and the Word.'[96] The spirit is God himself in creative and saving activity; the word presupposes the spirit, the creative breath of life. Every book of the Old Testament confirms the truth that God reveals himself by his word. The word is revealed in history; the prophet is the man of the word; law is the *debarim*, the words of God; the words of the wise were also a word of God. The theology of the word resulted in two crystallisations: the word fixed in writing and in tendencies towards its hypostasis.

Next Jacob turns to God the Creator of the world. The idea of creation is secondary to that of covenant. God the Saviour who brought his people out of Egypt is more directly the object of faith than is the Lord of heaven and earth. All the same, creation is already a prefiguring of the covenant. Creation is a beginning, it has a sequel; we can speak of *creatio continua*. Creation has an end: eschatology is a return to the beginning, but now with something additional. God's creative activity is regularly expressed in anthropomorphic language; however, the specific term for the creative act of God, *bara*, was not borrowed from anthropomorphic speech. Faith in God the Creator enabled the Israelites to have a coherent view of the world. Yet, in the Bible, the creation of man belongs to the order of redemption rather than to the order of creation. 'Because of the priority of the covenant, man can look creation in the face, for the covenant is eternal whilst the creation will come to an end.'[97]

The next section treats, at length, the nature and destiny of man. The Old Testament makes three basic affirmations about man: he is a creature, he is of eminent dignity through his peculiar association with God, he is a member of a group —the idea of corporate personality. Man is a creature of flesh, but he alone receives the vital breath (*ruach*) from Yahweh. *Nephesh* is what results when *basar* (flesh) is animated by *ruach*. The *heart* of man holds a paramount place in Israelite anthropology. Man is created in the image of God; this means a relationship with a dependence upon the God he represents. It is a matter of considerable significance that neither the fall nor the flood destroyed the image of God (cf. *Gen.* 5: 1, 3; 9: 6), 'and this from the outset puts the concept into the domain of anthropology and not that of soteriology.'[98] It follows, too, that the imitation of God is the principle of the moral and spiritual life. And man is destined for life which is at once a gift of God and a choice on man's part.

God is the God of history, and history is an essential field of God's revelation. In speaking of revelation through history we must be aware that the interpretation of facts is more important than the facts themselves; the Old Testament witnesses to the priority of the interpretation of history over its presentation. Since God has chosen to make historical events the vehicle of the manifestation of his purpose, the faith of Israel is founded in history. Two main events stand out from among the others, one at the beginning, the other at the close of history: the Exodus and the Day of Yahweh. The theological basis of all presentations of Israel's history was faith in one God who directs events according to his purpose. In the Old Testament, history is the most characteristic channel through which thought is expressed; the process of historicisation extends even to the fields of cult and law and subordinates myth to history. Election is one of the central realities of the Old Testament; it is the initial act by which Yahweh comes into relation with his people and it is the abiding reality which assures the constancy of that bond. Election is exercised within the framework of a covenant. The covenant is a gift that Yahweh makes to his people, a gift which forges with them a bond of communion and creates obligations which take concrete shape in the Law. The priestly and prophetic currents, each in its own way, helped to keep alive in Israel the reality of the covenant. Since God is both Creator and Lord of history, divine providence is exercised at the same time in creation and in history.

God acts on and among his people through institutions: the leaders and ministers, and the cult and Law. The king is the first representative of God, his son; his duties and obligations match his privileges. But the man of God *par excellence* is the prophet. He has a direct bond with God; he is God's spokesman. Where king and prophet had an immediate link with God, the priests' link with the deity is of an institutional nature. The wise men were counsellors to the king. It was the purpose of all these representatives to assure God's presence among his people. The king guarantees God's rule on earth, the prophet by his person and his message expresses God's action in history, the priest through the administration of sacred things reminds men of God's sovereignty over time and space, and the wise man teaches that there is no happiness outside God's love.

In the Semitic world in general the fundamental law of the cult was the distinction between the sacred and the profane; 'Israel's originality in the cultic field is shown in the priority of history over myth and of time over space.'[99] In the Old Testament the Law is one answer to the problem of God's presence; only at a relatively late period did Israel's religion become legalistic. Two aspects of Old Testament teaching about the Law correspond to two stages of its development: in the first stage *torah* can be defined as God's revelation to those who are in the covenant, while the second stage is characterised by the cleavage between the Law and the covenant. The covenant had been broken by the infidelity of the people, as the prophets had warned; the tendency was to find in the Law a substitute for the covenant or, at least, to regard the Law as the condition of the restoration of the covenant. The Law ended by becoming an end in itself, instead of remaining a means of walking in God's way.

In Part III Jacob considers the opposition to a final triumph of God's work; first he takes up the themes of sin and redemption. Sin is a refusal to choose God, it is rebellion; the Old Testament speaks of man as a sinner not because he is of human kind, but because he has rebelled against God. Since sin means separation from God it can only be effaced by an act of forgiveness; the motive for God's pardon is his love and *hesed*. Next he turns to a consideration of death and the future life. Throughout the Old Testament the various reflections about death are the result of two currents of thought. According to one death is a dissolution; but according to the other the individual dies but does not cease to exist. In this second viewpoint it was possible to conceive of the dead as still living on with their powers much reduced; and it seems that it was thought that the dead dwelt in the tomb and in Sheol at the same time. Victory over death by resurrection is the latest Old Testament solution to the problem of death.

To round off this third part and his whole book, under the general heading of 'The Consummation' Jacob treats of the eschatological drama and the messianic kingdom. 'The divine presence in the Old Testament may be defined as the presence of the God who comes,'[100] and Israel looked to the time when the divine presence would be made perfectly real. The world as we know it will end; but the idea of the end of the world is always secondary to Yahweh's coming. Though eschatology means rupture, the cleavage between history and eschatology is never radical; the essential place is occupied by the notions of a new creation and restoration. The great return, the turning-point of destiny, takes place in two stages:

judgement and restoration, hinged together by the idea of the remnant. It is a noteworthy fact that the eschatology of judgement and of the great return gave little or no place to the figure of the Messiah. The final pages of the *Theology* are a survey of messianism. We end with Jacob's own concluding words: 'We draw the conclusion that the notion of God's action in history to which the whole context of the Old Testament is referred could not do without his personal presence in men or a certain institution such as the Law and the temple. At the last stage of this history, the synthetic figures of the Servant of Yahweh and the Son of Man, which are among the most perfect creations of Israel's theological thought, will themselves be harmonised in a new unity.'[101]

IV. GERHARD VON RAD

Gerhard von Rad's *Theologie des Alten Testaments* was published in two volumes in 1957 and 1960 respectively.[102] The entire work is centred around von Rad's viewpoint that Israel's faith, based upon historical acts and continuously reshaped by living situations in which Yahweh's hand could be seen at work, is grounded upon a theology of history. Thus, the subject of his *Theology* is the testimony, the credal statements, Israel itself made concerning Yahweh—and in the very contexts of saving history in which she arranged them. Seeing these credal statements as completely bound up with history, von Rad considers the starting point of Old Testament theology to be in God's definitive acts of revelation. But, since Israel continually reinterpreted and re-avowed these acts in the light of future expectation, the Old Testament must be considered as an unceasing saving movement of promise and fulfilment. If it is to be understood properly as such, 'then it becomes apparent how the expectations it contains fan out even wider, then it is no self-contained entity, then it is absolutely open, and the question of its relationship to the New Testament becomes the question *par excellence*.'[103]

Thus, the entire two-volume work is an application of this, von Rad's particular historical approach to the saving events of the Old Testament culminating in the New. Volume I opens with a brief historical sketch of Israel's sacral institutions and phases of history in order to provide a firmer groundwork for the theological theses which follow. The primary contents of the volume are then divided into the theology of the Hexateuch, Israel's Anointed, and Israel before Yahweh—the latter section, drawn chiefly from the Psalms and Wisdom literature, dealing with Israel's personal response to Yahweh's great saving acts. Each section is introduced by 'methodological presuppositions' or considerations in which von Rad sets forth his personal approach to the following topics. A primary unique feature of his whole work is his conviction that Israel's prophetic traditions must be treated separately in a theology of the Old Testament simply because they are a denial, a 'smashing', of the efficacy of Yahweh's 'old' saving actions for the prophets' contemporaries; prophecy proclaims that God will rise up to completely new acts of history. Thus, it forms the backbone of volume II, and the questions of the reinterpretation of history and eschatology involved in prophecy lead on logically to the concluding section on the New Testament.

Perhaps the most comprehensive picture of von Rad's approach can be gained from his initial chapter on 'methodological presuppositions.' In this, he insists that there is only one proper subject matter for a theology of the Old Testament: Israel's own assertions about Yahweh, perceived and arranged by her own faith. These confessional testimonies cannot be ordered towards some systematic 'world of faith' because they did not point to such an abstraction, but rather to Yahweh and his action in history. 'The faith is not the subject of Israel's confessional utterances, but only its mouthpiece.'[104] Since Israel's theological thought cannot be divorced from her history, von Rad holds that one must submit to the sequence of events, the inner connections of history, as Israel's faith perceived them. For, in Hebrew thinking, historical grouping always took precedence over intellectual or theological grouping; 'event' took priority over *logos*. The revelation of Yahweh in the Old Testament is divided into a number of distinctive and heterogeneous acts; but the one principle unifying all of Old Testament thought is that of 'Israel', the people of God always acting and dealt with as a unit. Von Rad's own words are the best summary of his approach:

> If we divorced Israel's confessional utterances from the divine acts of history which they so passionately embrace, what a bloodless ghost we would be left with! If, however, we put Israel's picture of her history in the forefront of our theological consideration, we encounter what appropriately is the most essential subject of a theology of the Old Testament, the living word of Yahweh coming on and on to Israel forever, and this is the message uttered by his acts. It was a message so living and actual for each moment that it accompanied her on her journey through time, interpreting itself afresh to every generation, and informing every generation what it had to do.[105]

*Volume I: The Theology of Israel's Historical Traditions*
Certainly the longest chapter in the *Theology* is that on the Hexateuch. It is interesting, in relation to Eichrodt, that von Rad's first move is to show that covenant theology provides the time-division of the canonical saving history. Yahweh's covenants with Israel, those with Noah, Abraham and Moses, with their attendant promises and demands, are focal points in the divine action organising history into periods and setting the entire mass of Hexateuchal traditions beneath a 'three-fold arch of prophecy and fulfilment'.[106] Von Rad then discusses the primeval history, the place of creation and the earliest stories in Old Testament theology. He concludes with the enlightening observation that biblical primeval history does *not* end with the 'exhaustion' of God's grace at Babel, but with the call of Abraham; thus, the primeval and saving histories are welded together. This conclusion is based on the idea that 'the whole of Israel's saving history is properly to be understood with reference to the unsolved problem of Yahweh's relationship to the nations.'[107] Israel's election with the call of Abraham, indicating Yahweh's saving plan for all history, is the answer to this 'most universal of all theological questions.'

The chapter proceeds with discussions of the history of the patriarchs, the deliverance from Egypt, the divine revelation at Sinai, and the wanderings in the wilderness. In treating the significance of the commandments, von Rad notes how the Deuteronomist gathered all the divine traditions together to give 'a unified theological conspectus—one Yahweh, one (comprehensive) Israel, one revelation, one promised land, one place of worship, one Prophet.'[108] And, whereas Deuteronomy retells history from the angle of *applicatio* (that is, to teach the lesson of the permanent reality lying behind the events), the Joshua and Exodus editors throughout the Hexateuch were not concerned with using history as a guise for truth, but with the reality of the events themselves and Yahweh's presence there. Finally, von Rad finds the promise of Canaan to be the *leitmotiv* of the whole Hexateuch: 'then he brought us to this place and gave us this land, a land flowing with milk and honey' (*Deut.* 26:9). For Israel, to speak of this was not merely a recollection, but an 'avowal of Yahweh which every age had to reformulate in its own way.'[109] Indeed the 'good words' on which the Deuteronomist reflected (cf. *Jos.* 21:43-45) can be said to round off the Hexateuch theologically; for 'not one of the promises "failed": they were all fulfilled in history. Yahweh's great plan in history for Israel achieved its goal, and this is what the whole of the Hexateuch wants to say.'[110]

Thus, any new impulse in saving history could begin only when Yahweh addressed Israel anew. It is as just such a 'new address', occurring outside the already 'canonical' framework of saving history, that von Rad now treats Israel's monarchy. Whereas the hexateuchal material had consisted of enormous accumulations of traditions, the record of the monarchy is more a historiography; this von Rad follows 'backwards and forwards' according to its growth in tradition, trying to comprehend the different theological conceptions of the monarchy held within the sources. He considers first the covenant with David in the histories, especially in the succession document,[111] touches on the office of the Anointed as portrayed in the royal Psalms, and works back to Saul and the Judges. Finally, he considers the Deuteronomist's theology of history in the Books of Kings and the historical work of the Chronicler. He notes that the author of Kings was concerned with the problem of how Yahweh's word functioned in history: 'The Deuteronomist's theology of history was the first which clearly formulated the phenomenon of saving history, that is, of a course of history which was shaped and led to a fulfilment by a word of judgement continually ejected into it.'[112]

The final chapter of volume I, 'Israel Before Yahweh', sets forth Israel's answer to Yahweh's saving acts, its personal response both as a people and as individuals. When it had experienced the two great saving acts of the covenants at Sinai and with David, Israel was moved not only to record them in historical documents, but also to address Yahweh about them in praises, songs, and even complaints. 'For Yahweh had not chosen his people as a mere dumb object of his will in history, but for converse with him.'[113] Von Rad first discusses the various praises, songs and thanksgivings of Israel—the 'praises of Yahweh' being equated with life itself. Here we meet with Israel's encounter with 'the beautiful', an encounter all the more intensely inspiring because it took place in the religious sphere of contemplating Yahweh's revelation and action: 'because of this concentration of the experience of beauty upon the *credenda,* Israel occupies a special place in the history of aesthetics.'[114] He then discusses the righteousness of Yahweh and of Israel as being primarily a question of relationship. One of the most beautiful sections is that on the trials of Israel and the consolations of the individual. The nation took a realistic view of suffering and, through its faith, brought all such experiences of daily life into connection with Yahweh. The 'consolations of the spiritual' took their most sublime form when the idea of 'asylum' became spiritualised as a seeking of refuge in Yahweh, of a deep communion with him which would keep a man 'practically unassailable from the outside.'[115] The final, main portion of the chapter deals with the Wisdom literature, its origin in practical experience, its more theological applications. 'Wisdom consisted in knowing that at the bottom of things an order is at work, silently and often in a scarcely noticeable way . . . One has, however, to be able to wait for it, and also to be capable of seeing it.'[116] And von Rad speaks last about the scepticism which arose (e.g. Qoheleth) when man lost touch with the action of Yahweh in history and wavered in his faith that Yahweh could intervene either in history or in an individual's life.

*Volume II: The Theology of Israel's Prophetic Traditions*
　'Remember not the former things nor consider the things
of old. For behold, I purpose to do a new thing . . .' (*Is.* 43:
18-19). These words of Isaiah are prefaced to volume II of the
*Theology* and are echoed in the concepts and explanations
throughout its pages. As he expresses towards the end, von
Rad's concern is to 'put the prophets back into saving history'[117] where each occupied a place of his own at a specific
cross-roads in God's dealing with Israel. The words of each
prophet are bound up with the point of history at which
they were spoken, and after this point no message could be
repeated exactly in its original sense. Von Rad judges
prophecy's most important specific content to lie in the fact
that the 'new thing' was always *pre-figured* in the old, the
'former things', which were continually projected onto the
future and reinterpreted in its light. Thus, in defending his
method, he believes that this central aspect of Old Testament prophecy can be brought out most effectively by taking
the prophets and their messages individually and in
chronological order.
　The first part of the volume treats general considerations in
prophecy. Beginning with the observation that the break
between earlier Yahwism and the prophets is not so radical
as is supposed since the latter were conditioned by earlier
traditions, von Rad discusses pre-classical prophecy, the oral
tradition underlying the complexes of prophetic material in
the Old Testament, and the nature of the prophet's call. An
interesting chapter is devoted to the 'Prophet's Freedom',
showing how it was up to him to make momentous decisions
in revealing the divine secrets to the people in general. Moreover, in the prophets 'we are shown men who have become
persons because God has addressed them and they have had
to make a decision in his presence.'[118] A final chapter deals
with Israel's ideas on time and history and with the prophetic
eschatology, which shifted the basis of salvation to a future
act of God.
　The second part is a complete treatment of classical
prophecy, taking the prophets in chronological order and also
offering summaries of the different major periods of prophecy.
In the introduction to the first chapter, on Amos and Hosea,

von Rad further explains his view of the prophet's message as not a 'timeless idea', but as a particular, irreplaceable word relevant to a particular hour of history and delivered to specific men and women who stood in a special situation before Yahweh. In fact, he goes on to say, one cannot really speak of a prophet's 'message' to which every word is subordinate: 'All that we have are the various individual words in which, on each specific occasion, *the* word of Yahweh was proclaimed in a different guise.'[119] Three factors contribute to a tension giving birth to the prophet's *kerygma*: the new eschatological word, the old election tradition, and the personal situation of the people addressed.

The next chapter on Isaiah brings out the astonishing demand he made on his contemporaries—that they make their *present* existence rest on a *future* action of God, that they find salvation now by taking refuge in his future promise of deliverance. Von Rad goes on to summarise the new elements, the 'new departures', in eighth-century prophecy. He begins with the fact that these men were very lonely and isolated from their contemporaries because of the non-transferable word of Yahweh spoken to them. As they listened to this, 'these men became individuals, "persons". They could say "I" in a way never heard before in Israel.'[120] The prophets and their hearers stood on common ground regarding the old Yahwistic traditions, but they interpreted these in different ways. The prophets shocked their hearers by proclaiming that Yahweh had pronounced sentence on Israel because its history had been one long failure witnessing to its refusal. But the heart of the prophet's message is that, despite this failure, Yahweh would still not withdraw. They 'take as their basis the "No" pronounced by Yahweh on the Israel of their day, her relationship to Yahweh which had for long been hopelessly shattered. They were sure, however, that beyond the judgement, by means of fresh acts, Yahweh would establish salvation; and their paramount business was to declare these acts beforehand, and not simply to speak about hope and confidence.'[121]

We pass, then, to the Babylonian and Early Persian period of prophecy, highlighted by the work of Jeremiah, Second Isaiah and Ezekiel. Von Rad discusses the distinctive features of Jeremiah's mission, the seeming impossibility of the prophet's task in which 'there is not one single instance of hope, no occasion when he gives thanks to Yahweh for granting him redemptive insight or allowing him some success.'[122] Jeremiah's confessions are said to grow out of his specific call to serve Yahweh in a particular way, to have a relationship of unique intimacy with God, and they are characterised by a questioning reflection. 'On the one hand he is bound to Yahweh and remained subject to him more than any other prophet; on the other, however, he had to let his thoughts have free range.'[123] The most important feature of Jeremiah's prophecies of salvation is that of the new covenant in which 'Yahweh is, as it were, to by-pass the process of speaking and listening, and to put his will straight into Israel's heart.'[124] This will do away with the former problem of obedience since it envisions a 'new man' whose will is not confronted by the will of God as something alien, but is rather united with that divine will in the man's own heart. One new sphere of prophetic activity arising with Ezekiel, whose roots were in the sacral traditions of the priesthood, was his engaging in the 'cure of souls' (*paraclēsis*), giving exhortation, warning, and comforting address. He too sees that the saving event which Yahweh is to bring about in the heart of man is of the greatest moment. For Ezekiel the whole of canonical history can be explained in terms of the 'divine inconsistency' of Yahweh's lasting regard for the honour of his name amongst the nations, despite Israel's constant failure to comply with his will.

Von Rad portrays Second Isaiah as a skilled religious writer rather than a prophet, one who makes use of the Exodus, Zion and Creation traditions and takes Yahweh's creative word as the pivotal point of his preaching. It is here that we are introduced to the 'continuity of prediction': because the 'former things', the previous basis for faith, *had* come to pass, Israel could place her faith in the 'new thing', the saving act about to come to pass after a long pause in the saving history. In describing Second Isaiah's discourses with those of 'little faith', those who had grown weary and felt forsaken by Yahweh, von Rad states: 'Never before had Yahweh spoken in such a way by the lips of a prophet. Never before had he come so close to his people when he addressed them, laying aside anything which might alarm them in case he should terrify one of those who had lost heart.'[125] In his view, an understanding of the Servant of Yahweh depends upon grasping the nature of the office allotted to him; von Rad concludes that light on this subject can be shed by the Deuteronomic tradition which looked for a 'prophet like Moses'.

Summarising this period of prophecy, he links Jeremiah, Ezekiel and Second Isaiah by the ceaseless political crises with the Mesopotamian empires, the personal element and broader basis in their preaching, and the large part played by theological reflection—in particular, an absorption with the phenomena of their 'words' and the word of Yahweh. 'For these prophets, the hardest problem lies in the realm of anthropology—how can this "rebellious house", these men "of a hard forehead and a stubborn heart" (*Ezek.* 2 : 3-4), who are as little unable to change themselves as an Ethiopian can change the colour of his skin (*Jer.* 13 : 23)—how can these be Yahweh's people?'[126] The answer lies in the prophecy of a new covenant, a future saving act. The last two chapters of the second part deal with the prophets of the Later Persian period, and Daniel and Apocalyptic. Contrary to many accepted theories, but in accordance with his own entire approach to Old Testament theology, von Rad sees *no* possibility of apocalyptic's being rooted in prophecy since 'it no longer knows anything of those acts of God on which salvation was based and on which all previous accounts of the nation's history had been constructed.'[127]

The conclusion of von Rad's work, 'The Old Testament and the New', will be studied in a later chapter.

CONCLUSION

Walther Eichrodt's *Theology of the Old Testament* is widely, and with justice, regarded as the greatest work to appear in the field of Old Testament theology. A mark of this is that although his first volume appeared in 1933, the *Theology,* far from becoming dated, has grown in stature over the years. Eichrodt is certainly justified in his opposition to the use of the categories of dogmatic theology to provide an outline for a theology of the Old Testament since these neces-

6

sarily introduce a foreign element into the picture; however, if the Old Testament is to be related to Christian dogmatics, some kind of thematic presentation is desirable. His contention that the material must be arranged according to a pattern drawn from the dialectic of the Old Testament itself is eminently reasonable, and his division: God and People, God and World, God and Man, is undoubtedly more satisfactory than the traditional one. What he seems to do throughout his work is to reach a total picture of the Old Testament world of belief. He rightly claims that the activity of God in history must never be isolated from the response of the Old Testament community. He does justice to the priestly as well as to the prophetic strain, showing that these are not antagonistic but complementary elements in Israel's faith. He takes care to stress the forward movement in the Old Testament; he believes that, apart from its completion in Christianity, Judaism is a torso. Yet, Eichrodt's synthesis is, to some extent, artificial since the Old Testament is not very amenable to systematic treatment. Though this is the factor which appears to impart a powerful unity to the work, his organisation of the material around the central idea of 'covenant' is, in some respects, the greatest source of weakness. The idea of the covenant is by no means omnipresent in the Old Testament writings; to make it appear so is to place an undue strain on the arrangement and interpretation of the material. Besides, if we are to look for a central idea, it would appear that Wright may well be correct in seeing that the doctrine of election is primary, with the covenant confirming and clarifying the implications of election. At least, election is closely associated with covenant and should be given due prominence. Yet, whatever reservations one may voice, Eichrodt's study has become a classic and has set its stamp on subsequent work in the field.

T. C. Vriezen is quite sure that the subject matter of Old Testament theology is not the religion of Israel, but the Old Testament as a book which bears witness to divine revelation; he attempts a synthesis: a theology of the Old Testament in its essential lines. His choice and arrangement of themes are reasonably satisfactory; his plan lies somewhere in the middle region between a too tidy theological scheme which would distort the Old Testament evidence, and one which is too loosely knit to be a theology proper. His method, too, is fruitful; he admits the polarity, the complementary force of the concepts. It is a principle which does justice to the facts of the Old Testament better than other critical hypotheses. While Vriezen does not stress the importance of a dominating concept as strongly as Eichrodt does, his idea of an intimate relationship or intercourse between God and man is, in practice, such a central, dominating concept. It recurs as the great theme of the book and is manifested in concrete terms, thus escaping, in large measure, the danger of abstraction. This principle not only demonstrates the unity of the Old Testament message but offers a sound basis of the relationship between the two Testaments. The principle also enables Vriezen to include effectively in his scheme two subjects which have tended to be misrepresented or neglected: the cult and piety. And in his chapter on the intercourse between man and man he has found a natural setting for a treatment of ethics; here he brings out the special quality of the moral teaching of the Old Testament. In his last chapter the difficult problem of eschatology is expounded with singular clarity.

Vriezen's synthesis, however, is not free of a certain abstraction. His plan, in the beginning at least, is not really historical and dynamic, but conceptual: we begin with the idea of God, continue with the idea of man, and only then come to the encounter of God with man. Now, it has become increasingly clear that, in the Old Testament as a whole, God is known by what he does; it may be objected that this factor is not sufficiently represented by Vriezen in the structure of his theology. But, on the whole, it can be said that he has given a truly significant treatment of his subject, admirable in plan and presentation. It is a work of critical scholarship, marked by sound judgement and religious insight, besides being a work of great pastoral value.

Though the arrangement of Edmond Jacob's book may be said to be rather traditional, his plan has the advantage of centring all on God—on God as living and acting, and this certainly is a valid factor in a 'theology'. He recognises, from the start, the unity of the Old Testament, despite all appearances of diversity, and sees it as a preparation for the New Testament, thus affirming the unity of the two Testaments. In spite of its relative brevity, Jacob's *Theology* is no superficial treatment of the subject but one that is fundamentally solid. Indeed, many would regard it as the most satisfactory treatment of Old Testament theology for the theological student; that is precisely why it is important to point out its shortcomings.

Jacob's definition of Old Testament theology as 'the systematic account of *religious ideas*' found in the Old Testament is not too happy. He certainly understands that the faith of the Old Testament is centred not upon ideas about God but upon the interpretation of, and the response to, God's actions in history, and throughout his work the themes of the presence and the action of God are dominant. But, apart from his definition, it is not clear that the way he has chosen to organise his material preserves this perspective adequately. 'Will not the arrangement, in spite of the author's implicit statements to the contrary, convey to the unwary reader the impression that Israel's faith consisted first in a certain view of God, certain ideas about him, and only secondarily in the awareness of, and response to, the divine action in history?'[128] It may be that Jacob has been influenced by his belief that biblical theology has the task of supplying dogmatic theology with its 'raw material'—and we are faced with the thorny problem of the relationship between biblical theology and systematic theology. It seems, too, that he should have given greater prominence to the notions of election and covenant (election preceding covenant as a divine initiative) which, in the perspective of the Old Testament, command all the activity of God in the world until his triumph is fulfilled in the New Testament. Since it is Jacob's express intention to present all the essential features of Israel's faith, his exclusion of piety, cult and ethics from the scope of his study, is open to question. In fact, despite his statement of principle, he does not quite exclude them, but it is clear that, for him, they are not an essential feature of Old Testament theology. Here, certainly, Vriezen is eminently more satisfactory. While Jacob shows a commendable concern for the analysis of theologically important words, he has been justly criticised for laying too much stress on the etymology of words in attempting to arrive at their theological significance.[129] All these criticisms are valid, but they do not seriously detract from a balanced, comprehensive and clear presentation of Old Testament theology.

The three foregoing Old Testament theologies have a great deal in common; the work of Gerhard von Rad is distinctive and has opened a new phase in the discussion of the problems and methods of Old Testament theology. But, whereas the others have been favourably received, von Rad's *Theology* has stirred up considerable adverse criticism. We have seen that von Rad insists on the historical character of the faith of Israel: it is founded on the religious interpretation of events in which Israel had seen the hand of its God. This history is *Heilsgeschichte,* or history of salvation, and it is the basis of theological witness. The main task and method of an Old Testament theology is to re-tell this history. Consequently, von Rad's two volumes study successively the different groups of 'traditions' and are concerned with the 'theology' found in the historical traditions. His critics maintain that all this is very impressive—until we realise what he means by "history". He is entirely sceptical of the historical value of the interpretation of events, the *Heilsgeschichte.* There is a radical discrepancy between the theological expression of Israel's tradition and the facts of Israelite history. The 'acts of God in history' presented by the Old Testament narrators are pictures of Israel's history drawn without relation to or in contradiction of the facts and with the specific purpose of glorifying the God of Israel and his saving works. In other words, the 'salvation history' is presented by the different writers in accordance with their 'kerygmatic intention'; it is something quite distinct from a historical-critical view of Israel's history. Von Rad's position is quite like that of R. Bultmann, for whom the New Testament kerygma is independent of historical reality. Similarly, for both these scholars, an underlying conviction is that the existentialist interpretation of the biblical evidence is the right one; and in that case, the relation of the believer's convictions to history become immaterial.[130]

It would appear that such unfavourable judgements have

been unduly severe.[131] Von Rad himself[132] believes that he does not shirk a fundamental question: whether there is a true, objective salvation history, or only a religious reading of religious events. For the biblical writers the only events that count are those in which they see God at work, and their texts do deal with God's action in time. Biblical history, in short, is kerygmatic history—proclaimed by the religious traditions; it is a history of revelation, in deed and in word. The event is seen and proclaimed, the proclamation is re-read and readapted, all in the light of faith in Yahweh and his saving activity—but the proclamation in faith does not create the basic event. Von Rad has set out to present the varied proclamations of faith made by writers representative of the different religious traditions in Israel; he does not deny that there is a historically objective reality, that there is history as event, behind the kerygma. Hence, comparison with Bultmann is not fair to von Rad; the former does deny the reality of salvation history whereas, for von Rad, factual history and interpretation *together* constitute kerygmatic history. What is true is that the event takes on a new wealth of meaning as it progresses through the successive strands of tradition—and the tradition is itself a fact of the history of Israel.[133]

Von Rad has claimed that he has let the idea of *Heilsgeschichte* dominate the ordering of his subject; in fact, he has not really succeeded in bringing everything under its head. Thus, for instance, when he deals with Israelite thought about the world and man, he is in the 'idea world' whereas, by his his own canons, he should only be concerned with what Yahweh has done on the basis of what is directly enunciated by Israel. He claims, too, that he is letting the Old Testament speak for itself—but is he really doing so? For instance, he treats Deuteronomy as a late re-presentation of old traditions in a new form; but if he were to follow what Deuteronomy says of itself he would have to present it as a sermon of Moses spoken some forty years after the Exodus. Besides, he nowhere examines the concept of *Heilsgeschichte* critically and it is questionable that this concept is, in fact, the supreme controlling category in biblical interpretation.

Von Rad thinks that it is not possible to write *a* theology of the Old Testament: there are *theologies* which vary according to epochs and writings. The only unity which a theology of the Old Testament can seek is that which Israel itself has perceived. But surely one may reasonably maintain that if throughout the Old Testament we can discern the hand and hear the voice of the same God, we are perfectly justified in looking for an inner agreement in the 'traditions,' the testimonies of faith. We can discern certain common basic features which can be combined to form a unified system of belief.[134] Von Rad, on principle, rejects any systematisation of the elements of Israel's faith, any attempt to obtain a comprehensive picture of the Old Testament world of faith.

No one will deny that von Rad has made an outstanding contribution to Old Testament science; no one who studies his *Theology of the Old Testament* can fail to be stimulated by his brilliant insights and impressed by his erudition.[135]

We are left, then, with two quite different approaches to the theology of the Old Testament: that represented by Eichrodt, for instance, and that of von Rad.[136] The comment of J. Barr is apposite: 'It is possible that in the future Old Testament theology should try to work with something of both methods, on the one hand trying to state the central essentials of Biblical thought in Eichrodt's manner, and on the other working on the theological intention of the various passages in their historical setting, as von Rad tries to do; and in either case admitting that neither method will work at every point.'[137]

## 4. Roman Catholic Old Testament Theologies

In comparison with the immense work done by Protestant scholars in the field of Old Testament theology, the contribution of Roman Catholics has been slight. There are two main reasons why this should be so. In the first place, at the very time that so much progress was being made in the whole area of biblical studies, Catholic biblical scholarship was hampered by suspicion and restrictive measures; this was the situation right up to the liberating *Divino afflante Spiritu* of 1943. On the other hand, dogmatic theology as taught and studied in seminaries no longer found its source in Scripture.

It had become a text-book discipline, and the authorities were the accredited theologians of the past and official ecclesiastical pronouncements. There simply was no interest in biblical theology, nor even an awareness that such a discipline existed. Furthermore, the scriptural formation of the dogmatic theologian was hopelessly inadequate; and even if he did have some understanding of biblical theology, there really was no place for it in his neat scholastic system. As for the biblical scholars, they, for the most part, were engaged in fighting a rearguard action against the onslaught of 'rationalistic' methodology. Others, of broader outlook, had enough to do to assimilate the literary and historical achievements of the 'higher critics'. One advantage, however, Roman Catholics did and do have: a wider field of study. They accept as canonical the 'deutero-canonical' books, or Apocrypha; these are ignored, or explicitly excluded, by all the scholars we have considered up to now.

In the opening decade of the century, M. Hetzenauer made the first, lone attempt at an Old Testament theology.[138] It was the era of modernism and Hetzenauer is only too happy to describe himself as a conservative, carefully designating his work as a *Catholic* biblical theology; he takes issue throughout with the views of liberal Catholics—like M. J. Lagrange. He is obviously not the man to make any worthwhile contribution in the field of biblical theology.

Yet, Hetzenauer has been influenced enough by the prevalent dominance of *Religionsgeschichte* to devote more than half his book to a treatment of the history of the Old Testament, from Adam to Christ. If he does turn to extra-biblical evidence (his erudition is truly impressive), it is never in any constructive way. Thus, in his eyes, the Babylonian flood-story is an adulterated version of the original monotheistic form which the Hebrew tradition has preserved in its pure state.[139] The second part of his work is concerned with the religion of the Old Testament and is almost entirely devoted to what he calls the theoretical truths. In the first place, these regard the nature of God: the divine names, essence, attributes and persons (many Old Testament texts indicate obscurely at least a plurality of persons in the deity). In the second place come the truths relating to God's works:

the creation, redemption, and consummation of the world. In practice, Hetzenauer has adhered to the categories of scholastic theology and has given an exegesis of the traditional proof-texts. A very brief section on the 'practical truths' looks at the text of the Decalogue. For Hetzenauer these practical truths are the legislative material. In his view, and here he is correct, the ceremonial and civil laws belong in biblical archaeology; he feels that the moral laws are adequately treated by Catholic moral theologians. The most that can be said is that a Catholic had undertaken to write a theology of the Old Testament; we must wait thirty years for another to take up that task again.

In 1940 Paul Heinisch, professor at Nijmegen, published his *Theology of the Old Testament*.[140] He intended it primarily as a students' handbook, and it must be evaluated accordingly. In his Introduction he explains that while a 'History of the Religion of Israel' would show what the religious and moral conditions among the people actually were, a 'Theology of the Old Testament' should present in a systematic manner what the charismatic leaders and inspired writers required as to faith and morals. However, a theology of the Old Testament must have an eye to history and must take into consideration the development of doctrine.

The conception of the work as an aid to the theological student in his study of dogma was not the only factor which dictated the plan of this *Theology*; there is also the current scholastic understanding of revelation in exclusively conceptual terms. We find hardly any awareness that God reveals himself in and through history, that the actions of God, interpreted by his authentic representatives, are his self-revelation. Heinisch has arranged his material in five parts: God, creation, human acts, life after death, redemption. Apart from human acts (the field of ethics), the plan is that of dogmatic theology.

Heinisch begins by considering divine revelation, with Moses and the prophets seen as its chief organs; priests, psalmists, wisdom teachers, and the kings are the guardians of Israel's spiritual life. Then come the existence of God, our knowledge of him, and the names of God. Predictably, the phrase 'I am who am' is taken to imply aseity, that God possesses self-existence. Among the attributes of God is his immateriality: 'Since God is "being itself" and in no way subject to change or dissolution as are all material things, he must be a spirit. And because he is infinitely perfect, he must be a perfectly pure spirit.'[141] It is a typical example of how scholastic theology is read back into the Bible. There is also a study of God's immensity, omnipresence and omniscience—we are far removed from biblical categories. It must be granted, however, that God's righteousness, *hesed*, and the word of God are treated at relatively great length.

Part II, on creation, first takes up the spirit world (angels and demons) and then the visible world. Babylonian cosmology is used to illustrate the biblical creation stories. Though the biblical terms are adequately explained, the later dualistic concept of man (soul and body) tends to be read into them. Thus, belief in some sort of existence after death is not very happily presented in terms of the immortality of the soul: 'Israel at all times firmly believed that the soul, when separated from the body, does not cease to exist.'[142] The privileges of Adam and Eve in paradise are simply listed after the manner of dogmatic speculation.

Part III is a short treatise of moral theology, with a sizeable portion of it given over to a critique of Old Testament morality. The treatment of faith, the first of duties towards God, is hopelessly inadequate—because it is taken apart from hope and trust; the crippling effect of non-biblical categories is especially apparent here. The second part of the chapter, divine worship, is far more satisfactory. Heinisch does not dwell on descriptions of cult, sacrifices and feasts, but brings out the significance of sacrifice and has a good treatment of prayer. The final section deals competently with sin and suffering.

Part IV, on life after death, is very brief: it takes up the themes of Sheol, retribution and resurrection. Judgement is the first theme of part V, on redemption; it is explained that sin gave birth to the desire to be free from sin, which is an achievement of Yahweh. The Gentile nations must be brought to acknowledge their own helplessness and dependence on God and Israel must be disciplined that it might turn to Yahweh with a purified heart. 'Thus judgement was a preparation for, or an initial stage in, the redemption from sin.'[143] 'The new kingdom of God' is concerned with the restoration of Israel, the conversion of the Gentiles and, especially, the glory of the messianic kingdom. The final section takes up the person, mission, suffering, and glory of the Messiah. Here there is a tendency to interpret the messianic oracles in a too directly Christological sense, and it is surprising to learn that the divinity of the Messiah is an Old Testament datum. Suffering and glory are, of course, chiefly referred to the Servant of Yahweh and the Son of Man.

It is, perhaps, true to say that Heinisch would have been less conservative in his views if he had written after 1943; in fairness to him we must not overlook the fact that the publication of an Old Testament theology which, in many regards, shared the exegetical positions of Protestant scholarship was, at that date, a courageous enough venture. The legacy of *Religionsgeschichte* is observable in his consistent turning to non-biblical parallels. These are not always very helpful and the space so occupied would, with greater advantage, have been devoted to a study of such basic concepts as election and covenant—which are not discussed at all! The greatest defect of the work, already indicated, is its practical unawareness that God reveals himself in and through history. One might find here, too, a demonstration of the fact that the imposition of the scheme of dogmatic theology on the Old Testament material is not really the way to a satisfactory presentation of Old Testament theology.

The *Theologia Biblica* of F. Ceuppens is not really a biblical theology at all. The more immediately Old Testament part of it[144] is limited to the theme of God in himself, and follows the order of the *Summa Theologiae* of Aquinas. It offers a careful exegesis of the relevant Old Testament texts. Admittedly, on exegetical grounds, Ceuppens is very sound and, in many respects, his treatment is more satisfactory than that of Heinisch.

The outstanding Roman Catholic *Theology of the Old Testament* is that of P. van Imschoot.[145] In his Introduction van Imschoot outlines his understanding of the object, method and division of a theology of the Old Testament.

He sees biblical theology as an exposé of the religion of the Old Testament—that is, of the religious life, practices and beliefs of Israel down the ages. In practice, this could be no more than a history of the religion of Israel; if it is to be truly a theology, it must be a logical grouping, a systematic presentation of the doctrines of the Old Testament. It cannot, of course, ignore the history of the religion of Israel; on the contrary, it presupposes it, as it presupposes the literary and historical criticism together with the exegesis of the books of the Old Testament. The object of Old Testament theology is God's revelation as this is found in the inspired books. But if a presentation of this revelation is not to strain the perspective and to falsify the thought of the inspired writers, it must take account of the historical contexts and the stages marked by the heralds of the divine word from Abraham to John. It will also take account of the orientation of the old revelation towards the new. Moreover, while scrupulously respecting the proper character of the Old Testament, it will organise the doctrines of the Old Testament in function of the new revelation, since the latter is the crowning of the former.

There is not, in the Old Testament, a scientific, logical elaboration of the religion of Israel. However, it is permissible, without doing violence to Israelite thought, to extract and group ideas, to unite them in a synthesis. Such a synthesis, while respecting the originality of each author and the divergencies which they sometimes show, also brings into light first the basic unity of the revelation confided to the chosen people and committed to the sacred books, and then its continuity with the New Testament revelation, of which it is the preparation. Since the Old Testament has preserved the successive and fragmentary revelations confided to Israel, without furnishing any systematic exposé nor any ordered plan, it is necessary to introduce a plan, one which permits the logical grouping of the doctrines, without doing violence to the structure of Israelite thought. Van Imschoot believes that the simplest plan, the one which best reflects this object, is that adopted by E. Sellin and L. Köhler. It groups the doctrines under three principal rubrics: God, Man, and Divine judgement and salvation. His volumes treat, respectively, the first and second of these; a third volume has not appeared, so this *Theology* is incomplete.

## Volume. I. God

Van Imschoot begins his study by considering God in himself. The whole of the Old Testament presents God as the living, active and personal God, who has made himself known to Israel and continues to manifest himself by his interventions in the history of his people; anthropomorphic language reflects the personal character of God. The attributes of God are grouped in two categories: metaphysical (omnipotence, sublimity, eternity, omnipresence, omniscience and wisdom) and moral. The moral attributes are his goodness and mercy, truth and fidelity, and righteousness— the last one receiving by far the fullest treatment. At the same time, the Old Testament refers to God's human sentiments—such as love, repentance, jealousy and anger, sentiments which are understood to flow from the divine attributes. The second chapter turns to God and the world. God creates, conserves and governs the world; the divine providence, or the activity of God in the physical and human world, is exercised according to a plan and follows a determined end. God has subjected the elements to his laws; he equally well directs human events and history and each man in particular. The divine providence is manifested especially in the conduct of peoples, principally Israel, and of individuals. Since all natural phenomena were attributed to God, the idea of miracle is vague—it is the admirable, mysterious, terrifying, and so on. The space devoted to angels and demons illustrates an imbalance that pervades the work: 27 pages, as against 24 pages allotted to the attributes of God!

The author then takes up the theme of revelation. If man knows God it is only because God has made himself known; the origin of man's knowledge of God is always to be sought in an initiative of God. The means by which, according to the Old Testament, God reveals himself, or makes known his design and his will, are very diverse: theophanies, angels, oracles, dreams, word, name, glory, face—without speaking of his actions in the history of Israel. The prophets and the Spirit are dealt with at some length. Surprisingly, 'word' is

given only a few pages; the concluding section on hypostasis
is far longer—again that lack of proper balance. The final
chapter of the first volume, God and his people, is concerned
with the covenant and election. Covenant implies, in the
first place, the mutual relation of belonging which unites
the contractants, together with the rights and duties which
flow from this relationship. The idea of a covenant which
unites Israel with its God is fundamental in Israelite religion; always the initiative is God's. The idea of the election
of Israel is intimately linked to that of the divine covenant.
For Israel, as for Christians, election is a fundamental and
uncontested dogma which is an essential element of the
originality of the people of God and of its religion.

*Volume II. Man*

The Old Testament does not have a systematic doctrine of
man, nor a psychology as conceived in modern terms or even
in Greek philosophy. It is difficult to present any synthesis of
the anthropology and psychology of the Old Testament. It
is important to have in mind that the Hebrews did not think
of man or of a soul apart from a body; they always considered
man as a whole. Man is at once *nefesh* ('soul') a living being,
and *flesh,* a living corporeal being or a weak and perishable
being. Man is the image of God in his personal aspect, in his
faculty of thinking and willing. The whole study of the
nature of man is built on a study of the terms used to
designate the aspects of human being and life. The second
chapter considers the life and destiny of man. Life is not an
abstract concept but designates physical, organic life; and
includes not only individual existence but the power of
acting, of willing, of desiring. The mere fact of existing is
not, to the Hebrew mind, life; that is why, after death, even
though man still subsists, he does not *live.* Death is the
normal term of every life. The idea that death is a consequence of the sin of the first man is not prominent. We
should carefully distinguish between the following ideas:
the survival of man after death, retribution beyond the
grave, and the immortality of the soul. The first seems to have
been always present, the second occurs very late in the Old

Testament, and the third is found only in the Book of Wisdom.

Considerably more than half of the volume is given over to the duties of man. The Old Testament does not know our distinction between morality and religion: obligations towards man are imposed by Yahweh just like man's obligations to God; both are presented as the clauses and obligations of the covenant. The chapter is as long as it is because van Imschoot has devoted most of his space to considerations of the sanctuaries, sacrificial rites, and religious feasts. This is material which belongs in a study of the institutions of Israel; such an exhaustive treatment of the matter has no place in a theology of the Old Testament. On the other hand, the piety and prayer of Israel are lightly touched on. The chapter closes with man's duties and obligations to his fellow men: it is a short treatise on ethics. In the final chapter, 'Sin', it is noted that to designate sin the Old Testament has an extremely broad vocabulary; but the majority of the terms have not the exclusively religious and moral sense of our 'sin'. Much of the treatment is given over to the sin of the first man and the universality of sin. A relatively long treatment of expiation and forgiveness is again mainly concerned with expiatory rites.

The thought of the Old Testament is essentially a thought in continual progress; it is unceasing. The divine pedagogy developed slowly, and the duty of one who would wish to describe it is to respect its development and its different phases. Van Imschoot has indeed felt this, but he has allowed his plan to dictate his order of treatment, and so historical perspectives are blurred. An arrangement more congenial to biblical categories would have enabled one to see more clearly the marvellous growth of the faith of Israel and to discern the central values of this faith. The major part of his second volume is concerned mainly with morality and ritual; this rather gives the impression that the spiritual attitude of ancient Israel might be reduced to external attitudes or to a morality of precepts. Van Imschoot's work is a rich repertory of texts and of religious facts carefully classified and easy to find. The style, however, is too compressed; one is inclined to regard it as a book of reference, not as a book to be read with any ease. It altogether lacks the powerfully sustained interest found in Eichrodt and the others.

We can conclude this section by a brief reference to the work of two other scholars who have made significant contributions. *The Key Concepts of the Old Testament* by A. Gelin[146] studies first the Old Testament revelation of God: One, personal, transcendent yet close at hand. God's plan for mankind comprises promise, covenant, kingdom, messianic hope and Messiah. Under personal salvation the author discusses especially retribution and the sense of sin. Gelin's *The Religion of Israel*[147] treats of the covenant, Israel's life of prayer, the messianic hope and the yearning for a life after death. He also dicusses the missionary ideal of Israel and the nature of 'biblical man'. His *The Poor of Yahweh*[148], a study of the *anawim,* is a minor classic. It should be noted, however, that all three books are very slender volumes.

The other scholar whom we have singled out is J.L. McKenzie. His book, *The Two-Edged Sword,* sub-titled *'An interpretation of the Old Testament'*[149] has been hailed as the first significant work in English by a Roman Catholic scholar in recent decades. The author begins with the divine and human authorship of the Bible, the background against which the Old Testament was written, the Hebrew concept of history, and the literary form in which it is set down. Then he examines Old Testament beliefs on cosmic and human origins and the factors of covenant and election. He treats of kings and prophets, some elements of a biblical theology of history, and the hope for the future, the kingdom of God. After an analysis of man's personal combat with the forces of evil as pictured in the Old Testament, he concludes with a discussion of Semitic ideas about life after death, of Hebrew wisdom and biblical prayer; he gives a summary of the chosen people's understanding of God and the relation of the Old Testament to the New. His *Myths and Realities*[150] contains some important Old Testament studies: the word of God, God and nature, myth, and the Old Testament and royal messianism. Then there are the Old Testament themes in his *Dictionary of the Bible.*[151] Finally, his *Aspects of Old Testament Thought*[152] is an outline of Old Testament theology which is as important as that of N.W. Porteous and more extensive.

Accepting the fact that biblical theology does not lend itself to a synthesis, McKenzie is content to present a collection of essays on topics or themes, with no attempt to integrate them into a single whole. Biblical theology must create its own categories drawn from biblical thought itself; it must be historical in its methods and exposition. He arranges his material under four headings. First, he takes the God of Israel. The Old Testament, throughout, witnesses to practical monotheism: whether or not there are many *elohim*, there is only one Yahweh. In spite of the prohibition of images, anthropomorphism is prevalent; Yahweh is first and always a personal God. Mythical language and imagery are present in the Old Testament, and mythopoeic thought retains its validity in Christian belief and Christian theology. The themes of spirit, word, and creation are treated at some length.

Under the heading, Israel—God's Covenanted People, McKenzie first of all considers man. There is no consistent psychology of man in the Old Testament because the Israelites were more concerned with the relations of the collective group 'man' to the deity and to the world than with the species itself. The group has a twofold unity which reaches horizontally to all the members of a given generation and vertically through all earlier generations. It is now clear that the covenant was the principle of Israel's unity as a people; and the covenant was initiated through Yahweh's act of election. He discusses covenant and law, then covenant and cult, and notes that two attributes of Yahweh in particular are closely associated with the covenant: righteousness and covenant love (*hesed*).

When he comes to aspects of the relations between God and Israel, McKenzie first makes the point that in the Old Testament the anger of Yahweh occupies the place that justice occupies in modern thinking about the deity; he notes that there is a direct connection between God's anger and the sin of man. The conviction that Yahweh is a God of revelation is fundamental to Old Testament belief. Yahweh reveals himself chiefly in history; and the Old Testament might be regarded as a theological statement and interpretation of history. The character of Yahweh ensures that, in Israel, religion and morality are closely associated and ex-

plains, too, the peculiarly Israelite emphasis on the *heart*—
morality must be interior. There is a multiple Old Testament approach to the idea of sin, reflected in the variety of
Hebrew words for sin. Sin rises from evil inclinations within
man himself and is universal. The removal of sin and guilt
is a matter of vital importance in the religion of the Old
Testament. Sinful man must commit himself to the mercy
and forgiveness of Yahweh; forgiveness presupposes conversion, a true interior change of attitude and conduct. It is
extremely difficult to achieve a synthesis of the complex Old
Testament idea of salvation; perhaps the reign of Yahweh
may be seen as a central idea.

The Messiah is the first subject of the fourth and final
section, God's Future Plans for his People. McKenzie discusses
the term 'Messiah' and the development of royal messianism.
The question whether or not there is any eschatology in the
Old Testament earlier than the Exile is likely to be no more
than a question of semantics. Since eschatology in its simplest
form means at least the belief that history has an end, then
the early Israelite hope of the future is implicitly eschatological despite the absence of apocalyptic imagery. Always Israel
knew a kind of collective immortality: a man lives on in
his sons or in the people of Israel. When the hope of survival after death was finally expressed, it took the only form
it could take in view of Israelite anthropology and the Israelite conception of God and man: the resurrection of the body.
McKenzie's concluding observation is that the Christian
theological study of the Old Testament is truncated unless
the relation of the Old Testament to the New Testament is
taken into consideration. But this is matter for a later chapter.

## 5.  The Return of Histories of the Religion of Israel

We have noticed that, for a time, scholars had turned from
theologies of the Old Testament to histories of the religion
of Israel. When the reaction came, and the great theologies
began to appear, the histories of religion slipped altogether
into the background; in the most recent decade they have
made a return. But now there is no suggestion of conflicting

methods. Indeed the theological study of the Old Testament, with its emphasis on the historical dimension of revelation and on salvation history, has prompted the historical study of Israel's religion in the light of modern research. The Old Testament theologian of today needs a scientific history of Israel's religion as a foundation for his own theological work.

In a work of *haute vulgarisation* intended for the educated non-specialist,[153] H. Renckens aims at providing an outline of the religion of pre-Christian Israel. Working with the specifically theological aspects of the complex religious and historical culture of Israel, he proposes to discern and present the vital unity and organic growth of this religion. In the light of its divine election, he sees the very existence of Israel as a 'mystery'. He studies the passage from the conception of a national God to strict monotheism; he explains how the 'religion of the Bible' reacted on the 'religion of the people' and placed the imprint of faith on cult and history. In the following six chapters the author discusses, at some length, the fundamentals of Israelite religion: the patriarchs and the theme of the promise; the God of Israel, the revelation and the meaning of his name 'Yahweh'; worship—the cult and its officials, sacrifices, liturgical calendar, the cultic community; the king of Israel, his characteristics and his religious significance and influence; the prophets and the major themes of their preaching: woe and weal; the post-exilic community described according to the prophetic theme of the Remnant.

Renckens is anxious to bring out unmistakably the distinctiveness of Israel and of the religion of Israel. Israel is unique because of its monotheism, and it is vain to seek monotheism elsewhere. More specifically, the religion of Israel is unique because that one God is Yahweh: Israel's God is quite different in character from all others. Unique, too, are the messianism of the Old Testament and its eschatological perspective. The faith of Israel, a vital faith, came from contact with and experience of the one God who looked upon and chose his people. In general, we may say of Rencken's work that it is a useful synthesis, constructed along broad lines—but it lacks precision and tends to oversimplification.

Yehezkel Kaufmann has written, in Hebrew, a history of

the religion of Israel which he planned to carry to the destruction of the second Temple—eight volumes have been published. Moshe Greenberg's abridged English version[154] excludes the eighth volume and ends at the destruction of the first Temple and the Exile. The abridgement is drastic but it has been approved by Kaufmann and so can be taken as an accurate representation of his views. Kaufmann's basic position is that the religion of Israel occupies a unique place among the ancient religions, and that Israelite monotheism is an original creation which has been the common belief of the people at large and in all epochs of its history.

Part I studies the character of Israelite religion, and the first chapter is meant to demonstrate that Israel was utterly unaware of the nature and meaning of pagan religion. The Bible bases its whole polemic on the argument of fetishism. This means that the chief influence of foreign beliefs on Israelite religion did not involve mythological materials, while the age-long battle of the Bible with idolatry did not involve mythological polytheism. The Bible combats the cult of idols but does not combat mythology, which is the history of the gods. In short, the Bible's ignorance of the meaning of paganism is the most important clue to the understanding of biblical religion—it is a clear proof of monotheistic faith. Chapter two turns to pagan religion and finds its fundamental idea to be: 'the existence of a realm of power to which the gods themselves are subject';[155] this idea is given expression in mythology and magic. Kaufmann proceeds to demonstrate that this idea is at work in all the pagan religions, old and modern, but his brief and general treatment is so inadequate as to be misleading.

In contrast (ch. 3) the fundamental idea of Israelite religion is that God is supreme over all, with absolute sovereignty, and is utterly distinct from the world. 'He is, in short, non-mythological. This is the essence of Israelite religion, and that which sets it apart from all forms of paganism.'[156] The idea appears as an insight, an original intuition, and never received an abstract, systematic formulation in Israel. In chapter four Kaufmann seeks to show that this basic stand was characteristic of Israelite religion as it was practised by the people at large; but, in order to sustain his argument he has to do violence to the texts and explain away contrary evidence.

Part II treats of the history of Israelite religion prior to classical prophecy. Kaufmann finds himself obliged to contest the accepted relative dating of the Pentateuch sources; the crucial point for him is the dating of the priestly code, as this involves the relation of the Torah to classical prophecy. He argues that the centralisation of cult is a specifically priestly idea; it is the Torah that has influenced Deuteronomy and post-deuteronomic prophecy. From the viewpoint of the evolution of Israelite religion, the priestly stratum belongs not after but before literary prophecy. When, however, we observe that the centralisation of cult was explicitly promulgated in Deuteronomy, and yet the priestly code throughout presupposes a single sanctuary, we have a problem which Kaufmann cannot really solve on his premises. The next chapter turns to the origins of Israelite religion. The patriarchal age was not monotheistic, despite the fact that biblical tradition depicts the patriarchs as monotheists. The struggle with paganism began with Moses; he is the initiator of a religious revolution and the creator of the original, intuitive idea of monotheism.

From now on the consequences of Kaufmann's basic stand become glaring: in the face of the evidence, he continues to maintain that since biblical religion was ignorant of the nature of pagan religion, idolatry, in any real sense, was non-existent in Israel. Thus, in chapter seven, 'Conquest and Settlement', he conveniently disposes of the potentially dangerous pagan Canaanite influence by a radical *herem* of all Canaanites. And if the Bible does characterise the period of the Judges as idolatrous, that is 'part of the historiosophic idealism of the Bible, according to which every national distress is the result of apostasy.'[157] The biblical view of Israelite history sees a second idolatrous period lasting from Solomon's last days to the Exile; but again, this is only the result of the writer's generalisation of responsibility. The simple fact, he claims, is that the Bible does not know a popular cult of any foreign god. And even if the Baal worship of the northern kingdom cannot be explained away, it was limited to court circles and was soon eradicated by Jehu.

The stage immediately prior to literary prophecy can be illustrated by the materials of the Torah and of the wisdom writings.

The third part of the work is consecrated to classical prophetism. Kaufmann rejects the commonly held view that the prophetic literature is the product of a development involving the prophets themselves, their disciples and, often, generations of prophetic writers. He maintains that there are no grounds for assuming the literary role of disciples and there is even less reason to believe that the sermons of the prophets were transmitted at first orally and only much later set down in writing. Two rather brief chapters treat of the religious ideas and teaching of Amos and Hosea, and then of Isaiah, Micah and Habakkuk. With the final chapter, Jeremiah and Ezekiel, we are back to the basic problem again. For both these prophets, Jerusalem fell because of the sin of idolatry and its general moral decadence. But this biblical view cannot be justified: idolatry was non-existent, nor did moral and social dissolution prevail in Judah at the time of its fall (since the reform of Josiah still endured). What happened was, simply, that the small state of Judah had to yield to the overwhelming might of Babylonian arms. 'It is the inner necessity of religious faith, of theodicy, that has produced the biblical doctrine of Judah's sin. . . . This doctrine does not assume that Judah had sunk into the depths of a degeneracy that would in the normal course of things have led to its collapse. To the contrary, Israel's doom followed its own special law: when Israel's "measure" was filled, God visited on it the sins of all the generations.'[158] As for the Exile: the lesson of history is that the exiles did repent, because repentance was an internal process, while the exodus from exile was a longed-for release. Repentance and return came precisely because the exiles were *not* as portrayed by Jeremiah and Ezekiel; they were, at bottom, monotheists who could never adopt the religions of their environment.

Kaufmann observes, in his Epilogue, that during the golden age of creativity in pre-exilic times, the religion of Israel exerted no influence on its surroundings, while during second Temple times 'Judaism agitates the gentile world wherever it is found. Its influence gradually spread until by hellenistic times there were myriads of converts and "fearers of God" among the nations.'[159] Between these two periods came the fall of Jerusalem and the Babylonian exile; and thus it was precisely in the exile that the full stature of Israelite religion began to manifest itself.[160]

Helmer Ringgren[161] is quite explicit on the point that his book is not a theology of the Old Testament but a history of the Israelite religion, with the primary emphasis on a descriptive presentation of the religion during the period of the monarchy; his Introduction clarifies the distinction of the two disciplines. He would maintain that Old Testament theology, as a Christian discipline, is one aspect of biblical theology; it understands the Old Testament as part of the Christian Bible, a preparation for the definitive revelation in Christ. On the other hand, it would be possible to write a purely descriptive theology of the Old Testament in the sense of a systematic presentation of the religious ideas of the Old Testament without reference to New Testament teaching. This type of Old Testament theology, especially if it does not overlook the variations within Israelite religion, is not very different from a history of Israelite religion. And it is precisely because of the variety of religious phenomena in Israel that a strictly religious-historical study serves a purpose. Such a history of the Israelite religion will critically evaluate the Old Testament writings, taking full cognisance of the fact that our sources for the earlier periods are deficient. It will make full use of the comparative method. It will leave aside the question of divine inspiration and the revelational nature of the Old Testament simply because they do not fall within the scope of the history of religions. Ringgren's work falls into three parts: The pre-Davidic Period; The Religion in the Period of the Monarchy; The Exile and Post-exilic Period (Judaism).

All reconstruction of the religion of the patriarchs remains hypothetical. It is important to be aware that what we have been able to discover may not be classified as 'primitive'; the environment of the patriarchs was not 'primitive'. We really do not know much about Moses either. The whole story of the Exodus owes its form to its being a legend to be read at the Passover festival. How are we to understand the revelation of the name of God? In fact, the Old Testament conception of God does not in any way depend on the meaning of the name Yahweh. It would be wrong to call the Mosaic religion monotheistic because the existence of other gods is not denied. The scattered references to the religion of Israel in the period of the Judges cannot be combined to provide a general picture.

The introduction of the kingship was one of the three events of the tenth century B.C. that put a new stamp upon the Israelite religion; the others were David's transfer of the ark to Jerusalem and Solomon's building of the Temple. One of the distinguishing characteristics of the Israelite religion (originally monolatry or henotheism) is the belief that there is only one God of Israel, Yahweh, who claims exclusive devotion. We encounter a certain duality in the nature of this Israelite God: everything, good or bad, good fortune or ill fortune, comes from Yahweh. We might add that this conviction made belief in demons superfluous. Ringgren goes on to consider, in very much the manner we have found in the theologies of the Old Testament, the characteristics and manifestations of God. Then, in a similar vein, he takes up God and the World, Man, and Man before God. Two groups of texts are of primary importance as sources for our knowledge of the Israelite cult: the laws regulating the cult, and the psalms. The latter project a vivid picture of Israelite piety and its relationship to the cult. 'The cult is an expression of piety; conversely, the cult nourishes and encourages the piety of the individual. There is by no means a basic dichotomy between cult and piety; what we have is rather a productive mutual interaction between the two.'[162]

Ringgren has an important discussion as to what extent the Feast of Tabernacles possessed the character of a New Year's festival and was connected with other New Year festivals in the Near East. He evaluates the two main theories: Mowinckel's[163] theory of an enthronement festival of Yahweh, and the theory of a covenant festival supported by von Rad[164] and Weiser[165]. It is a question of divergent interpretations of what are, by and large, the same data. The basic difference is that Mowinckel would like to place the Israelite data in the context of the New Year's festival found throughout the Near

East but especially in Babylon, while von Rad and Weiser work almost exclusively with Old Testament material. Perhaps, after all, the two interpretations are not mutually exclusive. In the context of the celebration of Yahweh's kingship, we find the motifs of creation and battle; these cannot be harmonised easily with the theory of a covenant festival, but they have good parallels elsewhere in the Near East. On the other hand, the renewal of the covenant is specifically Israelite. 'From these two roots the Israelite New Year's festival arose, as it can be reconstructed from the psalms as one aspect of the feast of booths.'[166] For the rest of part II— the cultic functionaries, the kingship, death and the afterlife, and the writing prophets—it is enough to note that in an Israelite context, it is better to speak of 'sacral kingship' than of 'divine kingship', and that the basis for a doctrine of the afterlife was already present in ancient Israel in the conviction that Yahweh is mightier than death and Sheol.

The Exile forced Israel to concentrate on that portion of the ancient heritage which could be salvaged from the wreck of Temple, cult and kingship; the law became the sum total of these traditions. The codification of the Law gave rise to the idea of canonical Holy Scriptures. It now became an important task to apply the Law to the concrete details of daily life, and the scribe emerged. Furthermore, the new Temple could not compete with the Law: it was the place where the sacrifices and ceremonies prescribed by the Law were carried out. The Law is God's gift to Israel which gave to Israel, as the bearer of God's revelation, a special place among the nations. This created a tension which was clearly visible in the life of post-exilic Judaism: whether Israel must keep itself apart, free from contamination, or whether it must take seriously the doctrine of the one God who is Lord of all the world.

In the post-exilic period the ancient conception of Yahweh's heavenly court was transformed into a highly developed doctrine of angels. At this time too the figure of Satan makes its appearance as God's antagonist. A transformation can be observed in the anthropology of later post-exilic Judaism: soul and body now appear as essentially different components of man. This dichotomy, basically alien to the old Israelite conception, doubtless arose under hellenistic influence; it was a development associated with the ideas of the immortality of the soul and of individual retribution after death. But the hellenistic view that saw in the body something evil, a prison of the spirit, and the origin of all sin, never took root in Judaism. The post-exilic cult was in many respects very different from pre-exilic cult, as many elements dropped out and many innovations were introduced. The author closes with a consideration of eschatology and apocalyptic, and of parties and movements.

Ringgren has been at pains to point out that his book is not a theology. However, his own method—to present the religious ideas of the Old Testament, placing them in their proper context, and adding only what is necessary to clarify what is implicit in them—makes his work valuable to the theologian who desires to determine the proper context of the religous ideas of the Old Testament. On this score, too, and not only as a history of religion, this is an important work.

The history of the religion of Israel of Theodore C. Vriezen[167] is of special interest, coming as it does after his work on the theology of Israel. His first chapter (his Introduction) states his purpose of offering a picture of the religion of Israel which will depict not only its historical development, but also its essence and inmost character. It presents no clear-cut system of religious ideas, because it is a religion always on the move, always in process of change. It is a distinctive religion, and this fact is clearly seen when it is compared with the religion of the other peoples of the ancient East. Yahwism has a character all its own, solely because of the nature of Yahweh, its God; but one cannot bring it under a single formula because it is a dynamic religion with a vital, changing force.

The second chapter proceeds to set Israel's religion against the background of the religions of the ancient East. A proper use of the comparative method must recognise that religions may employ the same ideas and yet be profoundly different. So, for instance, the personal character of Israel's religion differs functionally from any counterpart in the rest of the Semitic world; and only in Israel did prophetism develop so distinctively as to emerge as a phenomenon without parallel in religious history. When we look at important religious elements found everywhere in the ancient East, we discover the consistent Israelite distinctiveness. The other religions know a pantheon, with a single divinity at its head; but Yahweh, the God of gods, stands quite apart from the other divinities. Yahwism took a resolute stand against religious ideas which reflected the notion of the god who dies and rises again. And even while accepting the common notion of the 'three-storeyed' universe, Israel insisted that all was subject absolutely to Yahweh. But in so defining its attitude to different religious ideas, Israel's religion became fully itself.

Comparative study sets Israel's religious distinctiveness in relief; and this is, ultimately, because Yahweh is unique. From the start he was a saving God. Man's relation to God was both personal, finding expression in prophetism and in God's attitude to the individual man of faith, and also social, in and through the cult. God's will is known because he has revealed it, disclosed it especially in the events of history. Since Israel's religion turned on a vital relationship between God and man, it was guided predominantly by practical considerations: men must act in God's service. Belief in the God who is at work in history leads to thinking that is markedly teleological; God's activities have a goal in view, his kingdom. Thus history leads to a renewal of Israel itself and, ultimately, to a re-creation of the entire world. Here Israel breaks clean away from the religious ideas of the contemporary world and by so doing came to influence, in a radical manner, the mental and spiritual life of mankind. Even more fundamentally Israel's religion stood out as the religion of will and obedience.

Vriezen goes on to give a phenomenological outline of Israelite religion in the heyday of its earliest phase, the Davidic period; his source is the document which tells the story of David's reign (1 *Sam.* 11; 13: 16-14: 46; 16: 14-23; 18: 1-2 *Sam.* 21; 1 *Kings* 1-2). The first striking factor is that the whole life of the nation stands under the rule of Yahweh alone; consequently, the Israelite lives by an absolute faith in Yahweh. Yahweh is the God of Israel; as a country and a people, Israel is his inheritance, his property. But there is yet no question of monotheism in a universal sense. What did obtain might be described as 'mono-Yahwism': Yahweh demanded the recognition and exclusive worship of Israel, but this situation did not yet lead to theoretical monotheism. The position of Yahweh as the one God of the new state was made quite clear when David brought the ark, the ancient sanctuary of Yahweh, out of the desert and into the capital.

The Yahwism of the Davidic period has a prehistory in the Mosaic religion and the religion of the patriarchs; Israelite tradition attests that this is an authentic development. Since every reconstruction of the two earliest periods must be hypothetical, it is extremely difficult to discern the characteristic traits either of the patriarchal religion or of primitive Yahwism. We can say at once, though, that the Mosaic religion is associated with the name 'Yahweh' for God, while the theism of the patriarchs is marked by more than one divine name. Vriezen ventures a tentative picture of how the religion may be thought to have developed. It would seem that the oldest typical element of the religion of the patriarchal age is a belief in the *theos patroios,* the god of the ancestor. The personal god, in direct relation with the god of the family, was well suited to the social conditions of the clan. When the old Hebrew tribes had settled in Canaan, their religion was accommodated to the worship of the Canaanite gods—particularly the chief god El, head of the pantheon; it was possible for an El-type to emerge which was characteristic of the Israelite tribes. The particular strain of the former ancestral god made possible an immediate relationship between El and the social group. This was not a bad preparation for the later breakthrough of Yahwism.

Israel's encounter with Yahweh took place in the desert: one has to accept the main features of the tradition on this score as being historically correct. Otherwise the tribal groups, coming in from the desert, could not have stood their ground against the culturally superior Canaanites. If the tag *Graecia capta Romam cepit* did not apply in their case, it was for one reason only: 'the peculiar religious character that marked the Israelite tribes coming out of the desert; and that character was determined wholly by the relationship of those tribes to the particular God whom they had encountered and who governed their lives.'[168] Etymological explanations are too uncertain to lead to a definition of Yahweh's essential being; the only profitable approach is to ascertain the functions ascribed to him and his relation towards those who serve him. The Hebrew tribes in Canaan could identify El with the Yahweh who came with the desert tribes; but Yahweh could never tolerate identification with Baal. At most, he could take over certain of Baal's features, especially that of the giver of earth's fertility. In the main, the Baal-figure was essentially and totally other than Yahweh, and conflict was inevitable.

Vriezen raises his voice in protest against the atomising of the *traditionsgeschichtliche* method and maintains that the general historical framework of the Exodus-story should be taken as seriously as the smaller-scale data within it; in other words, the framework of the Moses-story (and so the role of Moses) must have some grounds in history. He concludes that the Exodus-tradition offers a coherent picture of what took place among the refugees from Egypt. He finds the items which offer the firmest historical grounding to be: the connection of Yahweh with Sinai, the figure of Moses as Yahweh's prophet, the decalogue and the ark. These elements help to explain the course taken by Israelite religion in its later history. 'They give to Israelite religion a character which distinguishes it fundamentally from that of the Canaanites, and so confer upon the Yahwistic group the religious self-awareness that prevents its members from assimilating themselves to the Canaanite world.'[169]

Thus it was that the Mosaic groups clashed with the Canaanites not primarily on cultural grounds; the clash was between Yahwism and Baalism—we should not underrate the spiritual *élan* of the new Israelite groups. A significant symptom of the change was the centralisation of the tribes in an amphictyony. Yahwism gave a new content and meaning to the life of the tribes which from now on was to be controlled by Yahweh. While there was a rapid progress of Yahwism among the tribes, we must also admit a far-reaching process of assimilation, an undercurrent of 'popular' religion. Besides, there was also an attitude of aggressive Yahwism. But the conflict with Baalism left certain marks on Yahwism. For instance, this conflict accounts for the very stringent sexual laws laid down in Israel and the total exclusion of women from the official cult. At the same time an effective method of combating Baalism was to adapt acceptable elements, especially the idea of fertility—Yahweh was seen as Lord over nature. The so-called cultic decalogue (*Exod.* 20:23; 23:13-19; 34:14-26) is the oldest cultic legislation after the Yahwistic religion had become established. It illustrates the way in which Yahwism conducted itself in agrarian territory: on the one hand adapting to the new circumstances and on the other hand taking a fundamental stand against Canaanite religious influences. A number of fixed sanctuaries appeared. There were four kinds of holy place: private house-chapels, the older temple-sanctuaries of El, the *bamoth* (high places), and the new Yahwistic sanctuaries. The holy places grew more and more influential, and not only as cultic centres; for here, too, the *torah* was dispensed and the traditions took shape.

The Davidic dynasty introduced the second major period of Yahwism. Especially in Solomon's reign, the spiritual and intellectual life of Israel was greatly enriched. The kingship had brought a new element into the life of the nation and the king had become, in practice, the high priest of the state. The temple out-stripped the other sanctuaries because it was the 'royal' sanctuary, and its presence made Jerusalem the religious capital. After Solomon, Baalism found new opportunities; and Jeroboam's bull symbol helped to obliterate the distinction between Yahweh and Baal. The religious revolt led by Elijah eliminated the monarchy, in principle at least, as the decisive factor in the evolution of Israel's religion. When in the second half of the eighth century the Assyrian threat emerged, only the forces of religion remained steadfast and ensured a new future for Israel; religious maturity came with political eclipse.

The prophets have received a personal call from Yahweh and are conscious of their responsibility for the entire nation; they are, consequently, at once reactionary and revolutionary and are very much concerned with the present. If they are averse to the cult of the day it is because they seek a Yahweh-cult 'in spirit and in truth'. They are men of their own time who are acutely conscious that 'no service of Yahweh is the "real thing" unless it is actualised in absolute trust and heartfelt obedience to God's will in the here and now, and unless the life of this present time is lived in the assurance of God's good grace for today and for the future, which nothing, not even total ruin, is able to take away from men.'[170] The prophets gave Yahwism a new religious and ethical dimension, a new depth, making it a universal religion bearing the marks of what is common to all mankind. The prophets strike a new radical note in their proclamation of judgement and stress a new theme of confident trust and faith; yet the most typical feature of prophetism is the expectation of well-being in the future, beyond the judgement. The prophetic world of ideas is stamped by an attitude of unreserved hope in Yahweh and in him alone.

The process of renewal set on foot by the prophets was vitally important for Israel. In the first place they inspired, more often in later days, efforts at reform and restoration; their writings came to be seen as an expression of the word of God and became the source of the apocalyptic movement. In the second place, their eschatological message enabled Israel to withstand the coming crisis, to maintain its faith during the years of exile and to restore its national existence. In short, the influence of the prophets was far more marked in the future than in their own days. Their disciples came to form circles in which spirituality and obedience at the personal level developed. The prophets had furthered a consciously personal religion in order to build up the nation at large, and they helped to break down the overbearing influence of the official cult and its ministers. Israel's religion took the prophet, not the priest, as being the 'man of God'— a value-judgement thoroughly characteristic of Yahwism, and one which correctly assesses the true place of the prophet. 'The history of the eighth and seventh centuries confronts us with a number of great men, of whom the Assyrian world-conquerers, from Tiglath-pileser to Ashurbanipal, form one group and the prophets of the Old Testament the other. The clash of these two parties, which involved a clash of matter with spirit, of naked force with religion, for the soul of the people of Israel, proved to be an issue of significance for the history of the world.'[171]

The seventh century in Israel was, in the main, a period of political weakness and religious decadence. Yet the Deuteronomic Reformation shows that there was still a powerful movement loyal to Yahwism. The Reformation sought to bring into being the theocratic nation-state of Israel; it provided an impetus towards the evolution of the Yahwistic religion into the religion of the book of the Law, and ultimately of the Book. But, for the present, Jeremiah spoke with the most authentic voice of prophecy; he contributed, in a remarkable way, to the survival of Yahwism beyond the destruction of the Temple and the crisis of the Exile. With him, two other prophets, Ezekiel and especially Second Isaiah, made this period of material eclipse into a spiritual high-point in the history of Israel's religion. Second Isaiah discovered that the personal, saving God was the one God of all mankind, and his religion one of universal reference. Israel had a positive duty to be an active witness to Yahweh's revelation.

The rebuilding of the Temple within seventy years of its destruction was a factor of major importance for Judaism. The forms of religion current in an earlier period became normative again; the Temple became more than ever the focus of religious life and the priesthood and cult assumed a central place; Israel had become a 'hierocracy'. The cult was declared to be the aim of the whole revelation to Moses and the *raison d'être* of the covenant. The man principally responsible for this turn of affairs was Ezra, deservedly called the father of Judaism. In all this, however, the universal traits in the picture which Yahwism had presented, had gone to the wall. 'Isolation became a source of strength, and antithesis the mark of a devoutly religious approach to life. The national community thereby gained internally in unity and cohesion; but because it cut itself off and was tied down to a cultic-ritualistic pattern of religion, it was in danger of losing contact with the world around and becoming a sect.'[172]

The final chapter of Vriezen's work is significantly entitled: Centralisation and Disintegration. The writings of the fourth to the second centuries give evidence of a great diversity of spiritual and intellectual currents in post-exilic Judaism; yet one attitude was, in practice, to predominate. Now that Judah had regained self-reliance and inner assurance, it was determined to defend them. Modification of the religious structure could not be tolerated. In the face of the hellenistic world, the question of isolation or adaptation came up again; for it was seen that, once the culture of hellenism had been adopted, the Law had to be set aside—just when religion and the observance of the Law had come to mean the same thing. The Torah was the unalterable, unshakeable word of God; the activity of the Spirit ceased or was referred only to eschatological and messianic expectations. Prophecy disappeared, not through lack of spirituality, but because of the paramount authority of the written word of revelation, expounded by priest and scribe—though apocalyptic may have compensated in some measure and marked a reaction against the prevailing nomocracy and hierocracy. Fellowship with God was a matter of obedience to the Law. This outlook was profoundly serious and sincere, but its grave drawbacks were truly fatal. Fidelity to the Law could mean the loss of a forward-looking vision and could focus on a kingdom realised here and now. Election was less a call to be answered than a privilege conferred. 'Conservatism and separation became the hallmark of the Jewish community, which thus discharged with utter singleness of means and purpose its duty of obedience to God's Word and of loyalty to him.'[173]

At the close Vriezen draws together some impressions which have forced themselves upon him in his journey through fifteen centuries of history. The first is the great strength of Yahwism which enabled it to go on growing and evolving even beyond the political and social dissolution of Israel. Then he has found that Yahwism displayed an astonishing capacity for adaptation combined with a no less remarkable critical bent. The key to Yahwism's vital energy lies in the nature of its belief in and about God: God's dealing in history, interpreted by the prophets, made for a direct personal and moral relationship with Yahweh. Because Yahweh remains essentially the God of Sinai, his special relationship with Israel was an abiding factor, leading to a strong tension between what we call particularism and universalism. The final point is that Israel never completely managed to escape from this tension and, in Judaism, the religious state of affairs was such that drastic renewal, such as had taken place in the past, had become impossible. The only way out of the impasse was by the formation of various sects. This negative attitude determined the Jewish reaction to the Christian community and fixed the relationship between Judaism and primitive Christianity: 'they could only continue to exist as two ramifications of the *corpus Jahwisticum*, developing in contrary directions.'[174]

Vriezen's book is complementary to his theology of the Old Testament (its positions have been presupposed by the earlier work); together they give us an admirable presentation of Israel's theological thought and of the development and inmost character of Israel's religion. We are shown a picture of a faith in the making, subject to the impact of crucial historical event and bearing within itself a vital force that breaks out, time and again, in new growth.

These histories of the religion of Israel do, to some extent, treat of the religious institutions of Israel; we have said little about this factor because the institutions of Israel—the various forms in which the social life of the people found expression—have been thoroughly studied elsewhere. Here we shall simply introduce two works, both of them acknowledged classics in the field.

J. Pedersen's influential work[175] is in part a study of the psychology and thought-forms of the Old Testament people of Israel and in part a study of the institutions of Israel. It has also contributed largely to an understanding of the nature of Hebrew piety. The work has four parts: Part I—The Soul, its Powers and Capacity. The 'soul' in Hebrew thought is man as such, in his total essence. 'Blessing' is the vital power that makes the soul grow and prosper. The soul in its entirety, with all its blessings, finds expression in the 'name'. Part II—Common Life and its Laws. Man, to live rightly, must live in community, and community is characterised by harmony ('peace'), which is sustained by 'covenant'; like peace, 'salvation' is a free development of the soul, making for its fulfilment. 'Righteousness' is the health of the soul and the social health of the community. The opposite of righteousness is 'sin' and closely related to sin is the 'curse'—their mutual relationship is as righteousness to blessing. Part III—Holiness and its Upholders. Holiness is 'a force which is felt in all spheres of life, it is indeed at the root of all other kinds of energy'.[176] It is akin to 'blessing' because it is 'the extraordinary, the greatly increased strength of the soul'.[177] The upholders of holiness are the leader in battle, the king, the prophet, and the priest. Holiness attaches to holy places and to cultic objects. Part IV—The Renewal and the Source of Holiness. It is in man's power to contribute to the renewal of holiness which is brought about especially by the offering of sacrifice; Pedersen considers sacrifices, feasts and foreign cults. A brief chapter on God and man, the relation between the people and its God, leads to chapters on the conflict between Yahweh and Baal, the kingship of Yahweh, the prophets' fight for Yahweh, and the reforms of Yahwism from Hezekiah to the restoration of Ezra-Nehemiah. The closing chapter summarises the place of Yahweh in the life and religion of Israel.

It may be that Pedersen has been too theoretical and has not given a true account of the actual psychology of the Hebrews. A more obvious shortcoming is the fact that he has ignored the historical development of the basic beliefs of the Israelites and has gathered his data without reference to the epochs to which the data belonged.

The study of Roland de Vaux[178] has won universal acclaim. It too is divided into four parts. Part I, Family Institutions, considers the family, marriage, the position of women, children, succession and inheritance, death and funeral rites. Part II, Civil Institutions, deals with the population: freemen and slaves, the State, the king, royal household and officials, administration of the kingdom, finance, law and justice, economics, time, weights and measures. Part III, Military Institutions, covers army and armaments, the Holy War. Part IV is devoted to Religious Institutions (practically half of the whole text). Here de Vaux studies those institutions directly concerned with the external worship of God. His aim is 'to describe those cultic institutions which the Old Testament presents as legitimate institutions of true

Yahwism.' He describes 'first, the places of cultic worship, secondly, the persons involved in it, then the acts prescribed (especially sacrifice, the main act), and lastly, the religious calendar and its feasts.'[179] Since the study of cultic institutions is bound up with biblical theology and with the history of religions, this scholarly work, which carries the stamp (it is excellently translated) of its author's characteristic clarity of expression, is indispensable to the student of Old Testament religion and theology.[180]

## In Summary

*Now there are varieties of gifts but the same Spirit; and there are varieties of service but the same Lord; and there are varieties of working, but it is the same God who inspires them all in everyone* (1 Cor. 12:4-6).

Having surveyed the history of the biblical theology of the Old Testament, we reach a point of wishing to 'survey our survey'. It would seem, at first sight, that there has been such a 'variety' in the themes discussed, the approaches of the individual authors, and even the very wealth of the terminology employed, that it would be impossible to summarise the chapter with any degree of 'sameness'. And yet, upon patient reflection, we realise that certain unifying threads *have* appeared all along—threads which will have become even expected, strands whose colours will have become even predictable. These we shall survey under two main headings: recurrent ideas as to the nature and purpose of Old Testament theologies, and fundamental themes traced in the content of the Old Testament itself. We shall find that, for all the diverse, even conflicting, approaches of the different authors, there *is* a unity: the 'varieties of working' are, indeed, inspired by the 'same God' and in his service. And each has something to contribute to the whole—even if it be simply the personal conviction which could brave the undertaking of a biblical theology at all, no small task. To continue Paul's words, 'to each is given the manifestation of the Spirit for the common good' (1 Cor. 12:7).

*Recurrent Themes in the Approach of the Old Testament Theologian*

From the very birth of Old Testament theology as a field in its own right, there has been the effort to distinguish between 'biblical' and 'dogmatic' theology, the struggle to keep biblical theology free of 'scholastic' methods and categories. This was the basic concern of the pioneer Gabler and of Schultz a century later; however, both maintained the principle, generally accepted by most of the authors, that the two disciplines are complementary: biblical theology provides the working material, and the yardstick, for dogmatic theology and the continuing life of the Church. The work of Heinisch, on the other hand, revealed the devastating effect of imposing the dogmatic approach upon the biblical. Another distinction of which need was felt early, and which (or the absence of which) was to continually recur, was that between 'biblical theology' and the 'history of the religion of Israel.' Bauer felt compelled to define the two after his attempt to outline the 'religious ideas of the ancient Hebrews;' the post-Hegelian period of the late nineteenth century seemed submerged in writing histories of Israel's religion; van Imschoot, in his treating biblical theology as an exposé of the religious life and practices of the Israelites, was careful to group doctrines in a 'logical' order or synthesis to show his method as distinct from giving a history of religion. And we may recollect a criticism of von Rad that, by neglecting any such comprehensive synthesis or agreement in testimonies, neglecting the historical value of *Heilsgeschichte,* he seems to have produced a history of the religion of Israel rather than an Old Testament theology. *A propos* here would be Eichrodt's observation, based on Procksch, that whereas the history of religion traces stages of growth, what was needed instead was a 'cross-section' laying bare the marrow of Israel's faith, as it were.

Finally, among these more controversial issues which have accompanied and sparked the growth of biblical theology, we may note the varying influences of *Religionsgeschichte,* a word summarising all that is meant by an 'objective', 'scientific' approach to the Old Testament. Inaugurated, one might say, by Wellhausen, its theories and the drawing of parallels with non-biblical religions were incorporated in one form or another—sometimes successfully and in proper proportion, sometimes lamentably—in succeeding theologies.

It was really the reaction against *Religionsgeschichte* which re-awoke the self-proclamation of Old Testament theology from the stalemate it had reached in being the mouthpiece for the history of Israel's religion. As if moved by the very foundations of their faith, by their calling themselves 'theologians' at all, scholars began to realise that there was a higher criteria for historical truth than scientific 'objectivity'. There was the inner core of that history, the marrow or vital structure, consisting of permanent elements rather than accidentals. This core needed to be intuited and relived in terms of its abiding values for all ages. Already among the pioneers, de Wette had called for faith and religious feeling, for dedication on the part of the biblical theologian rather than rationalism; Hävernick had demanded the same thing in his cry for a 'theological aptitude'. Eissfeldt, describing biblical theology as purely 'confessional' in contrast with the neutral discipline of *Religionsgeschichte*, recognised that the biblical theologian's approach, while using scientific aptitude, would always be characterised by *witness*—valuable, really, only for those who share the author's own convictions. What we have called the 'pastoral' value of Vriezen's work could be mentioned here. Most recently, this idea of personal witness reached its highpoint in Wright's declaration of theology as 'the confessional recital of the redemptive acts of God in a particular history'—a recital free of seeing God in terms of propositional dogmatics or 'systems of ideas', a 'confession' true to biblical man himself.

This leads us to the recurrent insistence on *history* itself as the medium of revelation. Dodd found that the living God revealed himself in the movement of events—that history itself *is* revelation. Baab found historical continuity and human experience to be the unifying principle in an Old Testament theology; Jacob gave us his twofold definition of 'Theo-logy' as pointing to the presence and the action of God. Von Rad insists that an Old Testament theology must consist of the credal statements Israel itself made about Yahweh in the actual events of its saving history; and he tends to subordinate *Heilsgeschichte* to the 'kerygmatic intentions' he claims for the Old Testament authors. The conviction that Yahweh reveals himself chiefly in history can be summed up in McKenzie's definition of the Old Testament as a 'theological statement and interpretation of history'.

In the efforts of our theologians to define the nature of an Old Testament theology, we have seen again and again one very interesting (and inevitable!) conclusion: the Old Testament really does *not* lend itself to *any* complete synthesis, and the lines of thought or doctrine or even history within it are never 'straight'. Thus, Baab could find no 'complete' Old Testament theology; Porteous recognised different currents of faith and expression rather than uniformity; van Imschoot sought to introduce a synthesis into Old Testament thought but acknowledged that this would be something external to it, while McKenzie is content to collect his material into essays on various topics without attempting to integrate them into a whole. A classic statement of this feature in the Bible is Vriezen's awareness that not only is the 'line' never 'straight', the line of revelation running through both Testaments, but also that our own understanding is so imperfect: 'God's secrets' do not allow man ever to really copy the line. A corollary to this is the perennial difficulty many of the authors have encountered in attempting any systematic treatment of Old Testament material, in having to arrange it into a 'theology' at all. It was early met in the first attempt at categorisation, Bauer's dividing his work into theology and anthropology. We have seen how, at the outset, Eichrodt asserts that the Old Testament resists systematising, but then seems to go on to an artificial 'systematising' of his key covenant concept. H. Wheeler Robinson was to warn against any abstract presentation remote from the dynamic faith of Israel, and Knight warns that a system will render lifeless the reality of that living experience of encounter between Israel and its God which the Old Testament offers us.

So we are led to perhaps the most unmistakably clear and consistent theme within the various approaches to a theology of the Old Testament: that of *faith*—the faith of Israel, and the faith whose task is to interpret the biblical testimony.

110

This includes the necessity of understanding Israel's religion as a *living* experience, a history allowing for development and organic growth. Vatke and Hofmann early recognised that each period carried within it the germ of the succeeding one. One criticism of van Imschoot's work has been that in it such a growth of Israel's faith is indistinct. Dodd carried this dynamic unfolding into the continuing life of the Church, the most favourable context for biblical theology because through it there can be a participation in the biblical events and their application to our lives. A leading tenet of von Rad is the Bible's unceasing saving movement of promise and fulfilment, the 'new' always being a reinterpretation of the 'old' in which it was prefigured. This sets the tone for the final point in this part of our summary, one which will have its proper *Sitz im Leben* in a later chapter; and this involves the concern, repeated in almost all the Old Testament theologies, to point out the interdependent relationship between the Old Testament and the New.

### Recurrent Themes Traced in the Old Testament

We turn to survey the conclusions drawn as to the content of the Old Testament itself, and we may start with the trend of *biblical faith* as a linkword with our preceding section. We may stand side by side with Abraham, as Eichrodt portrays him, beneath the night sky—Abraham who took his stand on the promises of God and thus believed that the darkness of his will and word would be lit up as with the stars. We can recall Vriezen's deep insight: not only is the entire Old Testament message born in faith and in faith fulfilled, but also the God behind that message is so alive that knowing him surpasses even faith itself! Or, we could point to Baab's conviction that the key to understanding biblical religion and history lies in the faith of the men of the Bible; Wright's finding that to maintain faith and trust in God was the vital challenge offered to a chosen people; or Porteous' centring his entire theology around the words and deeds of men whose *faith* 'took God seriously', perceived his activity in historical events, and found expression in both word and deed.

In our view of the different authors' approaches through-out this chapter, we cannot fail to have been struck by the way in which each has striven to organise his material according to various *central ideas*, classifications, and divisions of one sort or another, and how these often overlap and contain repeated themes: 'Jehovah' and 'His people Israel' (Davidson), 'God's holiness' (Sellin), 'God as Lord' (Köhler), 'God and people', 'God and the world', 'God and man' (Eichrodt), 'The presence and action of God' (Jacob), 'What God has done' and 'What man has done' (Wright), 'God', 'Man', and 'Divine judgement and salvation' (van Imschoot). Almost all the authors treat at length in some way what Eichrodt calls the *'personhood' of God* or Vriezen his 'living' nature, and all deal with the familiar attributes of God such as his righteousness and *hesed*. For Dodd, this 'living God' is found in his word revealed in history; for Jacob, he is manifest in the idea of *presence,* his being *with* his people (although perhaps Jacob could at times give the wrong impression that Israel's faith rested solely in 'ideas' *about* God). A vital theme flowing from the nature of God is that of *communion,* of the relationship which God seeks with man. Eichrodt sees the covenant as the expression of Israel's faith in this communion, and Knight recognises that the inner heart of the covenant bond was covenant fellowship. Vriezen believes this communion, this 'intercourse' between God and man, to be the basis of all biblical testimony, and he makes it more specific and concrete than do the others by linking it with God's word, his judgement, the cult and piety. Many of the words touch upon two principles not always easy to reconcile: God as both spiritually transcendent and actively present.

Our theologies frequently overlap in their treatments of *man and his community,* agreeing in the first place that the Old Testament has no real systematic doctrine of man and, secondly, that the Hebrew attitude towards man is uniquely positive—assigning him to the 'marvellous purposefulness', as Eichrodt calls it, of the Israelite view towards creation. We must continue to ask the theological question 'why' God created man (Knight). The words also reveal similarities to one another in their emphases, to greater or lesser degrees, on the themes of *covenant and election*: they range from Eichrodt's subordinating all things to his 'covenant concept' to McKenzie's concentration on God's covenanted people as originating in Yahweh's act of election. Wright's understanding of the three elements unifying the core of Israelite faith ties together many of the themes we have looked at: *history* is the *revelation* of God, the first inference to be drawn from this is the doctrine of *election,* and the implications of election are confirmed and clarified in the *covenant.*

It remains for us to mention what can frequently be the most inspiring part of the theologies we have examined: their treatment of *God's reign or kingdom,* also expressed in terms of salvation hopes or eschatological expectation. Already in the late nineteenth century, Schultz had found the unifying principle of the whole Old Testament to be in the idea of God's kingdom on earth. Eichrodt gives this noble expression in discussing the salvation hope Israel had because the people had come to know and experience God, and thus to have the confidence that he would come to set up his perfect domain. As flowing from this, Eichrodt also discusses the indestructibility of man's relationship with God because *life* with God, the peace of direct and intimate encounter with him, came to be experienced as far more certain than death. Vriezen found the kingdom of God to be the golden thread running throughout the entire Old Testament, its highest assent to faith, its victory over 'repetition', and he has carefully outlined the stages of 'eschatology'. Finally, McKenzie has devoted most of his study to the central place held by the reign of Yahweh in the Old Testament idea of salvation—to the future, eschatological hopes implicit from the earliest times in Israel because of its view of history as having a final goal. Indeed, McKenzie's treatment of messianism can point the way in the end to the most meaningful, vibrant theme of all those we have found recurring in our theologies: simply, the entire Old Testament, or any 'theology' based upon it, is ultimately fulfilled only in Jesus.

Yes, if it is the 'same Spirit' who has called forth the 'varieties of gifts' in these authors, the same God who has inspired their 'varieties' of working, he has done so through his own Son—through one who, man as they, can understand the limitations involved in writing any biblical theology. And if, at times, we ourselves have found those limitations a cause for criticism or just a source of puzzlement, let us remember that the authors themselves were the first to recognise them. After all, Vriezen could apply to the whole task of the Old Testament theologian, as well as to himself, his awareness that 'we have this treasure in earthen vessels, to show that the transcendent power belongs to God and not to us' (2 *Cor.* 4 : 7). And one of the latest Catholic theologians chose for his theology a subject revealing that he understood the limitations of those who do feel 'least in the kingdom of heaven': he chose to write on the little ones, the *anawim, The Poor of Yahweh.*

## CHAPTER II

# A Survey of the Biblical Theology of the New Testament

## 1. The Beginning and Development of New Testament Theology

WE have traced, at some length, the beginning and development of Old Testament theology; the origin and course of New Testament theology are similar. For this reason, our survey of the earlier stages of New Testament theology can be quite brief: the general pattern is already sufficiently clear.

### I. A SHORT HISTORY OF THE GROWTH OF NEW TESTAMENT THEOLOGY

We may begin our survey in the last decade of the nineteenth century. The origin of New Testament theology is much earlier, but the turn of the century marks a new epoch of development. However, the work of one earlier scholar must be noted because of the influence of his views. F. C. Baur (1792-1860), professor at Tübingen, evolved a type of New Testament interpretation which is commonly called that of the Tübingen school. Baur made full use not only of Hegel's philosophy of religion, but also of his philosophy of history. In particular, he rigorously applied the Hegelian process of thesis-antithesis-synthesis to the history of apostolic Christianity. The thesis was represented by the Petrine faction with its Jewish-Christian particularistic and legalistic outlook. Hellenistic Christians of universalistic tendency, the Pauline party, represented the antithesis. The resultant synthesis, fruit of mutual concessions, gave rise to Catholicism. Each New Testament writing reflected one or another of these tendencies, Baur maintained.

H. J. Holtzmann's work[1] is a classic exposition of German liberal interpretation of the New Testament as it was worked out and formulated in the course of the last quarter of the nineteenth century. While working with the doctrinal content of the New Testament writings, Holtzmann also outlined the historical development of early Christianity. His division indicates this: Jesus and primitive Christianity, Paulinism, Deutero-Paulinism, Johannine theology—Pauline thought proved to be the most durable. The influence of Baur is evident.

W. Wrede[2] challenged the approach of Holtzmann: the method of 'concepts of doctrine' suggests that Christian faith is a system of thought rather than a religion. Wrede's essay is the programme of the *heilsgeschichtlich* school; H. Weinel[3] does his best to implement the programme. The sub-title, 'The Religion of Jesus and of Early Christianity', accurately describes his work. Weinel's purpose is not to study the doctrines of the New Testament but rather to study the religion of Jesus as it developed in the early communities. He regards the religion of Jesus as the summit of moral monotheism, a moral religion of redemption, and analyses it under the headings: the redemptive faith in God, the new man, the new world, the religion of redemption, the person of the redeemer. Primitive Christianity represents a first transformation of this religion; Paul inaugurated a second transformation; the Christianity of the emerging Church constituted the third stage of the evolution. The influence of Hegelian thought, mediated through Baur and manifest in this view of evolutionary development, is present, too, in Weinel's picture of a struggle between the moral religion of Jesus and the mystery religions as these are represented in Paul's thought. W. Bousset is another representative of the *religionsgeschichtlich* approach.[4] In his study of the main trends of Christian development, he goes beyond the New Testament canon, as far as Irenaeus. In his view, Christianity is syncretistic; it has borrowed heavily from the religious influences of its environment. In the Hellenistic communities, under Syriac and Egyptian cultic influences, Jesus became 'Lord' of the Christian cult. Paul's mysticism and his identification of Christ and Spirit evolved in the religious atmosphere of the mystery cults. John's mysticism, centred in the 'Son of God', marks another stage. In fact, Bousset's book is more valuable as a store of material for the study of comparative religion than for an understanding of New Testament belief.

The conservative Lutheran counterpart to Weinel's *Theology* was that of P. Feine[5] which presents the classic style of New Testament theology. It falls into three parts: I. The teaching of Jesus according to the Synoptics; II. The doctrine of primitive Christianity; III. The doctrine of the Johannine writings. It is a solid work. In Christology and soteriology and in his treatment of the Pauline doctrine of justification, Feine differs hardly at all from a comparable Roman Catholic approach. A decade earlier G. B. Stevens had published his work[6]—all the more worthy of note here because it has been recently reprinted. The aim of the volume is to set forth, in systematic form, the doctrinal contents of the New Testament according to its natural divisions. Thus it falls into six parts: The teaching of Jesus according to the Synoptics, according to the Fourth Gospel, and the primitive apostolical teaching; the theology of Paul, of Hebrews and of the Apocalypse. The influence of current ideas on the teaching of Christ and the apostles is given due weight, and account is taken of the historical conditioning of the truths and facts which constitute the gospel. However, Christianity is far from being a mere product of its age: 'I hold to the unique and distinctive originality of Jesus and to the supernatural origin of his gospel.'[7] Stevens is satisfied that this view of Christianity is not just an assumption but equally a conclusion which is established by his study.

A less satisfactory alternative to the *heilsgeschichtlich* position was the *Theology* of A. Schlatter.[8] The sub-titles of his volumes, I. Teaching of Jesus; II. Doctrine of the Apostles, became the titles of the volumes in their second edition. Schlatter presupposes the traditional position on the origin, character, and historical value of the New Testament writings. A feature of his work is his 'anti-intellectualism' and his religious and moral pragmatism. He denies that Jesus or the apostles were concerned to formulate doctrine and holds that it is vain to seek speculative doctrine of any kind in the

New Testament. All is practical; the primacy of the will is strikingly present in the Gospels. This position profoundly affects Schlatter's analysis and exposition of New Testament teaching; the dire result is most obvious in his Christology. F. Büchsel[9] presents his *Theology* as a 'History of the Word of God in the New Testament'. The first part of the work gives the teaching of the Synoptics and John. The second part is taken up with the teaching and preaching of Paul: Christ, crucified and risen, the Lord. The resurrection and the exaltation of Christ to God's right hand constitute a new revelation and a new point of departure in the history of God's word: man is justified by faith in Christ. Büchsel is content to sketch the broad lines of New Testament theology; but his analysis offers a solid contrast to more venturesome *religionsgeschichtlich* works.

Since the New Testament is a message of God, M. Albertz[10] maintained that the *Sitz im Leben* of each writing must be established not only by various historical factors, but also in relation to the activity of the Holy Spirit. His first volume offers a telling criticism of any interpretation of the Gospels which would see them only as a product of the Church's faith and not as continuing the authentic message of Jesus. In the second volume, 'The Unfolding of the Message', he describes the content of the New Testament message under headings suggested by 2 *Cor.* 13:13—'The Grace of the Lord Jesus Christ', 'The Love of God' and 'The Fellowship of the Holy Spirit'. His presentation follows the line that the eschatological event of Christ is an act of God who is love and who wills the salvation of men, while the Spirit is a witness to Christ in the Church. Albertz makes a distinction between the message itself and its accompanying theology—which is, in great part, a response to objections raised by the message. The work underlines the profound unity of New Testament teaching and brings out its richness; however, the author's highly personal views lessen its impact and its usefulness.

The Roman Catholic pioneer in the New Testament theology field, A. Lemonnyer,[11] favours a division of the New Testament material which he believes to be in harmony with the guiding idea that the revelation brought by Jesus and the work of salvation accomplished by him are the object of New Testament theology. Each of the three groups into which the New Testament writings may be fitted presents the thought and work of Jesus under a particular aspect. Each has its principal and characteristic theme: Synoptics—the kingdom of God and its Founder; Paul—the new economy of salvation; Johannine writings—the person of Jesus.

These three themes correspond, broadly speaking, to the three stages by which the disciples of Jesus arrived at a full understanding of the Christian revelation. But this must not be understood in an evolutionary sense—it does not mean real growth, much less a transformation of the initial Datum. To see that this is so, we need only note that the Pauline writings are chronologically earlier than the Synoptics and that the Fourth Gospel—the third stage—is a *gospel* which presents the words of Jesus. Yet the division is justified. The Synoptics present the teaching of Jesus in its most readily accessible form; the Epistles expound a soteriology which had its fulfilment in the death of the Master and in the great subsequent events; the Fourth Gospel presents the teaching of Jesus at its most profound. The three themes, then, represent, for the disciples of Jesus, three stages in their understanding of the Christian revelation and, for Jesus himself, the three levels of his divine pedagogy. A revision of Lemonnyer's little book, published in 1963, was edited by L. Cerfaux.[12] The editor did not make changes in the original text but added several lengthy sections. The result is a striking testimony to a firm tradition of New Testament interpretation which persists despite a radical change in the critical understanding of the New Testament.

The sub-title of the book of O. Küss[13] indicates that it is essentially an introduction to the theology of the New Testament; it is meant to open up the teaching of the New Testament to the Catholic laity and is correspondingly non-technical in style. The author combines introductions to the different writings with a résumé of their doctrinal content; he does not attempt a synthesis. It is a helpful book which, in a modest way, together with Lemonnyer, did something to fill a lacuna in Catholic New Testament scholarship.

## II. A BRIEF ASSESSMENT OF SOME RECENT NEW TESTAMENT THEOLOGIES

In his Preface F. C. Grant[14] explains that his book is not a New Testament *Theology* but an introduction to New Testament thought; his major aim is to provide a *total* view of the subject. In the midst of notable variety he finds a marked homogeneity and unity in early Christian thought. His first three chapters examine the fact, growth, variety and scope of New Testament thought and set out the fundamental theses which underlie the rest of his work. These theses are:

1. New Testament theology is not a rounded system but the developing theology of a growing Church; it displays much variety and some divergence.

2. It is a Christian Jewish theology steadily moving in the direction of Hellenistic thought.

3. It clung to the heritage of the Jewish Scriptures, interpreted now from the point of view of Christian faith and hope.

4. Early Christian thought grew out of early Christian experience; worship, piety, and the growing institutions of the Church were of central importance.

5. There are several theologies in the New Testament—reflections of different areas of thought, attitude and practice.

6. Christology was central from the start; but ethics and the growing institutional life were also fundamentally important.

7. The theological framework provided by apocalyptic-type eschatology soon gave way to a profounder and more philosophical pattern.

8. The antecedents of the various types of Christian thought represented in the New Testament are not exclusively Jewish.

9. In the New Testament as a whole the dominant tendency is seen to be christological. The Pauline and Johannine types of thought contributed most to the later evolution of Catholic dogma.

The remaining chapters take up the doctrines of God, man, Christ, salvation, the Church, and New Testament ethics. The New Testament had as its starting-point a

9

popular, untheological idea of God. This was soon left behind by the New Testament writers, principally Paul—they already moved in the direction of a Christian philosophy. There was a parallel development of Christology and pneumatology. The relationship of the risen, exalted Jesus, the *Kyrios* of Christian faith and cult, to the *Kyrios* of the Old Testament was a question which had to be faced. The answer may be summed up in a Pauline formula: the Lord of the Old Testament is 'the God and Father of our Lord Jesus Christ' (2 *Cor.* 1 : 3). Grant makes two general affirmations: (1) the thought of the Bible as a whole is orientated eschatologically. (2) In studying the great doctrines of primitive Christianity, it is not helpful to follow the order of classical dogmatics because a logical, scholastic arrangement of doctrines does not correspond to what we find in the New Testament.

The doctrine of man, like other New Testament teachings, is based solidly on the Old Testament; but Paul, especially, has made his creative contribution. 'Paul's real contribution to the doctrine of man is a tremendous deepening of the conception of human responsibility, a more profound and more subtly psychological interpretation of the meaning of sin, and a corresponding deepening of the significance and power of redemption.'[15] Paul's deepening of the conception of human nature laid the foundation for the most significant later work of Christian theologians.

Grant introduces his chapter on the doctrine of Christ by asserting that from the beginning of Christianity the figure of Jesus was theologically interpreted so that the New Testament conception of Christ is consistently theological. Similarly, the devotion to Christ reflected in the New Testament is theologically conditioned. Behind the Gospels and even behind all forms of the tradition, there is 'the purely religious, nonpolitical, nonsecular evaluation of Jesus; and back of that is the purely religious, nonpolitical, nonsecular, and even otherworldly, transcendent consciousness of Jesus himself.'[16] It is evident that theology of the Synoptic tradition needs to be studied more thoroughly than it has been up to now. The author singles out three great 'key' passages in Paul's letters as shedding light upon the Christology of Paul and of Gentile Christianity in general: *Phil.* 2:5-11; *Col.* 1:13-20; 1 *Cor.* 15:20-28. It must be said, in general, that the christological development of the New Testament was fundamentally religious—not purely historical and not philosophical or speculative.

Addressed to a world which was profoundly conscious of its need for salvation, the Christian doctrine of salvation, an eschatological reality, found its antecedents in the Old Testament. Many terms and metaphors were needed to convey the full meaning of this fundamental doctrine of the New Testament. Paul's doctrine of justification by faith is grounded upon the central experience of the Christian religion; for him salvation was both a future good and the present guarantee of it.

In Grant's view, the New Testament doctrine of the Church conspicuously illustrates three principles which he has kept in sight throughout: (1) eschatological orientation or relevance to the future; (2) the Jewish background; (3) the process of transition to a fuller expression by means of Hellenistic religious concepts. Baptism, going back to the earliest apostolic days, was originally a washing away of sins; it then became the sacrament of initiation and, under Pauline influence, the sacrament of a new life. Fundamentally, the Eucharist is a rite of fellowship first with Christ and then with Christians in him; but the doctrine of the Eucharist, in the New Testament period, does not depend upon a rigid formula or upon a precise historical datum. As for 'primitive Catholicism': the *principle* of the ministry was there from the beginning, in the role of the apostles. 'The "development" of Christian religious instruction is no late product of "institutionalised" Christianity, as opposed to an earlier free, "charismatic", noninstitutional religion or religious movement; instead it was a feature in Christian life from the first . . . The "growing Catholicism" of the second century really had its root far back in the first.'[17]

It may be said that the 'ethics' of the gospel are thoroughly Jewish and this accounts, in part, for the fact that the gospel is the 'the greatest agrarian protest in all history',[18] a protest against a tide of industrialism, power politics, and an economic reorientation of human life. Grant discerns a notable shift of emphasis from Jesus to Paul: where Jesus' religion is the noblest form of Judaism, the consummation of biblical revelation, Paul's is a Christ-centred mysticism conceived in terms of the Hellenistic longing for salvation. So, too, Paul's ethics have a different orientation from those of Jesus and mark a shift from the agrarian biblical emphasis to an urban and partly Stoic outlook. Jesus' most far-reaching contribution is to lay bare the inner motive behind the outward deed; his teaching is characterised by depth and realism. And the lesson was learned because the New Testament as a whole is concerned with principles rather than with details of application, with the right spirit behind ethical behaviour, and with a new vision of life.

Grant is right in his insistence that the Bible is the expression of the religious faith of a living community—first Israel, then the Church. And he is justified, too, in maintaining that Scripture, Old Testament and New Testament, has an essentially 'eschatological' value: it is a salvation history always orientated towards the blessed future whither God wishes to lead his creation. But the author is excessively sceptical with regard to the thought of Jesus himself; he too readily refuses to attribute to Jesus any of the conceptions in which the first Christians have sought to understand and express the mystery of his person; hence the christological titles are, all of them, regarded as Christian developments. Grant leans too much towards the historical scepticism of Form Critics like Bultmann, and this is a factor which is encountered throughout his stimulating and helpful book.

The greatest Roman Catholic New Testament *Theology,* that of M. Meinertz[19] was quickly followed by another significant one. J. Bonsirven divides his *Theology of the New Testament*[20] into four parts; Jesus Christ, Primitive Christianity, St Paul, The Christian Communities Grow Up. The first and third parts resume, in more condensed form, two of the author's earlier works.[21] Bonsirven first studies the self-consciousness of Jesus. In his use of the title Son of Man, Jesus gave intimations of his divinity. He saw himself as the only Son of God, as a person distinct from the Father who received all from the Father. Then the author turns to the kingdom which the Son came to establish. Against the background of biblical and Jewish conceptions of the kingdom, and under cover of a familiar term, Jesus promulgated an entirely new doctrine of his own. Bonsirven defines the reign of God thus: 'It is the society of men who possess in Jesus Christ the gift of divine sonship, preserved and developed by strife in this life, thanks to the mediation of their Saviour, and reaching its triumphant fulfilment in the next by total assimilation to their Lord.'[22] In his preaching Jesus emphasised the role of Messiah and the universal scope of the kingdom. He resolved that his kingdom would continue in the shape of a society, his Church, a supernatural society which was destined to act as a continuation of his personality. As a body with permanent members and a hierarchy, both destined to survive the Founder, it displays the essential features of a lasting society—it is the kingdom of the Son. Two chapters on The Way of the Kingdom of God consider, first, the duty of the children of God towards their heavenly Father and then the duties of the children of God towards their brethren. The duty to God is that of prayer: filial worship in a spirit of love and trust—the fruit of trust, its liberating effect, being a spirit of poverty. The faith which saves comes from the Father. Faith demands a surrender, without reserve, to Christ. It means bearing witness to Christ; its fruit is union with him. But faith is a matter of understanding too, and faith is in the will, because knowledge must always go hand in hand with love.

Part II, Primitive Christianity, is meant to cover the whole period during which the disciples grew in their grasp of the teaching of the Master and in their self-understanding. For our knowledge of this period we depend almost entirely on the first twelve chapters of Acts. In the primitive community, faith in Christ was expressed by means of the titles conferred on him, titles which convey the mystery of his nature and his mission. But his deeds and words are primary. The resurrection and exaltation of Jesus was the supernatural reality which proved his divinity; the suffering and death of Jesus, when seen as part of the divine plan, were the proof that he was the Messiah. The early Christians recognised that the gift of the Spirit was the distinguishing feature of the new order. The primitive community became increasingly more sharply marked off from Judaism, and the elements of an ecclesiastical hierarchy made their appearance in the space of a few years.

A lengthy introduction to the third part is devoted to Paul, his background and the foundations of his doctrine. His conversion, or the 'Damascene revelation' as Bonsirven prefers to term it, was a vision of the risen Christ which made the apostle an eye-witness of the resurrection and was his initiation into the mystical life. In his Christology, Paul's purpose is to bring out the whole meaning of Christ: his membership of the Trinity on the one hand and his relations with men on the other—his role as Mediator. The achievement of the Mediator is objective redemption, a triumph of divine grace. Christ obtained all the graces which are the effect of redemption by his whole life, but in a more important way by his death and in a decisive way by his resurrection. Redeemed men are raised potentially to glory in the Son; as free beings they benefit in so far as they come to him and are incorporated in him—this is brought about through faith and baptism. God distributes his graces through the Church founded by his Son. The Church has two sides: a mystical side, the body of Christ, and a social side, the Church as an organisation. Paul perceived two aspects of the relationship of Christ to the Church: Christ as identified with the whole body of Christians (the 'Body of Christ') and Christ as the principle of a Christian's life ('in Christ Jesus'). The Church, as Body, is an extension of the individual Christ because the Son, through his incarnation, incorporated mankind into himself. The expression 'in Christ Jesus' may have any of three meanings according to context: (1) Christ as the vital medium in which we receive the divine graces; (2) the result obtained by means of Christ; (3) the equivalent of the adjective 'Christian'. For Paul the Church had a hierarchy—apostles, prophets, presbyters; it had its worship and sacraments. The Christian, created anew in Christ, was guided by his union with Christ and his possession of the Spirit. He is called to holiness, he is urged to pray, he has duties in the family and social spheres.

The fourth part, The Christian Communities Grow Up, carries a deliberately chosen title which leaves chronological considerations out of the reckoning. The varied teachings of the more mature Christian writings are studied under the headings of theology, Christian life, and eschatology. Christ is the centre of theological reflection and the themes studied are: Christology, soteriology and trinitarian theology as well as Christian apologetics. In the later New Testament writings, the Church as such was rather taken for granted; what was of utmost importance was that Christians should lead lives in accordance with the gospel's teaching on conduct. The delay in the arrival of the end helped to correct any mistaken ideas about the imminence of the second coming. The Christians of the second generation held as firmly as Paul to the solidarity of Christian hope and to the certainty that they were living in the last days.

A serious defect in Bonsirven's plan and presentation is that John's unique place in New Testament revelation does not emerge at all. In the first part of the work his testimony is mixed in with that of the Synoptics. We might have expected to see him come into his own in the fourth part, but it is not so. The Johannine epistles and the Apocalypse are taken together with quite different writings: Hebrews, James, 1, 2 Peter. Thus the unity of the Johannine message is fragmented. Then, too, Bonsirven has allowed himself to be far too much influenced by the categories of systematic theology. His plan does indicate his attempt to follow a biblical pattern; but one soon recognises that the developments of scholastic theology are very much in his mind and have, more than once, coloured his interpretation of New Testament doctrine.

The modest size and unpretentious style of A. M. Hunter's Introduction to New Testament Theology[23] might lead one to undervalue this book. It would be a great mistake. In fact, we are offered a well-balanced synthesis of the most striking elements of the New Testament. This synthesis Hunter presents in three parts: The Fact of Christ, The First Preachers of the Fact, The Interpreters of the Fact. In the first place, it is clear that the kingdom of God is the dominant sphere of the Synoptic Gospels. If we look at a Gospel, that of Mark, for instance, we find that the events related have theological significance. Thus the baptism of Jesus

is the ordination of the servant Messiah, the opening of the
ministry is the sign that God has begun his reign, the
Galilean ministry shows the kingdom of God at war with
the kingdom of evil, with Jesus spear-heading the attack.
The episode of Caesarea Philippi means that the last battle
between the kingdom of God and the kingdom of evil must
be joined and that it will involve the death of God's Messiah. The Last Supper is a prophetic acted sign by which
Jesus says: 'I pledge you a share in the kingdom of God soon
to come with power by the servant Messiah's death'.[24] It
becomes clear, in fact, that without theology the story of
Jesus does not make sense. It emerges from a study of the
Synoptics that Jesus believed the kingdom to be present in
himself and in his ministry and that he saw his messianic
ministry as a fulfilling of the prophecies of the Servant of
the Lord. The nature and implications of the kingdom may
be set out in a series of propositions: The kingdom of God
is present in the ministry of Jesus; its King is a Father; it
implies a new Israel—the idea of the *Ecclésia* has deep roots
in the purpose of Jesus; it involves a new pattern for living;
it is centred in Christ; it involves a cross; though already
come, the kingdom is yet to be consummated.

Acts and the primitive traditions contained in the epistles
serve to describe the first preaching of the Christian fact.
The first preachers proclaimed the *kerygma*, the message of
salvation; Hunter follows the classic study of C. H. Dodd.[25]
It emerges that the primitive gospel was rooted in the gospel
preached by Jesus and that the pattern of the kerygma runs
through the New Testament giving it a deep essential unity.
Because the Resurrection gave a new dimension to the person of Jesus, new titles had to be found. The first Christians
discovered four: Messiah, Lord, Son of God, Servant of God.
The earliest Church never questioned the true humanity of
Jesus, and the cross was for it a central fact. The presence
of the Holy Spirit in the Church is an experience inseparably connected with Christ, a token that he is present among
his own. In the Christian life of the community, nothing is
older than the sacraments—they were there from the start.
It is not unlikely that, in the pre-Pauline Church, men already thought of baptism as union with the death and resur-

rection of Christ. Christians were committed to 'the Way', a new way of life; they turned to the Lord for moral guidance and found it in the Synoptic tradition of Jesus's sayings. The resurrection of the Lord gave substance to their Christian hope.

With Paul, Hunter gets on the right foot from the outset by pointing out that a great deal of 'Paulinism' is common, apostolic Christianity. Paul's debts to his Christian predecessors include: the apostolic *kerygma,* the concept of Jesus as Messiah, Lord, and Son of God, the Church as the New Israel, the sacraments, and belief in Christ's *Parousia.* Paul's 'gospel' is the good news of salvation which God has provided through the incarnation, death and glorification of Christ, and which he offers to all who will believe; his theology is that gospel as explained in his letters. His theology 'is not something we can separate from his gospel; it is his gospel as his mind grasped it'.[26] 'Justification by faith'—though it is his most distinctive doctrine—does not epitomise Paul's gospel (which is essentially the common apostolic gospel); the only term that can do so adequately is 'salvation'. Salvation is *from* sin but also *to* reconciliation and righteousness; it is a present experience: communion with Christ, life in the Spirit. Paul's teaching on Christian hope is that since 'D-Day' —the death and resurrection of Christ—has come, then 'V-Day'—the Parousia—is sure to come. The heart of Christian hope is to be 'with Christ'. Salvation points to a Saviour— Paul's gospel is Christocentric. His favourite title was 'Lord' (*Kyrios*); he also tried to set forth the theological significance of Jesus in other categories: the Second Adam, the new *Torah,* the divine Wisdom. Two things in Paul's distinctive doctrine of 'justification by faith' are of special and enduring importance: that true religion is a matter of right relationship with God, not primarily a matter of ethics and moral striving, and that the right relationship depends wholly on faith in God's historic act in Christ.

Turning then to Peter (1 *Pet.*) we find that faith, for him, is faith in God through Christ as mediator. For *Auctor* (the unknown author of Hebrews), the heart of true religion is 'access' to God, achieved through Christ's sacrifice. His doctrine of Christ's heavenly intercession is the necessary complement to faith in his atoning death.

It is becoming clearer that the roots of John's thinking strike into Jewish soil, though he has contacts, too, with Greek thought. He sets out to show the whole story of Jesus as the place in history where the ultimate truth of God is to be found. So, to a far greater degree than the Synoptics, the Fourth Gospel is an interpretation of the Fact of Christ. The theme which unifies the Gospel of John is the theme of life. Eternal life consists in *knowing* God, in personal communion with him; *faith* is a man's way of appropriating Christ and eternal life. The truth of 'realised eschatology' is more surely expressed in John than anywhere else in the New Testament. Eternal life is a present boon because Christ has come and died and risen, and because the Holy Spirit is here. The role of the Spirit is specific: he 'comes as Christ's *alter ego*, not so much to supply his absence as to complete his presence.'[27] The Spirit enables the Church to carry out its mission: to proclaim to the world Christ's word and to gather God's true children. Because the Word became flesh, material things may become vehicles of spiritual life and truth—this is the principle underlying John's doctrine of the sacraments. The Torah of the new Israel is the commandment of love. The Christ of St John is Jesus Christ the risen Lord, the omnipresent Saviour who, through the Spirit, abides with his people. The whole saving purpose of God was embodied in the person and work of Jesus of Nazareth, the dynamic and redemptive Word of God. John has shown us the ultimate meaning of the Fact of Christ.

In this brilliantly clear book A. M. Hunter has succeeded in showing that the same doctrine, while being deepened, remains identical throughout the New Testament from beginning to end.

Werner Georg Kümmel[28] shares the dominant view that a theology of the New Testament must begin with the thought of the individual writings or groups of writings. In this, the first of a projected two volumes, he presents the heart of New Testament theology in terms of the proclamation of Jesus, Paul's theology and the Christ-message of the fourth evangelist: these, Jesus, Paul and John, are the 'chief witnesses' of New Testament teaching. By 'Jesus' he means the presentation of the person and teaching of Jesus in the Synoptic Gospels.

Kümmel arranges his work in four 'chapters' or parts: I. Jesus' Preaching According to the First Three Gospels; II. The Faith of the Primitive Community; III. The Theology of Paul; IV. The Christ-message of the Fourth Gospel and the Johannine Letters. A Conclusion, 'Jesus-Paul-John: The Centre of the New Testament', rounds off the work. This Conclusion is of special interest because the author, having presented the contribution of the 'three witnesses' from their different standpoints, here shows what they have in common, their central, essential message. This sort of synthesis is a necessary feature of biblical theology; consequently, we shall concentrate on the Conclusion and be content with a broad outline of the main part of the work.

Facing up to the problem of the historical Jesus is an indispensable first step in the whole theology of the New Testament. Kümmel is quite firm in his view that without the reality of the person and teaching of Jesus neither faith in the risen Lord, nor the community's proclamation of God's revelation in his Son Jesus, makes any sense. Already before Jesus, John the Baptist warned his hearers of the imminent judgement of God, called for a change of heart and announced the coming of the 'mightier one'. Jesus proclaimed the imminent coming of the reign of God; but he also declared that God's reign was present in him, in his person and in his words and works. To understand the meaning of Jesus' proclamation we need to ask what he himself has to say about God, about God's demand and about his interpretation of his own person.

Jesus presents God as the future Judge, and as the Father who will care for his children and will grant forgiveness to men. However, he declares, too, that this loving and forgiving Father is active, already, in the present. In other words, Jesus' preaching of the imminence and of the presence of God's rule is the framework for his proclamation of God's judicial and fatherly dealing with men, and this divine activity becomes concrete reality for the believer in the person, teaching and works of Jesus. God makes demands: Jesus linked his proclamation of God's future and present activity with the demand for obedience to God's will, stressing the accomplishment of his will and pointing to reward and punishment.

Jesus' own explanation of his person and the claims he made are presented largely in terms of the titles either accepted or avoided by him. But first he made it clear that his works could be truly understood only if his accompanying message were heard. He demanded faith in God, not in himself—in Jesus' actions men see the activity of God. Jesus is not the Prophet: he is more than a prophet and with him the time of the Law and the Prophets is ended. The term Messiah (Christ) is not found, in the oldest Synoptic texts, as a self-designation of Jesus; he rejected the title 'Son of David' because of its political overtones. We cannot say with certainty, from the evidence, that Jesus knew himself to be Son of God in a unique manner (or even that he avowed it on occasion). As the presence of the kingdom of God is known only by faith, so the believer alone can recognise in Jesus the hidden activity of the Son of Man, of 'the Man'. God already meets as Father the one who has heard and accepted Jesus' claim to be 'the Man'. It is certain that Jesus foresaw a violent death for himself; and he understood his coming passion not as fate or as a burden but as part of his divine commission. He saw his passion not as an end but as a passage to divine glory and as a basis for his coming as 'Man' in the near future, and he had spoken in these terms to his disciples.

Kümmel goes on to consider the faith of the primitive community. This is important for two reasons: the primitive community asserts that the claim of Jesus was confirmed by God, and the faith of the community serves as a basis for the theology of Paul. The evidence indicates that between the burial of Jesus and the formation of the Christian community something of great importance had occurred. Because the witnesses of the risen Lord are relatively many (cf. 1 *Cor.* 15:3-8), something must really have happened to bring it about that all these men, quite unprepared for anything of the sort, became convinced that God had enabled them to see the risen Jesus. This risen Christ stands in eschatological glory and can give the gift of eschatological grace. Faith in the resurrection of Jesus and the proclamation of the risen Lord are the basis of the preaching of the primitive community. The characteristics of this faith of the

Palestinian primitive community can be studied in terms of the titles of Jesus. The title Son of Man was not exploited; instead the risen One was spoken of as 'the Anointed', the Messiah. The 'Servant of God' had its setting in the liturgical practice but otherwise did not remain long in use. It is hard to know when Christians first began to address Jesus as 'Son of God'; the title came from the highly-regarded Psalm 2, a royal messianic psalm. 'Son of God' does not indicate an essential relationship to God, but rather designates Jesus as the bringer of eschatological salvation—achieved through his life, death and resurrection. The Aramaic phrase *marana tha* makes it certain that the title 'Lord' was of Palestinian origin. But while the faith of the early Christians was grounded on the risen Lord, it would be a great mistake to think they had no interest in the person and teaching of the earthly Jesus. The riddle of the death of the Messiah was solved by the community in the light of the resurrection: they saw it as a vicarious redemptive death and recognised in it the saving activity of God. It is necessary to look, too, to the specific development of faith in Christ within the hellenistic community. For hellenistic Christians the title 'Son of God' designated a being who at all times belonged to God, who was sent from God's world into our world and who, after the completion of his task, returned to God's world; in him the lordship of God is already a present reality. Even during his earthly ministry Jesus was equipped with uncanny powers and occasionally allowed his real mode of existence to be seen (e.g. the Transfiguration). Kümmel sees the doctrines of the possession of the Spirit and the virgin birth as attempts to make the divine filiation of Jesus understandable. The early Christians did not regard themselves as a 'remnant' set apart for salvation, but as the new people of God of the 'new covenant'. But this new people of God is significantly not now designated as the 'community of God' but as the 'community of Jesus' or as the 'community of the Christ'.

Paul, for Kümmel, is the first theological thinker, the first theologian, of Christianity—but a theologian who had become one out of missionary concern and purpose. In his sources for the study of Pauline theology he excludes Acts, the Pastorals and Ephesians. He finds that the crucified and risen Lord is the centre of Paul's preaching. Yet, basically, one properly understands Paul when one realises that his fundamental view was that he regarded the present as the beginning of God's eschatological saving activity; in other words, Paul, like Jesus, proceeds from faith in the imminence of eschatological salvation. Paul looks to the proximate fulfilment of salvation and, at the same time, he is certain that, through God's saving activity in Christ, the end-time is already begun. Paul has seen the present as the commencement of eschatological salvation in this passing aeon; it was his theological task to understand the divine activity both in Christ and in Christian existence, from the standpoint of the faith-experience that God in Christ has brought about eschatological salvation. He had to grasp and present the truth that this salvation is a present reality although the fulfilment, with the appearance of Christ in glory, is still to come. Therefore he sees the Christ-event as a historical activity of God and he views the Christian in the context of *this* historical reality. Paul sees the historical reality of the man Jesus as part of the world-embracing activity of God whose end and goal has already had its beginning in the resurrection of Christ and will find its fulfilment in the coming appearance of Christ from heaven. 'The Lord' had come to designate Jesus Christ as the one to whom the community prayed and who encountered them in worship. But Paul has referred the title from the risen Lord to the earthly Jesus and back beyond that to his pre-existence; the man Jesus and the risen Lord are one and the same. By the title 'Son of God'—used relatively seldom, but significantly—Paul describes the 'history' of Christ from pre-existence to the Parousia; the title indicates unequivocally the connection between God's activity and the Christ-event; it shows God at work through Jesus Christ. Since the death of Jesus on the cross is central to Paul's soteriology, the man Jesus is decisively important for Paul's theology, though he seldom refers to his life and teaching. And though Paul can speak in identical terms of Christ and the Spirit, he does not identify the Spirit with Christ.

At this point Kümmel speaks of the 'mythical' language of Paul; in his view one must qualify as 'mythical' every declaration which bears on the action, in this world, of beings which do not belong to it; and so faith in the work of God operative in Jesus cannot escape 'mythical' expression. Thus we find that the declaration of the existence of Christ with God before his incarnation, like the confession of his resurrection, his return to the Father, the sending of the Spirit, the expectation of his coming, are all 'mythical'. The notion of 'pre-existence' safeguards monotheism: the mythical presentation of the eternal relation of the Son to the Father, of the incarnation of the eternal Son and of his installation in heavenly glory, marks the whole Christ-event as the work of *God*.

Kümmel proceeds to consider Paul's view of the state of man before Christ, the universality of sin, and the role of the Law. Then he treats of the salvation in Christ: deliverance from the 'powers', from the Law, from sin and guilt; there is a lengthy treatment of justification and a study of atonement. God's gift of salvation imposes an obligation on the Christian. The present reality of the Christian life presupposes baptism and membership in the Body of Christ; it involves dying with Christ, the presence of the Holy Spirit, 'existence in Christ' and the Lord's Supper. In considering judgement acording to works, Kümmel remarks that the dominant antinomy of biblical faith in God is that he is just *and* gracious; this same antinomy is evident in the formal contradiction, in Paul, between justification by faith and justification by works. He follows up with a consideration of predestination and of eschatology. A comparison of Paul with Jesus shows that any alleged opposition between them is more apparent than real. The true and essential difference is that Jesus is not only the preacher but the bringer of God's rule, while Paul is the messenger and slave of his Lord; that is why Paul has made Christology rather than the kingship of God the centre of his preaching.

In the fourth chapter Kümmel turns to the teaching of the Fourth Gospel and 1 John. He maintains that the fourth evangelist has set out to paint a perfect picture of Christ which will strengthen faith and bring about 'life', and his Gospel can be said to be the definitive witness to Christ. This Johannine portrait of Christ is spelled out yet again in terms of the titles given to Jesus. He is the 'anointed One', the Messiah, but this is not especially stressed. He is the 'Son'. In John the relationship of Son to Father *seems* to be one of identity, so that the Son stands as a divine being beside God and not really distinguishable from him. Yet it is clear that when John stresses the unity of the earthly Jesus with the Father he is not speculating about the human and divine 'nature' of Jesus Christ; rather the unity is to be seen in the *sending* of the Son by the Father, for, as the 'one sent' the Son does not act or speak independently of the Father. Jesus as 'Son' is the perfect presence of God because he takes part in the work of the Father and because God encounters men in a personal way exclusively through the man Jesus (cf. *John* 14 : 6). For John, too, the title 'Son of Man' emphasises the full presence of divine activity in the man Jesus. The 'Word' designates an eternal divine person of whom a human, historical activity is predicated; it is a mythical term which avoids identification of the pre-existent one with God. Jesus is the bringer of God's salvation which is operative in his person and in his word; we need to look to John's understanding of the salvation which has become reality in Jesus Christ.

The decisive message of John is that God in Christ has set men free from the domination of the world of death and of sin. The fate of men at the mercy of the world is recognisable especially through the presence of death, hence salvation is pre-eminently evident in the gift of life. John does not ignore the redemption from sin through the death of Jesus—as we find it in the primitive community and in Paul—but it plays no central role in his scheme. From beginning to end of his Gospel John emphasises faith as the way to the reception of salvation. Like Paul, John claims that Jesus received the Spirit at the baptism, and for him the gift of the Spirit is closely linked to the salvation-event. For John, too, the risen Lord is the sender of the Spirit, for the Spirit is the sign of the end-time. The Paraclete is the presence of Jesus: where the Paraclete is at work, there the words of Jesus are spoken again and interpreted, and the author of the Fourth Gospel understands his own gospel to be such a teaching of the Paraclete. John is not interested in the external form of the Christian community, but he does emphasise the significance of the Church for the salvation event; and, for him, the existence of the Christian community is closely linked to the saving action of God in Jesus Christ.

In his Conclusion, Kümmel outlines the common witness of Jesus-Paul-John: the 'centre of the New Testament'. It is evident from the foregoing that the chief witnesses are not quite unanimous; we can speak of *a* Christian message only if they agree in essential matters. And, in fact, these three forms of proclamation point to a common message, which is basic, and against which the witness of the rest of the New Testament can be measured.

*Salvation as Future and as Present.* Jesus proclaimed the imminent coming of the rule of God and expected its coming before the end of his generation. Yet, at the same time, he asserted that it was a present reality, present in his works and word. God, for Jesus, is pre-eminently the Father who will take his children into his coming kingdom, and who will forgive them, if they heed his call to conversion. But the Father of the future is already active in the works of Jesus, and sinful and despised men already receive his forgiveness as Jesus gathers them into his community; the presence of the end-time is closely linked to the person of Jesus. While apocalytic groups had proclaimed the nearness of the time of salvation, what was quite new in the message of Jesus was his proclamation of the present beginning of God's rule and of the present reality of eschatological salvation. And this salvation is bound up with the person of Jesus so that those who come to him can participate in it. Thus Jesus puts before his hearers a definite and concrete eschatological activity of God.

The first Christians, who believed that the risen Christ had been established as heavenly Lord, and experienced the activity of the Spirit in their midst, understood that the End-time had already broken in, although they still expected the imminent coming of God's rule. Paul's theology is built on the primitive community's experience of salvation. The coming of the Son of God into this passing world—his cross and resurrection on the one hand and the expectation of his imminent coming on the other—means, according to Paul,

that the present is already the time of salvation and that
the existence of the believer is determined by this reality
of salvation. The presence of salvation is manifest in the
fact that the risen Christ is present, through his Spirit, in his
community, and rules the life of the Christian. Thus Paul
has interpreted in a new and appropriate way the changed
situation, yet still remains in fundamental agreement with
the proclamation of Jesus.

A central theme of the Fourth Gospel is the sending of the
Son into the world and the close relationship of Father and
Son. John has depicted the appearance of Jesus as the
eschatological saving-event and reckons with the future fulfilment in the appearance of the risen Christ in glory. Yet, on
the whole, John has emphasised the presence of salvation
and speaks but seldom of the future fulfilment. But then,
the present is the time of salvation only because God had
sent Jesus as the 'Saviour of the world' and because the risen
Christ has, through the Spirit, given his own a share in this
salvation. So, for John too, salvation in the present is incomplete and the believer awaits the definitive casting out of
the prince of this world. Salvation is linked to the man Jesus
and to the divine activity in history. Hence in John also the
believer knows himself to stand in the *Zwischenzeit* between
the resurrection of Jesus and the eschatological coming of
the glorified Lord, while through faith he has a share in
the salvation inaugurated by Jesus and now awaiting its
fulfilment.

The Johannine message is not in every detail directly
influenced by the preaching of Jesus nor is it a continuation of Pauline theology. While these three chief witnesses
take their stand on the essential fact of faith in God's
eschatological salvation activity in Jesus there is also a clear
line of development. For Jesus the presence of salvation was
reality in his person only. Paul finds the presence of eschatological salvation also in the existence of the community as
the Body of Christ and in the Spirit-endowment of the
Christian; John further emphasises the presence of eternal
life and describes especially the existence of the individual
Christian. There is a corresponding weakening of the expectation of final salvation: Paul at one time reckoned with

the coming of the heavenly Lord in his life-time but then came to feel that it would be after his death; in John, the imminence of the end-time slips altogether into the background, though the expectation of future salvation is not abandoned. Thus, it is clear that the concurrence of faith in the presence of divine salvation through the sending of Jesus, and of expectation in a fulfilment of salvation through the coming of Jesus Christ in glory, is constitutive of New Testament theology.

*The Condescension of God.* This faith in the actual presence of the hoped-for future salvation is the framework for the message of God's condescension shown in Jesus Christ. It is in Jesus that the love of God the Father came to meet men because, in Jesus, the loving Father sought out his children precisely when they seemed to be lost. In Jesus the coming rule of God is made present because God had condescended to bring redemption through the 'Man'. Through faith in the resurrection of the crucified One and the experience of the Spirit, the primitive community had verified the claim of Jesus. In the light of their faith-experience the death of Jesus was understood as the crowning of God's condescension, of the divine offer of forgiveness; it was seen as a decisive factor in the salvation-event and as an unmistakable sign of the love of God.

Paul finds the present and future aspects of salvation united in God's salvation-activity in the historical person of Jesus Christ, and describes salvation as the setting free of believers from the 'powers' and, above all, as redemption from sin and guilt through God's justifying and reconciling activity in Christ. It is God's condescension towards lost and sinful men which has brought about the presence of future salvation and Paul lays special stress on the death of Jesus as the expiation-event effected by God himself. It is clear that for him too the presentation of eschatological salvation as at once present and future is the framework for the good news that God has come down to lost mankind in Jesus Christ, and for the proclamation of the divine love directed to men which would transform us into loving men.

Through his interpretation of Jesus as the eternal Son of God made man, John carries the Pauline proclamation to the point where the unity of the person and word of Jesus with God's saving purpose finds unsurpassed expression—to the point indeed beyond which one cannot go without undermining the reality of the humanity of Jesus. With such emphasis on the realisation of God's saving purpose, the significance of the death of Jesus has slipped into the background. For all that, the divine condescension has a central place in John too. The freeing of believers from the dominance of the 'world' and the promise of eternal life are the immediate consequence of the love of God who so loved the world that he gave his only Son and empowered believers to become his children. For John, also, the essential message is that God comes in the eschatological Christ-event to men lost in this world in order to set them free from the world and take them into his love and turn them into loving men.

*The Message of the Chief Witnesses.* 'Despite the development in thought which they show, the three chief witnesses of the theology of the New Testament agree in this twofold message: that, in Jesus Christ, God has begun his salvation promised for the end of the world, and that in this Christ-event God has encountered us and desires to encounter us as the Father who will rescue us from imprisonment in this world and free us to actively love. The historian clearly cannot establish that this "centre of the New Testament" is divine truth, which concerns us absolutely, and not human fantasy, which we may unmindfully overlook. But for one who believes that God in his redemptive love has encountered us in Jesus Christ, the joint view of the chief New Testament witnesses holds indeed a double message.

'Though we cannot share the expectation of Jesus and Paul for the imminent fulfilment of salvation, yet it is certain that our faith can really grasp the salvation-message of the New Testament only if we seriously regard the coming of Jesus as God's eschatological deed. Thus, we become aware that our present state is just as much determined by the once-for-all past occurrence of this deed as by hopeful looking towards the future fulfilment of his divine action.

'Even if the chief New Testament witnesses do not quite speak with one voice in their interpretation of the person and death of Jesus, yet we hear from them a common message:

that God, the Lord of the world, has come to us in Jesus. But this divine coming can be a personal reality for us only if we so allow ourselves to be seized by the love of God which comes to us in Christ Jesus that we become new beings. We become those who "let our light so shine before men that they may see our good works and give glory to our Father who is in heaven" (*Matt.* 5 : 16). The common basic perception of the chief witnesses of New Testament theology has found classic expression in *Heb.* 13 : 8 : "Jesus Christ is the same yesterday and today and forever." [29]

It is true that Kümmel might have included the author of Hebrews among his 'chief witnesses'; otherwise, no one will question that he has been right in seeking the centre of the New Testament where he has sought, and indeed found, it. And, of course, in fairness, we must remind ourselves that this volume is only the first, if the more important part, of a New Testament theology. One may feel that he has too easily attributed the origin of some of Paul's ideas to the hellenistic community; nor would it seem that he has done full justice to the historical value of the Fourth Gospel. At first sight it may seem strange that Kümmel has made so much of the future-and-present aspect of salvation, until one remembers that this is nothing other than the kingdom of God which Jesus preached. And the 'condescension of God' characterises the attitude of the loving Father who so loved the world that he gave his only Son. The author's gift for scholarly analysis and reflective synthesis makes this an important, and stimulating, contribution in the field of New Testament theology.

Karl Hermann Schelkle's work[29a] is the first part of a projected four-volume Theology of the New Testament. Significantly, he treats the contents of the New Testament in the light of the Old, for each of his major sections is prefaced by a careful and enlightening review of Old Testament thought on that particular topic. In Volume I, these leading sections are The World, Time and History, and Man. These are divided according to the synoptics, Paul, John and the other New Testament writings, for Schelkle recognises the differing insights and theology of each contributor to the New Testament. The notion of Creation underlies the entire volume.

While the whole of the New Testament can be synthesised into a single harmony by Christ's love, Schelkle also respects the various notes and tensions behind it. For instance, Paul claims over and over that he has become a 'fool for Christ's sake' (1 *Cor.* 4 : 10) and that he has chosen the foolishness of Jesus rather than the world's wisdom. Yet, he also teaches that Jesus is the 'wisdom of God' (1 *Cor.* 1 : 24) whom the Old Testament books of Wisdom describe as pre-existing with God and assisting him with creation. The synoptics present the world as alive with goodness, joy and hope. Yet, there is always the call for watchfulness amidst the present tribulation and the future 'unknown hour'. The disciples are called to leave behind all things in the world for the sake of Jesus. Yet, this is because all things will be restored to them 'a hundred-fold'. Their work of spreading the Good News will help to heal that world and to lead it back to a virginal state before its Creator.

Schelkle sees that, from the very beginning, this Creator provides the unifying point behind the various tensions in the New Testament. But, this is so because these different strands are gathered up beyond creation into the wider context of redemption. This is the unique beauty of Schelkle's vision. In the beginning, God directed the course of this world towards one end : Jesus Christ.

### III. NEW TESTAMENT ETHICS

Any treatment of the theology of the New Testament would be incomplete without a consideration of New Testament ethics. However, within our scope, it is not possible to give the subject adequate coverage; we are content to point to three recent and worthwhile studies.

The posthumously published work of T. W. Manson[30] is not extensive, but it does contain the distilled thought of a great biblical scholar on the moral doctrine of the New Testament and the early Church. He begins by looking at the Old Testament background. In Hebrew ethics the governing factor is the relation of human persons to a divine Person, and so the good is sought in the content of divine revelation. The Hebrews, too, regarded the commands of God, no less than his promises, as a gift to his people. The ultimate ground of Hebrew ethics is a call to the imitation of God: 'You are to be holy as I am Holy'. But God is King: there is an essential relationship between the kingship of God and the ethical teaching of the Old Testament. A Semitic king must be an effective leader, an administrator of justice and a guarantor of worship; in other words, the ideal king will give his people freedom from fear, freedom from injustice, and freedom to worship. The *Torah,* a body of instruction regarding man's place in God's world, is the divine guidance as to the right way in which man should behave as a subject of the heavenly king.

A saying of the pre-Christian rabbi, Simeon the Righteous, epitomises the attitude of Judaism to the place of the kingdom of God in the life and worship of the community. He declared that the world—a true and lasting civilisation—rests upon three foundations: the Law, worship, and 'the imparting of kindness' (*hesed*).[31] 'Imparting of kindness' is connected with the maintenance of relations between people linked by a covenant bond; it involves doing more than is required by the letter of the law. Thus the foundations of a true human society are the standard of conduct, worship, and brotherly feeling for one another. Judaism required, too, a correct attitude and spirit on the part of the doer: he must do what is right because it is right 'for its own sake'; more fundamentally, he must do it for the sake of God: to serve and obey him.

Manson maintains that the best focusing point for a study of Jesus' understanding of the Jewish Law as it existed in his day is the Sermon on the Mount. He makes the interesting suggestion that the threefold division of the Sermon is based on the fundamentals indicated by Simeon the Righteous (doubtless echoing an ancient and familiar maxim): Law, worship and 'imparting of kindnesses'. 'The Sermon on the Mount takes these fundamentals of Judaism and restates them as fundamentals of the New Israel living under the new covenant. So we have the New Law (*Matt.* 5: 17-48), the New Standard of Worship (6: 1-34), and the New Standard of Corporate Solidarity (7: 1-12).'[32]

Jesus summed up the New Law in the commandment: 'Be you perfect as your heavenly Father is perfect': his followers must show in their lives some positive quality akin to the positive creative goodness of God. It is important to note that the two great commandments—love of God and love of neighbour—are presented by Jesus as the quintessence of *Jewish* ethics. We must look elsewhere for the characteristic feature of his own ethic, and we find it in total self-giving. This is not merely an ideal, but is an act and deed which involves a more complete love of neighbour than the Jewish code. It goes beyond Jewish ethics but does not abrogate it. Besides, Christians live in the kingdom of God under the rule of Christ; we can look to him, the ideal king, for reliable guidance. Christians are not tied to a written code; for the living Christ is there to lead the way for all who are prepared to follow and gives the strength to follow the way.

The Church of Christ, the *kahal* or *ecclēsia,* is the people of God, functioning as a people in the full exercise of all their communal activities. In the New Testament we are presented with a picture of a community in which the elders or rulers exercise their authority by being its servants. We find that three factors loom largely in the life of the primitive Christian community: the *teaching* of the Apostles now regarded as the custodians of the Christian *Torah*; the *fellowship (koinōnia)* which is the same as 'the imparting of kindnesses'; the *breaking of bread* and the *prayers.* Thus we have the Law (instruction), the worship, and the brotherly feeling. The early Church was never just a worshipping society, but a community in a much wider sense.

The early Church preserved a body of Jesus' teaching. This is a teaching stamped with Jesus' acceptance of the Messianic vocation of suffering and with his declaration that he had come among men as a servant. It follows that as the Messiah sacrificed himself for the common good, so his people too must be expendable for the common good. There has always been a temptation for Christians to think of themselves as elected for privilege rather than for service, to make the words and deeds of Jesus the standard of their internal discipline rather than the inspiration of an apostolic mission.

The primitive Christian community strove hard to learn from the words and works of Jesus, and they found ways of applying to their own case what had been addressed by him to others. Manson illustrates this by reference to the studies on the parables by C. H. Dodd[33] and J. Jeremias.[34] He concludes his book by stressing that the ethic of the New Testament is the ethic of a kingdom, a society with a leader and ruler; the ethic comes from the Ruler himself. Inevitably the Christian ethic comes back to Christ himself, for it is from him that it derives its content, form and authority. 'Its force is most likely to be felt by those who belong to the community which he founded and maintains, the community which belongs to him. And the power to carry it into effect is most likely to be found in living association with that community and with its head'.[35]

We have two outstanding Roman Catholic works on New Testament moral teaching. That of R. Schnackenburg[36] is arranged in three parts: Jesus' moral demands, the moral teaching of the early Church in general, and the moral teaching of prominent individual preachers.

Jesus had come to inaugurate the kingdom of God. However, salvation, in part already realised, will be fulfilled only at the Parousia; hence there is a tension which conditions the moral imperative and stresses the necessity of watching in order to be found worthy to appear one day before God. For those who wish to enter into the kingdom, Jesus lays down certain conditions: radical conversion (*metanoia*), an internal disposition by which man submits himself to God; then faith, which is obedience to the will of God and acceptance of the message of salvation brought by Christ. He called men to 'follow him' by accepting the conditions of his life and by sharing in his destiny. The originality of Christian morality appears most clearly in the Sermon on the Mount: Jesus is conscious of having been sent by God in order to give back to the Law its true meaning and, where necessary, to give it a more perfect and definitive formulation. Taking a firm stand against legalism, he demanded interior disposition as the decisive factor in moral action; at the same time the moral obligation had become more radical in his teaching. Such morality is not thereby impracticable; Jesus did intend to establish a way of life for the time between his glorification and Parousia, the time of the

Church. It is true that it is an 'impossible ethic' when looked at from a human viewpoint alone; the decisive factor is that what is humanly impossible is possible with God (cf. *Mark* 10:25-27). Jesus concentrated all religious moral precepts in the great commandment of *agapé* which demands the final renunciation of self and utter devotion to God and fellow-men. It is almost paradoxical that the radical ethic of Jesus is marked by realism towards conditions in this world. This fact is illustrated by a study of his demands in regard to daily living, in his attitude to work and property, and in his attitude to marriage and the family. The principal motive that Jesus gave for his demands was the kingdom of God and its blessings; the motive of retribution is secondary in so far as it remains subordinate to the motive of the kingdom. The motive of imitating God was proposed by Jesus, and among his followers this quickly led to the imitation of Jesus himself.

The fundamentally eschatological outlook of the early Church was a major factor in its determination of ethical conduct. While the outpouring of the Spirit was the basic religious experience of early Christianity, it was Paul who first regarded the Spirit of God as the driving force of moral life. The first Christians were conscious of being the community of salvation of the last times; they lived in an intense expectation of the Parousia which placed a special stamp on their attitude to this world and their way of life. The thought of the Parousia could be used as a stimulus in exhorting the faithful. It explains the importance given by Paul to virginity and to the view that earthly things lose their importance; at the same time, Christians were not estranged from their worldly tasks. While Johannine Christianity lived in the serene awareness of having found salvation, conflict and persecution heightened the prospect of the Parousia and consummation (see 1 *John, Apocalypse*). Eschatological awareness summoned the believer to responsible action in the world, to combat against the destructive forces of evil, and to living hope and joyful confidence—this awareness needs to be re-established as a factor in determining our contemporary moral situation.

The early Christians saw themselves as the heirs of Christ

and the administrators of his legacy. They took Jesus' pronouncements as dynamic challenges to be *lived* according to the demands of a given situation, not as sayings to be treasured or principles to be watered down; but they did not hesitate to interpret and adapt his message according to circumstances. Their attitude to the Law changed when Gentiles entered the Church in great numbers: the new 'law of Christ' took the place of the Mosaic law. Christians had to take up a position on different questions: on the value of asceticism (in order 'to follow Christ'), on the requirements of piety and worship, in their attitude to the state and public authorities, and on marriage and the family.

In the third part Schnackenburg reviews the data of the previous two parts, now according to the particular genius of Paul, John and James. Paul saw that to be filled with the Spirit of God is the beginning of redemption, but that it is also a moral call to a new and real service of God. The moral precept is firmly anchored in the state of salvation bestowed upon us by the grace of God. Paul was very conscious of the Christian's struggle with the powers of evil still existing in the world. He saw that conscience, a moral endowment of all men, was the ultimate authority in moral judgement; therefore, it had to be formed and trained. He adapted his moral teaching to the requirements and understanding of his Gentile hearers. In general it may be said that Pauline moral teaching developed especially the mystique of baptism and presented a view of Christian life considered as a warfare with the forces of evil.

Johannine theology finds its focus in Christology, and John stresses the summons to man by the revealer and Saviour who has come into the world. He can present a synthesis of moral teaching in the commandment of faith and love. Johannine faith has assimilated two commandments of the Jesus of the Synoptic Gospels: repentance and discipleship. Strictly speaking, in John the plenitude of the moral commandments is summed up not in the double commandment to love God and one's neighbour, but in the 'new' commandment to love the brethren alone. Active love for the brethren is seen as the proof of communion with Christ and God. Ultimately, the Johannine Christians do not take up their position in relation to the 'world' on their own account but within the Church to which they belong. John is by no means oppressed by a sense of sin, but he does recognise it as a harsh and sinister fact in Christian life which it is impossible to ignore. However, God gives to the Christian powers which enable him and bind him to live a holy life without sin.

James puts forward the gospel as such, and more precisely the obligations it entails, as the perfect law of liberty; the message of salvation makes claims on men and imposes moral duties on them. But James was as concerned about 'works' as he was about the 'law of freedom'; he was concerned with negligent Christian conduct. 'The Christianity that James preaches is not a comfortable religion. But his practical, virile teaching will remain salutary as long as Christians continue to miss the path from knowledge to action, from faith to charity, from piety to moral proof'.[37] The first epistle of Peter, theologically more profound than James, inculcates a solid piety. We find in Hebrews, a paraenetic composition of the second generation, the ideas and forces which filled the early Church as a whole. In the letters of Apocalypse 2-3 the state of the Christian communities is judged by their 'works', the outcome of religious and moral action.

The conclusion of this study of New Testament moral teaching is that the proclamation of Christian faith and Christian morals has never, since New Testament times, attained the same profundity and power. This is, in great measure, because the dimming of the eschatological urgency of Jesus' message has weakened its impact. But there is reason for optimism: 'Our present generation of Christians seems once again more ready to accept the original words of the Bible, sensing in them the purity of a wellspring and the power of a root. But this means that they must be proclaimed without attenuation, and in the moral sphere this involves bringing the undiminished demands of Jesus into our own times and applying them to ourselves'.[38]

The moral theology of the New Testament which C. Spicq presents with his customary wealth of erudition[39] is described by him as 'a collection of *major themes,* common to almost all the New Testament writers, to which are attached *supplementary themes (thèmes annexes)* which receive their clarification and proper proportion from the former—but this is not to say that the supplementary themes are of secondary importance.'[40] The opening chapter of this extensive work makes a comparison between the morality of the new covenant and that of Judaism from which the latter does not emerge in a very favourable light; it would seem that Manson is more finely nuanced here. What characterises the morality of the New Testament is its baptismal character: baptism is the source of a new life, the life of Christ communicated to the believer. This life of Christ in him becomes the inner moral law of the Christian, a law summed up in the twofold precept of charity, love of God and love of men; here is found the essential feature of the imitation of Christ. The main supplementary themes are Christian devotion and Christian responsibility. This first chapter is fundamental and programmatic; the rest of the work exploits and details the different aspects of its content.

After this opening Spicq divides his matter in nine chapters, each given over to a theme or group of themes; we discover that he follows the plan of a systematic treatise of moral theology—more specifically that of the *Prima Secundae* and *Secunda Secundae* of Aquinas' *Summa Theologiae*. His chapters two to four are concerned with the basic themes of Christian moral life. Chapter two deals with the *new being* and the *new life*—that is, conversion and baptism with their consequences: reception into the Church and sonship. Then comes *grace* and the glory which is associated with it (the actual participation of the Christian in the divine splendour), and man's reaction to the gift of grace: to give thanks and glory. The following chapter treats of justification, sin and sanctification. The supplementary themes most notably dealt with are flight from the world, the spiritual warfare and mortification.

The next five chapters (five to nine) spell out the different aspects of this new life. The first three are given over to the theological virtues, faith, hope and charity. The supplementary themes of faith are: heresy and orthodoxy, fidelity and loyalty, hypocrisy, faith and authenticity; those of hope are: the prayer of petition (it is an act of confidence

in God), poverty and work; those of charity: purity and
virginity. A chapter entitled 'Pastoral instructions, formation of conscience and rectitude of conduct' deals, more or
less, with the moral virtues. The following chapter, 'The
liberty of the children of God', treats of a fundamental New
Testament theme—one sadly, and disastrously, lacking in
the classic manuals of moral theology. Spicq stresses the two
aspects: liberty, and openness to God and neighbour—not
freedom *from* but freedom *for*. Chapter ten returns to a more
general theme, that of the image of God with the stress on
its eschatological dimension: it involves the imitation of God
and of Christ. The concluding chapter outlines the major
characteristics of New Testament moral teaching: its con-
sistency within its varied expression in the different inspired
writings, its religious character, and its essential dimensions:
baptismal, filial, eschatological. Finally, a series of valuable
excursus forms an appendix to each of the two volumes.

Spicq has offered us a collection of monographs rather
than an exposition arranged in a rigorous pattern. There is
a plan—a very broad one—but it is that of systematic moral
theology and this is not the ideal arrangement of a work of
biblical theology. The author is conscious of the fact; he tells
us that his first intention had been to centre the moral theology of the New Testament around the theme of charity. His
work would have been more truly a *theology* if he had done
so[41] or, better, if he had built it around the theme of Christ
into whom the Christian is incorporated at baptism. He
eventually decided against this procedure. Instead, he declared just how his work is to be taken: 'Our intention is
not to expound a thesis, nor even an organically constructed
synthesis, but to build up an almost complete dossier of texts
and to exploit what they contribute while fully respecting
the hierarchy of values they represent, and thus to bring out
and explain the ideas expressed by Jesus and his apostles'.[42]
He still remains somewhat doubtful that such a procedure
constitutes a true *theology*—is it not rather a collection of
biblical themes? At the same time, the specific contribution
of each New Testament writer could have been more clearly
indicated; thus the different nuances of Pauline and Johannine 'faith' ought to have been brought out. But Spicq has

given, in his 'almost complete dossier', an indispensable tool for the exegete and the moral theologian.[43]

## 2. Four Representative Theologies

### I. RUDOLF BULTMANN

Rudolf Bultmann published his *Theologie des Neuen Testaments* in three instalments, between 1948 and 1953.[44] It has appeared in English translation in two volumes.[45] He has divided his work into four parts: I. Presuppositions and motifs of New Testament theology; II. The theology of Paul; III. The theology of the gospel of John and the Johannine epitles; IV. The development toward the ancient Church. In our outline of the salient points of the *Theology* we shall follow this division.

*Part I*. Bultmann asserts at the outset that the message of Jesus is not the subject of New Testament theology; it is a presupposition for the theology of the New Testament rather than a part of that theology. This is so because New Testament theology is 'the unfolding of those ideas by means of which Christian faith makes sure of its own object, basis and consequences'.[46] But since Christian faith is based on the *kerygma* which proclaims Jesus Christ, the crucified and risen One, theological thinking begins with the kerygma of the earliest Church and not before. At the same time, the message which Jesus proclaimed is an important presuposition of New Testament theology and merits consideration on that ground.

Jesus' message is eschatological; its dominant theme is the reign of God. What was really new in it was not the message itself but the certainty with which Jesus asserted that the time had come, that God's reign was breaking in. In the light of its dawning Jesus issued a call to decision. He did not found a sect, and certainly not a 'Church', but he did confront every man with deciding whether he will set his heart on God or on wordly goods. Jesus interpreted the demand of God and presented it with new vigour; his message became a protest against Jewish legalism which saw the will of God in the written Law and interpretative tradition. He demanded not the obedience that answers to a command but the radical, genuine obedience which claims man wholly for God. God's positive will is the demand for love and a man is ready for the salvation to come, the reign of God, only when he here and now responds to the demand of God which confronts him in the person of his neighbour.

Jesus' expectation of the near end of the world was not fulfilled—did this affect his idea of God? The answer is clear once we recognise that the essential thing about the eschatological message is not belief in the imminent end of the world but the assertion that God is a God at hand who directly confronts every man. For Jesus 'man is de-secularised by God's direct pronouncement to him, which tears him out of all security of any kind and places him at the brink of the End'.[47] The Synoptic Gospels make clear that Jesus' life and work, measured by traditional messianic ideas, were not messianic. There is undoubtedly a reinterpretation of the messianic concept, notably in the prediction of the passion, but this is the work of the Church; there is no evidence that this belief rests upon the self-consciousness of Jesus. For Bultmann it is not a matter of importance: 'The acknowledgement of Jesus as the one in whom God's word decisively encounters man . . . is a pure act of faith independent of the historical question whether or not Jesus considered himself as the Messiah.'[48]

Theology begins with the kerygma. In it the proclaimer has become the proclaimed; he who had been the bearer of the message has now become its essential content. Jesus is now proclaimed as the coming Messiah, as Son of Man; the Messiah-myth has been transferred to a concrete historical man. The importance of the Messiah-Son-of-Man lies in what is expected of him for the future. Already the coming of Jesus, his cross, resurrection, and exaltation have the meaning of eschatological occurrence. In quite the same way the earliest Church saw itself as the eschatological congregation of the end of days; it saw itself as the fulfilment of apocalyptic hopes. Baptism was the rite of initiation into the congregation; the common meals (the 'breaking of bread') received their character from its eschatological consciousness; it knew that it had been given the Spirit, the eschatological gift. Jesus' coming was the decisive event through which God called his congregation—Jesus' coming was already eschatological occurrence. 'That is the real content of the Easter faith: God has made the prophet and teacher Jesus of Nazareth Messiah.'[49] This necessarily implies a Christology. Jesus was understood as the one whom God through the resurrection had made Messiah, who was awaited as the coming Son of Man. But the scandal of the cross had to be surmounted; this was achieved in the Easter faith. The titles conferred upon Jesus were designations for the future salvation-bringer; at the same time it was recognised that, in a certain manner, he already exercises his sway here and now. But in the earliest Church the cult of Jesus had not yet developed. There was not, in any proper sense, an office of direction in the earliest Church; the Twelve were a symbol of the congregation as the true Israel. The sole appropriate institution could only be one founded upon the proclamation of the word.

In Bultmann's view, the historical presupposition for Paul's theology is the kerygma not of the earliest Church but of the Hellenistic Church. He seeks to reconstruct this Hellenistic kerygma from some few data in Acts, some inferences from the Pauline letters, and inferences from later sources, patristic as well as canonical. Christian missionary preaching to the Gentile world had to begin with the proclamation of the one God who is the Creator and Judge; the call to believe is simultaneously a call to repentance. At this point christological motifs emerge. With, or in place of, God, Jesus Christ appears as the eschatological Judge of the world and as the Saviour of those who belong to the congregation of the faithful.

Because the earliest Church saw itself as the eschatological congregation of the end of days, it took for granted that the salvation proclaimed by the Christian message was salvation not only for the individual, but also for God's people in fellowship. This 'Church-consciousness' stands behind a consciousness of solidarity with Israel and its history and includes a consciousness of separateness from the world. The Church's relation to the Old Testament raised a special problem, due to the fact that Hellenistic Christianity, while it had taken over the Old Testament, at the same time denied the validity of Old Testament Law for Christians. Early Christian literature answers the problem along the following lines: (1) the cultic demands of the Old Testament Law are abolished; (2) the whole Old Testament is regarded as a book of predictions; (3) the ethical demands of the Old Testament retain uncontested and valid authority.

Bultmann maintains that it was in Hellenistic Christianity that Jesus Christ figured for the first time as the cultically worshipped 'Lord'; the title *Kyrios* was first conferred upon Christ in the Hellenistic Church. The same is true of 'Son of Man': while the *title* was used by the Jewish Christians to denote the messianic king, it now came to mean the divine nature of Christ. Baptism had been practised as a rite of initiation into the eschatological congregation and had come to be understood as a sacrament which brought about purification from sins, the sealing by the name of the Lord, and the bestowal of the Spirit. The Hellenistic Church added another interpretation of the sacrament: it gives participation in the death and resurrection of Christ—this because it understood the initiation-sacrament on analogy with the initiation-sacraments of the mystery religions. For the same reason the Lord's Supper was understood as a sacrament and later came to be conceived of as a sacrifice. The bestowal of the Spirit (*Pneuma,* the miraculous divine power standing in absolute contrast to all that is human) was seen as a specific eschatological gift. Bultmann concludes the first part of his *Theology* by a consideration of Gnostic motifs and terminology which have contributed to the development of Christian theological language.

*Part II.* The Theology of Paul. Bultmann's presentation of Pauline theology is the most satisfactory part of his whole work. The foregoing reconstruction of early Hellenistic Christianity had been a preparation, for Paul's place is within Hellenistic Christianity. For a study of Paul's theology, only his undoubtedly genuine letters may serve: Romans, 1, 2 Corinthians, Galatians, Philippians, 1 Thessalonians and Philemon. Paul's theology is not a speculative system; he does not deal with God as he is in himself but with God as he is significant for man. The character of Pauline theology points to the proper way of handling it. 'Every assertion about God is simultaneously an assertion about man and vice versa. For this reason and in this sense Paul's theology is, at the same time, anthropology. . . . Every assertion about God speaks of what he does with man and what he demands of man. And the other way about, every assertion about man speaks of God's deed and demand. The Christology of Paul is likewise governed by this point of view. Thus, every assertion about Christ is also an assertion about man and vice versa; and Paul's Christology is simultaneously soteriology. Therefore Paul's theology can best be treated as his doctrine of man: first, of man prior to the revelation of faith, and second, of man under faith, for in this way the anthropological and soteriological orientation of Paul's theology is brought out.'[50]

Under the heading 'The Anthropological Concepts' the author considers *Sōma, Psychē, Pneuma, Zōē,* mind and conscience, and heart. Paul's most comprehensive term for characterising man's existence is *sōma* ('body')—a complex and difficult term. Man is called *sōma* in respect of his having a relationship to himself; he is so called as 'that self from whom he, as subject, distinguishes himself, the self with whom he can deal as the subject of his own conduct, and also the self whom he can perceive as subjected to an occurrence which springs from a will other than his own'.[51] It is as *sōma* that man has the possibility of being good or evil, of having a relationship for or against God. Man is a living unity, and the other anthropological terms express facets of his person.

Then Bultmann turns to a study of flesh, sin, and the world, which are taken as comprehensive. Sin means to miss what is good; it is rebellion against God. The ultimate sin is the false assumption that one lives from one's own self rather than from God. *Sarx* ('flesh') denotes corporeality; more specifically it designates the earthly-human in its weakness and transitoriness. For Paul, 'to live' or 'to walk' *in the flesh* means the fact of leading one's life as a man; the phrase 'according to the flesh', on the other hand, adds the further qualification of *sinful*—the pursuit of the merely human. Such sinful self-reliance finds its extreme expression in man's 'boasting'. The essence of human existence under sin is to be innerly divided, opposed to his true self. And because sin is the pursuit of the earthly and transitory, it leads necessarily to death; and sin, like death, is universal. *Kosmos* ('world') is very often a theological term meaning the sphere of the merely natural, the sphere of 'flesh' standing in antithesis to the sphere of God.

God is the Judge who demands good deeds of men; his demands encounter men concretely in the Law of the Old Testament—Paul thinks essentially of its ethical demands. And, in his eyes, the way of works of the Law and the way of grace and faith are mutually exclusive opposites. Paul's insight into the nature of sin has determined the teaching on the Law. He sees, firstly, that sin is man's self-powered striving to procure his salvation by his own strength and, secondly, that man is always already a sinner, already has a falsely oriented understanding of his existence. The reason why man must not be made righteous by works of the Law is that 'he must not be allowed to imagine that he is able to procure his salvation by his own strength; for he can find his salvation only when he understands himself in his dependence upon God the Creator.'[52]

Next comes the turn of Man under faith, which concerns the themes of the righteousness of God, grace, and faith. Righteousness, rather than a quality or something a person has as his own, is a relationship; a man is 'righteous' to the extent that he is acknowledged to be such. It is a forensic term which in the development of Jewish piety came to be also an eschatological term. Paul, however, declares that righteousness is imputed to a man already in the present, on condition that he has faith. Besides, God does not only regard a man as if he were righteous, but makes him righteous by absolving him from sin. What is most distinctive of Paul's view, however, is that, in direct contrast to the Jewish view, he asserts that it comes by or from faith and absolutely without works of the Law—it is sheer gift. Righteousness has its origin in God's act of grace accomplished in Christ. It is God's righteousness: its one and only foundation is God's grace. Another term can be substituted for righteousness: *reconciliation*; it is equally a gift which man 'receives'.

God's grace is not a quality; it is an event, and may be precisely defined: 'It is not a mode of dealing which God has decided henceforth to adopt, but is a single deed which takes effect for everyone who recognises it as such and acknowledges it (in faith)—"grace" is God's eschatological deed.'[53] God's deed of grace consists in the fact that he gave Christ up to die as a propitiatory sacrifice for the sin of men; the 'obedience' of the Son is his corresponding deed of grace. The deed of divine grace is the salvation-occurrence: the death and resurrection of Jesus.

At this point a distinctive view of Bultmann comes forcefully into prominence. He regards the proclamation of the salvation-occurrence not as a preparatory instruction which precedes the demand for faith in the occurrence; rather, he sees it as, in itself, the call, the challenge. More than that, the salvation-occurrence is nowhere present except in the proclaiming, and it continues to take place in the proclamation of the word. 'How can the salvation-occurrence be understood as an occurrence directed at man, reaching him, and happening to him? It takes place in the word, which accosts the hearer and compels him to decide for or against it.'[54] The further question, by what sign the cross of Christ is recognisable as salvation-event, receives the answer: 'It gets its scandal-and-folly character by the fact that a crucified one is proclaimed as Lord; and only in the fact that this proclamation occurs is the cross recognisable as salvation-event'.[55]

Similarly, for Bultmann, the mythological concepts of Christ's pre-existence and incarnation are present and active in, and only in, the Christian proclamation. Here again, it is preferable to quote directly. Pre-existence: 'There exists a divinely authorised proclamation of the prevenient grace and love of God; this is the fact that finds a mythological expression in what is said of the pre-existence of Christ. What the hearer affirms when he believes the pre-existence of Christ is that what has encountered him is the word of God.'[54] Resurrection: 'the resurrection cannot—in spite of 1 *Cor.* 15: 3-8—be demonstrated or made plausible as an objectively ascertainable fact on the basis of which one can believe. But insofar as it or the risen Christ is present in the proclaiming word, it can be believed—and only so can it be believed. Belief in the resurrection and the faith that Christ himself,

yes God himself, speaks in the proclaimed word (2 *Cor.*
5 : 20) are identical'.[57] The proclamation raises the historical
person and his fate to the rank of the eschatological event;
the meaning of the resurrection is not that Jesus has been
translated into the beyond, but that he is exalted to the
status of Lord (*Phil.* 2 : 11). The proclaimed word, the
*kerygma,* is personal address which accosts each individual;
it calls and gathers men into the *Ecclēsia,* the congregation
of those who are 'called' and 'saints'. In the Church, baptism
and the Lord's Supper, as well as the proclaimed word, make
the salvation-occurrence present.

'Faith' is the attitude of man in which he receives the gift
of God's righteousness. Paul understood faith primarily as
obedience. The fact is that faith, which demands acknowledgement of the crucified Jesus as Lord, demands the surrender of man's previous understanding of himself; it is the
radical surrender of man's will. As true obedience it is the
condition for receiving salvation. Precisely as obedience, faith
is trust and hope; but it is also accompanied by fear of losing
hold of the divine hand and falling back on oneself. Faith is
that acceptance of the *kerygma* which is a genuine obedience
to it. It includes a new understanding of oneself and leads
to the individually varied forms of concrete Christian living.
Faith as response to the proclaimed word is part of the
salvation-occurrence.

The surrender of faith and the new self-understanding
which it brings means *freedom*—the believer has yielded
himself entirely to the grace of God. Another way of expressing the freedom of the believer is to say that he has been
given the gift of the Spirit; by the term 'Spirit' Paul means
'the eschatological existence into which the believer is placed
by having appropriated the salvation deed that occurred in
Christ'.[58] Christian freedom means freedom from the Law and
sin; it also means freedom from death. Since Christ's resurrection is conceived as the origin of the resurrection-life of all
believers, then, in a certain sense, 'life' is a present reality
after all. The believer triumphs over suffering through his
'fellowship of suffering' with Christ; he triumphs over death
by sharing Christ's victory over death; he has freedom from
the world and its powers. In short, 'he who belongs to Christ,

and through him to God, has become master of everything
(1 *Cor.* 3: 21-33)'.[59]

The third part of the *Theology* takes up the Fourth Gospel
and the Johannine Epistles. Bultmann first considers the relationship of John and Paul: while they have certain things
in common, their development lies in quite different directions. Thus, while they agree to a certain extent in the use
of common Christian terminology, the specifically Pauline
terminology is missing in John. Again, the history-of-salvation
perspective as a whole is lacking in John; on the other hand,
in both, the eschatological occurrence is understood as already taking place in the present, though only John has
followed the idea through in a radical fashion.

For John the essence of the *kosmos*, the world of men, is
darkness; it is existence in bondage, a compound of false-
hood and darkness that is characteristic of it. The meaning
of 'truth' in John is not the teaching about God transmitted
by Jesus, but God's very reality revealing itself in Jesus. So,
accordingly, the 'lie' denies this reality, and the 'liar' falls
into the unreal, death. The world must choose between
bondage, the way of death, and freedom, the way of life.
'Each man is, or once was, confronted with deciding for or
against God; and he is confronted anew with this decision
by the revelation of God in Jesus. The cosmological dualism
of Gnosticism has become in John a *dualism of decision*'.[60]

The theme of the Fourth Gospel is the statement 'The
Word became flesh'. But this is a paradox, an 'offence',
since, according to John, the divine is the very counter-pole
to the human; and this is why the deeds and words of Jesus
are consistently misunderstood. 'The offence lies in the fact
that the Revealer appears as a man whose claim to be the
Son of God is one which he cannot, indeed must not, prove
to the world. For the Revelation is judgement upon the
world and is necessarily felt as an attack upon it and an
offence to it, so long as the world refuses to give up its norms.
Until it does so, the world inevitably misunderstands the
words and deeds of the Revealer, or they remain a riddle
for it.'[61] God encounters men in Jesus, and the paradoxical
authority of a human being speaking the word of God is
brought out by contrasting statements which declare that

Jesus has equal rights with God or that he acts and speaks only in obedience to the will of the Father. So too, Jesus' death takes on a double aspect in John: it is the completion of his obedience, but it is also the return to the glory that was his. And, since Jesus' death on the cross is already his exaltation, the resurrection is not an event of special significance. For John the entire salvation-drama (incarnation, death, resurrection, Pentecost, the Parousia) is concentrated into one event, the revelation of God's reality ('truth') in the earthly activity of the man Jesus; it demands the overcoming of the 'offence' by acceptance in faith. Consistently, in Bultmann's view, the sacraments play no role in John.

In Jesus there is a close unity between word and work: his actions speak, his words act. John, in his Gospel, presents the fact of Revelation without describing its content; what Jesus reveals is, essentially, the fact that he is the Revealer. And it becomes clear that the Revealer is a definite historical man, Jesus of Nazareth. Bultmann puts his viewpoint clearly: 'Jesus is not presented in literal seriousness as a pre-existent divine being who came in human form to earth to reveal unprecedented secrets. Rather, the mythological terminology is intended to express the absolute and decisive significance of his word—the mythological notion of pre-existence is made to serve the idea of the Revelation. His word does not arise from the sphere of human observation and thought, but comes from beyond . . . It is an authoritative word which confronts the hearer with a life-and-death decision.'[62]

The demand that one *believe* runs through the Gospel and 1 John; but faith is genuine only insofar as it is *knowing* faith; Christian knowledge is always believing knowledge. Faith is the overcoming of the 'offence'; it means accepting the life that Jesus gives, it means deciding for God against the world. Faith is *desecularisation,* a smashing of all human standards and evaluation and a transition into eschatological existence. Freedom and confidence follow on faith; and genuine faith provides the foundation for all one's future conduct. The possession of the Spirit is a final criterion of eschatological existence. The Revelation brought by Jesus is what it is by constantly occurring anew—the Spirit causes this to happen because it is the power which brings about knowledge and the proclamation of the Word. Bultmann's concluding words on Johannine theology bring out yet again his theological emphasis on the proclamation of the Word: 'It is not through a discipline of abstention from the world, an ascetic conduct of life, or a sacramental cult that this [Johannine] Church seeks to achieve its eschatological character, for it is the Church of the Word—the Word from which it lives, the Word which is also its commission to the world. Its life is impelled by the living Spirit within it: it is the power which brings forth both knowledge and the proclamation of the Word.'[63]

The long final part of the *Theology* (The Development Toward the Ancient Church) has not the absorbing interest of his treatment of the Pauline and Johannine theologies. Yet it is here we can find Bultmann's conception of the growth and progress of the Christian faith, from its beginnings in the *kerygma* to the organised Church of the second century with its doctrinal system and its ecclesiastical offices. The broad lines of the evolution traced by Bultmann may be summarised as follows: (1) the transition from the preaching of the Word by 'charismatics' to a sacramental and juridical order directed by 'ministers'; (2) the transition from an eschatologism which regarded the fact of salvation in Christ as the term of history to a historicism which set the person, life and teaching of Jesus in the midst of history. This postponed eschatological salvation to a more or less distant future and made of Christianity a 'new religion' side by side with others, one more concerned with individual than with community salvation; (3) the transition from faith to a search for knowledge with all that this involves of discussion, of 'true' and 'false' doctrine, of control by an authority, and of the canon of normative Scripture.[64]

Christology and soteriology formed the core of development. In all the churches Jesus Christ was worshipped as the bringer of salvation; but the crucial question was how the relation between the present reality and the futurity of salvation was conceived. In other words, in what degree is the Christian situation understood to be that peculiar situation of 'between-ness'—between 'no longer' and 'not yet'—

as it is found in Paul and John? Bultmann looks to the later
New Testament books and the Apostolic Fathers and finds
varied answers. In the main, the basic sense of 'between-
ness' has been paled down or, in some cases, is no longer
present. The passing of the tension of 'between-ness' gave
place to a sacramentalist regime. The fruit of the cross was
reduced to the forgiveness of past sins; the present became
the time of penance, of good works, of a new legalism. This
had a profound influence on Christology. 'The more Christian faith degenerates into legalism, the more Christ's significance is reduced to that of being at work in the Church's
sacrament. The less Christ is felt to be present in the proclaimed word, the more the Church becomes a sacramental
institution of salvation. Christology, as soon as it ceases to be
naïve and becomes a matter of reflection, will have to find
its task in furnishing a foundation for the sacramental
significance of Christ.'[65]

The final chapter of the *Theology* considers the problem
of Christian living, a problem which exercised the Church
from the beginning. This problem arises out of the paradoxical situation of the Church: an eschatological entity
belonging to the future world and yet leading its life between
the 'no longer' and the 'not yet'.

## II. ALAN RICHARDSON

Very different from Bultmann's *Theology* is the work of
Alan Richardson.[66] In his Preface he states explicity that his
principle of interpretation is that of historic Christian faith,
and he asserts that this gives a more coherent and rationally
satisfying result than do any liberal-humanist or existentialist
principles of interpretation. In his view, New Testament
theology must begin with a hypothesis which makes 'sense'
of the historical data of the New Testament; for Christians
the starting-point will be apostolic faith. So he declares: 'In
this book the hypothesis is defended that Jesus himself is the
author of the brilliant re-interpretation of the Old Testament
scheme of salvation ("Old Testament theology") which is
found in the New Testament, and that the events of the life,
"signs", passion and resurrection of Jesus, as attested by the
apostolic witness, can account for the "data" of the New

Testament better than any other hypothesis current today.'[67]

Richardson arranges his book in sixteen chapters; it is a thematic arrangement rather than one displaying a closely interlocking pattern. He thinks it is fitting to begin with a study of the fundamental concept of faith. In the Old Testament the prophets realised—especially in the need for a new covenant—that God himself must give the faith he demands; in the New Testament this happened through the covenant in Christ. In his own teaching Jesus issued a constant appeal for faith in God's reign, and in himself as the sign that it had come: the sign of the Son of Man. So, the object of faith of the apostolic Church is Christ himself. Faith is associated with hearing—which is the same as obeying—and it is always a gift from God. In the context of faith, repentance is seen as a constant awareness that all our faith and virtues are God's gift, not our achievement. And regeneration, the sense of being remade in Jesus, is an eschatological conception closely connected with Christian baptism.

In the Old Testament and then also in the New, knowledge through obedience and hearing is a personal relationship—it is 'existential' knowledge. Though the only explicit reference in the synoptics to knowing God is the 'Johannine logion' (*Matt.* 11:27 = *Luke* 10:22), that text epitomises what the apostolic Church understood of Jesus' and men's relationship to God. John's teaching on the knowledge of God starts with an act of faith in Christ; and for him 'believing' and 'knowing' are fully complementary. Paul is being wholly true to the biblical emphasis when he insists that not our knowledge of God but God's knowledge of us is the important thing. For that matter, any real knowledge of God must be revealed knowledge. It is always the *hidden* God who reveals himself—there is the utter mystery of God, and a mystery cannot be made less mysterious. So, too, the incarnation is necessarily a veiling as well as a revealing of the light. Jesus himself is the origin of the New Testament conception of the unveiling of the Son of Man, begun now by faith and to be completed at the Parousia. And the life of the Church, Christ's body on earth, involves an inner mystery veiled.

In the biblical view God cannot be known as he exists in

himself but only as he discloses himself by his activity. The
divine activity is variously expressed: power, glory, light,
life, wrath, righteousness and salvation. Christ is the power
of God unto salvation, the activity of God *par excellence.*
The New Testament sees the incarnate Lord as the first
instalment of the unveiling of glory at the end of the age.
Its use of the metaphor of light is thoroughly Jewish and
eschatological. Similarly, the conception of the wrath of God
in the New Testament is eschatological in the same sense as
are the conceptions of kingdom, glory and life; Paul in
*Romans* offers the most considered teaching on the subject of
divine wrath. 'If in the biblical view judgement is an inevitable consequence of God's righteousness, so also is salvation.'[68]
Jesus revived the whole Isaianic conception of salvation in
face of the distinctive doctrines of Pharisaism.

The New Testament conception of 'the kingdom of God'
has a long history behind it. Israel was appointed as God's
priestly ruler in relation to other nations and failed in the
task. Belief arose that God must again give the kingdom to
the faithful remnant in the latter days. John the Baptist
proclaimed it as at hand; Jesus showed signs by which it
might be discerned. He believed that after his death the
outpouring of the Spirit would take place, bringing in the
kingdom 'with power'. Thus it is given as an eschatological
reality to the saints. 'This is the fundamental conception of
the Church in the New Testament.'[69] And to enter God's
kingdom is more than to be a subject; it means a sharing in
the reign.

Our difficulty about the relationship of the Holy Spirit to
God is that we hold a different concept of personality than
that known to the biblical writers. 'We think of separate and
distinct personalities, hard and impermeable, each sharply
distinguished from the others: hence our "problem" of the
doctrine of the Trinity. In the Bible persons are not thus
separate and distinct; they flow into one another.'[70] The
eschatological character of the Holy Spirit is central in the
New Testament conception. The death and resurrection of
Jesus were to bring about the shedding abroad of the Holy
Spirit in the latter days. The Spirit is the Spirit of power,
giving deeds beyond our strength; his action is compulsive

but not coercive: he does not over-ride our human personality. As the Spirit of Christ, he is the Spirit of *truth*—which is something to be *done*, not merely thought or 'believed'. The Spirit is the interpreter of the Scriptures; without his inward testimony their message would remain locked up in the written or spoken work; the Spirit breathes life into 'dead letters'. The Holy Spirit is not a person existing independently of God; it is a way of speaking about God's personal activity in history or of the risen Lord's personal activity in the Church. 'The New Testament clearly regards the work of the ascended Christ and the work of the Holy Spirit as inseparably and indivisibly the activity of the one God, whose age-long plan for man's redemption and restoration is now made known, as in a mystery, to the enlightened eyes of those who believe in Christ.'[71]

For Richardson, the assumption that Jesus is the author of the New Testament's reinterpretation of Messiahship is the only hypothesis that does justice to the facts. Three kinds of Son-of-Man sayings are attributed to Jesus in the Synoptics: (1) in reference to himself as Son of Man at the time of speaking; (2) in reference to the coming sufferings and resurrection of the Son of Man; (3) eschatological: the affirmation of the future glory of the exalted Son of Man. The suffering of the Son of Man necessitated a radical reinterpretation of current Jewish notions about the Messiah and effected a brilliant new synthesis of Old Testament themes. Yet Bultmann maintains that Jesus was unaware of this and credit for the reinterpretation must go to an unnamed theological teacher in the Hellenistic Church. It is evident that it is far more plausible to see the bold new teaching as the work of Jesus himself. The grandeur and originality of Jesus' doctrine is this: the lowly Son of Man, with nowhere to lay his head and about to suffer shamefully, is the same Son of Man who will be seen sitting at the right hand of God. And he is still the afflicted one, identified with every man. The idea of corporate personality is present in the New Testament conception of the Son of Man who gathers up the new humanity into himself.

Chapter seven studies the Christology of the apostolic Church by taking up the titles: Son of God, the Lord, the

Wisdom of God, the Word of God. The meaning of 'Son of God' in the New Testament is based on its distinctive use in the Old Testament; so it is as the New Israel that Jesus is to be understood as Son of God, and not in any Hellenistic sense of a 'divine man'. At the same time, his intimate use of *Abba* points to Jesus' consciousness of being uniquely God's Son. By New Testament times the word *kyrios*, 'Lord' was regularly understood, throughout the Hellenistic world, as a divine predicate. For Christians it had further depth of meaning from its LXX use as rendering Yahweh; the title was universally available to the preachers of the Gentile mission. However, the Aramaic liturgical formula, *Marana tha*, 'Our Lord, Come!' shows that the title did not originate in the Gentile Church. Recognition of the pre-existence of Christ followed immediately on the worship of him as Son of God and Lord; the Old Testament concept of Wisdom was used, by Paul and John, to explain his pre-existence. It is a short step to John's pre-existent and incarnate Word. We may summarise the development of New Testament Christology thus: in the first place there is the appearance of Jesus as 'the Prophet' who startled the Jewish people and the rabbis by claiming to fulfil the Torah, by demonstrating through word and sign that the Prophet whom Moses had bidden them hear had arrived. Then there is the Messiah-Servant Christology: Jesus taught it to his disciples in the later stages of his earthly ministry; it was based on the scriptural insight that the Prophet would be rejected by those who should have listened. Thirdly, there is the developed Wisdom-Word Christology which, after the resurrection, went on under the illumination of the Holy Spirit to work out the conclusions that had been involved in the life, teaching, work, death and resurrection of Jesus.

Paradoxically, perhaps, contemporary radical criticism of the Gospels is prepared to take seriously the fact that the only 'life' of Jesus is the one to which the apostolic testimony bears witness. A chapter considers the birth of Christ, the Blessed Virgin Mary, the baptism of Jesus, the transfiguration and the passion-story. Then Richardson turns to the resurrection, ascension, and victory of Christ. The meeting of Christians to break bread as a joyful memorial is the strongest evidence of the certainty of the resurrection. The coming together of the disciples who had once left him and fled away, the existence of the Church at all, should convince us that the explanation given by the disciples themselves is the only one which can claim rational assent. The significance of the historical event of the resurrection is brought out by means of the doctrine of the ascension. Furthermore, 'the New Testament *doctrine* of the ascension of Christ teaches three fundamental truths concerning the risen Lord: that he is our Prophet, Priest and King'.[72] The resurrection-ascension of Christ is presented in the New Testament as a divine victory over the hostile powers of evil. And what is given in mythological form in the legend of Christ's preaching in Hades is that Christ's salvation is indeed for *all*.

The chapter entitled 'The Atonement Wrought by Christ' ranges over a wide field. The New Testament does not say that God demands satisfaction or that man (even Jesus) renders it to him. It positively affirms that God has reconciled rebellious man, who was unable by anything *he* could do to establish 'peace' or a right relationship with God. Two strands of metaphor go to make up the conception of redemption: sacrifice and ransom. The idea of purchase emphasises the cost of redemption, but the metaphor is not pressed in the New Testament and offers no solution to the 'problem' of atonement. 'The atonement in the New Testament is a mystery, not a problem. One can construct theories and offer them as solutions of problems, but one cannot theorise about the deep mystery of our redemption.'[73] As for propitiation—if there is propitiation at all, God, not man, provides it: God offering his own Son as a sacrifice for man's sins. The Pauline doctrine of justification is a way of expressing the truth, taught by Jesus himself, that salvation is the result, not of our meritorious works, but of the righteousness of God which brings salvation to hopeless sinners. The formula 'justification by faith' does not mean that faith itself is a work of merit; it means, rather, justification by the free and saving righteousness of God through baptism and incorporation into Christ—it is all the work of God. 'Justification' is God's objective act of conferring a new status upon us. 'It is not that God treats us "as if" we were righteous. In Christ we *are* righteous even now. But this righteousness must be understood in the light of the whole New Testament conception of eschatology: the righteousness of God is something which belongs to the end of history, but is revealed to faith and laid hold on by faith "even now"—so that it is really ours *now*."[74]

Since God's purpose is the gathering up of all things in Christ (cf. *Eph.* 1: 10), Richardson goes on to consider the whole Christ. St Paul represents the work of Christ as the creation of a new humanity; his conception of the Church as a new-created humanity in Christ is thoroughly eschatological. A closely connected conception is that of 'the last Adam' (1 *Cor.* 15: 45). The contrast between Adam and Christ leads to the conclusion that Christ is a corporate personality in the same sense as is Adam. 'Christ, like Adam, or Abraham, or Israel, is the "many-in-one" and the "one-in-many".'[75] The expression 'in Christ' is peculiarly Pauline; but its equivalents are found in John ('in me') and in other New Testament writings. They convey the idea that those who have come to believe in Christ and who have been baptised into him become part of the newly created humanity of the end-time which constitutes the corporate personality of Christ. Our relationship with Christ is a faith relationship, not one of mystical absorption. The gathering of the redeemed into Christ may be described as the 'fullness of Christ'; it is a reality subject to the 'even now' and 'not yet' of eschatological tension. 'It is the Hebraic conception of the one and the many, the Hebraic view of what we call "personality", which lies behind the conception of the Church as the body of Christ.'[76] The risen Lord, no less than the incarnate Christ, needs a body which can be the instrument of his gospel and of his work in the world. Though the language is metaphorical, it is right to speak of the Church as the resurrection body of Christ. And if the Church is called the Bride of Christ, this declares that our union with him is no merely 'spiritual' thing but is real and physical. The allegory of the Vine teaches that *agapē* is a real quality of life in Christ; God treats us as he treats his Son because we *are* the body of Christ.

Sons of God, brethren of Christ, Christians are co-heirs

with Christ: their inheritance is eschatological—the reign of God. The word 'heir' points to the heart of the paradox of New Testament eschatology: an heir is already in possession of something. One of the most striking displays of the New Testament reinterpretation of Old Testament theology is that the mixed community of Gentiles and Jews has become the new 'people of God'. This fact implies election; as in the Old Testament, election is a matter of service, not of privilege. Christians are elect because they are 'in Christ', the Elect of God. The fact of election shows the utter freedom and sovereignty of God's grace; and in the New Testament grace is primarily God's forgiving love toward sinful and strayed man. 'For Paul, grace and faith may be said to represent complementary processes in the whole act of salvation: grace is the objective, saving activity of God in Jesus Christ through the Holy Spirit, while Faith is the subjective aspect of the process in us; it is, however, not something that we do, but is itself a gift of the Spirit (cf. 1 *Cor.* 12:9)'.[77] Christians are 'members' of the one body of Christ and so of one another; hence to be out of communion with other Christians is to be out of communion with Christ. The Church, according to the New Testament, is not an invisible entity but an actual, bodily existence. The local churches are one Church because Christ is fully present in the whole and in the parts; conversely, the 'catholic' Church is always a local Church.

Since the ministry of the Church is a continuation of the apostolic and priestly ministry of Christ, the whole Church is apostolic, priestly and ministerial. Yet, within the Church, there is a particular apostolic ministry of those who exercise pastoral oversight. The New Testament speaks of a corporate priesthood of the whole Christian community: the priesthood of the laity. The Church is the appointed priest-nation to the 'Gentile', non-Christian world. Because Christ is the Servant, the Church is ministerial; the distinctively Christian virtue of humility or lowliness is closely connected with the concept of *diakonia*. It is clear from the New Testament that Jesus knew himself to have a divinely appointed mission of creating the Church, the new people of God. 'Christ is not so much the "Founder" of the Church as he *is* himself the

12

Church, since the Church is not a company of like-minded people, but the body of those who have been incorporated into the *persona* of Christ *totus Christus,* the head and the members.'[78]

From the first there have been ministries within the Church; this becomes even more clear when the New Testament writings are interpreted by the organic development of the Church's life. It is fair to look for the manifestation of the apostolic, priestly and ministerial character of the New Testament Church in the life and order of the churches or denominations of the world Christian community. The original ministry of the Church was a divinely appointed apostolic ministry; and though by the end of the New Testament period the word 'apostles' had come to signify 'the twelve apostles', the word is used in a wider sense in the New Testament generally. Once we have accepted the fact that Jesus did indeed establish a Church and appoint a pastoral ministry over the new people of God, we shall not be surprised at the hierarchical development within the Church. By the end of the New Testament period three orders had emerged in the Church's ministry: those of bishops, presbyters and deacons. 'The ministry of the Church is still essentially the ministry of Christ in the service of the world, acting through the appropriate members of his body the Church.'[79]

The two final chapters study the theology of baptism and the eucharistic theology of the New Testament. Baptism was, from the first, considered as the Christian's incorporation into the body of Christ, the only and indispensable means of becoming a member of the Christian *ekklēsia.* The only satisfactory answer to the universal and unquestioned place of baptism as the sacrament of initiation is that Jesus himself had taught his disciples the necessity of baptism into his death and resurrection. There can be no reasonable doubt that infant baptism was practised in the apostolic Church; infant baptism serves to underline the central gospel truth that faith is the response to God's saving act and not the condition of it. The ongoing celebration of the Eucharist from apostolic days is the most striking testimony of all to the truth of Jesus' interpretation of the significance of his own death. The Eucharist is the receiving of the life-giving Spirit of the risen Christ; thus, the closest union exists between the worshipper and Christ. It is certain that the Fathers understood the apostolic tradition to have regarded the Eucharist as a sacrifice. The three great themes of universal religious experience are finally fulfilled in the Eucharist: reconciliation, offering and communion. Richardson's closing sentence sets his subject in a living context: 'When everything has been written and rewritten, it still remains true that the best introduction to the theology of the New Testament is participation in the continuing, living tradition of the Church's eucharistic worship week by week and day by day.'[80]

## III. ETHELBERT STAUFFER

Ethelbert Stauffer published his *Theology of the New Testament* in 1941[81]; it first appeared in English translation in 1955—from the fifth German edition.[82] Stauffer has arranged his work in three unequal parts. The first part, 'The Development of Primitive Christian Theology', gives a short account of historical development. The main bulk of the book is in the second part: 'The Christocentric Theology of History in the New Testament'. It has five sections which follow the outline of a treatise on dogmatics: 1. Creation and fall, 2. Law and promise, 3. The coming of Christ, 4. The Church and the world, 5. The present and the future. Thirdly, there is a brief treatment on 'The Creeds of the Primitive Church'. Finally, in addition to lengthy notes, there are several appendices which set out in detail the evidence for some of the author's views. His purpose is to provide an introduction to the thought world of the New Testament. He does not propose, in the main body of his work, to follow the pattern of historical development he had briefly outlined at the start. Rather, he follows the sequence of the events of salvation, turning, on each point of importance, to the testimony of the New Testament as expressed in its different witnesses. The result is a historical theology of the New Testament which is christocentric in character.[83]

The first place to seek the antecedents of primitive Christian theology is the Old Testament. But we need to be aware, too, that apocalyptic has been decisive for the further advances of Old Testament thought, and so the pseudepigrapha assume importance. Stauffer proposes 'to use the ambiguous term "apocalyptic" in a strictly theological sense, and to mean by it that pre-Christian theology of history characterised by four presuppositions, namely the principle of primordiality [revelations about the primeval era], of conflict [with the forces of evil], of eschatology and of universalism.'[84] Besides, we find that the New Testament writers often use and interpret canonical texts in accordance with a post-canonical tradition; Stauffer calls such scripture references 'traditional'. Thus the exegetical and theological thought forms of the New Testament writers are rooted in a living tradition which runs from the Old Testament to the current apocalyptic; ultimately it can be maintained that 'the world of apocalyptic ideas is the one in which the New Testament writers were really at home.'[85] And the Baptist is the historical link between pre-Christian apocalyptic and the primitive Church.

The Gospels are not biographies of Jesus—rather, they put before us the Way of the Son of Man. We learn that the Way is laid out for him: it places a constraint upon him, its hour has struck and its range is vast. The meaning of Christ's way is summed up under three main heads: 'the doxological, the antagonistic, and the soteriological understanding of the Way of the Lord.'[86] This terminology recurs throughout the book; we may explain it as follows. The doxological sets forth the relationship with God (Christ and God); the antagonistic reveals the opposition to and victory over the Satanic forces that have usurped God's world (Christ and the devil); the soteriological deals with the restoration of the severed relations between God and man (Christ and the world). This threefold meaning of the Way of the Lord is sustained throughout the Gospels and is developed in the Christology of the New Testament.

Jesus himself meant to found a Church, to gather the new people of God about himself. Peter's central position among the Twelve marked him as of fundamental importance for the building up of the Church. The time is past when Paul can be thought of as a Hellenist and the originator of a turn to Hellenism in primitive Christianity. His strongest conviction is that 'Christ alone' is sufficient for the saving of the nations. Paul's principle was that 'anyone who proclaims the absoluteness of Christianity, any sort of Christianity, puts an end to the absoluteness of Christ.'[87] Stauffer sees John as 'an apocalyptist cast in a levitical-liturgical mould'.[88] The starting point of Johannine thought is a 'theological metaphysic'; and, like the other early Christian thinkers, John has his theology of history.

The first section of the main, central part of Stauffer's *Theology* is entitled 'Creation and the Fall'. The absolute priority of God over the world must be the fundamental datum of any theology of history—it is closely articulated in the Old and New Testaments. Taking its stand on this basic conception, the New Testament expounds, in christological terms, a complete theology of history. In both Testaments God's Word is creative, active and revelatory. In Pauline tradition, alongside the idea of the creative Word, there appears the theme that God created the world by his Christ: everything comes from God—but through Christ. John draws the ideas of God's creation through his Word or through his Christ into a unity by his identification of the creative Word with the creative Christ.

In creation, man is distinguished from every other creature in that he can hear God's voice and pray to God; in the Bible he is distinctly *homo orans* and stands at the very centre of creation. The course of human history is determined by wills: God's and man's. God, who delights in freedom, has established his world order in freedom; for that reason he permits the rebellion of Satan and the revolt of Adam. The primitive Church accepted, without question, the principle of demonic activity. Yet, God's omnipotence is unchallenged and, in reality, it turns out that 'the devil is the power in God's world who always wills evil and yet always effects good'.[89] The biblical doctrine of the Fall is conceived in terms of the idea of a historical heredity, a connection between man and man that is quite distinct from any notion of biological heredity. Man's rebellion is characterised by the threefold calamity of sin, sorrow, and death. While the New Testament does not reach the concept of original sin, it does stress the tragedy of having to sin. The history of man is the history of sin; Paul, especially, is conscious of the cosmic consequences of or accompaniments to the sinful history of man: sin, man's self-glorification, is a destructive attack on God's creation. Yet, against this sombre background, the New Testament sees God's universal plan of salvation coming to its fulfilment.

The next section, 'Law and Promise', opens with a study of the theology of civil power. First and foremost it is recognised that God is responsible for establishing the State; at the same time, the New Testament recognises the hidden tragedy of political life. The fact is that the State, by thinking too highly of itself, betrays its own mission and gives concrete expression to the fall of man. Natural theology is seen by Paul as falling under the divine permission: God has handed humanity over to itself until it reaches the point of destruction. Natural theology and natural ethics must fail—and then comes God's opportunity (see *Acts* 17: 29-31). The word of the cross marks the end of natural theology.

In his attitude to the Law, Paul builds on Jesus—basically the issue is the inadequacy of legalism. The legalistic outlook betrays a contradiction between teaching and life and an even more serious conflict between the inner and the outer which turns the proper function of the law into its exact opposite. Paul is clear why the more 'zealous' among his fellow Jews will have nothing to do with *sola cruce*: 'They seek to establish their own righteousness' (*Rom.* 10: 2-3). For New Testament writers it is clear that the Law and the Prophets have proclaimed Christ and his kingdom. 'The disposition to interpret the Old Testament christologically has come most decisively from Jesus himself.'[90] The New Testament writers agree that all pre-Christian history, pointing teleologically to the cross, is the prehistory of Christ's coming. As for Old Testament prophecy: Christ is both its subject and its object. He and the events of his life are not only foretold by the prophets, but also he is active in the history of the old covenant and even speaks in the prophets.

The third section turns to the coming of Christ. The old biblical tradition saw God himself as the deliverer, the saviour; later, a certain 'decentralisation' of divine power gave scope to heavenly and earthly agents. In three main ways the Christian message of deliverance was related to the traditional hope of salvation: Jesus was the fully authorised agent of God in salvation-history—God appears and acts in him; in him the offices of previous agents find their unity and perfection; his kingdom is not of this world. 'Son of Man', the title which Jesus himself used to indicate his significance for the theology of history, claims historical and theological primacy among all his names and titles. The paradox is that the heavenly majesty of the Son of Man belongs to a man who treads the way of suffering. In the course of time the title Son of Man was supplemented and replaced by a host of others; most of them include a reference to the passion motif. 'Of all the christological titles the richest is that of "Lord". Its history is a compendium and at the same time a *repetitorium* of New Testament Christology.'[91] Though the *kyrios* formula goes back to the primitive Palestinian tradition, Paul did deepen its meaning. He used the name *kyrios* in a wholly personal sense: it took on some colour from the theology of the passion; the emphasis fell on the unfolding of the power of the risen Lord; it had an antithetic character—Paul confessed *his* Lord.

Since the fate of the world is so radically bound up with that of man, the work of deliverance must be effected in terms of a human life: the Word was made flesh. The three modes of apprehension, the doxological, the antagonistic and the soteriological, find expression in the understanding of his becoming man: 'the pre-existent one renounces his own glory, so as to bring about the glory of God (*Phil.* 2), and he reveals the eternal glory of God in the broken forms of our historical existence (*John* 1). His coming into the world is an invasion of enemy territory (*Phil.* 2:7-8), and entry upon a state of war (*John* 1:11). He treads his earthly road so as to conquer the world's distress, and he does so for our sakes and for our salvation (*Rom.* 8:3; *John* 3:16).'[92] This threefold interpretation of Christ's life is sustained throughout the New Testament account of the life of Christ and his passion. Since the purpose of history is to establish the glory of God, this is, too, the purpose of the activity and desire of Jesus. The glory of God was the reality which was revealed in him; he preached God's glory in a world which sought its own glory. The Son of Man had to contend with the relentless hostility of the adversary who set all things against God. If the pre-existent Christ is the life of cosmic history, the incarnate Christ may be called the life of salvation history; he is the bringer of life in the history of salvation.

The cross figured largely in the primitive Church and different aspects of the *theologia crucis* may be discerned. The most elementary form is in the doxological understanding of the events of Good Friday; Jesus appealed to the old biblical theology of martyrdom. Its antagonistic form sees the cross as the decisive turning-point in the fight against the powers hostile to God. In the soteriological understanding of the cross the events of Good Friday were seen as giving the answer to the question of sin. 'It was Jesus himself who laid the basis for the *theologia crucis* as part of a theology of history.'[98] The descent into hell marks the deepest renunciation of the incarnation, the last act of Christ's self-humiliation before rising to his place of divine honour. The resurrection marks the first decisive step of the Son on the way to his final glory—this is the doxological interpretation of the resurrection. The antagonistic aspect finds in the resurrection the triumph of Christ over the powers hostile to him. The soteriological interpretation is decisive: it marks the completion of the work of Christ and the goal of salvation history. As for the ascension, the decisive theological factor is that it occurred. The doxological interpretation sees the significance of the ascension in that Jesus attained to the highest point of his return. The antagonistic interpretation sees that now the powers of hell are made the footstool of the Lord. The soteriological significance of the ascension is that from now on Christ is our advocate before God's throne.

But even after the coming of Christ the scourges of the world remain: death, affliction and sin. How then can Paul speak of a new creation and of the Christian as a new creature? The Old Testament background will help us to see the answer. In the Old Testament the problem of man's acceptance before God, the question of God's judgement, are of paramount importance. It is understood that God can make man 'clean', can make man acceptable before him. So, the New Testament understands that though death, anguish and sin still rule in the world, the question about guilt *is* solved, solved by the cross. 'So far as the actual state of affairs is concerned, everything can remain within the old order; that is the antecedent clause that saves us from romanticism. But everything has become new—forensically; and that is the consequent clause that saves us from nihilism.'[94] The coming of Christ has won a new situation for man before God. The basic idea of the forensically new situation brought about by the coming of Christ is expressed in the message of the peace of God for man. Paul's doctrine of atonement is a forceful expression of the message of God's grace and of the forgiveness of sins which derives from Jesus himself. Paul distinguishes between reconciliation and justification: reconciliation is the universal, and justification is the individual aspect of salvation. 'Reconciliation took place on Good Friday; justification takes place at baptism, or at the Last Judgement.'[95] The new relationship of God to man means deliverance from the enemy. The primitive Church was conscious of the coming of Christ as the fateful condition of human condition; it saw Christ as the prototype of Christian living. Now the vicarious bearing of burdens has become the office of those who are called by Christ's name. 'Suffering is no longer our fate; it is our office, our burden-bearing office as we minister to the many (1 *Cor.* 4 : 13).'[96]

Section four looks to the Church and the world. First there is a brief review of the concepts and images used by the primitive Christianity; the treatment of the Pauline image of the Body is surprisingly inadequate. The first task of the Church is to preach the Word; the content of the preaching of the primitive Church was the gospel of salvation wrought in the Christ-event. Christians are the new people of God—the new covenant sign is Christian baptism. Through its relation to the saving event the liturgical eucharistic act is a saving sign; John brought the eucharistic doctrine of the primitive Church to its completion. The Church is founded on the reality of the Spirit. Paul's distinctive contribution concerns the realisation of the Spirit in the personal life of the believer, achieved in prayer. John drew into one the conceptions which regarded the Spirit as operative in the history of creation, in the history of salvation and in the history of the Church.

Christian faith is firmly based on Jesus Christ. 'Such faith is the assertion of a possibility against all probabilities, in spite of any contrary indication provided by our experience of life or the realities of the world, and in constant battle against temptation. . . . Such a faith has nothing else than Jesus Christ in the middle of a world which scoffs at all of our hopes and fears.'[97] The challenge of temptation helps the vitality and growth of faith; the faith which has overcome temptation is true doxology.

The theological work of the primitive Church was not the construction of a system by an ordering of thought. The theology of history is the primary form of Christian thinking; history is ordered christocentrically because the Christ-event is at the centre of history. If the Christ-event was a stumbling-block to the Jews, it was foolishness to the Greeks. Paul challenged hellenistic philosophical presuppositions and demanded a radical reconstruction of philosophical concepts and categories: 'a break with a metaphysic of the "supra-historical", the construction of an understanding of reality in terms of a universal history, which has its centre in the Christ-event, but in which also the facts and problems of the Greek understanding of the world have their place, though properly related to the centre.'[98]

The life of Christ constitutes a prototype for the life of the believer; it finds most striking expression in the correlation between the passion of Christ and the sufferings of the martyr Church; the Church must hold itself in readiness for the imitation of his passion. The New Testament shows divergent answers to the problem of the Jews: were they now within or outside of the course of salvation history? In Paul we find the triumph of the spirit of Jesus: 'and so all Israel will be saved' (*Rom.* 11:26). The Church's vindication of God's glory must bring it into conflict with the self-glorification of the world. The Church must not let itself become embittered—its duty is intercession. The Church becomes most effective when it tells just what is at stake in the following of the cross. The mission of the Church in history is to give glory to God; its danger is the temptation to pious self-glorification; self-edification may supplant the glorifying of God. 'The Church becomes too important in her own estimation. She safeguards her historical existence instead of justifying it. She believes in herself and talks ecclesiology instead of Christology. She holds her form to be more important than her mission, and takes her dogmatics more seriously than her God.'[99] That is the temptation of the Church in history.

The last section of the central part takes up the theme of the present and the future. The New Testament writers discovered certain 'guiding principles' as they looked back upon the course of history. The first law of providence is the principle of freedom: God allows his creation to go its self-chosen way. All through history God chooses a few for himself: there is a law of selection. But the elect are called for the service of others, called to be mediators: there is a law of mediation. A law of retaliation, the justice of God, operates in God's providential rule. All the *leges providentiae* serve to reveal God's glory and are means to that end.

It was enough for the New Testament Church to sign the dying with the sign of the cross: death was a departure to the Lord. At the end the Church looked to the revelation of Christ in triumph, to his victory over all powers hostile to God. Then, in Paul's view, comes the *telos* when God himself will take over control and will reign over his saints forever. God's activity leads to a partition of souls, to a difference in destiny. Though the idea of eternal damnation finds clear expression in the New Testament, nevertheless the primitive Church held out hope that the mercy and power of God would overcome even the final 'no' of the world. Thus, while Jesus seems to take his stand on the basis of pre-Christian apocalyptic, Paul looks to the possibility of salvation for men after death. Though God's purpose for the future involves the destruction of the world in its present form, the realistic eschatology of the New Testament looks to a new created order and the redemption of the body itself.

The meaning of creation and history is the revelation of God's glory, or *doxophany*. The revelation of God's glory in Christ is doxophany and the glorifying of God in Christ is doxology—both point to another world. So it is that 'the final revelation of the *gloria dei* begins with the personal activity of God in the ordering of history.'[100]

The book ends with its short treatment of the creeds of the primitive Church. The New Testament gives ample evidence of the use and form of dogmatic formulas in the primitive Church. The most original species of theological speech in early Christianity was missionary preaching; it was further developed in the 'instruction'. A particularly important place for the origin of dogmatic formulas was in the baptismal practice of the Church; further development was occasioned by the needs and customs of the Church's worship. All the different currents flowed into the one stream of the dogmatic tradition.

It is not surprising that the christological formulas of the New Testament outnumber all other credal formulas put together: the coming of Christ constitutes the central theme of primitive Christian thought. The pre-Pauline credal formulas are passion formulas. The dogmatic development in the primitive Church reached its goal in John. The Gospel of John has 'more' to tell about Jesus than one Gospel can contain; Jesus has 'more' to say than any disciple could comprehend; that is why Jesus promised the Spirit, to lead the Church into the fullness of the truth about Christ. 'Whoever "confesses that Jesus Christ has come in the flesh" has the "Spirit of truth". This is the twofold confession that John makes and in turn demands, a confession of the true divinity and the true humanity of Jesus Christ.'[101]

### IV. MAX MEINERTZ

The *Theologie des Neuen Testamentes* of Max Meinertz[102] was first published in 1950 in two 'somewhat inequal' volumes—the second containing more extensive theological considerations. The author writes in the foreword to this work that it was actually finished in 1942, but that war-time intervened and thus gave him an enforced incentive to improve the whole before it could be published. It is his hope that the very long years put into the ripening of the work, as well as the crisis overshadowing the era, may have contributed to his—and thus the reader's—understanding of the New Testament. He also states in his foreword that his work bears all the features and weaknesses of a 'first draft' because it is the first general New Testament theology written from a Roman Catholic viewpoint. He adds, however, that his aim throughout is to present the theological contents of the New Testament *positively*—as briefly as possible and without any extensive ramifications; thus, he has not attempted to deal with any of the 'problems' in the field. Perhaps, too, this is because he has taken such a positive stand to centre his entire work around the person of Christ. Indeed, we may apply to Meinertz himself the words he applies to John the Evangelist: 'He knew by intuition, as well as by his own experience, that the ongoing, genuine Christendom depended on the ceaseless recognition of this Person.'[103]

It is precisely because of this unifying role of Jesus that Meinertz is free to state in his Introduction, and then to develop throughout the whole work, one of his leading principles. This is that since the New Testament is *not* a unified, systematic book of Christian teaching, nor can New Testament theology be a system of abstract thought and theory. The individual books of the New Testament are different records of the divine revelation in Jesus. A scheme of systematic theology would contain no understanding of these individual New Testament writings and persons, and biblical thought would be isolated from its living environment. Meinertz discusses the difference between biblical theology and dogmatic theology. He observes that dogma can never serve as a substitute for biblical arguments and, moreover, that many of the fine points and distinctions made in dogmatics simply cannot be made in biblical theology. Biblical theology (a term the author uses interchangeably with 'New Testament theology') has a definite historical basis—one which recognises that the early Christian community developed its own theological picture of the revelation which had come through Jesus.

Different forms of expression grew up to record this revelation: the teaching of Jesus differs, outwardly, from that of Paul, the earliest apostolic preaching from that in the later Johannine theology. These differences, Meinertz states, have been criticised and questioned because they contain seemingly contradictory material. But, he has written his work in answer to such criticism, for he says that it overlooks the one, great foundation and powerful source illuminating the entire New Testament: the personality, the personhood, of the Lord. 'Jesus is, so to speak, the sunlight which is divided into many colours in the prism of the various apostolic personages, but without impairing the original source.'[104] Christianity as a religion is born because of Jesus, on him is built its successive development, and with his work the New Testament opens with the presentation of the Gospels. These and the other books of the New Testament are deposits of historical thought and happenings flowing from the event of his coming. It is the task of biblical theology to recognise these different facets of New Testament expression as much as its great unity; to achieve this task, Meinertz has developed his own method.

He takes into account the literary uniqueness of the New Testament as the oldest record of Christianity, the original witness for its origin and growth. In discussing the requirements for a New Testament theology, he acknowledges the value of understanding Old Testament theology and revelation, but he feels that this is not as important a preparation for studying the New Testament as is often asserted simply because the old covenant has been taken into the new teaching. Exegesis merely provides the 'building stones' with which biblical theology erects the building, to then continually surpass the achievements of exegesis. Meinertz recognises that it is not easy to find an overall-satisfactory method for New Testament theology: insufficient would be methods (at least when dealing with the *whole* New Testament and not a single aspect or monograph) attempting to divide the material into 'motifs' or themes or to arrange its theological content in categories. Equally inadequate, he feels, would be any approach of 'accommodating' New Testament thought to a preconceived outline of biblical theology. And so, he arrives at what he sees to be the only true method of comprehensively grasping the theological contents of the New Testament.

He divides the material into four main sections. At the peak, and beginning, stands the person and teaching of Jesus, preceded by John the Baptist. This is followed by the section on the early Christian community in Jerusalem, the first step in the Church's development and activity. The third section, and beginning of volume II, deals with Paul, who took yet another step forward with his sweeping influence; this section is the most extensive because the apostle's penetration of the Christian revelation was so rich and profound. The concluding section deals with the Johannine theology, in the Gospel and Epistles, as the final development of Apostolic Christianity. The Apocalypse is treated in this section too as being most closely related to it, despite the book's unclassifiable nature. Thus, from Jesus to early Christianity to Paul to the Johannine writings, Meinertz finds first one point of view and then another emphasised, but the central message of Christ abides the same.

Describing in his foreword the actual presentation of his work, the author states that he has taken into account modern positions in New Testament theology and that he has repeatedly sketched various interpretations of a question. But he has neither mentioned many names of modern scholars (aside from in his extensive bibliographies at the beginning of each section) nor drawn citations from them, for he feels that the reader should not be weighted down by 'polemics'. He mentions that 'completeness' has certainly not been amongst the aims he valued most highly, simply because biblical theology cannot really embrace a 'concordance-like' completeness and must refrain from merely amassing material. He has 'struck a happy medium between tact and taste'.[105] However, he has certainly been 'complete' in another way. For he has fulfilled one of the requirements for a New Testament theologian that he himself put forth in his introduction—the requirement of having worked through the entire New Testament and come to understand it as the living Word.

Each of the four sections in the *Theologie* consists of many subdivisions carefully arranged to present its theological content in a unified way. (Meinertz is very skilful in making transitions to link each subdivision to the one preceding and following.) The first part in each section outlines the sources in the New Testament for it. For example, in the first division on 'Jesus' (pp. 8-211), the author notes that the Synoptic Gospels enable a New Testament theology to begin with the teaching of Jesus because they testify that he is the source upon whom everything else in New Testament revelation depends. At this source stands not a 'community theology' that has 'created' a picture of Jesus, but the Person himself recorded historically by evangelists completely in the service of the early Church. Jesus made such a powerful impression that it is not possible to divorce the picture we have of him from the actual sources—even from John's Gospel, which simply extends the Synoptic picture. Interesting, too, in this section is the author's linking of John the Baptist so intimately with Jesus; in the mind of Jesus and of the early Church, the Baptist and his work stood on the threshold of Christian thought. The remainder of this section treats in detail the kingdom of God and the Bringer of this kingdom, both as man and as Son of God. The next section on the primitive community (pp. 212-47), draws its theological content from the early part of Acts, especially the speeches of Peter, and from the epistles of James and Jude as exemplifying the Christian life.

The third section, on Paul (II, pp. 1-254), occupies most of the second volume and is a testimony to the apostle's own words: 'I worked harder than any of them, though it was not I but the grace of God which is with me' (1 *Cor.* 15: 10). For Meinertz, the apostle was the most influential figure in the development of early Christianity—though always his work was 'in the power of Christ', and he was as one only sent by his Lord. For, as Meinertz replies to critics who would make Paul the 'founder of Christianity', Jesus as the sinless man stands in direct contrast to his servant Paul, who knew so starkly in his own life the powers of sin and its effects. The cross and resurrection stood chronologically between Jesus and Paul and thus coloured the apostle's whole approach. Meinertz emphasises his familiar principle: the Pauline Epistles are not theological treatises, but letters directed to a living Christian community with its problems and weaknesses. He notes how it is nowhere clearer than in the Epistles how little one is justified in speaking of the 'self-sufficiency' of New Testament writings. For example, without the specific abuses connected with the question of food sacrificed to idols and the nature of the Agapē meals, Paul would have had no occasion for giving us the eucharistic tradition he knew (1 *Cor.* 11 : 23-32). One cannot develop a 'system' of Pauline theology: the Epistles may be *methods* of teaching, but that is vastly different from being parts of a whole system worked out in Paul's mind. That Paul was no systematic theologian is underlined by the emotional quality and inconclusiveness throughout his letters, in which not every thought can be defined with unequivocal certainty.

However, the theological *content* of the letters is a unity, free of gaps or contradictions, and it is this unity—rather than the messages of the individual letters—that Meinertz unfolds. It springs from Paul's complete devotion to God and his burning longing to spend himself entirely for Christ. The event on the road to Damascus was utterly transforming: Paul had seen the risen Lord, and henceforth for him to live *was* Christ (cf. *Phil.* 1 : 21) and the preaching of his death and resurrection for the salvation of men. This essential message remains constant throughout Pauline theology. However, its forcefulness and aliveness lie in the freedom of his 'christological' thinking, his devotional life and dedication which cannot be subjected to analysis.

In the final section on Johannine theology (II, pp. 267-338), Meinertz shows how John too, with his 'eagle's' vision of Christ, centres all his teaching around Jesus as the Sun—and the Son of God. John's work is seen to be the fruit 'in old age' of the apostle who, as the beloved disciple, was nearer than any other to his Lord. By this the author means not that it was 'senile' work, but that it had been spiritually matured through years of preaching, experience, and meditation. For, John saw the living effects of Jesus' personhood upon himself and upon a burgeoning Christianity; his vision beheld the divine light which had really irradiated the Man from Nazareth all the while he lived on earth. Jesus is indeed the perfect revelation of God; he is indeed the Word made flesh. Whereas the Synoptics had stressed the preaching of Jesus, the gifts and demands of his kingdom, John stresses the real identity of him who had brought the kingdom and was himself its eternal Life.

The concluding summary of the *Theologie* (II, 338-346) echoes the Introduction. Meinertz speaks of how many different lights fall on Jesus throughout the New Testament, and some may seem contradictory; however, all of them merely reveal new aspects of his great personhood. When this above-human standard of the whole Christ is kept in mind, then all New Testament theology falls into a 'great harmony in which his human life, work and sufferings find as much place as the eternal Word, the proclaimer of God's Kingdom, Son of God, High Priest, and Judge'.[106] There is one gospel, one Word, one Witness, one kerygma: the apostles were always conscious of keeping fast the original tradition as it had come from Christ. At first, no one thought of putting the gospel into set formulas because its great power seemed beyond set forms. Yet, precisely because it was 'the power of God for salvation to everyone who has faith' (*Rom.* 1 : 16), it 'longed for' a framework of words and forms by which it could reach the increasing numbers of believers. 'The source could not cease to flow, but had to be led into channels.'[107] The Church's thought and forms of communication had to be more firmly unified and fixed the wider Christianity spread, but always the central content remained unchanged. For, what Christ proclaimed was inseparable from his person—as is shown by the very title 'Christians'. 'All rays of the New Testament are ultimately united in the living Christ.'[108] With these words, Meinertz concludes his *Theology of the New Testament.* Truly, he had beheld, as he said of Paul, 'the light of the knowledge of the glory of God in the face of Christ' (2 *Cor.* 5 : 6).

CONCLUSION

The first part of his *Theology* sharply reflects Rudolf Bultmann's sceptical evaluation of the historical worth of the Synoptic gospels. He discounts altogether the theology of the synoptists and prefers instead to reconstruct, on fragile foundations, the kerygma of the Hellenistic Church. He has much to say about Gnostic influences, but his understanding of Gnosticism, here and throughout his work, is so elastic that he can virtually fit anything he chooses under this rubric. He is undoubtedly at his best in his treatment of the theology of Paul; thus his analysis of Pauline theological terms stands out even in his masterly handling of many New Testament keywords. Yet, here too, there is much that is open to serious question. In explaining Paul's theology as an anthropology, a doctrine about man, Bultmann's approach is too exclusively a development of the apostle's ideas in Romans—and even here he is selective. It is manifestly Paul's view that man can be understood only in terms of the Christ-event; Bultmann minimises the role of Christ because he is not prepared to admit an 'objective phase' in man's redemption and because he is concerned to recast Paul's theology in phenomenological terms. One cannot escape the uncomfortable truth that, for Bultmann, the salvation-occurrence is not a real fact of history, independent of faith and preceding faith. It is only in the word of the kerygma and in the faith which responds to it that the salvation becomes historical reality. Is this really the mind of Paul? It is not, unmistakeably, Bultmann?

Johannine dualism is traced directly to Gnosticism. Surely, today, we would look to the Jewish dualism of Qumran and then to its roots in the later Old Testament writings. If Bultmann so much stresses the 'offence' that God has revealed himself in a mere man, that is because faith must be a leap in the dark: the 'decision' cannot be bolstered up by any human values. Then, too, the revelation is without content; the Revealer reveals nothing but that he is the Revealer and demands unconditional surrender. This is the paradox of Luther, in its extreme Barthian form. While the concept of realised eschatology is a prominent feature in John, Bultmann makes it exclusive by labelling all references to future eschatology as later interpolations; he treats references to the sacraments in the same cavalier fashion. He is unashamedly cutting his cloth to his measure. Bultmann's philosophical and theological principles are not those of Paul or John or of Jesus, and he has allowed his principles to distort his understanding of their message.

The evolution in church order and doctrine which Bultmann has noted is incontestable; the development was inevitable in view of the delay of the Parousia, apart from the inherent needs of human society. In his eyes, however, all was retrogression. Especially, the tension of 'between-ness' which marked the *faith* of Paul and John had given place to a sacramental regime and the Church had become an institution of salvation. But, in order to maintain this view, he has to underestimate the sacramentalism of Paul and deny outright that of John. Again his theological presuppositions come into play. He puts all the emphasis on the *decision* of pure *faith* and does not pay attention to biblical realism—to the realism, for instance, of the union of the Christian with Christ realised in baptism and Eucharist.

Yet, whatever serious reserves one must harbour and voice, this is a very great work; it is fair to say that it remains the greatest New Testament *Theology* we have. It is a fitting monument to a man who, so often misunderstood, here emerges as the profoundly religious spirit he is. One cannot but admire the grandeur of his conception of faith, standing in its absolute nakedness and refusal of all human security. And though he seriously exaggerates the significance of the proclamation, attributing to it the ultimate reality of the Christian message, he has pointed to a powerful truth. 'Bultmann is right. The message of the Gospel is always *Kerygma*—it is always contemporary, and it is always challenge. For this reminder we shall always be profoundly indebted to him.'[109]

The sixteen chapters of Alan Richardson's book show a certain logical grouping of themes; it does emerge that Christology is at the centre of its plan and that the Church forms the climax. This arrangement brings to light at once a fundamental difference of opinion between Richardson and Bultmann as to what New Testament theology is really about. Where Bultmann maintains that it concerns man's self-understanding, Richardson maintains it is about the creation and mission of the Church. We may feel that Richardson has right on his side, but then he seems to make New Testament theology purely an ecclesiastical interest. Indeed, his work tends to be thrown out of balance by a vigorous polemic, mainly against Bultmann. (He describes Bultmann's *Theology* as 'heretical' and lists Karl Barth among 'all the great heresiarchs'.)[110]

Thus his reaction leads him to underestimate the creative work of the early Church in the articulation of its convictions. Time and again he disposes in a cavalier manner of what he regards as error.

Richardson vigorously champions a primarily Judaic background for much that used to be deemed 'Hellenistic', and one welcomes this emphasis. However, in filling in the Jewish background, he fails to use the Qumran materials. And he overlooks the fact, or at least the strong probability, that Greek thought sometimes provided a vehicle for early Christian beliefs.

Richardson achieves a powerful coherence in his presentation of the New Testament teaching, but at considerable cost. He imposes an artificial uniformity on the New Testament material by pulling together all sorts of passages, and he tends to sidetrack critical and exegetical problems. From his book one would never get the impression that the theological language of Paul and John differs considerably, nor become aware that they deal with different questions and even solve common problems in different ways. In reality, we have become aware of more, not less, diversity in the thought of the New Testament writers; it is clear that the unity of New Testament theology must contain the differences and not suppress them. Similarly, Richardson's method prevents one from seeing the genuine development of New Testament thought. The fact seems to be that, for him, unity and development do not constitute a problem because everything comes from the same source, Jesus; this is the unifying principle of his *Theology*. Here we come to another fundamental difference in outlook between Richardson and Bultmann. Where Bultmann would see the message of Jesus as merely a presupposition for a theology of the New Testament, Richardson has gone to the other extreme and presents Jesus as the profoundly original theologian who is the source of all the main New Testament teaching. A critic has commented, not unfairly: 'The Jesus who teaches everything Richardson attributes to him has been pasted together with New Testament texts; he is not a flesh and blood, first century, north Palestinian, Aramaic-speaking Jew. This Jesus is a Christian theologian, probably an Anglican.'[111] Christ undoubtedly stands at the source of the New Testament, but his person, deeds and words provide the material for the theology of the New Testament rather than the theology itself.

The final section on the Church (Chs. 11-16) is particularly effective and thought-provoking. One may reasonably question, however, whether the New Testament was as concerned about Church ministry and order as this book suggests. One would also look for something about New Testament ethics; the almost total avoidance of New Testament ethical teaching marks this *Theology* as incomplete. Despite the fact that 'eschatological' is perhaps the most frequently recurring term in the book, one cannot say that the treatment of eschatology is really satisfactory. For Richardson, it is almost entirely 'realised', expressed in the Church's sacramental life. This is hardly the complete New Testament view.

Ethelbert Stauffer has impressively demonstrated the unity of theological outlook and presupposition that is to be found in the New Testament; but, in the process, he has minimised the theological variety to be found there. It does not seem that the New Testament literature is properly amenable to the kind of systematic approach he has employed. Certainly, something is lost in the process: a sense of creative activity of the Word of God in the movement of history which is part of New Testament theology.

Stauffer emphasises the Christocentricity of the New Testament; for him New Testament theology culminates in the christological climax. The point is that Jesus Christ is not the ultimate goal but points to the Father. Christocentricity means that men look for and find God in Jesus Christ; for the fullness of New Testament faith, it is not enough to see Jesus Christ without seeing the Father in and through him. There is at least a certain ambiguity in Stauffer's christocentric emphasis. He believes that the New Testament writers were most at home in the world of apocalyptic ideas; and he is rather too free to posit lost apocalyptic sources where the Old Testament itself, or other influences, would satisfactorily provide the background of the thoughts and ideas in question. But his is beyond doubt an important book, a stimulating introduction to the wealth of New Testament theology written in a spirit of lively faith.

The plan followed by Max Meinertz has the advantage of respecting the concrete manner in which God has granted his revelation by placing the accent on the diversity of human minds who have transmitted the message to us. By relating the doctrine of each writing to that of the other witnesses, he safeguards the profound unity of the divine revelation. Thus, with admirable pedagogical method he has presented the richness of New Testament theological thought. He has followed the lines of traditional Catholic interpretation and has done so with a praiseworthy abundance of documentation and clarity of exposition.

On the negative side it may be admitted that Meinertz has tended to undervalue the influence of the Old Testament. A more profound use of the Old Testament would have enabled his treatment of New Testament theology to be less descriptive and more genetic in character. In view of the lengthy and admirable development of Pauline thought, one is rather surprised at the relatively short treatment of Johannine thought—but he has a thorough understanding of John and more than once warns against an 'intellectualist' interpretation of the dynamic Johannine message. Unquestionably, this is the best New Testament *Theology* by a Roman Catholic scholar and is worthy of a place among the leading *Theologies* in the field.

## 3. Development and Contrast

### 1. HANS CONZELMANN

A recent theology of the New Testament is the work of a disciple of Bultmann, one of the 'post-Bultmannians' who have departed in some measure from the positions of the master. Hans Conzelmann published his *Theology* in 1968.[112] Though the author declares that his book has primarily been written as a textbook for students, it is an important statement on the development of the existentialist interpretation of the New Testament.

An Introduction treats of the problem of New Testament theology and then of the environment of the New Testament: Hellenism and, especially, Judaism. The account proper starts with the kerygma of the primitive community and goes on to show how the traditional material about Jesus is worked out, first in the Synoptic tradition and later by the evangelists. In relation to the Gospels, the Epistles are seen to be a different kind of theological development of the kerygma. In this way the balance between unity and multiplicity within the New Testament is maintained. The fact of historical variety is apparent and unity is demonstrated by the relation of theology to its object, the Lord to whom witness is borne in the kerygma. This produces the plan: I. The kerygma of the primitive community and of the Hellenistic community; II. The Synoptic kerygma; III. The theology of Paul: the conceptual development of the kerygma; IV. Developments after Paul; V. The theology of John: the conceptual development of the tradition of Jesus.

Though we ought not make too sharp a distinction between the primitive community and the Hellenistic community, it is necessary to differentiate between them, especially if we are to understand the theology of Paul. In arriving at a self-understanding, the Church recognises that the life of Jesus is the presupposition for its origin and knows itself to be constituted by God's act of election. The nature of the Church is not guaranteed by a special ministerial office; its reality is achieved through preaching which narrates and brings about the saving event. Baptism, the rite of acceptance into the community, is the appropriation of the saving event by the person baptised; the understanding of the Eucharist is orientated to the Lord present in the community. Faith is the acceptance of the message of the saving event in Christ; it is the act and the state of being a Christian; it is decision but not achievement. 'In faith I cannot look at the fact that *I* have decided. I can recognise it only as a relationship to the word. In believing, I am not orientated to myself as a believer, but know that through grace I am what I am.'[113] The content of the kerygma is the person and work of Christ and the interpretation of his resurrection and death. The majority of the oldest confessional formulas are exclusively christological.

In his evaluation of the Synoptic tradition and the contribution of the evangelists, Conzelmann differs most markedly from Bultmann (for whom this material was not a proper element of New Testament theology). He considers the themes of eschatology, ethics and Christology with their common basis in the nature of God. Jesus did not teach a new idea of God; he made clearer who the God of Israel is. The designation 'my Father', attributed to him, and the absolute use of 'the Son', are a mark of the language of the community. The contradiction between the present and the future kingdom-sayings is an apparent one because the significance for human existence remains the same: man's attitude of the moment towards the coming kingdom. Jesus' ethical teaching corresponds with Jewish tradition; his criticism is not of the Law but of legalism; the absoluteness of his law does away with casuistry. The teaching of Jesus about God and about ethics is quite unrelated to an anticipation of the imminent end of the world. All of his teaching, whether it concerns God, eschatology or ethics, is stamped with an indirect Christology. 'We cannot understand Jesus' eschatology without him as proclaimer; we cannot understand his talk of God without him as the one who makes clear the relationship to God; we cannot understand his ethics without him as the one who expounds them.'[114] Eventually, this indirect Christology becomes the direct Christology of the community's faith. But Jesus did not express his understanding of himself by a direct christological concept; thus the titles 'Messiah', 'Son of God', 'Son of Man', 'Lord' are all formulations of the community. Jesus' understanding of himself is to be sought in his proclamation of himself as a sign of the kingdom of God. This second part closes with a consideration of the theology of the Synoptic Gospels—redaction criticism has brought about a needful corrective to the unfavourable evaluation of the earlier Form Critics.

The theology of Paul calls for and receives a fuller treatment. Conzelmann shows that it is quite misleading to regard Paul as the one who transformed the simple teaching of Jesus into a complicated theology. Paul did not invent Christology nor the doctrine of the sacraments. He came to a Christianity which already derived freedom from the Law from faith; his contribution consists in the way in which he thought through the faith theologically.

Faith is knowledge because it has a demonstrable dogmatic content; it is obedience because the message proclaims Jesus as Lord; it is the destruction of boasting about my freedom because its content is the cross. Man in the world is weak and guilty; the two most important concepts of existence are *sarx* (flesh) and *hamartia* (sin). The myth of the primal man helps me to discover myself as one who is already determined through sin. In Paul's argument, only a single point of Adam's existence appears: that through him sin came into the world. 'The doctrine of inherited sin is simply the consistent representation of the truth that my sin is there before me and that my lostness is inescapable.'[115] In Conzelmann's view the theme of inherited death is, of course, also mythological.

Conzelmann turns to the saving event and, in the first place, to God's saving action 'in Christ'. The christological titles are of special importance and particular christological schemata are associated with them: *kyrios*—resurrection and Parousia, *christos*—death and resurrection, *huios*—pre-existence and incarnation. The mythical idea of pre-existence means that salvation comes from outside the world and remains God's salvation founded on God's miraculous act; it means the objective priority of God's act to my faith. For Paul the most important christological scheme is that of the cross and resurrection; the resurrection is God's interpretation of the cross. The phrase 'in Christ' means that salvation has taken place in him; it expresses the objective foundation of Christian existence. The saving event must be made meaningful for me—preaching is the present communication of salvation which has taken place objectively; the communication becomes real in the Church.

Paul modifies the Jewish view of righteousness: the eschatological verdict of the judge has already been given 'in Christ', and righteousness without works is promised to faith. God's righteousness is experienced in the word; in hearing we recognise ourselves as really being made righteous. If righteousness is achieved without works of the Law, it might seem that the Law has lost all value. What Paul sees is that the Law is not a way to salvation, while it does remain in force as a moral demand. With the Law as 'pedagogue' man is led into sin and thus shown the way to faith: confronted by the gospel he must choose either works of the Law or faith. 'The Law does not lead to subjective despair about one's own wickedness, but into an objectively desperate

situation, which one understands on hearing the gospel.'[116]
The historical saving event is actualised in the word,
revealed in the present. But the preaching of the gospel
necessarily brings a stumbling-block with it: it is a scandal
to Judaism and folly to Greeks. The crisis brought about by
the gospel is developed in two directions: as the end of
righteousness by works and as the end of wisdom—two sides
of the effect of the cross, the destruction of self-glorification.

Paul envisaged the Church as the Israel of God, the new
covenant. The Church is an entity of the last age, set apart
from the world; it is a visible assembly, primarily for worship.
His specific contribution of thinking through the theological
significance of the ideas he had taken over is here shown by
means of examples: the eschatological understanding of the
Church, worship, the individual in the Church, and the
concept of the 'body of Christ'. Paul conceives of the body in
historical terms: it is the sphere in which the baptised live
together, experience newness of life, and put it into practice;
it is the sphere of Christ's rule. The ecclesial significance of
'body' is associated with the death of Christ; Christians stand
in the community in which the crucified One is proclaimed
as the universal Lord. As in the case of the formula 'in
Christ', Conzelmann rejects any mystical significance in the
concept 'body of Christ'. His view is put succinctly: *'sōma*
primarily means what embraces us; *en Christō* defines the
place of the saving event as lying outside us.'[117]

Paul's understanding of ministry in terms of preaching is
determined by his own call and experience as an apostle; for
him preaching is 'the word of the cross'. His authority as
aspostle comes from his subjection to the criterion of the
cross. 'It is the authority of service.'[118] Paul sees the significance of baptism to be in the fact that it is a sacrament which
brings about salvation by transferring the saving event to the
person being baptised. The Christian, in possession of salvation through baptism, can constantly taste it afresh by receiving the substance of the Eucharist—that means that each has
it for himself. 'The eating and drinking leads to the body of
Christ understood in historical terms, to responsible life
together.'[119] Paul considers freedom not in itself, but as the
freedom of faith—it is freedom in Christ. He particularises

it in two directions: over against legalism and against
libertinism. The Christian is not excused from God's demand
because he is free. 'Now I am really taken up into it. I am
not set down in an empty room, but transported into sonship: therefore I can only behave as a son.'[120] In his freedom
the Christian can afford to act against the letter of a precept
for the sake of its meaning, that is, for the sake of love; no
authority can deprive him of this decision. The cross and
resurrection of Christ give meaning to suffering and bring
about reconciliation to it. Besides, through suffering God
shatters the props of my self-assertion, leaving me nothing but
grace. The effect of suffering actualises what has happened
beforehand in Christ; Christ's own suffering takes place in
our suffering. 'In experiencing the dying of Christ, the apostle
communicates the life of Christ to the community. From this,
too, it is clear that we do not have a mystical exchange here;
Paul is simply describing the effect of the preaching on the
preacher and on the community.'[121]

Conzelmann's treatment of the development after Paul
provides a much-needed corrective to Bultmann's view. We
do not, after all, find a retrogressive transition to 'early
catholicism'. The notion of tradition is not an indication of
early catholicism: this notion is part of theology itself. Nor
is the fixed ordering of the ministry a sign of early catholicism; the decisive turning point comes when the ministry
has the quality of communitary salvation, when the Church
has become an institute of salvation. The theological situation
is that the third Christian generation is a new stage of reflection—and an extremely varied picture emerges. The creed is
the starting point and the rule of theology. Faith tends to be
understood as a timeless doctrine and the accent shifts to
doctrine about the revelation; the statements of the 'faith' are
handed down as ready-made truths. With the emergence of
false doctrine comes a preoccupation with 'orthodoxy' and
'heresy'. The claim of 'orthodoxy' that it alone represents the
original, unaltered faith points to a new relationship with the
object of faith. The original Christian worship was prayer,
stemming from the saving act. But worship soon became a
cult, with appointed ministers: the Church had become an
institution of salvation. It is the first stage on the way to the
Catholic institutionalisation of the Church.

The space allotted to Johannine theology is disappointingly limited. When he has studied the historical context of the Johannine writings—largely a comparison of Paul and John —Conzelmann turns to Johannine Christology. He finds the central themes of that Christology to be: (1) the Logos; (2) the development of the traditional christological titles; (3) the description of the revelation in the *egō eimi* statements. The statement 'Jesus is the Logos' is meant literally, as a direct description of the nature of Jesus—all the other christological titles serve to interpret this fundamental one. The significance of the Logos is not found in communicable notions about the being of the world and of man; its sense is Jesus himself, as the incarnate One. The word is not detached from the person of the Revealer; it is communicated so that anyone who believes in him, who has his person, has salvation.

The statement 'in the beginning was the Word' rejects any remark about God outside his word and points to where God can be found in the world. It is a positive interpretation of salvation: in the Son men see the Father. We are not presented with a doctrine about God, but are confronted by God himself, in the world. 'That the Logos is the creator means that God is accessible in him.'[122] Although the incarnation is revelation, it is also, and necessarily, a stumbling block: it shows that the revelation does not come from the world. The scandal lies in the manner of the manifestation of Jesus, his way into death; the unbelief which wants to see without faith and to subject revelation to its own criteria turns the incarnation into a stumbling block. John achieves a unity by considering the incarnation not in isolation but together with its presupposition, the pre-existence of the Logos, and its continuation, the career and work of Christ. Jesus appears as a *theios anēr* ('divine man') possessing wonderful knowledge and a wonderful capability expressed in his signs. The content of his teaching is that he is the revelation and that his testimony is true. In presence of him the world is given two alternatives: 'Either it can believe, in which case it is what it really is, world, creation, or it can remain as it is, and thus in face of the revelation make itself "world" in the negative sense'.[123]

John puts the proclamation of faith in Jesus on the lips of the historical Jesus because the revealed truth is the speaker himself, and he must be incorporated into his discourses. Thus, in hearing the discourses, through the present proclamation of the Church, the hearer can be led to Jesus himself. Revelation happens here and now as man comes to know himself through conversation with the Revealer. Knowing Christ is not knowing a definition of his nature: it is to understand who he is for me now. Jesus' presentation of himself has an eminently positive significance: 'the content of faith reveals itself in the process of my unveiling of myself, which becomes understandable to me as salvation . . . Faith leads to the particularization of freedom to live in the world in peace, which realizes itself as worldly insecurity and thus as the possibility of love.' [124]

John can say two things of the *cosmos,* the world of men: that the world already sinned before the appearance of Jesus and that the sin came about through encounter with him. The truth is that the world has always been confronted by revelation and has always sought to avoid this confrontation. It is here, too, that the conception of the pre-existent being of the Logos becomes comprehensible to the individual: it discloses to him his past, his solidarity with the world, his sin. John agrees perfectly with Paul in his understanding that the word, the message, does not offer a doctrine about salvation, but offers salvation itself—to faith. But salvation, once realised, must remain present in the world; it must continually happen anew, from above. Jesus has departed, but has left behind his word, that is his return—'present eschatology'. 'The one who departed has returned and makes possible the life of this community today, makes possible faith, and finally makes it possible to endure the world and in so doing already to have life in anticipation.'[125]

Conzelmann has written his *Outline of the Theology of the New Testament* as, in the first place, a textbook for students; he seeks to give a 'general report' so that the student can gain a 'general view of the New Testament'. This may be his intention; his achievement has been to bring Bultmann up to date. He can declare that, whatever else has appeared in German on New Testament theology, apart from Bultmann's *Theology* 'there is no other textbook, nor even another guide.'[126] This very restrictive scope certainly lessens the usefulness of the book. It is a helpful treatment of the existentialist interpretation of the New Testament; but Conzelmann is cavalier, to put it mildly, in his implied suggestion that this is the only valid approach.

Though he has paid attention to the Synoptic tradition, ignored by Bultmann, his historical scepticism almost negatives the result. He can casually declare that it is questionable whether Jesus regarded himself as Messiah and he has no qualms about pruning away elements which he regards as products of the early Church rather than the sayings of Jesus himself. The titles which purport to express Jesus' self-consciousness are, all of them, products of the community.

In his study of Pauline teaching he narrows the field by accepting only the 'indisputedly authentic' letters and excludes not only the Pastorals and Ephesians but Colossians and 2 Thessalonians as well. Very little is said, or presumably needs to be said, about Hebrews, 1 Peter, James, etc., and Apocalyse does not appear at all in the index of biblical references. In fact, these writings are regarded as a historically interesting but theologically unimportant group of New Testament addenda.

Then there is the general outlook. Theology is, in reality, anthropology; it does not speak objectively about God and the world but concerns me. Existence prior to and under faith is declared objectively by revelation communicated through the preaching. The hearer knows the message to be true because he has been brought to self-understanding through it. Faith is not not a matter of being convinced about historical truths; what happens to the believing hearer of the word here and now is both the truly historical and the truly eschatological . . . All this is Heidegger, through the medium of Bultmann; it is not Paul, or John—or Jesus.

## II. OSCAR CULLMANN

*Salvation in History*[127] is the most important book that Oscar Cullmann has yet written. It builds primarily on his *Christ and Time.*[128] He had wanted to follow this and his *Christology of the New Testament*[129] with an 'Eschatology of the New Testament'. He has not yet got around to doing this, but in the present work he shows the relationship in the New Testament between eschatology and salvation history. His first part deals with preliminary questions, then part II enters into the heart of the subject: 'The Genesis of the Salvation-Historical Approach'. Throughout five chapters Cullmann shows how the New Testament, following the lines of the Old Testament, is dominated by the idea of salvation history: under the pressure of events, events that are always new, the witnesses, prophets and apostles give an interpretation of the activity of God in history. Each time the event, together with its interpretation, forms a link in the chain of salvation history. Each new interpretation is itself reinterpretation of an interpreted past event. The centre of this chain of the saving acts of God is the Christ-event. An interpretation is attached to this event also: that of Jesus in the first place and then that of the apostles. In his third part, the author argues that the tension between 'already' and 'not yet' is the key to the understanding of New Testament salvation history.

Then comes part IV, 'The Main New Testament Types', the basis of the whole work. Cullmann shows, step by step, how salvation history is present in germ in the thought of Jesus. Next he studies how the extension of the intermediate period—the delay of the Parousia—influenced Luke's and the later New Testament writers' understanding of salvation history; finally he considers the Pauline and Johannine conceptions of salvation history.

With regard to Jesus, the two series of statements on the kingdom of God, those relating to the present and those referring to the future, must be allowed to stand. Jesus' essential message is that though the kingdom of God will come only in the future, it is already anticipated and realised in his person during his earthly existence. It is precisely this tension between 'already fulfilled' and 'not yet completed' which is the really new element in Jesus' eschatology. And it remains characteristic of all New Testament salvation history that an interval, determined by this tension, stands between Christ's resurrection and his return. In the proclamation of Jesus himself, the time before the End is given salvation-historical significance. At the same time it is true that in his preaching the present which extends beyond his death is already the end; yet, Jesus is not thereby the end of all salvation history. 'The end time is, on the contrary, understood as belonging completely to salvation history, since each of its periods, short as they may be, has its own significance and is distinguished from others.'[130] In Jesus' message salvation history is part of his self-consciousness, of his prophetic view of events at whose mid-point he himself stands.

The time after Jesus' death is characterised by the fact that salvation-historical thinking developed in the interpretation of new events; Luke's work expresses the final point in this development. He maintains the common conviction that not only the mid-point of time, but also the last temporal phase before the unknown end-time, have been attained in Jesus; he then proceeds to reflect about the periods of salvation history. Luke was the first to work out a complete salvation-historical perspective with its emphasis on the time of the interval, the time of the Spirit and the Church.[131] For Hans Conzelmann, following the Bultmann school, Luke's two-volume work, with the so-called Deutero-Pauline letters and other New Testament writings, belongs to the 'early Catholic' New Testament books, those oriented towards a history of salvation—a theme foreign to Jesus, Paul and John. Cullmann believes that the category of 'early Catholicism' as a principle for classifying the New Testament writings is misleading. Apart from the fact that the concept of salvation history is present in the thought of Jesus and throughout the whole of the New Testament, the characteristic tension between 'already' and 'not yet' is found everywhere. There are, indeed, differences among the New Testament books regarding the nearness of the end, but none over this tension. It is after the New Testament era, not earlier, that the crucial change took place. The biblical insight—that with Christ the end was ushered in temporally—was lost. The interval, no longer characterised by the tension between 'already' and 'not yet', ceased being an interval as the basic New Testament conception that the end time is already anticipated, and yet *only* anticipated, was lost. 'This attitude is, of course, characteristic of later Catholic conceptions in which the concept of the Church suffers from the fact that the "tension" no longer eixsts. However, Protestant theology has in the same way dropped this salvation-historical tension to a marked degree.'[132]

Paul undoubtedly speaks of salvation history, and his whole theology is dominated by its characteristic tension. It has fundamental significance for the apostle's concept of the Church, so that the Church is always for him a salvation-historical entity. His ethics can only be understood as an ethics of tension. The sacraments could have no meaning if the interval were not an object of salvation-historical interest. What of the importance for Paul of the 'now of decision' (e.g. 2 *Cor.* 6:2), an emphasis strongly advanced by the Bultmann school? The anwer is that it is Paul's very faith in salvation history which creates at every moment a basis for the existential decision.

While in the Johannine writings the 'already' is much more strongly emphasised in relation to the 'not yet' than in the rest of the New Testament, the situation of decision in John no less than in Paul is founded on salvation history. Indeed, in the Johannine writings, salvation history is not only present—it is stressed. The very fact of John presenting his theology in the form of a life of Jesus indicates his conviction that the historical life of Jesus is the centre of the saving process of God and the centre of all God's revelation. John's interpretation of the life of the incarnate Christ is a salvation-historical one because the lines are drawn from the events of the life of Jesus to other events in salvation history—that is, to the Christ event occurring in the Church and also, backwards, to events in the Old Testament. Christ acts in his Church through baptism and the Lord's Supper; these are related to episodes occurring during the life of Jesus. The fact that Christ is the mid-point of salvation history, and the connection of this central saving revelation with the whole saving revelation of God, includes faith in the pre-existence of Jesus. The Logos who has become flesh in Jesus of Nazareth must have existed from the beginning of salvation history. The reason why the 'relaxation' of the tension is more apparent in John is because the perspective of the Fourth Gospel puts the historical life of Jesus in its place as the decisive mid-point of history more emphatically than any other Gospel. Even in the Synoptics the kingdom of God is anticipated in the person and work of Jesus; this anticipation is the more marked in John because the person of Christ stands so much in the foreground of this Gospel. Thus the Bultmann school is quite unjustified in its exclusion of eschatology and salvation history from the Fourth Gospel.

It cannot be denied that salvation history is a perfectly valid expression of Christian faith in its most central aspect, for the simple fact is that salvation has been accomplished— revelation has been given—by God in history. God became man, entered into history, thus giving a centre and meaning to what one can rightly call the history of salvation. And even if some opinions of the advocates of salvation history may be open to question, it is certainly true to say that the salvation-historical approach of Cullman does greater justice to the teaching of Jesus and the apostles than does the existentialist interpretation of Bultmann or of Conzelmann.

III. JOACHIM JEREMIAS

The most recent publication of Joachim Jeremias is the first part of a projected New Testament theology.[133] He does not find it necessary to justify his decision to study at length the place occupied by the work and words of Jesus in the Synoptic Gospels, because he firmly believes that Jesus' own proclamation is a constitutive element of New Testament theology. Furthermore, he is convinced that the tradition about Jesus is more trustworthy than is assumed by many New Testament scholars, and his conviction is shown to be founded on solid and compelling arguments. Here is a badly-needed corrective to the scepticism of the existentialist school. For not only must we posit a unique creative genius behind the distinctiveness of the Christian religion; we can see that, in the light of a meticulous literary criticism of the Gospels, Jesus himself emerges more clearly as that unique creative figure. Jeremias can present his case with striking impressiveness, because he can speak with singular authority about the Gospels in their first-century Palestinian background.

In his opening chapter Jeremias examines the largely neglected area of the language and style of Jesus. Despite the fact that the sayings of Jesus are relatively not extensive, it is astonishing how clearly his personal characteristics stand out in them. Nothing in the literature of the time was comparable to the parlance of Jesus—in respect of its simplicity, its nearness to life, and its mastery of the short and striking description. In the first place we should note the ways of speaking preferred by Jesus. His *frequent* use of the 'divine passive' to circumscribe the name of God is distinctive. Antithetical parallelism expressed the urgency of his way of speaking and ensured that sayings were more readily remembered. When his sayings are rendered back into Aramaic the prevalence of alliteration, assonance and rhythm again points to a distinct characteristic of his. In the second place are unique characteristics, without analogy in contemporary literature— characteristics of the *ipsissima vox Jesu*. We can find nothing to be compared with the parables of Jesus. Rabbinical parables are notably inferior; the only worthy parallel is Nathan's parable in 2 *Sam.* 12. Teachers of the time did not teach in riddles, as Jesus did (e.g. *Matt.* 11 : 11f.; *Mark* 9 : 31). While *Amen* was commonly used as a response, assenting to the words of another, the Gospels show an unprecedented usage by Jesus: as either introducing or strengthening his own words; he speaks as a prophet, with authority. The most important linguistic innovation of all is the use, by Jesus, of the everyday word *Abba* as a form of address to God. Jeremias is so convinced of the weight of the linguistic and stylistic evidence that he feels justified in drawing up a principle of method: 'In the synoptic tradition it is the inauthenticity, and not the authenticity, of the sayings of Jesus that must be demonstrated.'[134]

Jesus has much in common with the Baptist, whom he recognised as the intermediary between the old aeon and the new; yet there is a fundamental difference between them. John proclaimed judgement, Jesus the kingly reign of God; John stood within the framework of expectation, Jesus claimed to bring fulfilment; John belongs in the realm of law; with Jesus the gospel begins. Yet, the starting point for an account of the message of Jesus is in his encounter with the Baptist: the call which Jesus experienced when he was baptised by John. Jesus was conscious of being authorised to communicate God's revelation, because God has made himself known to him as Father; his *Abba* as a form of address to God expresses the ultimate mystery of the mission of Jesus. His first appearance was preceded, too, by a quite different event: his rejection of the temptation of a political messiahship. 'In other words, the mission of Jesus includes not only the divine commissioning, but also Jesus' own acceptance of his mission in the form of his victory over temptation . . . The Jesus who confronts us is not the one who has been tempted, but the *one who has emerged from his ordeal*.'[135]

Though Jesus was conscious of being a prophet and bearer of the Spirit he did not simply take his place in the sequence of the Old Testament messengers of God. For, in the conviction of the synagogue the prophetic sequence had been broken off and the Spirit had been quenched. Now, with the Baptist and Jesus the long-quenched Spirit had returned; the presence of the Spirit is a sign of the dawn of the time of salvation, the beginning of the time of grace. God is turning again towards his people, and Jesus is his last messenger; God is speaking his final word. But Jesus comes into a world enslaved by Satan, not only to exercise mercy, but above all to join battle with evil. Jesus came with a proclamation, and the central theme of his message was the kingly reign of God. The *basileia* is always and everywhere understood in eschatological terms, it denotes the time of salvation. The really new element in Jesus' proclamation of the reign of God is that even now, *the consummation of the world is dawning*. The very heart of that proclamation, put in the form of a promise, is 'blessed are the poor'. According to the conviction of the time, the religious ignorance and moral behaviour of the disreputable and uneducated followers of Jesus stood in the way of their access to salvation. But when we look at the same people through the eyes of Jesus, they appear in another light. He calls them 'the poor', those who 'labour and are heavy laden' (*Matt* 11:28).

The infinite mercy of Jesus shown to those beggars before God finds special expression in the promise of the forgiveness of sins. Now, only twice (*Mark* 2:1-12 par.; *Luke* 7:36-50) is Jesus reported as promising the forgiveness of sins in so many words—and Jeremias establishes two principles of

major importance. Firstly, counting words in the proclamation of Jesus means nothing and only leads to confusion.
Jesus does not speak in an abstract way, but in pictures, and
in these the subject of 'forgiveness' is emphatically present.
Secondly, Jesus promised forgiveness not only in words, but
in actions. Because, in Judaism, table-fellowship means
fellowship before God, Jesus' inclusion of sinners in the
community of salvation, achieved through table-fellowship, is
the most meaningful expression of the redeeming love of
God. Indeed, when we respect the proper emphasis in *Luke*
6 : 20 and *Matt.* 5 : 3, the singular fact emerges : the reign of
God *belongs to the poor alone.* 'The first beatitude means
that salvation is destined *only* for beggars and sinners . . .
God does not give his revelation to learned theologians, but
to the uneducated (*Matt.* 11 : 25f. par.; *Luke* 10 : 21); he opens
the *basileia* to children (*Mark* 10 : 14) and to those who can
say *Abba* like a child (*Matt.* 18 : 3).'[136] Beyond any doubt, we
stand on the bed-rock of the tradition, for the accounts of the
proclamation of good news for the poor can be derived
neither from Judaism nor from the earliest Church—they
reproduce the *ipsissima vox* of Jesus.

The true prophetic message has two sides, the proclamation
of condemnation and the proclamation of salvation : grace
and judgement belong together. Thus, Jesus was convinced
that his mission was the prelude to the coming of the
eschatalogical time of distress. He was certain that the kingdom of God comes through suffering and only through
suffering. An important factor is that, in the earliest stratum
of tradition, the time of distress and the revelation of the
*basileia* are expected *soon*. Jeremias does not flinch from the
consequence of this fact; but he also manages to set it in a
broader, enlightening context.

> That raises an extremely serious question : must we not
> concede that Jesus' expectation of an imminent end was
> one that remained unfulfilled? Honesty and the demand
> for truthfulness compel us to the answer 'yes', Jesus expected
> that the end would come soon. But in conceding this quite
> frankly, we must immediately go on to make two further
> points. First, the sayings of Jesus in which there is a note
> of the expectation of an imminent end are not apocalyptic

speculations, forecasts of a date—Jesus rejected that quite firmly—but spiritual judgements. Their basic theme is: the hour of fulfilment has dawned, the reign of God is already being manifested here and now; soon the catastrophe introducing its definitive coming will arrive . . . If we want to sum up these spiritual judgements in one sentence, we might say that God has granted a last period of grace. The most important function of eschatology is that it keeps alive knowledge of this respite.[137]

An even more important point is the astounding qualification added by Jesus—that God can *shorten* the time of distress for the sake of the elect (*Luke* 18: 7f.). He takes into account the possibility that God may rescind his holy will.

Jesus censures his contemporaries for the carelessness with which they cast God's warnings aside and there are three groups of people which he particularly sought to shake into alertness: the priests, the scribes and the Pharisees. The pious men of the day stand in the gravest danger because theirs is 'the piety that separates from God'. Pharisaic Judaism had a markedly vivid consciousness of sin and yet, paradoxically, sin had been made innocuous by casuistry and the idea of merit. The result of casuistry is that sin is no longer seen as rebellion against God, and the idea of merit sets a counter-balance over against sin. Where sin is not taken seriously, men think too well of themselves; they become self-assured, self-righteous and without love. 'It was Jesus' view that repentance was hardest for the pious man, because he was separated from God not by crude sins, but by his piety. Nothing separates a man from God so radically as self-assured piety . . . This is the situation of those confronted with the catastrophe: they are stubborn and indifferent, and the pious live in self-righteous blindness, which makes them deaf to the gospel.'[138]

The urgency of Jesus' call to repentance is seen less in the use of the words *metanoia* and *metanoein* than in the clearer language of his parables. Thus, the repentance of the lost son consists in his finding his way home to his father. Repentance is putting one's trust in the heavenly Father, coming back to his home and his love, it is learning to say *Abba* again, it is joy. The one motive for repentance is God's good-ness which gives the personal assurance of salvation.

Jesus' proclamation always leads on to a personal appeal, a call to faith. His whole message becomes a single summons to accept the offer of salvation, an appeal to trust in his word and in God's grace. More than that, Jesus sought to gather together a community of salvation. Whereas the word *ekklēsia* occurs only in *Matt.* 16: 17-18, Jesus spoke constantly, in a wealth of pictures, of a new people of God that he was gathering—yet another confirmation that accounts of the proclamation of Jesus would not be limited to technical terms. His favourite, among the great variety of images, is that of the comparison of the community of salvation with the eschatological family of God, a family that finds its com-munion in table-fellowship, in anticipation of the Messianic Feast. The new people of God stood in contrast to other 'remnant' groups—Pharisaic and Essene groups, even the dis-ciples of the Baptist—because of one decisive element: a keen awareness of the boundlessness of God's grace. More impor-tant than anything else in the life of this people is the new relationship to God. God is Father, the disciples are his chil-dren; it is significant that Jesus spoke of 'your Father' *only* to his disciples, never to outsiders. In Jesus' eyes, being a child of God brings the certainty of a share in future salvation, grants everyday security and gives the courage to submit to what is unpredictable in the divine will. In particular, the disciple, the child of God, will see suffering in a new light. 'Suffering is a call to repentance, a call which goes out to all. Whereas his contemporaries ask, *"Why* does God send suffer-ing?"*, the disciples of Jesus are to ask, *"For what* does God send suffering?" In addition to God's purpose of summoning to repentance Jesus knows of another purpose for which God uses suffering: there is suffering which serves God's glory . . . Above all when one is a child of God the eternally unfathom-able riddle of *evil* is left in God's hands . . . Nothing happens without God. Jesus believes that unconditionally. Stronger than all questions, riddles and anxieties is the one word *Abba*. The Father knows.'[139] Children talk with their father —Jesus taught a new way of praying; he withdrew prayer from the liturgical sphere of the sacral and put it in the

centre of everyday life. He laid down one essential presupposition for the prayer of his disciples: forgiveness—one's
readiness to forgive, one's request for forgiveness where one
has committed an offence.

Discipleship, being a child of God, the belonging to the
reign of God, transforms a man's whole life, affecting his
relation not only to God but also to man. In other words, the
disciple stands under the new law of God which replaces the
divine law of the old aeon. Jesus himself lived in the Old
Testament—only when we have grasped this basic attitude
can we appreciate the significance of his making more radical,
his criticising, and indeed his superseding words of the
written Torah. Jesus' attitude is anything but antinomian:
he is not concerned with destroying the Law, but with fulfilling it, bringing it to its full escathological measure. His
attitude to the oral Torah, the *Halakah,* is quite different: he
rejected it in a radical way. *Mark* 7: 6-8 gives the reason for
this rejection: it is because this lawgiving is entirely the work
of man, contradicts the commandment of God, and puts
casuistry above love. It is quite certain that love is the law
of life in the new age but, since the commandment of love
is found also in the Old Testament, we look for the new distinctive element and find it to be in the *motive.* The ethical
attitude of Judaism was dominated by the notion of merit
and when Jesus speaks of *misthos* ('reward') he takes up the
terminology of his time. But though he uses the terminology,
Jesus is not concerned with the claim to a reward but with
something quite different—the reality of the divine recompense. 'Merit has an eye to human achievement; recompense
looks to God's faithfulness.'[140]

Membership of the *basileia* leads to the sanctification of
everyday life; the most striking characteristic is 'an indefatig-
able capacity to forgive the brethren.' The disciples are a community of men who have themselves experienced forgiveness
and therefore must extend it to others. Jesus has taken over
and developed the social demands of the prophets and loving
understanding of the poor permeates the Gospel accounts.
More characteristic is the fundamental attitude towards
women and children expressed in the sayings of Jesus. He
'accepts women into the group of disciples because he expects

his disciples to control their desires . . . Nowhere in the social sphere does the new life make so striking an incursion into everyday affairs as here.'[141] Likewise, he introduces a new view of children and brings them nearer to God than adults. Yet the individual demands of Jesus are obviously *incomplete*: he does not offer a moral theology or a code of behaviour. Instead, he lays claim to the whole life of the disciple. Proving one's discipleship, indeed, will consist in staying by Christ in his temptations. The law of the kingdom is that the reign of God comes through suffering, and this law applies to the disciples of Jesus.

At the beginning of his penultimate chapter, 'Jesus' Testimony to his Mission', Jeremias gives his own summary of the preceding four chapters:

> I remarked at the beginning of this book (ch. II) that Jesus' appearance on the scene was preceded by a call, which presumably took place at his baptism. From this time on, Jesus knew that he had been commissioned to share with others the knowledge of God that had been granted to him. With this commission, Jesus saw himself placed in the series of heralds of God, but the attempt to outline his preaching showed us that his awareness of his authority transcended the category of the prophetic. For Jesus proclaimed that with his coming the time of salvation and the conquest of Satan had begun (ch. III). The decision for or against God and deliverance at the last judgement depended solely and simply on obedience to his word (ch. IV). He presented discipleship as true life, set a new law of God over against the *Torah* and had the dawn of the time of salvation proclaimed by his messengers (ch. V). In short, he designated his preaching and his actions as the eschatological saving event. An awareness of mission of this kind can no longer be kept in the prophetic sphere. Rather, all these statements mean that Jesus believed himself to be the bringer of salvation.[142]

To find Jesus' own understanding of his status and his claim to authority we turn not to the christological titles, which are almost all post-Easter, but to his pictures of the symbolic call of the redeemer. Jesus' view of his status is expressed even more emphatically in the remarkable accumulation of the emphatic *egō* which permeates the whole tradition of his sayings. Through the imagery of symbolic language and the prevalence of the emphatic *egō* it becomes strikingly clear that Jesus was conscious of himself as the bringer of salvation and, further, that his testimony to himself was part of the good news that he proclaimed.

It is the unanimous testimony of all four Gospels that Jesus spoke of himself as 'Son of Man' and this is the only title used by Jesus of himself whose authenticity is to be taken seriously. Though it can be shown that the majority of the fifty-one Son of Man sayings in the Gospels carry the title as a later addition, a notable residue of sayings held the title from the beginning. Indeed, the fact that the use of the title was extended in the gospel tradition is quite remarkable when we recall that even at the time of Paul, the Greek-speaking Church avoided the title Son of Man. 'How is it that the instances of it increase, but the usage is still strictly limited to the sayings of Jesus?There can only be one answer; the title was rooted in the tradition of the sayings of Jesus right from the beginning; as a result it was sacrosanct, and no-one dared to eliminate it.'[143] Jesus spoke of the Son of Man in the third person, thereby making a distinction between himself and the Son of Man. (This is a clear indication that the designation dates from before Easter; for the community Jesus simply was the Son of Man.) It is impossible that Jesus should have in mind a future saving figure who was to be distinguished from himself; the distinction he makes is between his present and future state of exaltation. 'The third person expresses the "mysterious relationship" which exists between Jesus and the Son of Man: he is not yet the Son of Man, but he will be exalted to be the Son of Man . . . Evidently the reference to *Dan.* 7 still does not bring us to the heart of Jesus' awareness of his mission. That lies deeper: not in *Dan.* 7, but in *Is.* 53.'[144]

In the faith of the Church, the passion is not the end but the goal and crown of the earthly activity of Jesus, but we still have to ask whether Jesus himself gave his own death a place in his preaching. The Synoptic Gospels agree in giving three predictions of his passion by Jesus (*Mark* 8:31; 9:31; 10:33f. parr.); as they stand, those predictions have been formulated *ex eventu* and, furthermore, are better designated as variations of the passion prediction. Jeremias finds the ancient nucleus which underlies the passion predictions in the *mashal* of *Mark* 9:31a—'God will (soon) deliver up the man to men'. Again he adverts that the evidence that Jesus did treat of his future suffering is not to be sought only in a few 'key' texts. He complains of the 'extremely unfortunate and quite unjustified' practice of scholars who have, in investigating whether or not Jesus had announced his sufferings beforehand, concentrated almost exclusively on the so-called passion predictions, and have ignored the variegated and much more important material in the Synoptic Gospels. When all the evidence is taken into account (and the eucharistic words are the most important allusions to Jesus' suffering) it is no longer reasonable to deny that Jesus expected and announced his suffering and death. 'Uncritical scepticism can unintentionally lead to a falsification of history, as here, if the apt observation that individual phrases and *logia* have been formulated in retrospect, looking back on the course of the passion, leads one to regard all the material as the construction of the community.'[145] The evidence also shows that Jesus had found the answer to the necessity of his death in Scripture, primarily in *Is.* 53. Finally, it is not at all surprising that the instances of Jesus' interpretation of his sufferings are limited; he had spoken of this only to his disciples and only during the last period of his ministry.

It is quite evident that the early Church regarded the resurrection of Jesus as the divine confirmation of his mission. His resurrection is not represented as a return to earthly life but as a resurrection to *doxa* (glory); it stands quite apart from any accounts of raising from the dead. Resurrection to *doxa* meant the dawn of God's new creation, and the disciples must have experienced the appearances of the risen Lord as an eschatological event. Thus we find that the resurrection of Jesus was bound up with his enthronement, his taking his place at the right hand of God. This, then, is how we should understand the disciples' immediate experience of the resurrection of Jesus: 'Not as a unique mighty act of God *in the course of* history hastening towards its end . . . but as the dawn of the eschaton. They saw Jesus in shining light. They were witnesses of his entry into glory. In other words, *they experienced the parousia.*[146] The earliest community, through its life of faith, had a real experience of the dawning of God's new world. The history of the Church began on this basis.

## 4. An Emerging Trend

We have insisted, more than once, that it is not our purpose in this book to give, or even to attempt to give, an exhaustive coverage of work on the theology of the Bible. We aim at being reasonably representative, so that the reader can discern the main trends and may be in a position to form a fair evaluation of what has been achieved. In the final section of this chapter we shall suggest that a recognisable trend is emerging. The ground is being laid for the new theology of the New Testament, one which is likely to be more satisfactory than any which have appeared to date—worthwhile though they are.

By now it is manifest that the New Testament writings must be taken according to their natural groupings, or be studied individually where it is necessary to do so. It is also needful to study major themes—Christology for instance—throughout the whole of the New Testament. A fruitful New Testament *Theology* will emerge from a marriage of the historical and the thematic, a theology which will be seen in its true stature when the various doctrines, traced from the kerygma to their development in the later writings, are built into a flexible synthesis. Here it is our modest purpose to point to some of the converging lines. We feel that we may do so, adequately and yet within our limited scope, firstly, by turning to three recent and deservedly acclaimed single-volume commentaries on the New Testament, and then, in order to give the thematic approach its due weight, by looking at some important works on New Testament Christology.

### I. THE KERYGMA

P. Grech[147], following the historical method, treats the theology of the New Testament as the outcome of the preaching of the apostles. The preaching began with the simplest form of the *kerygma* and then, under the influence of various causes, and incorporating the life and teaching of Jesus into the living faith of the Church, developed into the rich theology of Paul and John. New Testament theology should endeavour to describe this development, indicate its causes and its ramifications, and also point out how certain concepts of the New Testament evolved to the theology of the post-apostolic age. The endeavour is to follow the growth of New Testament theology from *kerygma* to *paradosis* (tradition). It may be seen that that supreme law which guides the development is the necessity of adaptation: apologetical, pastoral and circumstantial. The starting point of all theological development within the New Testament is the kerygma. Grech examines this theology under the various heading of the kerygma: the Holy Spirit, the Last Days, Jesus of Nazareth, the Christ, the cross, the new Israel, and salvation.

The whole New Testament maintains that our faith in Christ does not rest on worldly wisdom but on the witness of the Spirit. The Old Testament doctrine of the Spirit of God is readily taken up by the primitive Church and applied to itself as the new people of God. The Spirit is the messianic gift *par excellence,* the surest sign that the messianic age is here. This doctrine is manifestly Lucan; but it is also Pauline and it receives its fullest development in John. The activity of the Spirit is 'redemptive-historical' (*heilsgeschichtlich*), especially in Luke's presentation: he is God's agent in leading historical events to their destined end; thus, he guides the spread of the Church. The power of the Holy Spirit within the Church can best be studied in the theology of St Paul. For John the reception of the Spirit is the logical outcome of the glorification of Jesus. He is the Spirit of truth who enables the Church to achieve a deeper understanding of the words of Christ.

The outpouring of the Spirit at Pentecost led the first Christians to the conclusion that the last days had come. If we wish to trace the evolution of the eschatological consciousness of Christians of the New Testament age, we begin by asking what Jesus had thought about the kingdom of God. Grech groups the sayings of Jesus about the kingdom under eight different headings; in this way both the doctrine of the

Lord and the preoccupations of the primitive Church may be discerned. The sayings were certainly retouched or expanded —'but to suppose that Jesus' *logia* were created *ex nihilo* is as unscholarly as it is arbitrary.'[148] Luke's interpretation of the kingdom is especially important. In his view the kingdom was ushered in at Jesus' glorification—Passion-Resurrection-Pentecost; the end will come at the Parousia, and with it the final and full salvation. Calvary is the end or *eschaton* in so far as it closes a period of promise and forms one theological whole with the ultimate fulfilment. 'Both Jesus and Luke considered Calvary-Parousia as one event, theologically speaking. Jesus preached salvation in prophetic language and stressed the theological reality. Luke repeated Jesus' message but was more explicit by subjecting it to a historical analysis in the light of events.'[149] The *eschaton*, the kingdom of God, is a single theological reality which touches history at two points: at the incarnation and at the Parousia; between them the kingdom is operative in history through the earnest of the Spirit. Paul is an excellent theological interpreter of Christ's prophetic message. His contribution is the insertion of the resurrection of Jesus into the pattern of the doctrine of the Last Days—our resurrection has begun with his. Christ has been declared 'Son of God' at his resurrection; at his Parousia he will be triumphantly revealed as the only King. John, of course, is the master of realised eschatology, which takes place in history; the eschatological themes are fully transported into the present, without any denial of their futurity.

Jesus of Nazareth figures largely in the kerygma: the early Christians had no inhibitions about the 'Jesus of history'. What they wanted to know was: who in reality is Jesus? They asked what Scripture had to say about him, what his mission was, and how it was being fulfilled. The New Testament books represent various stages in the attempt to answer these questions. Though reluctant to accept the title of Messiah, Jesus consistently strove to lead his disciples and the Jews to the understanding of the real nature of his mission and the identity of his person. He did this by selecting a few passages of Scripture which referred to 'him that cometh' and by moulding their different aspects into one idea. In particular he introduced the 'humiliation' motif into the concept of the Son of Man by linking the text of *Daniel* 7 with the Servant of Yahweh poems of Second Isaiah. Thus he provided the apostolic Church with all the material for producing the sequence: pre-existence—humiliation—death —glorification—judgement of its christological kerygma. While Jesus never called himself 'Son of God' in direct terms, he clearly considered the father-son relationship between God and himself as particular. The apostles found in 'Kyrios' a ready and apt title for the risen Christ, the Lord of the Church. He was so obviously the promised Messiah that 'Christ' quickly became his proper name. The idea of divine Sonship was elaborated by St Paul. He understood that if God had 'sent' his Son, it means that even before the fullness of time the Son pre-existed. The main problem then was: what is the relationship between the pre-existent Son and God? To answer this question and to construct a coherent theology, New Testament theologians borrowed material from rabbinic, Philonic and Hellenistic sources. The Christ-ology of the New Testament reached its highest peak in John. In the Johannine writings the accent is not metaphysically motivated; rather, it is required by John's way of presenting the place of the incarnation in redemptive history. Grech remarks that the modern theologian will do well to revive the neglected aspects of New Testament teaching on Christ and reset it in its redemptive-historical context.

The Jews objected strongly to a crucified Messiah; the Christians sought an answer in Scripture and in the words of Jesus; in this way the sufferings of Christ were related to the purpose of God. Jesus' own interpretation of his com-ing death provided the apostles with a set of soteriological ideas which could be referred back to him: the will and purpose of God, ransom, vicarious suffering, the new coven-ant, the supreme hour of redemptive history; the theme of sacrifice is implicitly present. The Church could turn, too, to the Scriptures indicated by him. New Testament authors who wanted to penetrate deeper into the meaning of the sacrifice of Christ could stress the value of the death of Jesus as a bloody sacrifice or could stress the aspect of obedience—not that these views are mutually exclusive; it is a matter of emphasis. Paul develops the soteriological doctrine of Jesus by taking into consideration the aspects of death, covenant and obedience—with his main stress on obedience. Hebrews, which is the greatest soteriological epistle of the New Testament, underlines the significance of the blood of Jesus. The annunciation of the fact of the resurrection belongs to the most primitive stratum of the kerygma. The Church used it as a proof that Jesus is the Christ, and from the beginning it was affirmed that faith in the risen Christ brings salvation. The soteriological significance of this event emerged later, and the efficacy of the resurrection was placed on a par with that of Jesus' death. The doctrine of redemption through the death of Christ and the place of the resurrection are so developed by Paul that later writers have little to add. Even John, whose contribution to Christology is enormous, has little original material in his soteriology.

Jesus established his *qahal* (his *ekklēsia*) so that it and its institutions (unlike the Old Israel) could truly become a vehicle of the kingdom. The conditions for entry into the New Israel were faith, *metanoia*, and baptism. It was the eschatological community; by becoming a member of it, through baptism, the believer also acquired a special relationship to Christ and became a participant in his death and burial. This fellowship finds its clearest expression in a phrase which must have arisen early in the Church but which received its fullest development in Paul: 'In Christ Jesus'. 'We can conclude that "in Christ" all that happened to Jesus —death, resurrection, glorification, gift of the Spirit—also happens to those who become one with him through baptism. Whatever Christ has done or has received, is likewise done or received by the Church.'[150] Participation in the messianic blessings of the Spirit is referred to as *koinōnia*, 'fellowship'; the apostles provided the foundation for this fellowship; the bond of *koinōnia* is the Eucharist. The entry of the Gentiles into the Church marked the first turning point in New Testament ecclesiology. Problems were raised: what would be the Church's relationship with the Old Israel? how could the new converts fit into the new structure? The answers were sought in the direction of the prophetic doctrine of the eschatological people of God. Gentiles stood on the same footing within the Church as the convert Jews. Paul saw the

15

revelation of God's mystery: Jews and Gentiles form one 'body' in Christ—'body' referred directly to the glorified body of the Messiah as well as to his eucharistic body. A parallel idea developed in Paul's mind, that of Christ as Head. These independent concepts he brilliantly knit together in Colossians and Ephesians. The Pastoral epistles particularly reveal another facet of ecclesiology; here we find an almost completely de-eschatologised organisation which looks forward to a long life in history before the final end comes. We find evidence of confusion of thought, life and order which called forth a threefold reaction: insistence on the unaltered retention of the deposit of faith, an exhortation to the practice of virtue, and a greater emphasis on Church order and authority. The Church of the Pastorals is not a break with the Church of Paul, but the development of a second theme which serves as a balance to the first main theme.

The kerygmatic discourses in Acts promise salvation. The Old Testament saw salvation as an utterly free gift of God's love; there was no place for grace in rabbinic soteriology— good works possessed an intrinsic meriting value. Thus it was that the gospel always met with a divided reaction. The legalistic-minded took scandal at the cross, the self-satisfied had no room for a redeemer. The pious accepted the coming of Christ as yet another mighty and merciful deed of God. Salvation, in a Christian sense, is specifically the mighty act of God in Jesus Christ. In its comprehensive sense it is eschatological; yet it has an earthly aspect between the two salvific acts of God, resurrection and the Parousia. Deliverance from sin is the first and primary effect of salvation in the interim period; and the next step is reconciliation. Paul called justification what the first Christians called salvation; for John it is eternal life. In his doctrine of justification through faith, Paul's preoccupation is to vindicate the absolute righteousness, fidelity and transcendence of God. God's loving initiative in sending his Son for our deliverance from sin is so inconceivably great that nothing must be allowed to minimise its significance. That is why the righteousness of God is needful not only for those who have sinned but for those who have kept the law without reproach, because those who rely on their own righteousness are 'in the flesh'. Those justified by God are 'spirit'; the foundation of the transformation is faith. And faith is man's acknowledgement of his utter poverty in relation to his Maker. Paul does not answer the question why one man accepts the gospel while another rejects it. Luke answers that it is the Lord who opens the heart (*Acts* 16: 14)—but a certain disposition is presupposed. The same principles of election and moral disposition are upheld by John. The Pastorals, with their insistence on right doctrine transmitted by the Church, see faith as an intellectual reception of these truths and obedience to their practical implications.

## II. THE SYNOPTICS

The *Jerome Biblical Commentary* article of D. M. Stanley and R. E. Brown, 'Aspects of New Testament Thought',[151] concentrates on the thought of the Gospels, especially that of the Synoptic Gospels. The themes selected are: titles of Christ, New Testament eschatology, the kingdom of God, the Gospel miracles, the parables of Jesus, the resurrection of Jesus, the Twelve and the apostolate.

An examination of the titles or epithets given to Jesus in the New Testament will reveal the development undergone by Christology throughout the apostolic age. A theology of the Name (*Kyrios*) began to emerge in the earliest days of the Jerusalem community. The apostolic faith quickly found that the title *kyrios* attributed the desired aura of divinity to the glorified Christ. The title *Messiah* underscored the Christian belief that Jesus was the divinely given answer to the messianic hopes of Israel. The title *Servant* characterises the most primitive Christian reflection on the meaning of salvation. As one continues a study of these and other titles through the Synoptic Gospels, the Pauline writings (including Pastorals and Hebrews), and the Johannine literature, a rich Christology emerges, one which is more functional than ontological. Always, the concern is with the role or function of Jesus in regard to men (*pro nobis*). Of course, this implies an ontic affirmation about him, what he is in himself (*in se*), but this factor is never a primary concern.

Eschatology is concerned with God's definitive intervention

in history through Jesus Christ. Generally speaking, the New Testament presents it in two distinct phases marked off by Christ's first and second coming. The crucial events of New Testament sacred history, the set of occurrences by which salvation has been essentially accomplished in the death and resurrection of Jesus Christ, underpin the New Testament expectation of 'the end'. The theme of eschatology is followed through the preaching of Jesus, apostolic preaching in Acts, Paul, Synoptics, and Johannine literature. The conclusion of this section is an important statement which deserves to be quoted in full: 'What gives the New Testament eschatology its characteristic cachet and originality is the unflagging awareness of its inspired authors that he who comes, the judge who exercises cosmic judgement, is not only already victor and Saviour of mankind, but a person familiarly known from the Gospel record of his earthly life of humiliation and suffering. The Old Testament Day of Yahweh, in consequence, has been transformed into the Day of Christ; and its nature has been essentially revealed to men by Jesus' life, death and resurrection. Indeed this day is not so much something ordained to be the termination of this world, but rather a reality already dynamically present in history. And this history becomes fundamentally salvation history; for the value of the present time, as also the significance of the future, has been created and revealed to us by Jesus Christ.'[152]

The synoptists agree in their presentation of Jesus as proclaiming the imminence of the kingdom of God right from the beginning of his public ministry. They attest, too, his conviction that he had an unprecedented role to play in the coming of the kingdom. As for the individual synoptists, they seize on different aspects. The Old Testament idea of the kingdom of God as a heavenly reality that descends into human history is a prominent theme in Mark. Matthew has two characteristic modifications of the kingdom theme: he calls it the 'kingdom of the heavens' and he distinguishes between the 'kingdom of the Father' and the 'kingdom of the Son of Man', which is the Church. The presence of the kingdom of God, this divine reality, in history is a favourite theme for Luke.

If we are to understand aright the meaning of the miracles

in the Gospels, we must de-emphasise the traditional apologetic assessment of them. Far from Jesus' miracles being essentially external confirmations of his message, the miracle was rather the vehicle of the message. Word and miracle, together, gave expression to the breaking-in of God's kingly power into time. The miracle is not principally proof, nor criterion, but is an intrinsic part of revelation. Besides, the miracles were Jesus' weapon in his struggle with Satan; they were the very means of establishing God's reign. The symbolic use of miracles leads to the 'signs' of John. The parables of Jesus are treated in the light of the approach of C. H. Dodd and J. Jeremias.[153]

J. Marsh, too, centres his attention on the theology of the synoptists.[154] However, he opens on a wider note. In a general way, it may be said that the New Testament 'tells a story'; it is the theologian's task to draw out and systematise the truths contained in, or implied by, the story. Because of that, New Testament theology must be firmly based on exegesis. It must be sure that the doctrines about God, man and the world which it propounds must follow from and truly explain the story, and it must give full weight to the theological forms in which the New Testament story is itself cast. The New Testament writers, in their turn, made use of the rich theology and the forms of the Old Testament. In the Old Testament the Exodus is a fundamental and pervasive event which is presented in a consistently theological manner. It is meant to say that what God did on that occasion can be properly understood only in the light of what had been done before, what had been done afterwards, and what was yet to follow. The centre of the New Testament is the Christ-event which is deliberately related to the Exodus story as both fulfilling and transcending it; the Exodus and other Old Testament elements provide the narrative form for many New Testament events. That is why, whatever about other influences, the Old Testament is the basic and indispensable instrument for interpreting the New Testament.

Christ is necessarily the centre of New Testament theology. Each New Testament writer bears witness to him in his own way; all are concerned with a Jesus of history who is the Christ of faith. In their testimony to the divine person and work of Christ, the New Testament writers make statements and narrate stories in such a way that the theologian can discover and formulate what their witness to Christ means for the whole range of theological enquiry. The common theological interest in Christ is the unifying principle of the different theologies and theological languages found within the New Testament. This is why Marsh thinks it proper to begin his outline of New Testament theology with a theological evaluation of Mark, our earliest Gospel. He then finds that the Marcan themes recur throughout the New Testament.

Mark tells the story of Jesus who fulfilled a specific role, that of Messiah, in the life of the people of God and was himself related to God in a unique way as 'Son'. He tells the story of the beginning of a new Israel in the divine and human person of Jesus. He turns to the story of the Exodus for categories and forms in his interpretation of the life and death of Jesus. He tells of Jesus' proclamation of the kingdom of God as a present reality and of his miracles, the signs of its presence. At the beginning of his ministry, the Messiah withstood the Adversary and carried on the warfare in his exorcisms. His power is adequate to work effectively beyond what sin and death can do to men; he defeated the assault of death upon himself. The Son, from the beginning, was the centre and the life of a community; his death was a shattering experience for the community, his resurrection filled them with awe. They had learned that the disciple shares his Master's destiny; it was understandable that their hearts should quail at what had been done and what was being asked of them. 'As a book which is intended to explain the Christian community to itself, Mark has the seeds of all later theology in it, as it sets the seal upon all that has been wrought hitherto.'[155]

When the theological dimension of the Synoptics is understood, John no longer appears in the role of a perverse theologiser of a simple story—rather, he carries on the theological interpretation of the fact of Christ. 'John has told the Synoptic story so that neither docetism nor adoptionism can explain it, indeed so that only a Chalcedonian Christology is adequate; and he has told it so that nothing less than a Trinitarian theology will bear the weight of the good news that the Gospels contain.'[156] Where the Gospels had told the story of the coming of the people of God in the person of Jesus with an eye to Exodus analogies, Acts tells the story of the coming of the people of God in the community of the Church with an eye to Exodus and Gospel analogies. Acts gives a clear-cut picture of the kerygma of the early Church which is quite like the theological structure of the Gospels. Acts is the book of the Spirit who guides the spread of Christianity; Acts is also the book of the Church. As the risen Lord among his people, Christ rules his Church; it is he who reigns—not James, nor Peter, nor Paul.

The basic Marcan themes are all substantially developed in Paul. Understandably, the ecclesiological theme receives much attention since Paul is writing to the churches. Paul's doctrine of 'justification by faith' may be regarded as the theological counterpart of the gospel narrative: salvation is an act wrought by God in Christ—hence the great duty of preaching is to 'preach Christ crucified' (1 *Cor.* 1 : 23). His image of the Church as the 'body' of Christ is a more theological way of indicating the organic unity which Christ's presence with his own bestows. For Paul, as for the evangelists, the 'end' has come; Christians are 'the kingdom of God's beloved Son' (*Col.* 1 : 13)—yet he can look to the day when 'Christ will appear' (*Col.* 3 : 4). This certain hope and the awareness of the justifying act of God lead to a new formulation of the moral life, one which is christological and thus fundamentally eschatological. In Hebrews, 1 Peter, and even in Apocalypse, we find interesting appearances of the Marcan themes or, at least, many characteristics in common with Mark.

The New Testament, then, is not a treatise in theology: it is a story with a theological commentary. The conviction that God has acted in history is basic to Christian faith, and so the story is necessary. The fullness of the good news cannot be conveyed in a one-dimensional telling of the gospel story, and so the commentary is necessary. The evangelists themselves make theological comments on the story as they tell it; the other New Testament writers develop further theological aspects of it. But the very life of the Christian Church provides an essential commentary. 'Thus, though the New Testament is not itself a treatise in theology, it is without doubt an exceedingly theological document.'[157]

The task of the New Testament theologian is in principle no different from that of the New Testament writers themselves. He traces a theme (or themes) of Scripture and explores its theological significance, just as they show that the story of Christ and his Church is the fulfilment of the story of God and his people in the Old Testament. And if, by examining the great themes of the Bible, the theologian finds himself constantly being directed to Jesus Christ as the final point of reference and of fundamental meaning for all such themes, he will have understood why biblical theology must flower into something essentially systematic. But the story remains basic to and distinctive of Christianity; it might be said that the whole purpose of Christian theology is to make articulate what the Christian story requires us to believe. Biblical theology points to the central place of the person of Jesus Christ in that story, and points to him as the origin and inspiration of the ideas that are involved in the telling.

### III. PAULINE THEOLOGY

We return to the *Jerome Biblical Commentary* for the excellent treatment of Pauline theology by J. A. Fitzmyer.[158] He works with ten letters of the Pauline corpus, excluding Pastorals and Hebrews, and arranges his material under the dominant perspectives of soteriology, anthropology, and ecclesiology and ethics. But first an introductory section deals with Paul's background. In the main, five factors may be said to have influenced Paul's theology: pharisaic rabbinism, hellenism, the Damascus revelation, the early tradition, and Paul's apostolic experience. All else—the heritage of his Jewish background, the wider outlook of his contacts with hellenism, whatever he had received from the tradition of the early Church, and his own missionary experience—was transformed by his insight into the mystery of Christ granted in the moment of revelation on the Damascus road.

Paul's theology is emphatically Christocentric. It is functional in character: he preached 'Christ crucified', Christ as significant for men. The content of his gospel is Jesus the Christ, the risen *Kyrios*; that is why he sees the gospel as a salvific force which spreads abroad to men the redemptive event of Christ's death and resurrection. In it the 'mystery', the divine plan of salvation, is revealed. The author of the saving plan is God the Father, thus Paul's theology (in the strict sense) is closely associated with his soteriological Christology. His conception of the relationship of God to Christ brings out the relation of the Father to man's salvation. In this wide perspective of salvation history, Paul's Christology acquires historical, cosmic and corporate dimensions: historical, since it embraces all human history and is rooted in the intervention of Christ in history; cosmic because it relates all the created *kosmos* to man's salvation; and corporate because it gathers Jews and Gentiles into one body.

We turn to the role of Christ in salvation history. When Paul calls Jesus the 'Son', he most often wishes to express only his divine election; he uses the title in a functional sense. Sometimes, however, he uses it to express something about Christ's origin and relation to the Father. *Kyrios,* which expresses the actual dominion over men of the risen Lord, is Paul's title *par excellence* for Jesus. A characteristic of Paul's theology is the linking of Christ's death and resurrection as the salvation event; it is through passion, death, and resurrection that Jesus became the 'Saviour' of men.

Although Jesus is the power and wisdom of God, he is never called outright 'the Spirit of God'; yet several times, the Spirit is not clearly distinguished from Jesus. On the other hand, there are triadic texts which set God (Father), Christ (Son) and Spirit in a parallelism that is the basis of the later dogma of the Trinity. Paul's conception of the relation of the Spirit to the Son displays a lack of clarity. Throughout, he is concerned with the functional role of the Spirit in man's salvation. The effects of the salvation event— Christ's passion, death and resurrection—are the reconciliation of man with God (the main effect), the expiation of his sins, his redemptive liberation and his justification. The whole process is coloured by the gracious and loving initiative of the Father and the love of Christ. Justification is by no means as important to Paul as it has been made to seem in later theology, and it is by no means the key to Pauline thought. It is an aspect of salvation that emerged in polemic with judaisers and it gives salvation a judicial aspect which is not characteristic of the Christian reality. Paul fits the metaphor to a Christian context by insisting on the utter gratuity of justification.

Paul understood that Christian reconciliation brought about a new union of man with God, a 'new creation'; it introduced a new mode of existence in which Christ and the Christian enjoy a kind of symbiosis. Man appropriates to himself the effects of the Christ-event through the experience of faith, a vital, personal commitment. The basis of the Christian experience is a new union with God in Christ, an ontological reality which is not immediately and consciously perceived by man. 'The lively commitment of faith must so influence his conscious conduct as to integrate his psychological activity with the ontological reality within him. This is integrated Christian living.'[159] Faith is a gift of God; it is man's acceptance of, his response to, God's initiative. Paul's stress on the role of faith is adequately understood only when it is linked to his teaching about baptism; it was he who brought out the real significance of this rite. Salvation is not a mere individualistic experience for a Christian—by baptism he is incorporated into the 'body of Christ'. This intimate union of Christ and Christian is expressed by prepositional phrases; the most important of these is *en Christō* ('in Christ') which is most commonly used to express an inclusion or incorporation that becomes a symbiosis of Christ and the Christian. However, the most typical Pauline figure to express this corporate identity is 'the body of Christ'. And his meaning is unmistakable—somehow Christ and the Christian share a union which implies one flesh; a union that is not so much corporate as corporal. The ontological reality that stands as the basis of the union is the possession of the Spirit of Christ. The theme of the Body developed independently of that of the Church; they merge only in the Captivity Letters. The Head theme, too, appears at first independently of the Body theme. In the Captivity Letters for the first time Paul links the themes of 'body', 'head' and 'church', and the Church is identified with the 'Body of Christ'. The Christian experience is a living, dynamic union with the individual risen body of the Lord, while the corporate union of Christians must grow to fill out the total Christ—the *plērōma* of the cosmic Christ. Paul also uses 'the body of Christ' in another sense, to mean his eucharistic body, but he is still explaining the intimate union of Christ with Christians.

The word *ekklēsia* is found abundantly in the Pauline letters; the notion of *ekklēsia* plays a very important role in the Captivity Letters. We may detect a certain growth in Paul's awareness of what 'the Church' really means for man; in a sense it is a development of his understanding of Christ's role in salvation. 'The unity of the Christian community in the Church is Paul's great contribution to Christian theology —a unity that he derives from the single purpose of the divine plan of salvation.'[160] Christian living makes demands. The baptised Christian has become a 'new creature'; he lives, but it is really Christ who lives in him; he must integrate his conscious conduct into this new ontological mode of existence. The Christian lives a life with a double polarity; that is why, Paul insists, the Christian, activated by the Spirit of God, can no longer live a life limited by a merely natural, earthly horizon. That is why, too, the Christian is free from law, sin, death and self. If there is a 'law of Christ' it is a law of love; Christ has not imposed a legal code. The Spirit's law of love is the ontic principle of vitality which interiorises the ethical conduct of the Christian. Yet Paul can still find a place for exhortation to virtue and for detailed instructions regarding ethical conduct. But his ethical teaching is always Christocentric. What Paul recommends to his readers, contemporary and modern, is growth in Christ. Yet, ultimately, he refers the Christian to the Father—through Christ.

## IV. JOHANNINE THEOLOGY

We remain with the *Jerome Biblical Commentary* for an outline of Johannine theology.[161] In John's thought and in Paul's, we have the two most important of the diverse theologies that emerged from apostolic Christianity. Vawter sets out to synthesise the dominant perspectives of Johannine theology. When he has indicated the significance of Johannine thought, he turns to Christology, eschatology, and the theology of Apocalypse.

The first point taken up is the relation of Johannine theology to other New Testament thought. The one element in John that most strikingly differentiates it from the Synoptics is the transfer of interest from the kingdom to the person of Jesus. On the whole it is accepted today that there is far closer connection between John and the most primitive formulations of Christian thought than was formerly admitted. Comparison with the other outstanding New Testament theologian, Paul, is inevitable. Between them, they have done most to influence the course of early Christian thought and represent parallel developments of it. John's originality is seen most markedly in his fresh synthesis of existing ideas. He has set emphasis on the elements most revelant to the Christianity of his age and has put them into a language comprehensible to that age—his work truly meets the test of a theology.

The Johannine world is characterised by a great dichotomy. Yet it is clear that John's dualism has nothing to do with a philosophical speculation on good and evil, but is a component of salvation history. The warfare between light and darkness in this world is not cosmic but a struggle within man in his search for truth and light. In the Johannine view, truth has come whole and entire through the coming of the Son of Man. In him the meeting of God and man takes place; he is the communication of divine life. John stresses equally the divinity and the humanity of the Saviour: the truth, light, and life which men need have been brought from above by the Son, but they are given only because he is one with mankind, who through him can enter into the divine sphere. 'The reality of the incarnation is not simply an affirmation of Christian dogma, but constitutes the essence of salvation.'[162]

When he identifies Jesus as the creative Word of God, source of the light that is man's life, John presents him as the revealer of God; but the conception of revelation is dynamic—the idea of the Word is eminently soteriological. The revelation made by the Word gives knowledge of God; the revelation is found in the example and imitation of a life that has been led, the life of the Son of Man. The incarnation is the supreme grace of God. The Word is preeminently the revelation of God's love; hence Jóhn's stress on love. It is the essence of discipleship, of what it means to be a Christian, and is shown in obedience to the law of God and Christ. The 'signs' of Jesus comprise his words and works—the words give determination to his works and show them to be the works of God. The 'signs' of Jesus constitute the communication of God to men, and so they are truth and life; they are abiding realities. The glory of Jesus is something that has been seen by men and in him they have found the glory of God.

The incarnation is a beginning; it has to be fulfilled in the work for which the Son has been sent into the world: the glorification of the Father that in turn is his own glorification. The 'hour' of Jesus, the hour of his suffering and death, is one phase of his 'glorification', the other phase being his resurrection and return to the Father. In contrast to the synoptists, who reflect the common tradition, John has underlined the glorification aspect of the passion story. It is an hour of triumph because, despite appearances, it is the world that is being judged and the power of evil broken. The incarnate Word has glorified God by his words and deeds; God, in turn, has glorified him by the same words and deeds. By thus glorifying Jesus Christ, God has entered the human sphere and has enabled man to enter the divine sphere.

Faith plays an important part in John's theology. 'It is by faith that man is set free from his own hopelessness and brought into contact with that otherness that can save him. For John, that otherness is God as he has revealed himself historically in Jesus Christ. Here is the enduring "scandal" of Christianity.'[163] Faith and knowledge are often associated, but they are not identical. Knowledge comes from faith and faith leads to knowledge—that is to say, the believer is led into a true knowledge of God to the extent that he can possess it. Knowledge, in so far as it concerns salvation, comes through faith. Besides, knowledge is not passive but eminently active —and 'active' as embarking on a new experience, since the real object of this knowledge is a Person. Believing is also seeing; more than any other New Testament writer John has laid stress on faith as vision; it is a true vision of God and of truth. Because faith is the assent of man to revelation, and the revelation of God in Christ is pre-eminently the revelation of his love, there is the closest possible connection between faith and love.

In his treatment of the Spirit, John has brought out more clearly than any other the implication of the New Testament revelation that the Spirit of God is a true person standing in relation to the Father and the Son. The Spirit is presented as the divine power that continues and completes Jesus' ministry; the Spirit is the perpetuation of Jesus' presence among his followers. The Spirit is the principle of the divine sonship that Jesus has made possible for men; John's emphasis is on the Spirit as sanctifier and principle of the life of the Christian. John's more elaborate triadic theology (of three divine salvific agents, Father, Son, and Spirit) still remains largely functional rather than ontological. The activity of the Paraclete (John's designation of the Spirit) is to reveal the mind of Christ. We live not by the words of the 'historical' Jesus alone, but by the words of Jesus as made known through the Church enlightened by the Spirit. John's theology of the Spirit means that his eschatology could hardly be other than 'realised'. Hence it appears that it is not so much the 'delay' of the Parousia as the Church's consciousness and experience of the presence of the Holy Spirit that was responsible for the development of 'realised eschatology'.

Men find in the Church not only the teaching of Jesus but also his works of salvation; and the works of Christ perpetuated in the Church by the Spirit are chiefly the sacraments. The sacraments draw their efficacy from the sacrificial death of Christ. The presence of the Spirit is manifested in Christian life, most obviously in the Christian virtues, specifically fraternal charity. John's concept of the judgement is in line with his realised eschatology: while not denying the final judgement, he insists on the present realities of judgement, on the importance of the existential moment of decision. The coming of Jesus is and remains an occasion of judgement; men must decide whether to accept or reject him. In making this decision man judges himself. The 'division' caused by the appearance of the Light continues into John's Church and the Church of our day.

## V. CHRISTOLOGY

In the introductory chapter of this very important study of the Christology of the New Testament,[164] Oscar Cullmann makes a point which he sustains throughout his work: Christology is functional. 'When it is asked in the New Testament "Who is Christ?", the question never means exclusively, or even primarily, "What is his nature?", but first of all, "What is his function?" '[165] It is by investigating the different titles which the first Christians conferred upon Jesus that one can most closely attain to 'the Christology of the New Testament'. Cullmann arranges the christological titles in four groups accordingly as they designate primarily the *earthly* work of Jesus, or his *future,* eschatological work, or his *present* work, or the work completed in his *pre-existence.* The arrangement brings out the basic truth that Christ is connected with the total history of revelation and salvation. Christology demands a *Heilsgeschichte* which unfolds in time.

The first of the titles which refer to the earthly work of Jesus is the 'Prophet'. It is only in John and the first part of Acts that Jesus is considered as the eschatological Prophet who prepares the way for God. The concept is inadequate because it cannot really be referred to the stages other than the earthly. The title 'Servant of Yahweh', on the other hand, takes us straight to the heart of New Testament Christology. It had its origin with Jesus himself—not because he designated himself as such, but because he applied to himself the ideas of vicarious suffering and death and also the idea of the Servant's restoration of the covenant between God and his people. Yet this 'Servant' Christology, one of the oldest and most important, soon receded into the background. The 'High Priest' concept is present not only in Hebrews but also stands behind the christological statements of other New Testaments passages. It is surprising that Cullmann includes this title here; it surely belongs in part three, among the titles for Christ's exalted work.

'Messiah' is the first of the titles which relate primarily to the eschatological work of Christ—the adjective 'messianic' is almost a synonym for 'eschatological'. Jesus, however, showed extreme reserve toward the *title* Messiah. In decisive passages he substituted 'Son of Man' for 'Messiah' and set the ideas relative to the Servant of Yahweh in contrast to the current political conceptions of the Messiah. This reserve was not shared by the Palestinian Church, which quickly elevated the expression 'Jesus is the Messiah' to a confession. Jesus' sayings about the Son of Man fall into two categories: those in which he uses the title with reference to his *eschatological* work and those in which he applies it to his *earthly* task. His use of the title expresses his consciousness of having to fulfil the role of the Heavenly Man both in the glory of the end time and in humiliation of the incarnation among sinful men. The title is particularly important in John, while Paul gave the *concept* greater theological depth.

The most important of the titles which refer to the present work of Jesus is 'Lord'. It points primarily to the exalted Christ and asserts that he is not only a part of divine *Heilsgeschichte* in the past, nor just an object of future hope, but is a living reality in the present. The confessional expression *Kyrios Iēsous* refers to his post-Easter, present work fulfilled in his state as exalted Lord. It is one of the most ancient formulas and expresses the whole faith of the early Church. The title, with its central place in the theological thought of the first Christians, rests upon the acceptance of two essential elements of *Heilsgeschichte*: Jesus is risen, and yet salvation history is not interrupted. Christ continues to exercise his role as Mediator in the 'between-times'. The title 'Saviour' is rare, but the idea was already present in the earliest Church that Jesus is not only named but *is* Saviour.

In his fourth part Cullmann turns to the titles which refer to the pre-existence of Jesus. For John, because the incarnate One, the Son of Man as he appeared in the flesh, is the centre of *all* history, the question of his pre-existence arises. The Prologue of John offers one of the few New Testament passages which speak of the 'being' of the pre-existent Word. Yet even here, with his eye on the Word becoming flesh, the evangelist is already thinking of the function of the Word. The Word *is* God and he is *with* God—this is the paradox of all Christology, and the New Testament does not resolve it. The New Testament paradox that the Father and Son are at once one and yet distinct has its source in the fact that while one may speak of the Son only in connection with the revelation of God, in principle one can speak of God also apart from revelation—though the Bible speaks of God *only* in his revelatory action. 'The Logos is the self-revealing, self-giving God—God in action. This action only is the subject of the New Testament. Therefore, all abstract speculation about the "natures" of Christ is not only a useless undertaking, but actually an improper one. By the very nature of the New Testament Logos one cannot speak of him apart from the action of God. One can say of the being of the Logos only what the Johannine prologue says and no more: he was in the beginning with God, and he was God.'[166]

Jesus' consciousness of being the Son of God refers both to his person and to his work: his work of salvation and revelation shows that the Father and the Son are one. Cullmann finds in the description of the final fulfilment of all redemptive activity as a total 'subjection of the Son' to the Father the key to all New Testament Christology. 'It is only meaningful to speak of the Son in view of God's revelatory action, not in view of his being'.[167] We find that according to John the Son of God is God in his self-relevation; while according to Paul he will be absorbed in God when redemptive action has reached its goal. Hebrews unequivocally applies the title 'God' to Jesus. It is thus true to say that the New Testament teaches Christ's 'deity'—provided it is understood strictly from the standpoint of *Heilsgeschichte*. Without a divine *Heilsgeschichte* it would be senseless to speak of Jesus' 'deity' and senseless to distinguish God the Father from the Logos, his revelation, his 'Son'.

Throughout, then, Cullmann understands Christology as a redemptive history which extends from creation to the eschatological new creation, the centre of which is the earthly life of Jesus. The experience of the Lordship of Christ first gave the real impetus to a consistent formulation of Christology in terms of *Heilsgeschichte*; it is in these terms, too, that the connection was made between the incarnate and pre-existent Christ, involving the recollection of Jesus' words about his unique sonship. The principal themes of the New Testament Christology were already known and developed by the earliest Church, and we must discard the rigid scheme: Judaistic-original-Church—Hellenistic-Christianity.

16

The faith which regards Jesus Christ as the Revealer implies a statement about his person, but in such a way that one can speak of his person only in connection with his work. The first Christians saw God's redemptive revelation in Jesus Christ, fundamentally in the central work accomplished in the flesh. 'Functional Christology is the only kind which exists. Therefore all Christology is *Heilsgeschichte* and all *Heilsgeschichte* is Christology.'[168]

In his study of the Christology of the New Testament,[169] Vincent Taylor employs two methods, the exegetical and theological and accordingly, his work falls into two parts. In the first, the exegetical section, he examines the various New Testament writings singly or in groups. He begins by describing the primitive beliefs expressed in the Gospels and finds that the outstanding feature of the Christology of the Gospels is the combination of traditional teaching with doctrinal ideas which foreshadow later developments. A fully human life of Jesus is described in all the Gospels and all of them affirm his Messiahship. All four evangelists use the name 'Son of Man' freely, though it had dropped out of use when the Gospels were written. The four Gospels support the view that the name 'the Lord' describes Jesus as risen and glorified, recognises a close connection between the Holy Spirit and Jesus, and affirms the divine Sonship of Jesus. The Acts of the Apostles reveals that in the primitive preaching the reality of Christ's manhood was assumed and shows a deep interest in the Messiahship of Jesus. Characteristic of its teaching is the belief that Jesus is the Servant of the Lord and, even more so, the conviction that Jesus is Lord.

Paul is the first Christian teacher to develop the traditional christological teaching. There is no doubt that for Paul, Jesus is the Messiah; but this is not a central and dominating thought in his theology. Though it too is taken over from primitive usage, the conception of Christ as 'Lord' is that dominating idea. Paul speaks less frequently of Christ's Sonship. What he means by it can be appreciated by considering his teaching concerning the relationship of Christ to man, to the universe, to the Spirit, and to God, and is estimated best in terms of its functions. In Paul's teaching the relationship between Christ and the Spirit is singularly close in range and function. Though Paul does not call Christ 'God' when he thinks of his relationship with man, with the universe and with the Holy Spirit, he brings him within the orbit of deity; in particular he separates him as an object of worship. But he does not call him God. 'The instructive paradox of Pauline theology is that he does not identify the pre-existent Christ with Deity'.[170] Taylor pays special attention to the christological hymn in *Phil.* 2:6-11 in view of his presentation of the doctrine of the kenosis in part three. It is clear that Paul says nothing about the abandonment of the attributes of God; the kenosis he describes is very different from the kenosis as a christological hypothesis.

Of the other writings, the Christology of 1 Peter is important because it combines primitive Christian data with elements which foreshadow later developments. The main interest of the unquestionably important epistle to the Hebrews lies in its soteriology. Nowhere else in the New Testament is the humanity of Christ set forth so movingly. But no other New Testament writer has contributed so richly to the doctrine of the Person of Christ as the fourth evangelist. The basic ideas reflected in John's portrait of Jesus are: that he truly appeared in the flesh; that he is the divine Son of God; that he is the eternal Logos; that the Holy Spirit, while distinct, is his *alter ego*; that he is the 'Lamb of God', the Saviour; and that, as the risen and Living Lord, he is the subject and object of a communion which exists between himself and the believer. The Christology of the Fourth Gospel is essentially a doctrine of divine Sonship, but its association with the idea of the Spirit-Paraclete implies distinctions within the Godhead to be worked out in later Christian theology. The Pastoral Epistles show us how the Person of Christ was interpreted in circles in which practical and ecclesiastical interests were uppermost; they reflect a practical and unspeculative type of primitive Christianity in which Christ is tacitly assigned the powers and functions of God. The Apocalypse is remarkable for the way in which it combines primitive elements with a lofty Christology.

In the second, the historical and theological part of his book, Taylor sets out to trace the movements of thought in relation to the doctrinal issues which are involved. In the

first place he examines the emergence of the divine consciousness of Jesus. From the evidence we may conclude that his
consciousness of divine Sonship is the key to the presentation
of Jesus we find in all the Gospels; and this consciousness
emerged in the mind of Jesus as described in the Synoptic
Gospels. The Christology of the primitive period is reflected
in the life and worship of the early communities; it is this
that compels us to believe that primitive Christianity
regarded Christ as divine.

The three great New Testament theologians, Paul, the
author of Hebrews and John, inherited a much larger
element of primitive Christology than was commonly recognised. They proceed to set right the limitations of this
tradition: a failure to appreciate the christological importance of the work of Christ and failure to relate the high
claims made for Christ to the doctrine of God. In Paul,
Hebrews and John we find the association of Jesus' person
and work: the work illuminates the person and the person
explains the work. Then, too, each of them believes in the
pre-existence of Christ and sees him as a divine person, the
Son of God, appearing in a true humanity. Each of them
presents Christ within a doctrinal pattern in which he, as
divine Redeemer, descends to earth to be the Saviour of men.
Each of them can bring the person of Christ into close contact
with his belief in God. But in fact the shaping of the doctrine
of God was influenced not so much by teaching concerning the
person of Christ as by the growing appreciation of the work
of Christ—this supports the functional aspect so stressed by
Cullmann. To appreciate the true nature of New Testament
teaching concerning the person of Christ, we must not overlook the relationship between Christology and the Trinity.

A distinctive feature of Taylor's work is his argument that
some form of *kenosis* is essential to any worthy doctrine of the
incarnation. The New Testament makes clear that the life of
Christ on earth was unambiguously human. Equally clearly
he is divine, Lord and Christ, Son of Man and Son of God.
The problem is the co-existence of the two manifestations of
his divine-human personality. It seems necessary to conceive
the divine nature as limited by the human conditions of the
incarnation. A true Christology must find the divinity of

Christ in a life lived on the human plane, in a particular time and place; and this requires some form of self-emptying. This self-emptying is implied in Pauline and Johannine teaching and is suggested by the primitive records of the earthly life of Jesus. Thus, it would seem that a Christology which is in accord with the teaching of the New Testament is one which accepts that the Son of God, in becoming man, willed to lay aside the divine attributes of omniscience, omnipotence and omnipresence in the sense that, during the Son's earthly existence, these are potential and latent rather than continuously operative.

Taylor states his case thus: 'Only on the assumption that the divine attributes are potential rather than active does a true incarnation seem possible. If the Son comes into the world omniscient and omnipresent, his coming is a theophany; if he completely strips himself of these attributes, he is down-graded to the level of a man. In the one case the humanity is a semblance; in the other the divinity is lost; in neither case is there a veritable incarnation of the Son of God. This dilemma is resolved in a Christology in which these attributes are latent, conditioned in operation by the circumstances of a truly human existence.'[171] To avoid misunderstanding it is well to note the author's assertion that this christological view 'unequivocally accepts the divinity of Christ, its trinitarian foundations, and the possession of two natures, or modes of existence, each appropriate to the conditions of his existence. It affirms the divine Ego of his Person which manifests itself by a supreme act of self-limitation within the confines of a humanity which is complete in every respect.'[172] Put like that, it is not really possible to maintain that the form of kenosis which Taylor propounds is untrue to the christological view of the New Testament. At very least, the theologian must look closely at this kenotic hypothesis.

R. H. Fuller[173] sees Christology as a confessional response to a particular history in that men confess their faith in what God has done in terms of a Christology. He sees it as a kerygmatic response in that the disciples of Jesus, by means of Christology, proclaim Jesus as the one in whom God has acted redemptively. Christology is the Church's response to its total encounter with Jesus. The Church made this response in terms of whatever tools lay to hand. Chapters two to four of Fuller's work deal with the tools of Christology derived from the three successive environments in which the early Church was operating: Palestinian Judaism, Hellenistic Judaism, the Graeco-Roman world. Chapter five deals with the earthly history of Jesus and chapter six with the effect of the resurrection faith on the disciples' assessment of Jesus' work and mission. Chapter seven traces the christological response of the Christian mission in its preaching to Greek-speaking Jews, and chapter eight traces the christological formulations of the Gentile mission. The final chapter indicates the three christological patterns which form the foundations of New Testament Christology.

In this résumé we begin with the self-understanding of the historical Jesus. It emerges that Jesus himself understood his mission in terms of eschatological prophecy and knew that the coming Son of Man of the End will vindicate his work. As eschatological prophet (though he did not *define* himself as such), he was already initiating in his words and works the future coming of salvation and judgement. The basic datum of New Testament Christology is the proclamation and the activity of Jesus which confront men and women with the inbreaking presence and saving act of God. It was the task of the post-Easter Church to interpret this datum in explicit christological terms. In the Church's kerygma the Proclaimer became the Proclaimed.

This kerygma of the earliest Church presented a Christology with two foci: the historical word and work of Jesus, and his Parousia. Both foci were related to the present life of the Church: Jesus' word had present authority; his work had present soteriological significance. This admirable Christology of the earliest Palestinian Church, which saw Jesus as the Mosaic prophet in his earthly life and as the one who was to come shortly as the Son of Man to vindicate his word and work, made explicit what Jesus had implied about himself throughout his ministry. This Christology enabled the history of Jesus to be interpreted in terms of the redemptive event which had occurred in history, yet which awaited consummation. Fuller questions Cullmann's judgement of the inadequacy of the Prophet concept and urges that the prophetic Christology brings out effectively the soteriological aspect of Jesus' mission. However, he admits that it did appear inadequate in the Hellenistic world.

In the Hellenistic Jewish Mission the two foci Christology was transformed into a two stage Christology. The kerygma was now orientated chiefly upon the present work of the exalted One, now evaluated for its own sake; and the historical ministry was seen as a preliminary stage in his Messiahship. However, the question of pre-existence was barely raised and the kerygma was not concerned with the nature of Jesus; it is yet an entirely functional Christology. The missionaries to the Gentiles took a major step forward in affirming the Redeemer's pre-existence and incarnation. Thus the Hellenistic Gentile Mission developed a three stage Christology: it produced a threefold christological pattern of pre-existence, incarnation and exaltation. A full-blown doctrine of incarnation evolved as the redeemer was thought of as a divine being who manifested his deity in the flesh and was subsequently exalted to heaven. 'Thus the quintessence of the Christian message is variously interpreted to the succeeding environments of the Christian mission. But it was essentially the same message throughout, the message of the divine salvation in Jesus of Nazareth.'[174] This is the foundation upon which the theologians of the New Testament (Paul, John and the others) built their Christologies.

Fuller grants that much of the Christology of the New Testament is functional, but he believes that Cullmann has gone too far in maintaining that all New Testament Christology is purely functional. He maintains that the Gentile mission did make ontic statements about the Redeemer. The ontic Christology of the Gentile mission gave rise to ontological problems: how can the pre-existent One and God share the same being? how can he be God and man at the same time? how can the exalted One be one with God and distinguishable from God? The answer of the Church was the doctrines of the Trinity and the incarnation. However, this answer was given in later theological development, and it would seem that Cullman is justified in his view that the New Testament does not resolve the paradox of all Christology.

The Roman Catholic study of L. Sabourin[175] testifies to the prevalence of the view that the most rewarding approach to New Testament Christology is through an examination of the titles given to Christ by the early Christians and their first theologians. This is not surprising since 'for a Semite, the name represents and embodies the man that it designates.'[176] Thus it is that to make an inventory of and to analyse the various names given to Christ in the New Testament is, by that fact, to acquire a more profound knowledge of the person of Christ. Sabourin has examined about fifty names and titles of Christ which he has divided into five categories. Commencing with a consideration of the names of Jesus (Jesus, Son of Joseph, Son of Mary, Master) and the simple messianic titles (He-Who-Comes, Christ, Prophet, etc.), he moves on to what he classifies as the communal messianic titles (Way, Truth, Life, Good Shepherd, Vine, etc.), the soteriological titles (Saviour, Servant, Lamb, etc.), and the properly christo-logical titles (Son of Man, Son of God, Lord, Logos, etc.). The very extent of the field covered involves some super-ficiality of treatment; but then, the book is not addressed to theologians.

Sabourin acknowledges his indebtedness to Taylor and Cullmann and makes clear that his book serves a different purpose from theirs, for he has written for 'a cultivated public anxious to deepen its faith and eager to learn about the Christology of the New Testament.'[177] Yet he has made a contribution by consistently setting each of the titles of Jesus in its Old Testament background. And he has underlined the fact that the names of Jesus reveal what traits of his person and activity held the attention of the primitive Christian community. These titles (as Fuller has shown) fixed the pattern which was to guide the Christology of the later ages, down to our own day, and beyond.

### 5. The Jewish Background to the New Testament

The immediate environment of nascent Christianity was not precisely the Old Testament itself but contemporary Judaism, a living and variegated religion. The histories of the religion of Israel, when they move into the epoch of later

Judaism, already document the general religious setting of primitive Christianity. However, it is well to look at it specifically here, if only to draw attention to an important area of study for a better undertanding of New Testament theology.[178]

The Jewish conception of God is based on the Old Testament, but the approach to God had become less simple and direct. It had become a concern to preserve the transcendence of God and so the divine name Yahweh was not uttered; instead God was designated by circumlocution: Heaven, the Power, the Shekinah (dwelling), and so on. This attitude would suggest too a more remote sense of the divine personality and presence. The angelology of the period, particularly prevalent in apocalyptic, also preserved the immanence of God, his presence in the world, while safeguarding his transcendence; indeed the interest in angels was a result of the feeling that God was remote. It would be wrong, however, to deduce from all this that the predominant note was one of fear before God. Judaism laid emphasis on his goodness and had deep faith in his divine mercy. Three divine attributes were singled out for special emphasis: majesty, spirituality, and holiness—though holiness is not so much an attribute as divinity itself, that which distinguishes God from creatures, his transcendence. The strict monotheism of Judaism made it intolerant of Gentile culture, which it judged to be based on polytheism, and blind to any element of good in it.

Universalism was, of course, implicit in the awareness of one God, but it co-existed with particularism: there was a relationship of peculiar intimacy between God and his people Israel. The gift of the Law, in particular, gave Israel superiority over the nations; for the Law was the condition upon which Israel had been chosen to be the people of God. *Torah* ('law') is not merely legal in its connotation but stands for teaching of a religious kind, and is not too far removed in meaning from 'revelation'. *Torah* could be applied to the Decalogue, the essential part of the whole Law, most often to the Pentateuch, and even to the whole Old Testament. Because of the necessity for accommodating or adapting the Law to changing circumstances, the 'oral Law' developed (though it was never accepted by the Sadducees). The oral law enjoyed the same authority as the written Torah and it, too, was traced back to Sinai; in practice it was authoritative tradition. The central place of the Law in Jewish life and the need for its study led to the institution of the Synagogue which encouraged the growth of personal piety, furthered Pharisaic influence, and helped to preserve the unity of Judaism. But the Law affected the life of the Jew still more directly; it ruled his whole life and demanded his complete obedience to the will of God. Observance of the Law, and especially of the oral law, inevitably led to segregation and particularism.

We can assume that Judaism was familiar, too, with the prophetic tradition. The earnestness of the prophetic tradition and the 'exquisite sensitivity' of Pharisaism can be discerned even behind the intricate rabbinical casuistry. Jewish morality had its secure foundation on the moral character and justice of God; its motivation was not only reverential fear of God but also love of him. It is true that with such emphasis on the Law, sin was conceived of as a legal transgression. Jewish family morality was immeasurably superior to anything in the contemporary world. The Temple worship had an important place in Judaism—it signified the perpetual presence of Yahweh among his people. Prayer occupied a large place in the life of the Jew who, indeed, lived in close personal communion with God. 'In summary, Judaism did impose upon its followers a standard of morality which was far above anything in the world of its times. The average Jew was by all known standards a good man and a religious man.'[179]

Messianic hope, which pervades the Old Testament, found its fullest extra-biblical development in the apocalyptic literature. In New Testament times messianism was predominantly material, temporal and national. The messianic future was termed 'days of the Messiah' (looking principally to the national restoration of the Jews), or the 'end of days' (looking rather to the universal consummation of the world). The coming of the Messiah was, in general, associated with the end of the world; the messianic kingdom was visualised in various ways. In the main, the messianic kingdom was expected at the end of days (though in some quarters a preliminary messianic reign on earth was envisaged) with the present world being transformed into the world to come. The 'kingdom of God' was the basis of messianic hope. It presupposed a moral renewal of the people—the wicked had no place in the kingdom. In popular expectation, the Messiah was a warlike figure who would establish the kingdom of God on earth. Rabbinical literature tended to stress the transcendental and superhuman qualities of the Messiah. But Judaism had no place for a suffering Messiah.

Jewish eschatological beliefs were closely linked to its messianic hopes. The establishment of the messianic kingdom will be preceded by God's judgement. Judgement is universal and based on ethical principles but especially in apocalyptic, it tended to be the judgment and destruction of Israel's enemies. The idea of Sheol, the common abode of the dead, survived; but now, for the just, it was regarded as a state of quiet repose while the wicked would be punished after judgement. Belief in the resurrection of the dead arose late in Judaism, though it was common Pharisaic belief in the first century. The thought of Judaism was influenced by the past, especially by the great Exodus-event, and memory of this past event coloured eschatological expectation also. 'The mark of Judaism of the time of Jesus was variety and change within a context of memory, anticipation, and present obedience to the Law.'[180]

In recent years the contribution that the Dead Sea Scrolls can make to a more profound and accurate understanding of the New Testament and the milieu in which it took shape has become increasingly more evident. The Qumran writings emerge ever more clearly as the writings of a thoroughly Jewish sect, deeply concerned with the proximate eschatological crisis and preparing for it by a conscious return to the past. This attitude is an accurate reflection of the mentality of Judaism as it was immediately before Christianity; hence the literature of Qumran is of great help to us in our study of primitive Christianity. Very much has been written about Qumran and its literature. Happily, we have two recent collections of articles[181] which, between them, make available, in English, most of the really noteworthy contributions that have been made in this domain.

The collection edited by Krister Stendahl consists of articles which, for the most part, have been revised and brought up to date for this edition—therefore it is a provisional synthesis of Qumran studies. The editor indicates the different perspectives which are offered for the study of the relations between Qumran and the New Testament and he situates the different contributions in relation to these perspectives. Three articles consider aspects of the relationship of Qumran to primitive Christianity, those of O. Cullmann, S. E. Johnson, and Bo Reicke. W. G. Kuhn offers three articles, on the Messiahs of Aaron and Israel, on the Lord's Supper and the Qumran communal meal and on the new light thrown by the Scrolls on temptation, sin and flesh in the New Testament. W. H. Brownlee considers John the Baptist, and K. Schubert the Sermon on the Mount in the light of the Scrolls. W. D. Davies studies Paul and R. E. Brown the Johannine writings in relation to the Scrolls. Some of these articles give the impression of having over-emphasised the resemblances between Qumran and the New Testament without taking sufficient account of the profound differences which exist. And it is not clear that the resemblances underlined are always characteristic of the Scrolls and of Christianity; they may well be explicable by reference to parallel trends.

The nine essays of Jerome Murphy-O'Connor's book[182] concentrate on the institutions, words and ideas found both in the writings of Paul and of the Essenes. It is inevitable that further research will modify some of the views put forward in these essays (and the same is true of the other volume, of course). Some suggested contacts may seem less likely, whereas other, new ones, may be discerned. At any rate, a strong case is made for the influence of Qumran on Pauline language and concepts. Two points emerge clearly, nonetheless: the originality of the Christian message and the fact that the influence of Essenism on Christianity took place in its later development rather than during its early years. We may linger over the opening essay[183] because in it Pierre Benoit lays down solid principles on which should be based any fair attempt to draw parallels or to conclude that there is real contact between the New Testament and the Qumran Scrolls.

Benoit puts forward three reflections on method. His first is a 'warning against an imprudent tendency to accept as immediate contacts from direct influence what in fact may be no more than independent manifestations of a common trend of the time.'[184] An important and necessary distinction is that between the doctrines which are truly characteristic of the Qumran sect and those which came from wider movements and were shared by other groups. This means restricting research on the relationship between Qumran and the New Testament to a narrower field than has been customary. Yet Essenism had some direct influence on Christianity. The questions are, *when*—whether at its beginning or at a later stage, and *how*—whether in essential or in secondary matters, whether through passive reception or in a more positive way.

The next methodological reflection takes up the first of these questions. 'In the measure that direct influence of Qumran on the New Testament appears to be established, it does not necessarily follow that this influence was exercised at the very beginning, so that Christianity would derive from Essenism as from its source. This influence could rather have been exercised at a later stage, and would have assisted the new movement only to express and organise itself, but would in no sense have created it.'[185] Benoit suggests that the second alternative is more often the truth. The contacts with Qumran have come not through John the Baptist and Jesus but rather through Paul, John, and even through Christians of the second generation. Thus it is that the influence of Essenism is visible not in the realm of basic inspiration but rather in the area of community organisation and theological speculation.

But if we admit, as indeed we must, that Paul and John used Essenian ideas, then we seem to say that these ideas have penetrated the entire system of Christian theology. Benoit answers this problem (it is his third 'reflection on method'): 'Firstly, the themes which are borrowed are secondary and do not form the essence of the christian message. Secondly, when they are used, they are profoundly transformed, precisely because they are put in the service of a new and original reality.'[186] In short, while the New Testament can share with Qumran certain themes and expressions, yet everything has been transformed from within and endowed with a new significance.[187]

## In Summary: The 'Gospel' of New Testament Theologians

INTRODUCTION

'For I am not ashamed of the gospel', Paul proclaimed; 'it is the power of God for salvation to everyone who has faith' (*Rom.* 1:16). It is through these words that Meinertz has explained why this gospel 'longed for' set forms, frames of words, in which to reach believers through 'channels'— channels from the one source and 'good news' embodied, Jesus himself. And it is through these words that perhaps we can attempt to survey the work of New Testament theologians as we have studied it: each in his own way 'unashamed of the gospel', of the glad tidings stirring in his own heart, has sought a framework, a means of expression, for his understanding of the meaning of that gospel. Each in his own way has understood the salvation to be found in Jesus, the power of God alive in him, and each has reflected upon the invitation to men to respond to that salvation through faith.

The gospel flowed into the 'channels' or forms of the various books of the New Testament, and it is with these in their natural groupings or individually that our theologians have been concerned. But we, in this summary of their thought, shall make out groupings according to the authors' recurrent interests and preoccupations among New Testament themes, regardless of where they may actually occur within the New Testament itself. Just as Hunter found the theology of Paul's epistles to be his gospel (the good news of salvation through Christ) 'as his mind grasped it', so shall we find the theology of the books we have studied to be that same gospel as grasped by each of our authors. And just as Meinertz found that the different New Testament records are not really contradictory because their one foundation is the personhood of Jesus, so shall we find that all the concepts of these theologians, diverse and far-ranging though they be, ultimately must and do converge in the living Christ.

'I AM NOT ASHAMED OF THE GOSPEL'

Each of the authors we have studied seems to be moved by Schnackenburg's conviction that there is cause for optimism today from a new awareness of the pure wellspring to be found in the Bible, in the New Testament, but that this optimism must be based on presenting the absolute, un-compromising demands of Jesus (which, as we shall see, come down to the 'law of love'). Let us recall again some of the ideas concerning the *aims* of New Testament theology, the purposes containing our authors' convictions. There is Weinel with his purpose of studying the 'religion of Jesus' as it developed in the early community, or Schlatter with his anti-intellectual, practical approach (to be echoed much later in Cullmann's notion of 'functional' Christology), or Grant with his major aim of providing a total view of New Testa-ment thought. There is the existentialist approach of men like Bultmann and Conzelmann, who find the concern of New Testament theology to be man's self-understanding. Or, there is the approach of *Heilsgeschichte* early outlined by Wrede and fully developed by Cullmann in his view of every New Testament event with its interpretation forming a link in the chain of salvation history, a chain of which the centre is the Christ event. Richardson takes historic Christian faith as his principle of interpretation and concentrates on the mission of Christ, presenting Jesus himself as the original theologian. Meinertz maintains that his aim is to present the contents of the New Testament 'positively'—briefly and free of problematic ramifications. He also stresses a conclusion we noted among the theologies of the Old Testament: namely, that since the New Testament is not a 'system' of Christian teaching, New Testament theology cannot be a 'system' of abstract thought and theory. Marsh expresses this through his standpoint that the New Testament, rather than being a treatise in theology, tells a story, a story with a theological commentary to convey the fullness of the Good News. It is up to the biblical theologian to draw out the truths contained in that story, and his task is similar to that of the New Testa-ment authors themselves. Kümmel presents the heart of New Testament teaching in terms of its 'chief witnesses'.

This points us towards reviewing some of the *methods*

employed by our theologians in proclaiming their 'gospel'. We recall some of the pioneers: Baur with his application of the Hegelian process to apostolic Christianity; Albertz with his endeavour to determine the *Sitz im Leben* of each writing both historically and in relation to the action of the Holy Spirit; and Lemonnyer with his thematic approach according to the stages in the disciples' understanding of Jesus' teaching. The interpretations of Bonsirven are coloured by scholastic theology, as are those of Spicq, whose intention is not to give an organic synthesis but to build up an 'almost complete dossier' of texts bringing out the ideas expressed by Jesus and the disciples. Likewise, Stauffer approaches his material systematically to produce a 'historical theology which is Christocentric'; but his system does not show the variety of theological outlooks in the New Testament and loses the sense of the creative activity of God's word. Meinertz, on the other hand, accentuates the diversity of the personages who have transmitted the New Testament message to us, and he adds that biblical theology cannot possibly embrace a 'concordance-like completeness' and must refrain from merely amassing material. He speaks of a 'requirement' for the biblical theologian: the requirement of really working through the entire New Testament and understanding it as the living Word.

One helpful way to perceive the authors' methods and intents is to survey the divisions of their material. The different topics and sections in the books are telling because they reveal various attitudes towards the gospel, towards the message of Jesus—but also because they reveal how the same patterns and concepts cannot help being repeated by the different authors simply because they are working with the one body of the New Testament. We have those who divide their works according to historical development: the basic synoptic—Pauline—Johannine division (such a Lemonnyer or Meinertz); the Fact of Christ, the first preachers of the Fact, the interpreters of the Fact (Hunter); the message of Jesus and Kerygma, the theology of Paul, the theology of John, the development towards the ancient church (Bultmann); the proclamation of Jesus, the faith of the primitive community, the theology of Paul, the Christ-message of the

Fourth Gospel (Kümmel). We have the tracing of New Testament theology from kerygma to *paradosis* (Grech), or the following of basic Marcan themes throughout the New Testament (Marsh), or the following of the 'Way of the Son of Man'—the 'doxological', the 'antagonistic' and the 'soteriological' (Stauffer). Stauffer also arranges his material according to themes, as does Richardson, while Conzelmann develops his historically around the kerygma. Those whose works are more specialised divide their works accordingly: Schnackenburg with the different moral demands of the New Testament, Cullmann with the relationship between eschatology and salvation history or the titles of Christ in his work on Christology, and Taylor with his two-fold division of the exegetical and the theological.

Most of our authors give at least some consideration to the role of the Old Testament, in particular to Jewish background and the 'Old Law', in their treatments of New Testament theology. (It is interesting that of course the Old Testament theologians, by contrast, had to devote more of their works to showing how the Old Testament is 'fulfilled' in the New Testament.) Manson looks to an Old Testament background for Hebrew ethics: the call to the 'imitation' of God, the foundation of 'Law, worship, and the imparting of kindnesses'. For Marsh, the Old Testament, and in particular the Exodus event, is the basic instrument for interpreting the New Testament, and Stauffer finds both the Old Testament and apocalyptic literature important antecedents of the New Testament. Meinertz, by contrast, feeling that the old covenant is not that important because it has been taken into the new preaching, has undervalued Old Testament influence.

In this our survey, we cannot hope to give an 'almost complete dossier' of the points of concentration to which the authors have been led by their different approaches. But we can touch upon some of the themes on which they converge to proclaim their 'gospel'—the contexts in which they feel the message of salvation is set. As theologians speaking to a Christian community they are interested in the role and meaning of the *Church*. For Grant, it was the experience and growing institutions of the Church which gave rise to early

17

Christian thought, and religious instruction was not an 'institutionalised' development but was present from the first. Bultmann sees this as 'retrogressive': the preaching of the word has given way to a juridical order, pure faith has been sacrificed to a search for knowledge and to the controls of authority. Conzelmann corrects this view by describing the Church not as a retrogressive transition to 'early Catholicism', but as a new stage of reflection handing down truths of the faith. Richardson, preoccupied with the mission of the Church, stresses its actual bodily existence. Its ministry is still the ministry of Christ in the service, *diakonia,* of the world—a service to be rendered in his own humble and lowly spirit. Stauffer, discussing the Church and the world, makes the important point that the Church's danger and temptation is its own self-edification rather than God's—a placing ecclesiology over Christology, dogmatics over the divine love. And Grech, picking up the idea of service, saw that Jesus founded his *qahal,* his *ekklēsia,* that it might be simply a vehicle of his kingdom; and Jeremias points out that in Jesus' eyes, the law of the kingdom is that the reign of God comes through suffering.

Intimately connected with the role of the Church is that of the *kerygma* and its theological interpretation. For Bultmann, the kerygma, the proclamation of Jesus, of the early Church is the starting point of theology because upon it Christian faith is based. Sceptical of the historical worth of the Synoptics, he constructs a 'Hellenistic Kerygma' instead; and although we may not agree with the extent to which he carries his tenets, yet he has had the powerful insight that the gospel is always kerygma, always a challenging proclamation. Hunter finds that the unity of the New Testament is achieved by the pattern of kerygma running through it. Grech's whole work is organised around the basic headings of the kerygma and traces its growth into fixed traditions. And he too brings out the vital truth that the law guiding this growth was the necessity for adaptation and re-interpretation according to new situations. The kerygma is really the proclamation of the *kingdom* which Jesus has brought. The kingdom is the society of men possessing divine sonship in Jesus, preserved by strife in this life and looking towards triumph in the next (Bonsirven). It is present in Jesus, the Father is its king; it is a new Israel involving both rebirth and the cross, and it is yet to be fulfilled (Hunter). The future and present aspect of salvation so much stressed by Kümmel is nothing other than the kingdom of God which Jesus preached. The kingdom is the eschatological reality given to the Church, the fundamental concept in the New Testament (Richardson); different aspects of the kingdom are emphasised in the Synoptics, but all agree that Jesus proclaimed its imminence from the beginning (Stanley and Brown). And John transfers the centre of interest from the kingdom to the person of Jesus himself (Vawter).

The kingdom, and in particular its 'unfulfilled' nature, leads us to consider a striking convergent theme in our theologies, a final one to be looked at in this part of our summary of the authors' basic view on the 'gospel'. This theme is that of *eschatology,* both 'future' and 'realised', and the accompanying 'tension' contained in it. Grant finds the whole of the New Testament oriented eschatologically; for Schnackenburg, the thought of the Parousia was a stimulus to the faithful, while eschatological awareness can lead to responsible action in the world. Bultmann's emphasis on 'decision' derives from his seeing Jesus' message as eschatological—characterised by the certainty of the inbreak of God's reign. This does not mean that the world ends, but that God places man 'at the brink of the end' by tearing from him all human security and confronting him as a 'God at hand'. For Richardson, all eschatology is realised in the sacramental life of the Church; for Vawter, 'realised eschatology' grew out of the Church's awareness of the presence of the Holy Spirit. Further, we cannot help but note that our authors repeat the idea of the 'tension' in eschatology, the time of waiting until the Parousia and the fullness of the kingdom. For Schnackenburg, it is a time of 'watching'; for Bultmann, this tension of 'betweenness' gives place to a sacramental regime and a new legalism, and problems in Christian living arise because of the paradoxical situation between the 'no longer' and the 'not yet'—or the 'even now' and the 'not yet', as Richardson calls it. For Cullmann, the new element in Jesus' eschatology is that in him the kingdom is 'already fulfilled', yet 'not yet completed', a fact uniting all the books of the New Testament beyond their individual differences. Paul's whole theology is dominated by the 'tension' of salvation history, while John's placing the historical life of Jesus at the mid-point of history relaxes this 'tension'. Kümmel sees that the twofold aspect of salvation, as present and as future, is central to the New Testament message.

A beautiful and simple definition of New Testament eschatology is offered by Stanley and Brown: the Jesus who has and shall come is not only the victorious Saviour, but also the familiar friend known from the gospel record of his earthly life of humility and suffering. And Stauffer presents eschatology in the light of *hope*: though the New Testament does contain the idea of 'eternal punishment', yet the early Church held out the hope that God's mercy and power would overcome even the final 'no' of this world. This is the same hope, 'faith's nevertheless' (to borrow one of Eichrodt's phrases), expressed in Psalm 73:23: 'Nevertheless, I am continually with thee. Thou dost hold my right hand.' It is the same hope Jesus gives us in his assurance, 'Take heart! I *have* overcome the world.' (*John* 16:33). And so, having surveyed the various attitudes towards the gospel which are ancillary to the Good News himself, we turn now to this One who has 'overcome'—the One who is the real focal point of all New Testament theology.

THE POWER OF GOD FOR SALVATION

Jesus—the bringer of salvation, 'Saviour'. The title is rare in the New Testament; but just as, according to Cullmann, the early Church was filled implicitly with the idea that Jesus *is* the Saviour, so may we centre this part of our summary about the implicit foundation of all our theologies: that this Gospel, this Good News, is the Saviour—the 'power of God for salvation'. We cannot possibly, of course, do justice to all the ideas about Jesus in these works; but, once again we can look at some recurrent themes and points of convergence. Taking 'salvation' itself, Hunter finds this to be the epitome of Paul's gospel—salvation as a present experience pointing to the Saviour with whom we are in communion. For Bultmann, the salvation occurrence, originating in

God's grace alone, is the death and resurrection of Jesus— not an 'instruction in faith', but a present challenge continuing to take place in the proclaming of the word. We recall the wise perception of Richardson that redemption or salvation is beyond all theorising because it is a deep mystery. Or there is Fuller's thesis that the divine salvation in Jesus of Nazareth is essentially the same message throughout the different stages in New Testament Christology: the foundation of all theological thought in the New Testament is the proclamation and activity of Jesus which confront men and women with the *saving* presence of God. And what could be a more all-embracing view of the meaning of salvation than Stauffer's teaching that the coming of Christ, this 'forensically' new situation, means the message of God's *peace* for man? For Kümmel it is God's condescension towards lost and sinful men shown in Jesus Christ that has brought about the presence of future salvation. God comes in Christ to men lost in this world in order to set them free and turn them into loving men. And Jeremias shows that Jesus' whole message becomes a single summons to accept the offer of salvation.

This leads us then to the place of Christology in our theologies—which are all, at root, christologically orientated, though but a few are classified as such. Among the latter are Cullmann with his understanding of 'functional' Christology as a redemptive history centred on the earthly life of Jesus and fulfilled in his 'subjection to the Father'; Taylor, with his finding the key to the gospel presentation of Jesus in his own self-consciousness of divine sonship; and Fuller, with his defining Christology as the Church's response to its total encounter with Jesus. Christology has been included in the other works. In the early days, Stevens touched upon it with his noting the 'distinctive originality of Jesus'; Grant found that Christ, and devotion to him, was always theologically conditioned in the New Testament; Conzelmann claimed that *all* Jesus' teaching was stamped with an indirect Christology which became the direct Christology of the community's faith. He also, in the existentialist approach, claimed that to know Christ is *not* to define his nature, but to understand who he is for 'me' now—that is, man comes to know himself by 'conversation' with the revealer, and this constitutes 'revelation'. Fitzmyer understands Pauline theology as christo-centric and functional. 'Christ crucified' means Christ as significant for men, and growth in Christ refers the Christian to the Father through him. Meinertz centred his whole work on Christ because, as he said of John, he realised that 'on-going Christendom depended on the recognition of this Person'. And Kümmel maintains that we can really grasp the salvation-message of the New Testament only if we seriously regard the coming of Jesus as God's eschatological deed.

When we break it down, we find that Christology must be concerned with the events and meaning of Jesus' life. Hence, the theme of the *incarnation* is a recurrent one in our theologies. By becoming man, Jesus proclaimed that he came as one who serves—and this is the basic Christian ethic (Manson). This same ethic is marked by Jesus' realistic atti-tude towards the world and its conditions because he, too, has been man in our midst (Schnackenburg). The incarnation must necessarily be a veiling as well as a revealing of the light (Richardson). The Gospels are simply a presentation of the Way laid out for the Son of Man (Stauffer); John views the incarnation as both revelation and stumbling block—the world can either believe and enter into its fullness, or not believe and be merely 'the world' in a negative sense (Conzel-mann). And the incarnation is not a 'dogma' but the very core of salvation (Vawter).

The incarnation necessarily involves one of the most poig-nant themes of New Testament theology—that known as its paradox or 'scandal', the mystery of Jesus as both God and man. The Johannine word-made-flesh is the 'offence'; the revealer comes as a man who cannot and must not prove to the world his claim to be the Son of God. This 'offence' must be overcome by accepting Jesus in faith (Bultmann). The bold grandeur of the Son of Man is that, while he is still the afflicted one identified with every man, the earthly person with 'nowhere to lay his head' and about to suffer, he is also the same Son of Man to be seated at God's right hand (Richardson). The paradox of the incarnate Christ, the life-bringer, is that he must tread the earthly road of distress to conquer that distress, he must assume human life to deliver humanity, and he must suffer in order to be raised from suffering into glory (Stauffer). The man Jesus is decisively important for Paul's theology; the decisive message of John is that God in Christ has set men free from the domination of the world of sin and death (Kümmel). Finally, the enduring 'scandal' of Christianity is that the total 'other-ness' which alone can save man is *God* as he has revealed himself historically in the *man* Jesus (Vawter)—a truth parallel to that of some form of *Kenosis* being essential to any doctrine of the incarnation (Taylor).

And so, we notice that emphasis on the *cross* must occur throughout New Testament theology—simply because it is the heart of the New Testament. For Hunter, the kingdom of God had to involve the cross, just as the cross was a central fact for the early Church. Stauffer, following the Old Testament idea of God's power to make clean and whole, finds that though sin and anguish and death *are* still in the world, the question of 'guilt' *has* been solved—by the cross. Paul, Conzelmann notes, understood his ministry through his own personal, humanly painful experiences; and so, for him 'preaching' meant 'the word of the cross': by experiencing the dying of Christ, the apostle communicates Christ's *life* to the community through the effects of his preaching. Or, we may recall a similar necessary emphasis on the resurrection—understood not as a return to earthly life but as a resurrection to *doxa* (Jeremias): Büchsel saw the resurrection as a new revelation in the history of God's word; Richardson found the resurrection—ascension to mean final victory over evil, and the joyful meeting of the early Christians to break bread together was the strongest evidence for the certainty of the resurrection. Conzelmann, simply but forcefully, defines the resurrection as 'God's interpretation of the cross.' Or, finally, we may pause to look at words concerning one fruit of the resurrection—ascension: Jesus' sending of the *Holy Spirit*. The Spirit's activity shapes the *Sitz im Leben* of New Testament writings (Albertz); in John, the Spirit comes to complete God's presence rather than to supply for his absence (Hunter). The person of the Holy Spirit as one with the person of Jesus is quite a natural biblical concept because, according to the biblical view, 'personalities' are not hard, distinct and impermeable, but flow into one another (Richardson). Jesus promised the Spirit because he had much to say that his disciples could not yet bear or comprehend (cf. *John* 16: 12); to confess that Jesus *has* come in the flesh is to receive the Spirit of truth (Stauffer). For Paul the presence of salvation is manifest in the fact that the risen Christ is present, through his Spirit, in his community, and rules the life of the Christian (Kümmel).

Finally, among those interests in Jesus himself shared by New Testament theologians, we may mention their preoccupation with the *titles* by which he is known. The titles and their usage in the New Testament writings remain constant, but different authors have stressed different aspects of them; ('Son of Man' is the only title used by Jesus of himself —Jeremias). During the period of 'primitive Christianity' when the disciples grew in their grasp of Jesus' teaching, they expressed their faith by means of the titles they conferred on him, according to Bonsirven. For Richardson, likewise, titles reveal the Christology of the Apostolic Church: Son of God, *Kyrios*, Wisdom of God, Word of God—all developed through a three-fold stage of understanding Jesus as Prophet, as Messiah-Servant, and as Wisdom-Word. Stanley and Brown make the point that the titles given to Christ are concerned with his 'function' in regard to men—*pro nobis*. Cullmann too discusses the different titles as 'functional'— with special emphasis, as shared by the other theologians, on 'Son of Man' implying both glory and humiliation and on 'Lord', *Kyrios*, implying that Jesus is a living reality here and now. Of course, it is the work of Sabourin, with his treatment of some fifty names and titles, which is the most comprehensive approach to this Semitic notion of the 'name embodying the man'. For him, the names of Jesus reveal just what traits of his person and activity held the attention of the early Christian community and provided a pattern down through the ages.

## TO EVERYONE WHO HAS FAITH

We have seen the theologians' different methods and standpoints on the gospel; we have seen their varying understandings of Jesus. But, this 'power of salvation' calls for a response from man, a response embodied in the word 'faith' and its effects. And so, in this part of our summary, we include those themes in the theologies which treat of the role of Christians themselves in relation to the gospel—its call to them and their answer. We may start in a negative fashion by noting how often the 'downfall' of man is seen to be his own efforts to 'stand alone', his own *'self-reliance'*. According to Schnack-enburg, the 'radical moral obligation' of the Sermon on the Mount is an 'impossible ethic' indeed—but *only* if viewed from a human standpoint, since 'with God, nothing will be impossible' (cf. *Luke* 1 : 37). Bultmann groups together Paul's concepts of 'flesh', 'sin' and the 'world' as the single evil of 'self-reliance', a striving to procure salvation by one's own strength or by works of the law. Stauffer notes that, while not teaching 'original sin', the New Testament does teach the tragedy of man's having to sin—sin being his own 'self-glorification'. Yet, the New Testament holds out salvation beyond this: even though the 'devil' is the power in God's world who always wills evil, he always effects good (cf. *Gen.* 50 : 20, where Joseph tells his brothers, 'As for you, *you* meant evil against me; but *God* meant it for good . . .'). In reacting to the gospel, says Grech, the legalistic minded were scandalised by the cross, whereas the self-satisfied felt no need of a redeemer—there was 'no room in their inns'. And, in Conzelmann's view of Pauline theology, the value of suffering, of sharing in the cross of Jesus, is that it shatters the 'props of self-assertion'.

Turning to a more hopeful note, the very opposite of 'self-reliance', we may observe the recurrent interest among the theologians in the two Pauline themes of *'the body of Christ'* and *'in Christ Jesus'*. In passing, we may pause to recollect the observation of how the 'Damascene revelation' utterly transformed Paul: it was his 'initiation into the mystical life', impelling him to bring out the whole meaning of Christ (Bonsirven). It was a moment of revelation affecting utterly every other aspect of Paul's background (Fitzmyer); it fostered his complete dedication to Jesus and his longing to spend himself for him, a dedication so great that it gave his message a forcefulness and a freedom far beyond 'analysis' (Meinertz). And so, it was through this transforming experience that the great theological concepts of Paul were born, concepts—rather, living realities—such as the 'body of Christ'. The 'body of Christ', the first aspect of the Christ-Church relationship, signifies his identification with the whole body of Christians (Bonsirven). It is the sphere of his rule in which the baptised live together (Conzelmann); it is the presence of eschatological salvation (Kümmel); it is a union implying one flesh, and this union is not so much corporate as corporeal (Fitzmyer). Above all, the phrase is simply Paul's way of indicating theologically the organic unity bestowed by Jesus' living and moving amidst his own (Marsh).

Turning to the phrase, 'in Christ Jesus', we are struck by the way in which almost all our theologians have been moved towards an interpretation of it. For Bonsirven, it is the second great aspect of the Christ-Church relationship; as the principle of a Christian's life, it means Christ as the medium of divine grace, Christ as the effect of his grace, and Christ as embraced by the very name 'Christian'. Hunter describes the 'salvation' theme in Paul's 'gospel' as communion in Christ: to 'be *with* Christ' is the heart of all Christian hope (cf. Jesus' choice of the disciples 'to be with him', *Mark* 3 : 14). 'In Christ' (or, as John would express it, 'in me') means participation in the newly created community of the end time, according to Richardson. According to Conzelmann, 'in Christ' refers to the salvation brought by him and is the objective foundation of Christian living. For Grech, it means that all that happened to Jesus happens also to those who are one with him through baptism; for Fitzmyer, *en Christō* is simply the symbiosis of Christ and Christian. Meinertz could sum up his whole understanding of Paul by saying that the apostle, while being the most influential figure in early Christianity, was always conscious of being but 'one sent'—*apostolos*—of doing everything 'in the power of Christ'. 'I worked harder than any of them, though it was not I but the grace of God which is with me' (1 *Cor.* 15 : 10). And the phrase *en Christō* can also remind us of the use of the term *koinōnia*—'fellowship' or 'communion'; *koinōnia* in the community inherits the 'imparting of kindnesses' of the old covenant (Manson); it is participation in the messianic blessings of the Spirit, and its bond is the Eucharist (Grech).

The Eucharist does not depend on a rigid formula or historical datum (Grant). The Last Supper is a prophetic acted sign of our share in the kingdom and, as a sacrament, epitomises the Johannine teaching that, because the Word became flesh, material things may become vehicles of spiritual truths (Hunter). The 'breaking of bread' and the prayers of the new community inherit the worship of the Old Israel (Manson); it is salvation 'tasted afresh' (Conzelmann). Bultmann, by contrast, would seem to neglect the reality of union with Christ in the Eucharist in his stress on the pure 'decision of faith', his view of the sacramental regime as being 'retrogressive'. Richardson takes the opposite point of view: the greatest testimony of faith, of the certainty that Christ *has* risen, is the joyful meeting of Christians to break the eucharistic bread together. And he concludes his whole work with the comforting thought that, for all that is written and pondered over in words, the *real* 'introduction to New Testament theology' is a receiving of *the* Word himself, a sharing in the 'living tradition of the Church's eucharistic worship week by week and day by day'.

This leads us to look again at *Christian living* briefly and to note the recurrent emphasis on the one principle of love, *agapē,* guiding that living. We have seen the various works entirely devoted to the ethical teaching, the moral theology, of the New Testament. We may recall from them Schnackenburg's finding the whole meaning of Christ's call 'Follow me' to be in accepting the conditions of *his* life, sharing in *his* destiny. We have seen Grant's helpful conclusion that the great new contribution of Jesus to Jewish ethics was to 'lay bare the inner motive behind the outer deed'—and thus that the New Testament is concerned with the right *spirit* rather than with legalistic details of application (a conclusion which fits in well with the idea of the necessity for adaptation of Jesus' original teachings and the kerygma according to the changing situations of a living community). We have seen Fitzymer's words that Christian living makes demands and that, because he is a new creature in Jesus, the Christian can no longer live a life limited by an earthly horizon. The very title 'Christian', as Meinertz says, means that what Jesus proclaimed is inseparable from his person.

Hence, the real guide for Christian living, the one 'law

of Christ', is *love*. Love is the 'new Torah' (Hunter); it yields
the 'liberty of the children of God'—which means 'not freedom *from*, but freedom *for*' (Spicq)—a freedom which, in
James, is equated with the demand, the love-obligation, of
the gospel (Schnackenburg). For the sake of love, the Christian can act against the 'letter' of precepts and cannot be
deprived of this decision by any authority (Conzelmann); in
John, active love for the brethren is seen to be a proof of
communion with Christ and God (Schnackenburg). Jesus'
call to 'decision' means precisely to live wholly in God's demand for *love* (Bultmann). The characteristic of Jesus' own
ethic is the love which means total self-giving. The sermon
on the Mount teaches that Christians are bound to this love,
rather than being tied down to any written code, and that
they need not fear the demands of total self-giving: Jesus is
there—here—to lead the way for all who will follow him,
and he himself gives the strength to walk in that way
(Manson). Finally, as in John, love is connected with *faith*—
since faith is the assent to God's revelation of Love himself
in Jesus (Vawter).

And so, we are brought back to our beginning: the gospel
is 'the power of salvation to him who has *faith*'. Together
with love, *this* is the Christian response, and this shall be
our final 'discovery' in this summary of our authors' themes.
Faith includes the trust whose liberating effect is poverty
(Bonsirven). Indeed, it is man's acknowledgement of his utter
poverty before his Maker, and Paul's concept of 'justification
by faith' means a reliance upon God rather than upon oneself (Grech). Repentance, too, is trust, putting one's trust
in the heavenly Father, coming back to his home and his
love; it is learning to say *Abba* again (Jeremias). For Richardson, to be *en Christō* signifies a faith relationship rather than
any mystical absorption. We have spoken of the grandeur
of Bultmann's conception of faith, its refusal of all human
security: believing means primarily obedience, the surrender
of man's own will in trust, hope, and even the piercing fear
of the loss of God's hand; believing is the means of overcoming the 'offence' and, as 'desecularisation', leads beyond
human standards into the eschatological realm. Ultimately,
for Bultmann, faith—knowing faith—means simply accept-

ing the life that Jesus gives. An equally inspiring description of faith is Vawter's in relation to John: faith sets man free from his own helplessness by bringing him into contact with the only 'other-ness' which can save him, the 'other-ness' of God's historical revelation in Jesus. Or, finally, Stauffer's view seems to reach to the very core of Christian faith: it is the 'assertion of a possibility against all probabilities', in the midst of very real and hard life experience. And 'such a faith has nothing else than Jesus Christ in the middle of a world which scoffs at all our hopes and fears'.

## CHAPTER III

# The Theology of the Bible

BY now we have a reasonably comprehensive view of the work done in the fields of Old Testament theology and of New Testament theology. It might appear that our procedure in this chapter would be firmly determined by what has gone before—that we would give rather full summaries of the important theologies of the Bible. Unfortunately, this cannot be, and for a sufficiently good reason: there are practically no theologies of the whole Bible. This state of affairs is significant and is not wholly explained by the fact that scholars tend to specialise in one Testament or the other. It would seem, rather, that the complex relationship between the Testaments has not been satisfactorily worked out. There can be no doubt, however, that the relationship exists and all Christian scholars agree that the Bible, in one way or another, forms a unit. We must look at this unity and note the links that bind the Testaments. Again, it is a fact that the Old Testament is part of the sacred scripture of the Christian Church; this means that the Old Testament is read in a Christian context. We need to enquire how it is subject to Christian interpretation; this will lead us to a study of the theory and practice of Christian interpretation of the Old Testament. At the same time, we must surely recognise that the Scripture of Israel has abiding values of its own.

## 1. The Unity of the Bible

The work of H. H. Rowley on the unity of the Bible[1] is concerned, in the main, with the unity within the Old Testament. One of his six chapters, the fourth, does, in a special way, treat effectively of the unity of the Testaments;

we may deal with the preceding chapters briefly. He begins by insisting that any unity to be found in the Bible is unity in the midst of diversity. Indeed, that diversity is obvious enough. It is the unity that needs to be sought out. The kind of unity that is discerned is a dynamic unity which recognises development and, in particular, development from the Old Testament to the New Testament. It follows from the nature of the Bible as God's revelation that if God reveals himself there should be some unity about the revelation. And there is room for diversity too: God chose to reveal himself not only to men but through men and thus he was limited by the medium that he choose. The Old Testament looks beyond itself to a fulfilment that lay in the future; the single hypothesis that the finger of God is to be found in expectation and in fulfilment is an adequate explanation, and there is no other single explanation. The unity of the Bible is like that within a man's personality, the unity of a process of development; it is the unity of the divine revelation given in a context of history and through the medium of human personality. The dynamic unity of the Bible leaves neither God nor reason out of account.

Rowley finds a correspondence between the Old Testament and the New Testament but is careful to point out that this is quite different from a typology which would find in the Old Testament a prefiguring of the New. He finds that there is a continuing thread and a process of development leading from one Testament to the other and so it is not surprising that there should be recurring patterns. Hence diversity and dynamic unity must be perceived together— as well as a continuing thread (election) that runs through the Bible. The Book finds its unity in something of enduring significance which has meaning for us.

Recent study has considerably softened the once sharply maintained antithesis between prophet and priest. Today it is clear that the pre-exilic prophets denounced not cult and sacrifices but sacrifices which were hollow and ineffective, while the Law, in prescribing sacrifices, yet presented sacrifice as secondary to obedience and to rightness of spirit. The Old Testament does not teach that sacrifice is valid without relation to the heart and dispositions of man and it nowhere teaches that sacrifice is of universal validity. The ethical religion found in both Law and Prophets is a significant bond of unity in diversity. And it is remarkable that the deepest word on sacrifice in the Old Testament, the sacrifice of the Suffering Servant that transcends any in the Law, stands in the most spiritual of the prophets.

While the unity of the Bible is a unity of growth, it does not mean that we always begin with primitive ideas which become more sophisticated. Certainly this is not true in the Bible's teaching about God and man. There is a developing richness of meaning, of course, but the idea of God and man taken for granted in the New Testament is that which is characteristic of the Old Testament. The most significant things learned about God's character spring from Israel's Exodus experience of God and in this we encounter a fundamental biblical factor. Peculiar to Israel is the idea of a God who reveals himself in history and experience. This does not imply first history and then interpretation; the pattern is: first the prophetic announcement of the fact of history, then the fulfilment and finally the interpretation of the event. But what is of prime interest here is the fundamental, dynamic unity in the thought of God that runs through the Bible. The real bond of unity between the Testaments is not to be found in the repetition of the message of the Old in the New, but in manifest threads running through and uniting the whole. Paradoxically, the most significant bond of unity is found not in the continuity of development but in the basic differences between the Testaments.[2]

This brings Rowley to his key fourth chapter, 'The fulfilment of Promise'. We have noticed that the bond between the Testaments is consistent with wide differences between them; the special bond forged by promise and fulfilment unites the Testaments in the very act of distinguishing most clearly between them. Though there is much in the Old which no longer belongs to the New, yet they belong indivisibly together; the New Testament cannot be understood without the Old and neither can the Old Testament be fully understood without the New. The link emerges more clearly when we compare both post-biblical Judaism and the New Testament with the Old Testament. Judaism is a development from the religion of the Old Testament and is unintelligible without the Old Testament but the Old Testament is not unintelligible without post-biblical Judaism. The Old Testament continually looks forward to something beyond itself and this expectation and the promise set forth in it is not fulfilled in post-biblical Judaism, which is a development out of the Old Testament and not a response to its hopes. The Old Testament hope of the Golden Age, in which people of every age should worship Israel's God, follow his Law and acknowledge his kingdom with its Davidic leader, is in no sense realised in Judaism. Nor does the latter observe the law of Moses since, for nineteen centuries, Judaism has not known animal sacrifice, or any sacrifice, and this suspension of sacrifice is not by divine revelation but by sheer force of circumstances. 'Not in any spirit of hostility or of controversy, but as a simple statement of fact it must be observed that with all its cherishing of the high ethical values of the Old Testament post-biblical Judaism is an interlude that neither continues to obey the law of Moses, nor yet offers in itself the fulfilment of the hopes which the Old Testament holds before men. It is an interlude that is worthy of high respect and marked by a noble spirit which calls for deep admiration. Nevertheless it is an interlude, in which the sacrificial element that is of such importance in the thought and teaching of the Old Testament is suspended, and Israel's task to win the world to the worship of her God is also suspended.'[3]

When we turn from Judaism to the New Testament and the Christian Church we find how different is the relation to the Old Testament. We discover in the New Testament a new revelation, but it is from the same God and the basis of revelation is still the same. The new revelation, like the former, is given in a combination of personal and impersonal factors; it is given in a person and yet is guaranteed by historical events. In other words, we find here too that unique quality of biblical revelation: the structure of the combination of mediation through history with mediation through prophetic personality. Again Rowley insists that, in finding the same pattern of revelation in the New Testament and in the Old Testament, he is not resorting to typology.

Rather, he finds the signature of God in the common pattern of revelation in personal and impersonal factors. But when we speak of similar patterns we must recognise that in the New Testament the pattern is on a new level or in terms of new conditions and carries a new message.

We have seen that the deepest word on sacrifice in the Old Testament speaks of no Temple sacrifice but of the death of the Servant of the Lord. It is clear that Jesus thought of his own death in terms of the death of the Servant and his followers came to realise that with his death all other sacrifice was superseded. In this we have the fulfilment of something that was promised in the Old Testament, for 'of no other than Christ can the terms of the fourth Servant Song [Is 53] be predicated with even remote relevance.'[4] Promise and fulfilment bind the Testaments together. At the same time, the contrast with post-biblical Judaism is sharp: the Christian Church suspended sacrifice not by force of circumstances but because the sacrifice of Christ, which corresponded to one promised in the Old Testament, transcended in significance and effect all other sacrifices and was valid for all men. No other sacrifice was needed. 'The one suspension had no relation to the Old Testament and none to the revealed will of God; the other is closely knit to the promise of the Old Testament and rests on a new revelation of God.'[5]

The investigation of promise and fulfilment is then pursued in terms of the themes of kingdom and remnant. It is seen that other Old Testament streams of thought run to Christ and to his Church; those that do not run to him run nowhere. In short, the New Testament not only springs out of the Old Testament but responds to its faith and promise. While neither Testament can be explained from the other alone, both find their sufficient explanation if the hand of God is in both. But if reference has been made to a common texture in the revelation of both Testaments, there has been no resort to typology, no suggestion that the purpose of the former revelation was to prepare the way for the other. 'From both the community of pattern and the interlocking we may reasonably conclude that there is a profound and important unity running through both Testaments and that it is the unity of the thread of the revelation of the one

God.'[6] The concluding chapters, 'The Cross' and 'The Christian Sacraments', do not really carry the main point of the book's theme, the unity of the Bible, very much further. They serve to highlight some of the correspondences which bind the Old and New Testaments together and they help to illustrate the fundamental conception of the nature of religion which is common to the whole Bible.

While scholars have turned out their theologies of the Old Testament and theologies of the New Testament, the factor of the unity of the two Testaments has tended to remain at the theoretical level. However, the American scholar Millar Burrows has moved beyond theory and has written a work which presents the theology of the Bible as a whole.[7] He is careful to point out that his use of the term 'biblical theology' does not imply a complete, logically articulated system of doctrine derived from the Bible; indeed, the term could not have such a meaning since the religion of the Bible is not something finished and static but is a living historical movement. One's point of view in interpreting it must be historical. This means not only distinguishing earlier from later stages and tracing developments but also studying religion in connection with the life and culture of the people. When one recognises the great diversity within the Old Testament and the New Testament it might seem appropriate to speak of the religions of the Bible; yet there is an underlying unity which is both historical and theological. 'With full recognition of the differences within the Bible, biblical theology may judge everything by its relation to the truth as it is in Christ.'[8] The practical purpose of his study demands a topical order of treatment but each topic will be considered in its chronological development and with reference to the historical background.

A preliminary chapter faces the problem of the authority of the Bible and its revelatory value. It is clear that in the Bible itself authority is a matter more of what must be done than of what must be believed; the first question is always, What must I do? God's will is paramount and the authority of the Bible depends upon the reality of its inspiration. As a Protestant, Burrows cannot accept the Roman Catholic position that the testimony of the Church is the sufficient

and final guarantee of the inspiration of the Bible; he falls
back on the inherent truth and value of what is revealed.
'The only ultimate basis of assurance is the witness of the
Spirit with the believer's own spirit . . . This does not mean
that the individual may interpret the Bible as he pleases
and claim divine authority for his interpretation. The meaning of the Bible is what its writers meant by it and that is a
question for objective exegesis.'[9] The Bible is the word of
God in the sense that it contains the record of a long series
of authentic and supremely important revelations, each to be
understood, evaluated and applied on its own merits. The
Bible can be a reliable guide only when it is rightly used
and interpreted in the light of the central revelation in
Christ.

Most modern scholars agree that the Yahwism of Moses
was still henotheistic or monolatrous; the final emergence
of monotheism is probably the result of the prophetic interpretation of history. The biblical conception of God is
always strongly personal. Any idea of God that makes him
anything other than a distinct and real person is a radical
departure from biblical thought. In addition to the idea of
the Spirit, the Old Testament and Jewish sources use also
other concepts to express the presence and operation of God
in the world; for the New Testament and later Christianity
these are important chiefly because they afforded means for
expressing christological ideas and finally the doctrine of the
Trinity. For its part, though the New Testament has all the
elements of this doctrine, it has no statement of it. Burrows
puts forward an interesting reinterpretation of the Trinity.
God is made known in three ways: he reveals himself in
nature, in history and in the experience of individuals. The
God revealed in nature is the Father, the Maker of heaven
and earth; the God revealed in history is the Son, the eternal
Logos, speaking by the prophets and incarnate in Christ; the
God known in personal experience is the Holy Spirit. By
these three channels of nature, history and inner experience
we learn of God, and by faith we combine what is revealed
to us in these three ways as all coming from and pertaining
to the one God. 'The distinction of Persons is true only for
our knowledge of God, not for his inner Being, which we
cannot know.'[10]

While the idea of Jesus as prophet is much more true to his own purpose and much more fruitful for the Christian life than the conception of him as lawgiver, the truth of the latter idea must not be forgotten—to follow Jesus in love for God and man does fulfil all that was good in the law of Moses. The Gospels indicate that Jesus saw in the figure of the Servant a picture of himself and his mission and, indeed, the identification of Jesus with the Suffering Servant is constant in the New Testament. It seems clear that Jesus called himself the Son of Man, that he also spoke of the coming apocalyptic Son of Man and therefore that he identified himself with the apocalyptic Son of Man. Yet, no designation of Jesus comes nearer to including the whole meaning of New Testament Christology than 'Son of God'. For Paul this is basic and it is for him something entirely different from the Old Testament conception of the king as God's son. The title 'Lord', again especially for Paul, came to express the very essence of faith in Christ. John's idea of the Logos is a metaphysical or substantial rather than a personal concept and metaphysical, substantial concepts are sometimes suggested by Paul's language. However, for both Paul and John the personal point of view is clearly primary. This follows from their common Jewish background and their knowledge of the person, Jesus; their use of substantial concepts is 'hardly more than a pedagogical point of contact in presenting the gospel to people of Greek background and way of thinking.'[11] Though by the end of the New Testament period the process of the deification of Jesus had gone far, the New Testament never quite puts Christ in the place of God. Yet, the basic experience was that in and through Jesus the disciples were somehow dealing with God himself.

The revelation preserved in both Testaments is necessarily presented in terms of a prescientific, mythological world-view. Burrows is careful to explain what he means. The sense in which he speaks of the Hebrew and early Christian world-view as mythological 'involves the personal, even anthropomorphic element, treating as the act of a personal being or beings what a scientific world-view sees as the operations of impersonal forces or laws. . . . Much of the ancient Hebrew and early Christian thought is obviously mythological in this sense. The mythological element must be distinguished and eliminated before we can accept whatever spiritual truth may be hidden behind it.'[12] In general, the cosmography of both Testaments remained popular and for most of the practical purposes of religion, the geometric, anthropocentric point of view of the Bible is still adequate. Post-biblical sources (including the Apocrypha) show an exuberant growth in angelology; though Jesus apparently accepted the current beliefs, he made little use of them. On the whole, it seems best to regard the idea of such divine messengers as a part of the ancient mythological framework of biblical religion which we have discarded. The same applies to demons. 'Used frankly as mythological the figure of Satan may still serve to symbolise everything in the universe that is contrary to God's will and therefore to be fought by the Christian.'[13] The biblical faith of the Bible saw the universe governed by a personal God; miracles might be seen in especially significant events and in events not predictable by known causes.

In the context of the people of God, the idea of the righteous remnant as a holy community approaches the idea of the Church: in general it seems close to what Jesus taught. The idea of a community of disciples is rooted in his life and teaching, but not that of an organised institution. For Paul salvation is primarily an individual experience, but the shared experience welds Christians into a community. The main point of his characteristic figure of the Church as Christ's body is unity in diversity. 'The appeal for unity in the New Testament is based on the principle of Christian love. What is urged is not that all Christians should be of the same opinion, but that they should be of the same mind in the sense of sharing the attitude and spirit of Jesus himself. . . . There is nothing in the New Testament that would require a single, united ecclesiastical organisation.'[14]

The first concern of biblical religion is what God requires of man; it becomes imperative to know what the will of God is. This is the function of the Law and the reason for its existence; it led to the formulation of the Old Testament law codes. But to regard the Gospels as merely a new law, not essentially different from the Mosaic law, would destroy the whole point of Jesus' ethical teaching. Jesus taught a single basic attitude, not precepts, or a philosophy of values; yet that attitude provides a positive ethical ideal. He demands a doing of the will of God in specific situations, not mere good intentions. Paul, too, while rejecting legalism, is careful to repudiate antinomianism. We must ask whether Jesus' ideal is actually practicable in the world as we know it. The answer is that the Christian way of life does work. But to understand this, four points must be borne in mind: The ideal of Jesus is not to be judged by its power to bring worldly success; his ethical teaching cannot be enacted into legislation; Jesus demands not emotion but an attitude of will; he demands that we do what love requires in each given situation.

The Old Testament has two conceptions of the nature of sin. One is impersonal, combining the ideas of the 'unclean' and the 'accursed'; the other, far more characteristic, is personal: sin is disobedience to the will of God. In the New Testament the impersonal conception of sin has dropped out entirely. Jesus never speaks of sin in the abstract, but always of specific sins. His interpretation of the will of God in terms of love for God and one's neighbour makes his idea of sin more searching and strict than anything in the Old Testament or in Judaism. Paul often speaks of sin in the abstract, as an alien power tyrannising over man. The stress laid by later theology on the fall of man as necessitating redemption is not found in the Bible. 'This does not, of course, make sin unreal or redemption unnecessary. The reality of sin and the need of redemption are not dependent upon any theological doctrine. They are facts of experience which a realistic theology must take into account.'[15]

The religion of both the Old Testament and the New is dominated by the conviction that every human life is subject to judgement, here or hereafter. The biblical terminology of salvation is varied and is used very broadly. Thus, the themes of justification, reconciliation, redemption, adoption and forgiveness are not disparate, but mark one and the same experience: the entry into life. For Paul salvation must include victory over the power of sin in the flesh; the Christian must become a new creature. The Old Testament has little to say about this; it assumes that the individual or nation is free to stop sinning. Some passages, however, do approach the sort of experience with which Paul deals, and speak of the need for a 'new heart' and a 'new spirit'. Salvation, according to Paul, is past, present and future: the believer *is* already saved—he has been justified; he *will* be saved—in the life to come he will be free from the power of sin; he is *being* saved—in Christ he is overcoming the power of sin in himself. The conception of sanctification offers the final explanation of Paul's attitude to the Law and his idea of Christian freedom. The Christian is above the law, not under it; he is not subject to it because he accepts the values it defends. The Spirit is his motive power and makes the law inapplicable to him.

The main interest of Burrows' discussion of eschatology and the future life is his conclusion regarding Jesus' conception of the kingdom of God, which he sums up in seven propositions. The basic meaning of the concept is the eternal sovereignty of God. Because God's sovereignty is not fully realised on earth, the kingdom is still to come. Its final coming will be eschatological, hence in many sayings, the kingdom of God means the future age. The power of the kingdom is already at work in the world: the expulsion of demons is the sign that Satan's power is doomed. Jesus' followers accept God's sovereignty; the power of the kingdom is manifest in their lives—they already are in the kingdom. Jesus' idea of the kingdom was not that of a Christianised social order in the world; however any real advance in that direction is a demonstration of the power of the kingdom. For Jesus, the kingdom of God represents the sum total both of individual salvation and of the divine cosmic redemption of all creation.

Though the idea of atonement is understandably prominent in the priestly legislation of the Old Testament, the most characteristic biblical conception of atonement is that of a redemption which proceeds from God himself. No systematically developed doctrine of the atonement is given in the New Testament, but *Is.* 53 is much used in explaining the problem of the cross. Paul's conception of dying with Christ and rising to a new life with him has the spiritual dynamism of his idea of becoming a new person in union with Christ.

Throughout the Bible there is an emphasis on responsibility, which implies freedom of choice. Post-biblical Judaism continued to stress both the divine sovereignty and human freedom to choose between good and evil. Motives such as God's sovereignty and a humble sense of gratitude for undeserved blessings underlie the idea of the election of Israel in the Old Testament and the call of the individual Christian in Paul and John. In the Bible, too, it is clear that election to privilege implies election to service. The conception which best does justice to the biblical representation is that the possibility of salvation is God-given. Faith in the sense of confidence in Yahweh's power and his fidelity to his promises is exalted throughout the Old Testament. In the New Testament Paul makes faith the primary and sole condition of salvation; by faith he means not only trust in God, but also self-committal to Christ and devotion to him.

In the Old Testament the word 'fear' as applied to the right attitude toward God indicates reverence and obedience; in general, the New Testament attitude toward God may be characterised as reverent love. The presence of Yahweh in the midst of Israel was a source of confidence; the individual Israelite valued the presence of God. In the post-exilic age the tendency to make God more transcendent, the development of the cult, and the legalistic trend all increased the difficulty of a personal relationship with God. In both the Old Testament religion and early Christianity, the controlling conception of the individual's relation to God is that of the relation between two persons: servant to Master, child to Father. The New Testament added the idea of communion with Christ. Joy is a marked feature of the spiritual life throughout the Bible; the characteristic New Testament term for the message of Jesus comes from Second Isaiah, the 'good news'. Whereas in the Old Testament the group is primary, and the emergence of the individual is gradual and incomplete, in the New Testament the main stress is on the individual, though the individual is never apart from the community of the saved. Jesus' idea of the kingdom includes the community of those who enter it.

Burrows devotes two chapters to a consideration of special offices and functions and of public worship, then finally goes on to treat of Christian service and of moral and social ideals. Jesus was not a social reformer. If the New Testament looks for a redemption of all creation, it does so by means of an eschatological and not by a social and political transformation. This does not mean that the Church has no responsibility for social welfare and justice; active effort for the good of society is involved in the gospel as long as Christians live in this world. The Bible teaches that the good things that God has made are to be received and used with thanksgiving; asceticism has no place in the moral teaching of the Old Testament or the New. Thus, throughout the Bible, fasting is not commended as a means of mortifying the flesh but as an act of self-denial, related to sacrifice in its motives. The healthy biblical attitude to sex and marriage has much to offer us. The value placed by the Old Testament on large families must be assessed in the light of very different modern social conditions. The Bible can bring us to a greater realisation of social responsibility in marriage and parenthood. The New Testament follows the prophetic tradition of social justice, but with greater stress on otherworldly ends; and the whole Bible inculcates the principle of respect for the personality and rights of every human being.

The conclusion sums up the nature of biblical religion—though a brief summary is necessarily inadequate in view of the rich variety of the religion of the Bible. Through the Bible's various directions and currents runs a perceptible continuity and unity, for in and through it the one God is always speaking to his people. Man is completely dependent upon God and, alienated from God by sin, he is freely delivered by God who has provided a way by sending his Son. If we accept by faith the free gift of eternal life in Christ, we pass from death to life and are delivered from all fear and judgement. Faith overflows into a life of loving service of God; biblical religion is the affair of a group as well as of individuals. 'The faith of the New Testament contemplates not merely a relative amelioration of life in this world, but new heavens and a new earth. . . . Christian faith will always boldly affirm, with the Old and the New Testaments alike, that God's goodness is inexhaustible and eternal, and therefore nothing can separate us from his love as it is revealed in Christ Jesus our Lord.'[16]

On the whole, Burrows' work is a satisfactory synthesis of the theological concepts of the Bible and does justice to the evolution of biblical ideas from their first emergence in the Old Testament on to the New Testament. He has avoided a rigidly systematic plan and has adhered to biblical categories. Of course, a Catholic will not be happy with his view of authority and revelation, and Scripture scholars will not always accept his interpretations. Besides, the Old Testament has rather suffered—the emphasis is very much on the New. One particularly misses a treatment of the divine revelation in history. In fairness it must be observed that the author himself is the first to be conscious of this lack: he has presented an *outline*, the dry bones of biblical doctrine.

## 2. The Christian Interpretation of the Old Testament

I. THE GENERAL APPROACH

The final section of Gerhard von Rad's *Theology*,[17] dealing with the relationship between the Old and New Testaments, forms not only a conclusion to his work but is also the culmination of his theological credo and methods. In his preface to the volume he asks the reader not to take these final chapters in isolation from all that he has previously said— especially regarding history and its continual reinterpretation. The same principle of reinterpreting old material in the light of a new saving event is operative in both Testaments: Isaiah's 'remember not the former things' can be compared with Jesus' words in Matthew's Sermon on the Mount, 'But I say to you . . .' Perhaps we can indicate best the broad horizons of von Rad's thought by quoting his 'final word', the end of a recapitulating postscript appearing only in the English edition of his work:

> Only when Old Testament theology takes this final step to the threshold of the New Testament, only when it makes the link with the witness of the Gospels and the apostles perfectly openly, and when it is able to make men believe that the two Testaments belong together, will it have the right to term itself a theological undertaking, and therefore 'Biblical theology'. If instead it analyses the Old Testament in isolation, then, no matter how devotedly the work is done, the more appropriate term is 'history of the religion of the Old Testament.'[18]

In short, von Rad feels that the way in which the Old Testament is absorbed in the New is the logical end, the final reinterpretation, of a process initiated by the Old Testament itself.

How, he asks in a chapter entitled 'The Actualisation of the Old Testament in the New', could the apostles, the early Church, and Jesus himself see the whole Old Testament as pointing to him? The answer lies in the history of Yahwism itself, a history characterised by repeated breaks, fresh beginnings, the inauguration of new ideas and acts, and a vast sense of expectation which swelled Yahweh's promises and transmitted them for generations on end. As the prophets did with the old traditions, selecting from them, giving them new content and breakthroughs, so did the evangelists and apostles do with the Old Testament. They were filled with a sense of wonder, of standing at a new threshold where the kingdom *had* truly come. 'Thus, a new name was once again proclaimed over the ancient tradition of Israel: like one who enters into an ancient heritage, Christ the Kyrios claimed the ancient writings for himself.'[19] Von Rad analyses the different methods by which the New Testament writers 'actualised' the Old Testament. The Old Testament was now read as a divine revelation which was the precursor of Christ's advent and was full of pointers towards the coming of the Lord: this led to a completely new interpretation of the Old Testament. The New Testament took as its starting point the contrast between this new event and the whole of Israel's previous experience, and this must always be the starting point for a Christian interpretation of the Old Testament. One particular way by which the Old Testament was understood as a prediction pointing forward to Christ is the well-known typological interpretation which the New Testament applied in various ways. The Christ-event led to a fundamentally new interpretation of the Old Testament, which was read as dominated no longer by law, but by saving history. In the last analysis, it was the risen Lord himself who 'opened up' the Scriptures to his own (cf. *Luke* 24:32, 45). And, it must be clearly understood that the foundations of Christianity rest on the Old and New Testaments together.

In the following chapters von Rad shows how the foundations of Christianity lie in both Testaments together. His starting point is his 'still hotly disputed' proposition that 'it is in history that God reveals the secrets of his person, a proposition valid for both Old and New Testament ideas alike.'[20] He finds that the terms and concepts derived from the Old Testament's understanding of the world and men, of God's revelation, provide the real link between the Testaments. A phenomenon calling for theological explanation is that the Old Testament does not supply Christianity just with single ideas but with whole 'texts' in which Christianity did and still does find its own expression. Language forms a special link: the New Testament uses Old Testament terms and concepts. Old Testament language was a language appropriate to a world exposed to God and the primitive Christian community availed gladly of this fitting linguistic tool. Indeed, this factor accords the Old Testament a preparatory function of great scope: 'These terms and concepts belonged to a faith which was constantly reshaping them and which was warranted only by God's revelation of himself in Israel. Here is the real link between the Old and New Testaments; it is in this that the "preparation" took place.'[21] The 'preparation' began with the first revelation of the secrets of Yahweh's person; and all the Old Testament witnesses who taught men to understand the world and themselves as creatures in the sight of God are to be seen and understood as pointing to the coming of Christ. They express insights in the context of a particular saving activity which reaches its true goal with his coming.

We find in the Testaments an unmistakable structural analogy: the peculiar interconnection of revelation by word and revelation by event so characteristic of them. Typological understanding of the Old Testament put its correspondence with the New in a theological frame of reference. Events in the Old Testament can be recognised as pre-figurations of Christ's coming if they are understood in the light of a movement towards a fulfilment—a fulfilment to which they are already inherently open. It is in this way of looking at Old and New Testaments that correspondences and analogies between the two appear in their proper light. But the chief connection lies in the saving history, for Jesus is the supreme saving event. 'The coming of Jesus Christ as a historical reality leaves the exegete no choice at all; he must interpret the Old Testament as pointing to Christ, whom he must understand in its light.'[22] And that is why our present-day situation of having independent theologies of the Old Testament and of the New Testament which ignore each other is false. A theology of the Old Testament can confine itself to the Old Testament only at the price of disregarding an essential characteristic of the Old Testament—the way in which it points forward to the Christ-event of the New.

The final chapter deals with the Law, in particular with the prophets' handling of the old regulations to make them the basis of Yahweh's new demands upon Israel. Von Rad directs his discussion towards the great New Testament proclamation that all the Law is fulfilled in Jesus, God's true covenant partner, with whom he spoke 'face to face as a man speaks to his friend' (*Exod.* 33 : 11).

> In fact, God's whole relationship with Israel had not 'fallen into the void', nor had it ended in posing an absolutely intolerable question to God. In Jesus Christ, there at last entered into the history of the chosen people one who was 'perfect' with God; and in this One, God drew near to his people in the most personal way possible, more personally or directly than could be through any of the institutions or offices in the old Israel. Yet Jesus Christ was also the one in whom, again in accordance with the ancient prophecies, the limitations of God's covenant were removed, and who made the blessings of salvation extend beyond the things of this earth.[23]

Von Rad concludes by saying that just as the interpretations of the Old Testament given by Paul, Matthew, Mark or the author of Hebrews show different viewpoints and marks of the Spirit, so too there is really no absolute norm in present-day interpretation. For, 'every age has the task of hearing what the old book has to say to it, in the light of its own insights and its own needs.'[24] The vital thing is to remain open to the Spirit's guidance into 'all the truth' (*John* 16 : 13).

The first part of Theodore Vriezen's work[25] is given over

to five chapters in which the author discusses questions con-fronting the Christian theologian and puts forward the key concepts in his own approach to Old Testament theology. In the opening chapter, 'The Christian Church and the Old Testament', we read of how Christianity stands historically and spiritually on the shoulders of Judaism, and of how the authority of Scripture was an incontestable fact to Jesus him-self, although he did not feel committed to its letter. The Christian theologian who starts with the revelatory character of the gospel *must* maintain the same revelatory nature of the Old Testament; however, he needs to apply the tools of critical research and he needs to ferret and sift out the original message of God, the basic spiritual ideas, within the Old Testament writings. In doing so, 'the theologian will meet with men of like passions with himself, men who know that God has spoken to them . . . For essentially it is these people who have come to know him and who have heard the Word, who speak in the Old Testament.'[26] The second chap-ter, 'The Historical Character of Old Testament Revelation', describes the life and death struggle between two different Old Testament interpretations: the approach of 'mere his-toricism', which secularised Old Testament religion in terms of history and culture, and the approach of Christian faith, which sees the Old Testament as a record of divine revela-tion. Although the first approach *per se* cannot be acceptable to the Christian theologian, yet he cannot afford to ignore the factual data provided by the historical sources and must frankly admit the historical character of Israel's religion, in which the Old Testament is rooted. Vriezen emphasises here, and throughout his work, that the Old Testament is a product of the ancient Near East and bears marks accordingly. He offers an interesting view on the question of whether or not the early Israelite belief in God can be called monotheistic. This question must be answered by both 'Yes' and 'No', for Moses gave to Israel something *other* than a teaching on monotheism or a 'conception of God': he proclaimed God as Yahweh who intervenes directly in Israel's history—thus stressing his saving character rather than his uniqueness. Hence, it was from 'mono-Yahwism' to monotheism that the step was made. In a summary outline of the development of

Israel's religion, Vriezen notes that there was never any basic change in Israel's knowledge of its God, but rather a deepening of this knowledge through conflicts, suffering, and God's continual guidance. 'By the influence of his Spirit, the creed of Israel is purified and amplified more and more.'[27]

Chapter IV, 'The Old Testament as the Word of God and its Use in the Church', contains Vriezen's chief considerations on the relationship between the Old and New Testaments. His final words on the Church's homiletic use of the Old Testament summarise his viewpoint: the preacher is to look on the Bible as a *unity,* both historically (in that both Testaments originated in the same milieu and involve temporal continuity) and 'organically' (in that both share a fundamental spiritual outlook). The parts of this unity, however they may differ in origin, form, and *Sitz im Leben,* are yet one because they offer the same eschatological perspective of the kingdom and because in them the same Spirit speaks of the same God. Vriezen, however, first discusses the tensions and difficulties experienced in the Church, beginning with Paul himself, regarding the 'authority' of the Old Testament. With Paul, two lines become clearly visible: one is that of absolute acceptance of the Old Testament as the revelation of God; the other is that God has created a new relationship to himself by the revelation in Christ. Hence, there is an ambivalence in his appreciation of the Law, and therefore of the Old Testament, which consists in retaining its revelatory character, while subordinating it to the word of God revealed in Christ. Ultimately, the authority of the Old Testament and its real value lie in its truth—that is, in the existential validity of what it has to say about God and man. It is fully authoritative when it shares in the truth revealed in Jesus Christ, that is, when it is in harmony with the New Testament

Yet the twofold relationship which appeared to Paul remains. On one hand we admit the organic spiritual unity of Old Testament and New Testament because the life of Christ rested on the foundation of the Old Testament message of the Law and the Prophets; but on the other hand there is also a historical relationship, and there is an obvious difference between some parts of the Old Testament and the message of the gospel. As that which presents the oldest material—God's message to Israel—underlying the life and purpose of Jesus, the Old Testament belongs to the material bearing witness to him and as such serves a vital function. This entire witness is what constitutes the *Bible*, which Vriezen defines as 'essentially the documentary foundation of [the Church's] message concerning Jesus Christ and his gospel, her previous history, her revelation, her future.'[28] Placing the Old Testament and the New Testament side by side, a single spiritual thread can be seen running through both towards Jesus, the last phase of revelation in Israel. And this 'golden thread', the true heart and most profound motif in both Testaments, is the thread of the 'eschatological perspective' or prospect of the coming of the kingdom of God. 'There is ultimately but *one* hope and *one* certainty: that God shall be with them and that they shall live with him. This complete dependence on God, this faith in his holy and loving desire for re-creation, is characteristic of the message of both Old Testament and New Testament.'[29]

For Walther Eichrodt, the action of the one God, with his one purpose of establishing his kingdom in this world, is the unitive fact in the whole of biblical theology, binding both Testaments together. In his Appendix added to volume one of his *Theology* in response to the publication of G. von Rad's *Theologie des Alten Testaments*, he firmly upholds his conception of this unity: 'There is one task which Old Testament theology can never abandon, namely that of pressing on from the Old Testament evidence to a system of faith which shall, by its unified structure and consistent fundamental attitude, present a character unique in the history of religions.'[30] Already, in the very first chapter, Eichrodt states that part of the task facing him was to see that the comprehensive picture of Old Testament belief which he hoped to present also did justice to its relationship with the New Testament, for the uniqueness of Judaism could be grasped only when seen as a *movement towards Christ*. Thus, in keeping with his purpose, this movement is voiced in almost every succeeding chapter. For instance, in discussing sacrificial worship in the cult, it is seen to attain its full meaning only in the relationship between Father and Son, only in the primitive Christian com-

19

munity's faith in the intercession of Jesus. In the 'Nature of the Covenant God' (ch. 6), only Jesus is able to combine both God's spirituality and his immediacy; only he can reconcile the priestly-prophetic tension between the God who has come and is to come, the God both revealed and hidden (ch. 9). In discussing the Judges (ch. 8), Eichrodt notes that these charismatic leaders furnished the colours for the portrait of the one, final Redeemer who would truly bring order and peace to a weary, torn land, as they had done in their own smaller measure. We have seen how the whole message of the prophets was a 'reaching out in faith toward an as yet unseen Coming One'.[31] The divine name of God is most perfectly revealed in the work of Jesus; indeed, it is most concisely expressed in his own name. In a final example here, the word of God comes fully into its own in the New Testament—in the word as the Good News of salvation, and in Jesus himself as the Word become flesh (ch. 14). Here, Eichrodt remarks what a complex demand it is to be able to sum up all the features of biblical revelation—biblical theology—in *one* Word! The only way is to apply the fullness of the Old Testament concept of God's word to the person of the Redeemer, the Word himself.

Finally, we return to the concept of 'Fulfilling the Covenant' which concludes the first section (ch. 11); in this lies the ultimate link between the old and new covenants, a link forged by the hope for the consummation of God's sovereignty or dominion. Upon the establishment of this reign, for Eichrodt, turns the whole of biblical theology. He affirms that the work of Jesus, as revealing God's sovereignty, is indeed the fulfilment of Old Testament prediction. And yet, this fulfilment is still perceptible only to *faith* and personal decision! For, despite the historical event of redemption through Jesus, there is a temporary postponement of the complete new creation and perfect reign of God. This postponement, at first an occasion for anguished perplexity for the early Christian community, led to a deeper faith—faith in the hidden kingship of Jesus, who had indeed overcome the world despite the mystery and contrary appearances which *still* remained as they had throughout the Old Testament. Thus, the 'fulfilment' of the Old Testament by the New is not a logical conclusion, but a call for personal decision— for believing without seeing. That Jesus unites all the strands of Judaism can be theoretically understood; but there remains the need to accept him as doing such, to personally answer the question as to whether or not he is the Son of God. Eichrodt concludes by saying that Jesus himself intended that 'recognition or rejection of the "fulfilment" of the Old Testament prophecy in the New Testament gospel must proceed from men's attitude to his own person—and without personal decision, this is inconceivable.'[32] The Jewish leaders made their decision No against him; Eichrodt—and those of us blessed to share his faith—have clearly made ours Yes.

Ethelbert Stauffer[33] maintains that the New Testament looks to the Law and the Prophets to find what God has announced and finds this answer: Christ and his kingdom. Jesus himself initiated the christological interpretation of the Old Testament; the fourth evangelist shared this conviction (*John* 5:39), and Paul gives it expression in terms of his metaphor of the veil over the face of Moses (2 *Cor.* 3:13-18). Pre-Christian history is the prehistory of Christ's coming and points teleologically to the cross, and we find that the Testaments present a typology of salvation history. A proper understanding of Scripture leads one to grasp the fact that since the Old Testament has found its end and fulfilment in Christ, it is thereby, theologically speaking, outmoded.

John L. McKenzie[34] observes that the Christian values of the Old Testament have been a problem for Christians since apostolic times. The primitive Church presented Christianity as the fulfilment of Israel. It regarded Christ as the Messiah of Israel; this title alone did justice to him. The apostles were aware that only a Jesus who was Messiah of Israel, and therefore a focus of God's historical saving purpose, would be an object of genuine faith. 'A Jesus who was not the Messiah of Israel would not have been for them—to use a modern term —the Jesus of history, just as he would not have been the Christ of faith.'[35] The Messiah of Israel emerges from Israel of the Old Testament; he can be understood only in terms of Old Testament traditions. The proclamation of Jesus in these terms was the only way open to the apostles. In view of this, it is not surprising to find that almost every important religious word in the New Testament has an Old Testament background and a definite traditional meaning. The Christian message had to be proclaimed in this largely inherited religious language if it were to be uttered at all when and where it was uttered. 'The Christ event, mysterious in any language, is most accurately set forth in its original language.'[36] McKenzie observes that New Testament themes are easily distorted when, without sufficient attention to their original form, they are translated into other idioms. Modern theology has become more conscious of the importance of the biblical background.[37]

## II. THE METHODS

A book of essays edited by Claus Westermann[38] conveniently gives the view of leading German scholars on two important matters relevant to our study in this chapter: the theme of promise and fulfilment, and the validity of the typological interpretation of the Old Testament. Though opinions and even fundamental standpoints vary, these valuable studies do make a real and, in general, a positive contribution. They serve as a starting-point for a study of other important aspects of this question.

### i. Promise and Fulfilment

As is to be expected, R. Bultmann takes a controversial stand, in line with his own existential interpretation of Scripture. He takes three central concepts of the Old Testament —the ideas of the covenant, of the kingdom of God, and of the people of God—and argues that they could never become historical possibilities and could only be realised eschatologically. In this tension between eschatological hope and empirical reality, there is a contradiction and a miscarriage of history. Thus he illustrates his main thesis that Old Testament history can only become promise in the sense that it is a history of failure. He explains that 'this miscarriage is, of course, to be understood as a promise only on the basis of its fulfilment, that is, on the basis of the encounter with God's grace, which makes itself available to those who understood their situation as one of impossibility.'[39] In fact, Bultmann's position is one of radical denial of the true relevance of the

Old Testament to the Christian. W. Zimmerli has shrewdly discerned Bultmann's concern to be that of stripping the Christ-event of historical value; to do this he has to strip history away from the Old Testament promise. 'Does Bultmann not do this in order to elevate the Christ-message purely out of history in existential interpretation?'[40] C. Westermann, too, observes that, for Bultmann, the history of God's people, recorded in the Old Testament, is nothing more than an *exemplum* of human existence: an example of the failure of the history of salvation meets the believer and strengthens him against temptation.[41]

Though Friedrich Baumgärtel[42] cannot accept Bultmann's thesis of a total failure, he, too, accepts that, in fact, the traditional understanding of the Old Testament in terms of promise-fulfilment has no relevance today. His first point is that the Old Testament is a witness out of a non-Christian religion. The simple Christian's understanding of the Old Testament is based on *a priori* understanding: it is because he has been grasped by Christ that the Christian can receive the Old Testament word with understanding. This is in fact the way in which the New Testament has understood the Old Testament. But today our thinking is historical thinking and so we must understand the Old Testament on its own terms. Our contemporary historical thinking has recognised the Old Testament as the witness of a religion outside the gospel; and the contemporary hermeneutical problem is to win it back into a Christian context. This cannot be done by typological and christological methods of interpretation since these methods have no place in modern historical-critical thinking.

Baumgärtel maintains that the fundamental experience of the Christian who, through his faith in Christ, knows himself confronted and grasped by the reality of God, can be expressed in this way: 'the Lord my God'. The fundamental experience of the Old Testament is the same: 'I am the Lord thy God'. In each case the experience is foundation and promise in one; in this fundamental promise the Old Testament and the New Testament witness find common root and 'togetherness'. Theologically, this 'togetherness' of the Testaments must be understood in two ways: the Old Testament witness together with the gospel is powerful for us; the Testaments stand together in a perspective of salvation history, because the Old Testament event can be comprehended as saving event from the standpoint of the gospel and not from the standpoint of the self-understanding of the Old Testament. Only on the basis of this fundamental promise and in this perspective is the Old Testament of theological relevance to the Christian.

Wolfhart Pannenberg roundly asserts that history is the most comprehensive horizon of Christian theology. It is a presupposition of theology that theological questions and answers are meaningful within the framework of a history which moves toward a history already revealed in Christ. Hence the connection between the Old and New Testaments 'is made understandable only by the consciousness of the one history which binds together the eschatological community of Jesus Christ and ancient Israel by means of the bracket of promise and fulfilment.'[43] Jesus himself is understandable only against the background of the Old Testament; the doctrine of the incarnation is to be judged on the basis of Jesus' connection with Israel's history of promise. This same history is the basis of and the justification for the New Testament proofs from prophecy.

Pannenberg fully endorses the typological exegesis of the Old Testament. However, he warns that the connection between the Christ-event and the Old Testament must not be sought primarily in the structural similarity of the Old Testament type to its New Testament counterpart. Rather, the relationship between the anti-type and the type is understandable as a temporal continuity and not as a purely structural correspondence. It is this historical unity, seen in the continuity of the promises, which assures the old covenant its place alongside the new. The connection between the Testaments is the one history which includes both Testaments; but then, on this foundation, one can establish all kinds of typological connections and structural agreements. In this way the Old Testament maintains its place as an independent basis for the Christian faith. 'In Christianity there is in fact an interest in the past which cannot be surrendered, because it contains the promise which will be fulfilled in the future. Historical experience of reality is preserved only in the biblical understanding of history, in the biblical faith in the promise.'[44]

Walther Zimmerli observes that the New Testament expresses the relationship of both Testaments in a particularly striking way through the language of promise and fulfilment. But then, rather like Pannenberg, he insists that there must be a basis in the reality and continuity of history. Without such a history the category promise/fulfilment is inconceivable—'Anyone who knows of promise and fulfilment is responsible to a yesterday about which he has heard something, and he walks toward a tomorrow.'[45] Yet the historical path stands under a tension because promise and fulfilment mean veiled purposes and distressed waiting. In the Old Testament we find that prophecy lived from the certainty that history stood under the informing word of Yahweh; and so, the element of promise/fulfilment emerges as a major theme in the great prophets. Indeed the Old Testament as a whole presents the flow of a great history of movement from promise to fulfilment. We find, too, that each Old Testament event receives a character of fulfilment—yet looks to a deeper fulfilment and thus receives a new character as promise. But the Old Testament remains open-ended, and only in the New Testament is it asserted that the promise has become wholly event; in Christ the Old Testament is at an end. This has to be correctly understood: 'The Old Testament history does not simply extend into the New Testament history in an unbroken line. Christ is the end of the old covenant and its promise . . . Christ is at the same time the fulfilment of the Old Testament . . . now he alone can be the legitimate interpreter of the Old Testament language of promise.'[46] Zimmerli has seriously depreciated the predictive element in prophecy —prediction is, in fact, an important aspect of the prophetic standpoint. Then, too, he offers a general and restricted theology of promise that is far removed from the text-related connections we find in the New Testament.[47]

Gerhard von Rad finds a tension between promise and fulfilment within the Old Testament itself: a statement is to be understood as standing between a particular past and a particular future. Israel recorded the fulfilment of promises which occurred within its own saving history, yet the fulfilment was not regarded as having given final effect to the promise: there was still a looking to the future. The accumulated promise of the Old Testament looks to fulfilment; Christianity answers that it is found in the Christ-event. There are, in fact, two ways of looking at the Old Testament. 'If I view the Old Testament "genetically", that is, as a comprehensive process of religious and spiritual evolution, I can view it as, to some extent, a self-contained entity. But if what I principally see in it is the ceaseless saving movement of promise and fulfilment, then it becomes apparent how the expectations it contains fan out ever wider, then it is no self-contained entity, then it is absolutely open, and the question of its relationship to the New Testament becomes the question *par excellence*.'[48] This second way, of course, introduces a new element of interpretation which does not derive from the Old Testament itself. For the Christian the Old Testament texts speak in a new way, and Old Testament events can be recognised as prefigurations of Christ's coming. The tension constituted by promise and fulfilment, characteristic of Israel's whole existence before God, has found a new dimension. If the exegesis of Old Testament texts must always strive to understand them in the light of a movement towards a fulfilment, that demand has found a fresh urgency. It has to be kept in mind that the New Testament fulfilment is not a literal realisation of the promise, but a fulfilment which far surpasses the promise. It is evident that the early Church's reinterpretation and application to itself of Old Testament material is, in principle, a perfectly legitimate procedure. However, we recognise that the interpretation of the Old Testament, in pre-Christian terms, is not thereby precluded.

R. E. Murphy[49] feels that von Rad, Zimmerli and Westermann have given effective expression to the promise/fulfilment aspect of the Bible, and he finds this category to be the most satisfactory way of explaining the interrelatedness of the Testaments. The basis for it is the historical experience of Israel as a people and the historical growth of the message revealed to Israel. It does not, in any sense, involve a mathematical equivalence between the preparation and the realisation, but the unity of the Testaments emerges from this general typology. 'Fulfilment is wholeness, the flowering of what was set in motion by the word (or event).'[50] We have noticed, too, that H. H. Rowley favours the promise/fulfilment relationship.[51]

J. D. Smart[52] pleads for greater precision in this discussion. 'There is an important distinction between the categories "promise—fulfilment" and "prediction—fulfilment" that has not always been properly recognised. Promise—fulfilment is a basic biblical category that is rooted in the prophetic understanding of God's relation to history. God has a purpose for his people that embraces the events of history. The revelation of that purpose is understood by Israel as a promise for the future, but in the promise itself the divine purpose is revealed and is already at work. It is no bare word about a future event, but rather it is a word that contains within it a very real foretaste of that future.'[53]

He points out that already, in Israel, all history is seen as a movement between promise and fulfilment. God fulfils what he promises but, because the fulfilment is no more than partial, it contains within itself an unfilled promise that points forward to a new fulfilment. Thus, when the New Testament Church speaks of fulfilment and points to Old Testament promises it is not looking to predictions of New Testament events in the Old but rather it is interpreting the whole of the Old Testament as the beginning of a work of God which finds its completion in Christ and his Church. 'When we speak of the Old Testament being fulfilled in Jesus Christ, it is not a formal pattern of promise and fulfilment that is being superimposed on the materials, but rather it is a recognition that in the most intensely personal way the purpose of God that was at work in Israel through the centuries came to its full revelation and triumph in Jesus Christ.'[54]

## ii. Typology

(a) *Typology*. According to Gerhard von Rad,[55] typological thinking is an elementary function of all human thought and interpretation; evidently he is going to acknowledge the validity of the typological interpretation of the Old Testament. He finds that the Old Testament is dominated by a form of typological thinking—that of the eschatological correspondence between beginning and end. The New Testament applies this theological thought-form to the Old Testament; we must stress the great importance of the New Testament's typological way of understanding things (while allegory falls quite into the background).

Von Rad's primary aim in the article under consideration is to raise the question of the redemptive significance of the the Old Testament witness to past and present. I may ask what part I, as a Christian believer, can have in the Old Testament if I cannot identify myself, at least partly, with the religion of Israel. I can only do this when I see in this history brought to pass by God's word the prefiguration of the Christ-event of the New Testament. Typological interpretation leads the Christian to this deeper understanding of the Old Testament; it has to do with the entire Old Testament and finds that the number of Old Testament types is unlimited. Typology, however, is not concerned with historical or biographical details but confines itself to the *credenda*. 'There can be no question of declaring certain persons or objects or institutions as, in their objective and, as it were, static essence, types.'[56] And typological exegesis is never oblivious of the difference between the redemptive benefits of the Old Testament and those of the New.

Von Rad insists that though typological intervention goes beyond the self-understanding of the Old Testament text, there should be no sharp separation of typological interpretation from the historical-critical exegetical process. Typological interpretation enables Old Testament exegesis to be more theologically relevant by going beyond the meaning inherent in the event. No pedagogical norms can be set up to handle the typological interpretation of individual texts: 'it cannot be further regulated hermeneutically, but takes place in the freedom of the Holy Spirit.'[57] This means that the exegete is free to establish new typological connections between the Testaments in a great variety of ways. The validity of typology assures us of the witness of the Old Testament to Christ, and our knowledge of Christ is incomplete without the witness of the Old Testament.

Hans Walter Wolff[58] too, agrees that typology is not intended to suspend historical-critical work, but to support it in a relevant manner. Typology leads to an exposition of the Old Testament which brings out the fact that the God of Israel is our God and that the message of the Old Testament has meaning for us. It underlines the relation of the Old Testament to the Christ-event, a mutual relationship. On the one hand, the history of Israel is incomprehensible without its proper conclusion, which is found in Christ. On the other hand, the great concluding chapter of the witness of faith, the New Testament, needs to be read in the light of the preceding Old Testament context. The permanent, fundamental significance of the Old Testament for Christianity lies in the fact that the Christ-event can be fully understood only in the light of the Old Testament.

Our approach to the Old Testament must first of all ensure our reading the Old Testament text according to the meaning it has in its Old Testament context; but then, we must go on to take the New Testament context into consideration. 'That does not mean superimposing on the historical meaning of the Old Testament text a second meaning, an allegorical one . . . That would ruin everything. Rather we are to listen to how the historical meaning of the text continues to speak in the New Testament situation.'[59] If we ask what the Old Testament can say to men living in the fulfilment of the Christ-event, we get a number of answers. It brings us the insight that *God* is acting in Jesus Christ and so guards against false isolation and historicisation. It makes clear the uniqueness of the sending of Jesus and prevents the witness to Christ from being corrupted into philosophy about Christ. The Old Testament fixes the Christian message in the context of a people, emphasises its concern with this world and so saves it from false individualisation and false transcendentalism. The concern of typological exegesis is to give the Old Testament its proper place in the Christian economy. 'It knows it can deal properly with the Old Testament only by practising exposition which is historical, which compares the Old Testament with the New, and which is thus proclamation.'[60]

The most comprehensive and valuable contribution in the typology debate is made by Walther Eichrodt;[61] he has no doubt that typological exegesis is a perfectly appropriate method. Where the other scholars had been vague (and it is not easy to be quite sure what exact meaning 'typology' has for them), Eichrodt is precise. In the first place he asserts that types are 'persons, institutions, and events of the Old Testament which are regarded as divinely established models or prerepresentations of corresponding realities in the New Testament salvation history.'[62] As for the antitype, it does not correspond to the type in every respect, nor is it a photographic copy of the type—'on the contrary, the argument envisages only a few analogies, but these of special importance, between the two realities in question.'[63] For that matter, there is always a certain element of contrast between type and antitype. This is because each type, like the entire salvation history of the Old Testament, marks a preliminary stage of the salvation in Christ and lacks the fullness of the latter. The persons, events and institutions of the Old Testament do not become types through some discovered similarity with corresponding New Testament realities. 'Rather it is the intercourse of God with his people, represented, warranted, and actualised by them, that validates them. In other words, their religious and theological significance in the historical revelation of the Old Testament gives to them their significance as divinely established prerepresentations of important elements in the salvation manifested in Christ.'[64]

This peculiarity sets the typological view of Old Testament events in the New Testament clearly apart from other ways of considering biblical material. In the first place, it differentiates it from allegory which disregards the historical value of the text—an essential presupposition for the use of typology. In the second place, typology looks to the Old Testament realities as pre-representations of present salvation, while paranesis uses the realities as models of warning or exhortation for the present community. The third point is the relation between typology and prophecy/fulfilment. Here, again, Eichrodt's precision is very helpful. He acknowledges that there is a close relationship between these two approaches since each of them finds in the Old Testament the announcement of God's completion of salvation. 'But while in prophecy the messenger of God proclaims the future which has been opened to him and seen by him, a type possesses its significance, pointing into the future, independently of any human medium and purely through its objective factual reality; and in many cases its function is still hidden for contemporary people and is disclosed only when the gaze is turned backward from the New Testament time of salvation. From this point of view one might designate typology as "objectivised prophecy".'[65]

The basic conviction of the New Testament, that Old and New Testaments belong together in their witness to the revelation of God, remains the foundation of typology; however, the typological methodology of the New Testament writers cannot simply be taken over into our modern exegesis. In other words, we have to test, in the light of our understanding of history, the typological interpretations of the Old Testament which we find in the New Testament. This is important because typology emphasises the continuity and purposefulness of the divine action in history. Then, too, typology points to 'a constancy in God's relations to men, one which adds to the vertical of the divine act of revelation the horizontal of a history of salvation. This history of salvation binds the Old and New Testament communities together through all the changes of time into one people of God, because the continuity of the divine act of love guarantees that they belong together.'[66]

Finally, Eichrodt can reassert that typology has its place in an exegesis that knows the whole compass of its task. However, typology, of its nature, will play only an ancillary part in exegesis; it can never become the dominating conception in exegesis. If von Rad proposes to make the whole exposition of the Old Testament into typological exegesis, it can only be because he understands typology in a way notably different from Eichrodt's definition of it (and the same might be said of Wolff).[67] Eichrodt is quite firm in his rejection of a one-sided definition of the relation of the two Testaments in terms of typology.

(b) *The Typical Sense.* As understood by Roman Catholic scholars, typology is taken in much the same way as it is by Eichrodt. The typical sense of Scripture differs from both literal and fuller senses.[68] These two (whether we regard the *sensus plenior* as a distinct sense or as a secondary literal sense is immaterial) are concerned with words; the typical sense arises when the persons or events or things designated in the primary sense typify persons or events or things of a higher order and when this signification is intended by God. For example, we know from the New Testament that Melchizedek is a type of Christ the Priest, that the crossing of the Red Sea is a type of baptism, and that the brazen serpent raised up by Moses is a type of Christ on the cross.[69] The typical sense is not a literal sense because it is concerned with things and not with words. Nevertheless it is firmly based on the primary literal sense, for the significant facts or 'types', which are the object of the typical sense, find their place in the Bible and are known to us only by means of the words; even though the human writer is unaware that he is describing a type, the type does emerge from his words. Abraham sacrificing his son and the manna feeding the people in the desert are types of Calvary and the Eucharist only insofar as these facts are recorded by the sacred writer and under the form in which he has recorded them. A biblical type is founded not only on a historical reality, but also on a literary existence. The latter may be the more important; for example, Melchizedek is a type of the heavenly priest (*Heb.* 7:3) not because he had no parents, but because Scripture has not stated that he had. It may happen that the literary existence is the only real one (for example, Jonah is a literary, not a historical, figure). But the essential factor is that the typical sense, precisely because it is a *scriptural* sense, must be sought and found in the words of Scripture.

Raymond E. Brown[70] offers a definition of the typical sense: it is 'the deeper meaning that the things (persons, places and events) of Scripture possess because, according to the intention of the divine author, they foreshadow future things.' The criteria for recognising the typical sense are a correspondence between type and antitype, and the divine intention. But can there be any real correspondence? We cannot overlook the vast distance and the diversity between type and antitype, between the brazen serpent and Christ on the Cross, for instance. Yet they do meet in the religious significance with which both are clothed in the message of revelation, a significance that is brought out in the words which sketch them. Thus the brazen serpent and Christ are both 'raised up' and both bring 'salvation' to those who gaze upon them in faith. Always there is a real, although mysterious, connection established by God, which is expressed by the fuller sense on the level of the text and by the typical sense on the plane of history. We still have to seek the evidence that God really planned the relationship between type and antitype. Here there is real danger of subjectivism, and the history of exegesis, with its excesses in this direction, should give us pause. In practice, it is best to be guided by the New Testament. We can really be sure of the divine intention in the case of the types indicated by the New Testament writers.[71]

III. THE FULLER SENSE

In this century and, for practical purposes within the past two decades, the pursuit of a secondary sense of Scripture has taken a particular turn in Roman Catholic circles. In 1925 Andres Fernández[72] introduced the term *sensus plenior* in a classification of scriptural senses. It was some time before the term and the theory of 'fuller sense' were taken up by others. The three outstanding exponents of the Fuller Sense have been J. Coppens, P. Benoit and R. E. Brown; the latter has documented the continuing debate in a thorough manner.[73]

In 1948 Joseph Coppens presented a treatise on the senses of Scripture in the perspective of the relations between the two Testaments.[74] In chapters one and four of his work, he insists on the primacy of the literal sense and on its fundamental importance in establishing a comparison between the Old Testament and the New Testament. However, it has seemed that the true accord between the Testaments cannot be seen on the basis of historical-philological exegesis alone; thus, the second and most important chapter of the book is devoted to an analysis of the proposed *sensus plenior*. Coppens marshals a series of arguments in favour of the existence and validity of a 'fuller sense'. He proceeds to distinguish three types of fuller sense: 1. A *'périchorétique'* fuller sense which is perceived when a passage, or even a book, of the Bible is set in the context of the whole Bible. 2. A 'historical-typical' fuller sense based on the continuity between the text of Old Testament and New Testament, as well as on the inchoative character of the Old Testament: it is the earlier part of a process which leads to fulfilment in the New. 3. A 'prophetical-typical' sense which is the fuller meaning that we find in prophecy in the light of its fulfilment. Coppens maintains that the Old Testament author can have a certain knowledge (through revelation) of the fuller meaning of his words in the third case; this is not so in the other two cases. The question of the sacred writer's awareness of the fuller sense is treated again in later articles;[75] he continues to regard the fact that the *sensus plenior* seems to escape the awareness of the sacred writer as a major difficulty. In facing this problem he pictures two situations. The sacred writer may have possessed the charism of prophecy; in that case, the texts which derive ultimately from such a charism could contain a meaning which went beyond the full religious awareness of the writer. On the other hand, the author who does not enjoy the prophetic charism still moves in the realm of the supernatural and enunciates declarations of faith. The act of faith deepens his awareness. The thrust which is characteristic of the act of faith goes beyond the explicit import of his words, giving them a greater depth of meaning; this thrust of faith is not entirely lost to one's awareness.

In the *Concilium* article Coppens gives a definition of the fuller sense. 'The *sensus plenior* is the supernatural depth of the literal meaning. It arises from the totality of Revelation and, in particular, from the New Testament fulfilment of scriptural texts—to the extent that this meaning was intended by God, the principal author of Scripture, and aimed at by the sacred writer's act of faith. The writer's act of faith may be regarded in itself, or in combination with an accompanying process of prophetic intuition.'[76] He concludes that the fuller sense (understood as something which results from prophetic intuition or the thrust of supernatural faith, and as enriched by a living tradition) seems best able to move us beyond the literal meaning into the 'spirit' of Scripture. Thus it is an important factor in the elaboration of an Old Testament theology and in bringing out the harmony between the Testaments.

In 1947 Pierre Benoit treated, briefly, of the 'fuller sense.'[77] However, his main contribution to the debate has been a long article in the *Revue Biblique*.[78] We have had occasion elsewhere to indicate the significant features of his treatment of the fuller sense;[79] it will be adequate for our purpose to reproduce this outline. In the first place, Benoit prefers to describe the literal sense as the *primary* literal sense: this leaves room for a treatment of the *secondary* senses (typical and fuller) that are also found in the letter of a biblical text, although they were not perceived by its human author.

The fact of secondary senses stems from the very nature of the Bible and, more precisely, from the relationship between divine Author and human authors. The former is the Author of the whole Bible, while each sacred writer is responsible for no more than a restricted portion of it. Moreover, God embraces the whole course of sacred history and of revelation, while the human writer is only one link in a chain. The divine Author outstrips the human author in three ways: [80]

1. The human writer speaks in one book only and then for a determined age and milieu; the divine Author speaks in all the books, from one end of the Old Testament to the other and from the Old Testament to the New. *Genesis, Isaiah,* and *Mark* are just so many distinct works when one thinks of the men who wrote them; but when one thinks of the God who inspired them, then they are seen to be so many chapters of the same great Book which he has directed from beginning to end.

2. It follows that the same God, although he has spoken throughout the centuries under different pens, has maintained enriching relationships between the succeeding stages of his unfolding word. Under his guidance, words written by some have been taken up by other, later writers and now have fresh resonances not perceived by their first authors, although foreseen and prepared by him.

3. The God who inspires the written revelation guides also the sacred history which it mirrors. He is master of events as well as of minds, and he can have raised up persons or events or things which have the value of signs. 'He can speak a creative, concrete, existential language in which beings and events speak more eloquently than do the abstract terms of

20

ordinary speech, a language of which God alone is capable and which he has used in a revelation that was lived and spoken before being set down in a book. It is a language which could not have been fully understood by its first interpreters, because the real portent of it can be grasped only at the close of the final act of the drama, when the roles of the various actors are at last clearly revealed in the light of the dénouement.'[81]

In view of the circumstances we have described, we may say that, in the Bible, beyond the primary literal sense, there is present—to an extent not easily determined—a deeper literal sense, contained in the letter, but foreseen and intended clearly and directly only by God. We may speak, therefore, of a *fuller sense*: that fuller and deeper significance of a text which is intended by the divine Author and which is discovered in the light of further revelation, particularly in the light of the New Testament. The fuller sense, which is no more than a deeper insight into the primary literal sense, can be readily seen in the messianic prophecies of the Old Testament; they are clear to us because the Messiah has come, but the full meaning that we now perceive was intended by God from the first. Ultimately, the discernment of the fuller sense depends on the quality of the light in which one views a text. It is something like the process of infra-red photography. Some of the Dead Sea Scroll fragments, for instance, are illegible to the naked eye, but the infra-red camera reveals letters and words that were hidden. Nothing is added to the fragments, but the special light has brought to view something that was there all the time. So, too, the development of revelation reveals the hidden depths of earlier texts.

While there may be a close connection between fuller sense and typical sense, these remain distinct. What is specific in the typical sense is the correspondence, willed by God and expressed in his Scripture, of two concrete realities, each of which, although they have a common meeting point, is marked off from the other: manna and Eucharist; Noah's ark and baptism; the brazen serpent and Jesus on the cross—the type and its antitype. The link factor in each case is a common religious value which sustains the correspondence (for instance, the divine gift of manna which nourished the chosen people and the spiritual food of the Eucharist which feeds the new people of God). 'It is on this continuous plane of religious values that the fuller sense is situated, while it is between the two planes of existence, the old and the new, that the typical sense comes into play.'[82] The fuller sense follows on and accompanies the typical sense, but it is not identical with it.

The fuller sense may exist independently of a particular type, but it always has its roots in a general typology. Although the fuller sense does imply the homogeneous maturing of an idea, and not, immediately, the appearance of a new person or event, the growth of ideas that we have in mind could not occur without the emergence of something quite new on the plane of history. This new event is the fact of Christ: he has made all things new. It is in the sphere of this re-creation that the religious values of the old Law find their accomplishment. In short, the whole of the old economy may be considered as one single, complex type, whose component parts are particular types: not only persons and facts, but institutions like the Law, the Temple, the kingship. Over against this, God has raised the antitype of the new economy, with its personages, its facts and its institutions—the whole of it centred in Christ who gives to the old economy its decisive fulfilment. For, with Christ, all has, in principle, been given; God has nothing more to add to this definitive word. 'The fact of Christ constitutes a decisive leap forward, a radically new departure, a passage to a new plane which continues along the line of the old only after a vertical change of levels. We are not now on a higher step with other steps yet to climb; we have passed into a definitive order, into another world. In face of this decisive change in which God has "made all things new" (*Apoc.* 21:5), all the former stages represent only one and the same level of history, that of the old things.'[83] For this reason, the fuller sense and the typical sense are not found within the Old Testament taken by itself, or within the New Testament, but only within the Old Testament in the light of the New.

The conditions required for a secondary sense, typical or fuller—and therefore also its criteria—are *homogeneity* and *reproduction (reprise)*. In the first place, it is necessary that

the secondary sense and the primary sense be *homogeneous*—
that is, that the former should be a prolongation of the other
in the same direction. The fuller sense, which is indeed a
literal sense—although a secondary one—is substantially
identical with the primary literal sense. 'It adds to the latter a
plus-value, but one that was already included in the objective
meaning of the notion in question, although it had escaped
the subjective perception of the author . . . If, from the point
of view of human psychology, we must distinguish between
the primary sense and the secondary sense, from the point of
view of God and of his Scripture we can say that these are
one and the same literal sense.'[84]

The second condition and criterion is *reproduction (reprise)*.
The divine Author alone is capable of preparations in history
and in the text of his Scripture, which he then brings to fulfilment on a higher level. But if we are to be sure that he has
done so, he himself must let us know, for this is an element
of the mystery of salvation whose secrets are his alone. God
must point out to us that a particular situation of the new
economy had its authentic preparation willed by him, in a
particular situation of the old. It is in the New Testament
that God has manifested his fulfilments; there he has commented on his own word. This is done by 'reproduction', by
reproducing the figures and words of the preparation in the
new context of fulfilment. Thus, for instance, the manna is
the 'bread from heaven' (*Ps.* 78:24; 105:40) and the Eucharist
is the 'true bread from heaven' (*John* 6:32); the brazen serpent was 'raised up' on a pole that the man 'who sees it shall
live' (*Num.* 21:8), and the Son of Man 'must be lifted up
that whoever believes in him may have eternal life' (*John*
4:14f.). At the making of the Sinai covenant, Moses poured
out the blood of the victim upon the people, saying: 'Behold
the blood of the covenant' (*Exod.* 24:8); and Jesus said: 'This
is my blood of the covenant, which is poured out for many'
(*Matt.* 26:28).

In all similar reproductions of the word of God, there is
a fuller sense. Indeed, much of the vocabulary in which the
New Testament authors have expressed the mystery of Christ
has been taken from the Old Testament. God guided them in
this, just as he had guided the choice of words of their distant

predecessors. Hence it is God who has brought about the homogeneous development of biblical language, in this way powerfully underlining the harmony of the two Testaments.

Benoit maintains that, in his opinion, the fuller sense is no exceptional meaning of the Old Testament but is, in fact, frequent and rather easily discovered. The secondary senses of Scripture are, in a special way, the field of biblical theology; in order to perceive them, the light of faith is necessary. Indeed, every Christian believer reads the Bible with the eyes of faith so that the normal, habitual manner in which a Christian understands the Old Testament is according to its fuller sense. It follows that while the term 'fuller sense' is recent, the reality is anything but new; it has been present in the Church from the first century onwards. Benoit feels that recent complicated classifications of the secondary senses have not really helped matters. He would wish for something very simple: literal sense on the one hand, typical sense on the other. The literal sense would be primary and secondary (fuller) according as it had been perceived by the human author or by God only.

More than any other, Raymond E. Brown has contributed to the study of the *sensus plenior*; his 1955 doctoral dissertation was an exhaustive treatment and his *CBQ* articles have indicated later developments.[85] His own views can best be presented here in terms of his latest handling of the subject.[86] Brown notes that the New Testament exegesis of the Old Testament was extraordinarily varied. It is not possible to classify it as one type of exegesis but, to a large extent, it might be characterised as more-than-literal exegesis. The question then arises: is there any place for a more-than-literal sense of the Old Testament in our day of scientific exegesis? Brown finds that the question might be approached in any of three ways: a) An attempt to preserve past symbolic exegesis. This would be a retrograde step and has no future. However, some serious scholars would maintain that, despite the assured place of modern literal exegesis, the spiritual exegesis of the past is still valid today.[87] Few have been convinced that such symbolic exegesis has anything worthwhile to offer. b) The acceptance of a 'modern' more-than-literal exegesis—this is the approach under consideration here. c) Rejection of more-than-literal exegesis—we shall consider this attitude later in the section.

Brown then turns to a direct treatment of the *sensus plenior* and begins by proposing a definition of it. 'The Sensus Plenior is the deeper meaning, intended by God but not clearly intended by the human author, that is seen to exist in the words of Scripture when they are studied in the light of further revelation or of development in the understanding of revelation.'[88] Brown would regard the demand for the consciousness of the human author as a pseudo-problem: how would we determine the nature and origin of this vague awareness? He agrees with Benoit, but prefers to be less categorical with regard to the human writer's lack of awareness. In two other important points he differs from Benoit: he will admit fuller senses within each Testament, while Benoit confines the fuller sense to an Old Testament-New Testament relationship; he would admit the possibility of uncovering fuller senses through a development in the understanding of revelation after the end of the biblical era, while Benoit would reject this possibility.

Brown distinguishes two especially important types of the fuller sense. The first is more restricted and is connected with the Old Testament passages which have been classically identified as prophecies referring to Christ and to the Christian dispensation; the theory of Sensus Plenior permits the Christian to retain at once the literal Old Testament sense and the Christian prophetic sense of these passages. The second form, the General Sensus Plenior, pertains to the field of biblical theology: it is the fuller meaning uncovered when a text has been placed in a wider biblical context—it is quite the same as the *périchorétique* sense of Coppens. Like Benoit, Brown establishes two criteria of the fuller sense. Both scholars agree that the more important one is that of homogeneity—the Sensus Plenior must be homogeneous with the literal sense, developing what the author wanted so say. Their other criterion is basically the same for each: the authoritative interpretation of the words of Scripture. For Benoit this means the 'reproduction' of the Old Testament words by a New Testament writer; Brown, with his broader view, extends the scope of the criterion to encompass the interpretation of Scripture in the later authentic tradition of the Church. These criteria are not always easy to apply. With regard to the extent of the Sensus Plenior, Brown is more cautious than Benoit (who would find a fuller sense in very many passages of the Old Testament). He would regard the 'majority' of the Old Testament texts cited in a more-than-literal sense in the New Testament, as well as the 'over-whelming majority' of the patristic and liturgical citations of Scripture, as failing to meet the criteria for a valid Sensus Plenior.

Brown concludes by considering some arguments against the fuller sense. The contention that the deeper meaning is not contained in the text itself but is acquired at the moment of further revelation boils down to a fuller understanding on the part of the exegete rather than to a fuller sense of Scripture. He argues that this would involve a dichotomy in God's plan of action. Furthemore, the literal sense leads to a fuller understanding—the fuller sense is not an addition to the literal sense but part of its organic growth. Brown is much more concerned about the dependence of the theory of the Sensus Plenior on a scholastic understanding of inspiration and, especially, on the principle of instrumental causality. This factor precludes sympathetic understanding in non-Catholic circles and, increasingly, in Catholic circles too. Elsewhere, he wonders whether the theory can be liberated from 'the scholasticism in which it was conceived . . . otherwise it may not survive the contemporary shift in the study and understanding of inspiration.'[89] Yet, the majority of Roman Catholic exegetes are willing to accept the Sensus Plenior as a theory.[90] It is significant, however, that the proponents of the fuller sense seldom appeal to it in practical exegesis but keep it for discussion on the theoretical level. Perhaps its greatest value is as a reminder that historical-critical exegesis of a scriptural text does not exhaust its full meaning.

The idea of a Sensus Plenior has met with opposition from some notable Catholic scholars.[91] Perhaps the most interesting critique is that of Bruce Vawter; it will suffice here to indicate his position.[92] Vawter is unhappy about the theory of a fuller sense because he sees it as a threat to the hard-earned primacy of the literal sense in scientific exegesis. While the exponents of the Sensus Plenior maintain that there must be an organic continuity between the 'first' and the 'second' literal sense, does not the insistence on a fuller literal sense inevitably involve some depreciation of the historical sense? He is prepared to accept some such term as 'fuller sense' to designate the ultimate course of a prophetic word which we know through later revelation—and which was unknown to the prophet; he would prefer to think of it as a fuller understanding. But Scripture as such is not the work of prophets but of writers who know what they intend to convey and who speak their own minds. There is no scope for a 'fuller sense', of which they are unaware, in their words. He makes the point that in our theory of inspiration, the factor we are sure of is that the writers are *human*; 'instrumentality' is the deficient analogy, and the theory of Sensus Plenior has leant too heavily on it.

Vawter observes that the examples we are offered of the 'General Sensus Plenior', notions like sin and justice, are illustrations of the development of scriptural ideas rather than of the deeper meaning of biblical texts. He feels that fuller senses might be sought more profitably in ideas rather than in texts. If he were prepared to accept the theory of fuller sense, he would regard it as more logical, with Brown (against Benoit), to find a fuller sense also in a New Testament text elucidated by authentic tradition. But, since in fact, Benoit explains such later Church development of doctrine as a better understanding of the primary literal sense by means of the 'consequent explicative sense',[93] Vawter wonders why, then, there is any need to demand a new literal sense in the text of Scripture itself to explain the deeper understanding of the Old Testament enjoyed by the New Testament authors. He believes that further study will lead to fewer and not more scriptural 'senses'. We may note in conclusion that J. L. McKenzie believes that the hypothesis of a fuller sense is no more than 'a complicated statement of the truth that the meaning of the whole Bible is greater than the meaning of any single passage.'[94] And Lionel Swain would prefer to see the light thrown on the Old Testament by the New regarded as an extrinsic relation to the literal meaning of the Old Testament. He feels that it does more justice to the data in question 'to speak not so much of a fuller sense, or meaning, as of a *fullness of understanding*.'[95] He justifies the preference for a term which designates a subjective condition rather than an objective meaning by pointing out that 'it is the constant and repeated relevance of the original *meaning* to the different historical and existential circumstances which make such an understanding of the text "objective".'[96]

Though discussion on the pros and cons of a Sensus Plenior is carried on almost exclusively within Roman Catholic circles, there has been at least one significant contribution by a Protestant scholar. J. M. Robinson[97] observes that the Sensus Plenior does help to reach what critical historical research fails to find in the literal sense and does help to show that such material still pertains to the meaning of the passage. In his view, a basic achievement of R. E. Brown's study of the fuller sense has been the demonstration that a Sensus Plenior has always been involved in the Church's interpretation of Scripture. He would regard the discussion about the Sensus Plenior as a current Roman Catholic form of a debate inevitable in the Church—the whole question of 'Scripture and the Church'. The rejection, out of hand, of the Sensus Plenior is not necessarily scholarly; the theory is a feature of a basic problem which ought to be subject to scholarly discussion. Robinson agrees with Brown that the meaning expressed in terms of the Sensus Plenior cannot be confined to the use of the Old Testament in the New Testament but must include the use of the Bible in the Church. He fears that the Sensus Plenior may be used as a peg to hang new doctrines on. His fear is not unfounded: the theory has come as a God-send to those who would see the doctrines of the Immaculate Conception or the Assumption in the fuller sense of a passage like *Gen.* 3:15.

But Robinson is not sympathetic to the substitution of a 'fuller understanding' of the text for a fuller sense. The alleged addition of meaning, and so fuller understanding, neglects the dynamic factor in the literal sense. 'Once one recognises that any discussion of the "sense" of Scripture is a discussion of its understanding then or now, the distinction between sense and understanding as a meaningful classification tends to disappear, and the study of the text becomes a study of its life as word event from its original composition until now.'[98] He does not share Vawter's fear that the literal sense is 'depreciated' by the theory of fuller sense. The literal sense, adequate and 'full' in the situation in which it was spoken, must be translated into new meaning if it is to make its point today. However, he too would reject much of what Vawter finds unacceptable, feeling that any advocacy of the Sensus Plenior today and in the future should share Vawter's criticism of much that it has meant in the past. But still, Protestant exegesis, no less than Roman Catholic exegesis, has to involve itself in hermeneutical discussions as to the meaning of the biblical text then and now.

## IV. RESERVATIONS

James Barr[99] asks the question how we, understanding the Old Testament as we do, may state valid connections between it and the New Testament. He replies by distinguishing aspects of the ways in which the New Testament related itself to the Old. As regards methods employed in the New Testament, such as typology and allegory, the modern scholar can respect the interpretative processes and forms of the time, yet he cannot maintain that the methods are mandatory for him. On the other hand, we may not reject the value of the theology of the New Testament writers because allegorical exegesis has been admitted into it. But Barr is not happy with the attempt to rehabilitate typology: it may fail to meet with modern scientific requirements without relating itself to the exegetical practice of the early Church. He surely makes a pertinent comment when he suggests that 'we have to separate the question of stating how the Old Testament is used in the New from the question of how *we* are to relate ourselves to the Old and its use in the New.'[100] He has doubts, too, about the practicality of typological exegesis: a really typological approach will not work in the context of modern critical exegesis. Here, of course, he has in mind the sweeping typological exegesis envisaged by von Rad.

Barr is satisfied that the relationship of the Old Testament to the New Testament is extremely complex; he indicates some of the levels at which the Old Testament operates in relation to the New. In the first place, we should recognise that the religion of later Judaism formed the religious framework for the New Testament. Then there is the fact that the Old Testament is a text read and meditated upon; the text is different from the religion and was open to the production of something different. Another level may have been the mind of Jesus: his understanding of himself and of his work is formed upon biblical patterns; a further feature is the authority with which he used the biblical text. Similarly we may mention the minds of the apostles, in their coming to understand Christ and in their use of the Old Testament. In general we find that when the New Testament quotes Scripture, it is imaginative and constructive in its choice and combination of passages. The New Testament writers were concerned less with methods than with results. This means, in short, that 'the use of the Old Testament in the New was a rather different sort of operation from what we call "exegesis" altogether.'[101] The object is to let the meaning emerge from the text by looking at every aspect of the text.

But while we may thus come to a better understanding of the New Testament use of the Old, the question remains: can we, in our context of historical exegesis, affirm that Christ 'fulfils' the Old Testament Scriptures? Barr's answer is quite firm and hinges on the distinction between the irregular methodology of the New Testament writers and the essential values involved. The modern Christian can come to understand that Christ came from what had been done and prepared in Israel and can affirm this with certainty. That is why he is sure that the historical-critical method does not discern the total meaning of the Old Testament text. Even if we are not happy with methods like typology and allegory, we should not fall back on a purely 'historical' way of stating meaning. We should keep in mind that while the New Testament may have been arbitrary in its use of texts, it has not been arbitrary in its general interpretation or in the connections it makes between the Old Testament and Christ.

We must not overlook the fact that the Old Testament is pre-Christian. Barr finds in this fact a theological ground for a decision against a 'christological' interpretation of the Old Testament. 'Though the God of the Old Testament is the

Father of our Lord, the Old Testament is the time in which our Lord is not yet come. It is as the time in which he is not yet come that we ought to understand it.'[102] Thus, while it is true that the sending of Jesus Christ is the culmination of God's purpose, this does not mean that Jesus is the criterion for the meaningfulness of what God has done before he came. The reality of God's original contact with Israel demands that we should show interest in the original setting of the texts. The situations of Israel are real in themselves—it does them less than justice to talk of them as 'prefigurations'. God's purpose, indeed, works towards what happens in Christ, but it works towards it in situations of actual contact with God. The setting in Israel is central, irrespective of later interpretation of Old Testament texts even in the New Testament itself.

Thus Barr questions the statement that the Old Testament can be understood only 'in the light of Christ' or 'in the light of the New Testament', and does not think that we can really consider Christ as the 'key' to the Old Testament. He points out that the concern of the apostles was not to understand the Old Testament but to understand Christ: they turned to the Old Testament in their striving to know and explain Christ. We too facilely believe that we can come to know the Old Testament from the standpoint of our understanding of Christ. The question is: do we know Christ? It would seem that only bad Christologising can follow from trying to take the 'known' Christ as a key to the understanding of the Old Testament. He maintains that other generalities, such as the idea that the Old Testament is 'incomplete' or 'a torso', are also misleading. He points out how the idea that the Old Testament cannot be understood without Christ can easily be tautologous; it is obvious tautology to say that the Old Testament cannot be understood as part of the Christian economy of salvation apart from Christ. And if such a statement means that the non-Christian finds the Old Testament unintelligible, it is untrue. 'The proper strategy in the Church is not to take Christ as the given and argue from him to the authority or meaning of the Old Testament; it is rather, taking the Old Testament as something which we *have* in the Church, to ask in what ways the guidance it affords helps us to understand and discern and obey the Christ more truly.'[103]

G. Ernest Wright[104] raises his voice in protest against certain Christocentric theologies of the Old Testament which dissolve theology into Christology and so leave nothing to say about the independence of God; this tendency he labels 'Christomonism'—a unitarianism of the Second Person. He does not suggest that every form of Christocentric piety and theology is Christomonism; his target is the sharp narrowing of religious attention that would rule out talk about God in favour of talk about Jesus. The fact is that *Christo*centricity is meaningless without a prior *theo*centricity. Wright is especially critical of the 'existentialist Christomonism' of Rudolf Bultmann. For Bultmann Christianity stands apart from Old Testament religion as the faith which perceives in Jesus Christ the revelation of God. The specifically Christian content of the New Testament is 'the idea that man's relation to God is bound to the person of Jesus'[105]; and the idea cannot be eliminated that God is accessible only in Jesus Christ. From such a Christomonistic standpoint the answer to the question of the significance of the Old Testament for the Christian faith is obvious: the Old Testament can be proclaimed in the Church as God's word only when the Church finds in it 'what is already known from the revelation in Jesus Christ'.[106] In fact, Christomonism plays a real role in Bultmann's dehistoricising of the Bible.

Wright's conclusion is that 'in any event, existential Christomonism is no more helpful than any other Christomonism for the problems of faith and its articulation today'.[107] He feels strongly that an Old Testament scholar must protest against Christomonism as a substitute for 'a theology of the divine initiative in history, the only theology that can handle the Old and New Testaments together'.[108] He then proceeds in chapters 3 to 5, the centre of his book, to examine certain primary assumptions and assertions about God in the Old Testament (God as Creator, Lord and Warrior) and gives reasons why they must be taken seriously by all who would keep in touch with the biblical understanding of reality. Because human life is mostly concerned with the sociopolitical realm, with the *means* whereby human beings relate to one another, he contends that what is basically biblical is a special political understanding of the universe. In this perspective the conceptions of God as Creator, Lord, and Warrior maintain an abiding relevance. In short, the Christian theologian must take the Old Testament seriously, not solely as a historical document which gives the background of later movements, but as of vital serious moment for present faith and life.

Roland E. Murphy[109] is concerned that the word of God to Israel should be taken for what it is and ought not to be too hastily Christianised. This factor must be kept in mind in any attempt to lay out the lines of continuity and discontinuity in the relationship of the two Testaments. In the first place he asserts that the relationship is not adequately conceived in terms of biblical inspiration. In particular he feels that the 'fuller sense' approach has not been as successful as had been hoped and, already, there is a swing away from this kind of analysis. Then the idea of fulfilment needs to be spelled out. A Christian notion of fulfilment should not blot out the Old Testament reality, nor should it become an abstraction. Perhaps our preoccupation with historical-critical exegesis has caused us to overlook the concrete manner in which the Old Testament was understood by the primitive Church. We should pay more attention to the meaning of the Old Testament for the people of Christ's own age. Finally, the lines of continuity and discontinuity between the Testaments must be delineated. Murphy feels that the phrase 'the unity of the Bible' ought to be interred! In fact it is not possible to give conceptual expression to the unity of the Bible. One cannot ignore the discrepancies between different parts of the Old Testament and of the New Testament, and the problem is compounded when one puts the Testaments together.

In the Christian perspective the Christological approach has been the most obvious centre of unity. As it is commonly worked out, it has not been successful because it virtually eliminates the historical development of the Old Testament material and reduces the vitality of Old Testament thought which becomes only a pale reflection of the Christ to come. It would seem that the most fruitful approach to unity is by the way of promise/fulfilment. Properly understood, this means that the Old Testament contains the history of the promise which comes to fruition in the New Testament; the dynamic, historical hope of Israel abides, even after its 'fulfilment' in the New Testament.

If ever an Old Testament scholar and historian has spoken with conviction on behalf of his field, in a defence of the Old Testament's 'authority', it is John Bright.[110] In his work, he first clearly states the nature of the problem and the 'classical solutions' which have been proposed. This is followed by his own answer, his almost polemical stand, that the key to the problem is to be found in the discipline of biblical theology in its capacity to 'distinguish the normative from the incidental and transient, the central from the peripheral, *within the biblical faith itself.*'[111] Bright has an intense, almost passionate conviction that we must confront the Old Testament witness *as a whole,* even the 'offensive parts', and make our peace with *that*—since no part of the Bible is without authority. In some way or another, the whole always reflects some facet of the structure of faith normative for Christianity. Although we shall be content here to survey only the first part of his work as it sets forth his thesis, perhaps we can pinpoint the source of his conviction by a statement which he makes in the latter part of his book, which deals with 'Hermeneutical considerations' in the preaching of the Old Testament to the contemporary Church. There he says that we shall never be able to hear the Old Testament aright unless we hear it all—that is, in its full humanity. For, in biblical revelation, 'there is a drive toward incarnation'—a drive which reached its goal when the Word became flesh and shared our very human condition, our thoughts and feelings and daily life. It follows that 'we cannot demand that God's word be always spoken from heaven with the tongues of archangels. We cannot demand that the Bible give us nothing but correct teachings and safe moral instructions, and be offended at it when it does not. We must receive the biblical word in its humanity, and as a whole, or we cannot rightly hear it at all.'[112]

Because of the very nature of the Old Testament, its difficulty and strangeness which have offended many a sensibility, the authority of the Old Testament and its place in the Christian's Bible have always been debated. Bright differentiates three different classical solutions to the problem which have been found in various forms throughout history. He notes that all of them have this in common: they take the New Testament as the point of orientation and evaluate the Old Testament from that perspective. Now although this does seem a reasonable procedure for a Christian to follow, and all who have followed the lines of these solutions have done so in all good faith, grasping clearly the nature of the problem, yet the results have been unfortunate because the approaches have been misguided. The first solution Bright classifies under the general title 'Marcionism' after the second century heresy which, under Gnostic influence, devalued the Old Testament as the product of 'evil', of another and hostile god. Bright would label as 'Marcionists' all those Christians who, because of the great differences in the Old Testament as compared with the New, would depose it or rank it as second-rate Scripture. He traces the Marcionist strain from those who would overtly complain that there is so much in the Old Testament which is 'unedifying' for Christians (e.g. Harnack and Delitzsch—who thought that the 'great deception' was the identification of Yahweh with the Christians' God), to those who practise Marcionism unawares (e.g. the layman or pastor who, troubled by the Old Testament, treats it as if it were not in the Bible). He mentions the era in which theological courses offered in seminaries or elsewhere treated the Old Testament like an 'unwanted guest whom one can neither send away nor entertain properly'.[113] As an example of those who would accord a secondary value to the Old Testament, he names Bultmann—who saw the Old Testament as a historical 'miscarriage', a history of shattering failure yielding nothing but the great contradiction that belongs to human existence: 'to be called by God, yet to be bound to earthly history'.[114] Indeed, Bright claims, Bultmann saw in Israel's history a reflection of his own dilemma and the failure of his own hopes.

Bright summarises the Marcionist fallacy thus: 'wherever the law-gospel antithesis is pushed to the virtual equating of the Old Testament with law, wherever the discontinuity between the Testaments is stressed to the virtual exclusion of the continuity, wherever the Old Testament is accorded the exclusively pedagogical function of preparing man for the hearing of the gospel, the danger exists that the Old Testament will be reduced to a position of secondary importance.'[115] He says that the Church must continue to resist the Marcionist tendency not only by retaining the Old Testament, but by actively using it as a part of normative Scripture. For, the Old Testament was authoritative Scripture for Jesus himself, who knew no God save its God and who found in it the key to his own person. 'I find it most interesting and not a little odd that, although the Old Testament on occasion offends our Christian feelings, it did not apparently offend Christ's "Christian feelings"!'[116] Moreover, to loosen the bond between the Testaments always somehow results in damaging the gospel. 'The Old Testament holds the gospel to history. It is the surest bulwark against assimilation with alien philosophies and ideologies, against a flight into sentimental and purely other-worldly piety, and against that disintegrating individualism that so easily besets it.'[117]

The second solution is that of 'saving' the Old Testament by reading a Christian meaning into all its texts. This began with the early Church Fathers, who resorted to allegory and typology in order to define various levels of meaning. Although patristic exegesis did 'save' the Old Testament (by making it a Christian book), it strayed beyond control into an 'exotic jungle of fanciful interpretation'. The Reformers objected to this quite rightly, asking what authority the Old Testament could have if each individual could read *any* meaning into it, and they defended the text in its 'plain meaning'. Yet, they thought that this included a 'prophetic sense' in the light of Scripture as a whole (*sensus literalis propheticus*), and this too tended to become subjective. More recently, the trend in biblical scholarship has been to abide by the historical meaning of the text as the author intended it.

Then, asking if the Church can really rest content with the 'plain historical meaning', Bright discusses still more recent views: the Roman Catholic stand on the *sensus plenior*, the christological interpreters, and others who feel that the Old Testament must be read beyond its historical sense. 'All are alike expressive of the strongly held conviction that, on the one hand, the Church *needs* the Old Testament and

21

cannot do without it; and that, on the other, she cannot be asked to "take it straight"; some meaning over and above its plain historical meaning must be added if she is to stomach it.'[118] However, the text *must* be allowed to speak its own word: typology or 'interpretation' are not to act as substitutes for straightforward exegesis, whose task is to make clear the precise meaning of the text. 'Let us say it clearly: the text has but one meaning, the meaning intended by its author; and there is but one method for discovering that meaning, the grammatico-historical method.'[119] Bright concedes that there *may* be meanings beyond the obvious sense of the Old Testament text: who can confine or limit the one God of both Testaments? However, this does not change the exegetical task. 'To put it bluntly but quite fairly, one can make an exegesis of texts, but one cannot make an exegesis of the Holy Spirit's intention.'[120] As Jesus says, the Holy Spirit is like the wind, blowing where it wills, and cannot be probed (or prodded!) by the exegete's tools. In short, Bright concludes, interpretation must go *beyond* the historical meaning of a text, yes; but, it must be controlled by that meaning.

The third and final classical solution, a kind of *via media,* is associated with liberal Protestantism. It consists of making a value-judgement on the basis of New Testament teaching which is then imposed upon the contents of the Old Testament, separating the elements of abiding validity from those too 'ancient, sub-Christian or outworn' to concern us. This liberalism (associated with Wellhausen) stressed the human aspect of the Bible and the social and moral aspects of its religion; it was seen as a historically conditioned book, as God's self-revelation progressively 'developing' towards Christianity. Hence, all of the Old Testament was to be evaluated according to the norm of its highest level: Jesus himself. But, this meant that large parts of the Old Testament were seen as irrelevant to the Christian and thus slipped into disuse, and also that what remained tended to be spiritualised or moralised. Granted, Jesus is the crown of revelation; but, to test the validity of Scripture by deriving a 'norm' from him can easily become too subjective. In fact, to make such value-judgements leads to the breakdown of scriptural authority because, as a result, the individual formulates his own beliefs and practices; his own mind and heart become the final court of appeal. However, 'the Christian faith is a historical phenomenon: it is what it *was*', Bright points out.[121] In other words, it is not what a given individual believes it to be by trying to isolate elements in Scripture by 'value judgements'. Thus, he concludes, these three classical solutions, all taking the Old Testament as a point of orientation, seem to be the only logical possibilities in answering the problem of the Old Testament's authority. And since, as he has demonstrated, none of them is acceptable, we seem to be at an impasse. But, we shall see in our final chapter, Bright's way out of the impasse is found in the study of biblical theology.[122]

### 3. The Old Testament as a Christian Book

The Christian meaning of the Old Testament is the subject of two important books which, to some extent, synthesise the views discussed so far in this chapter. First, however, we shall take warning from another work: if we exaggerate the Christian sense of the Old Testament we may undermine the true values of both Testaments.

The Christocentric interpretation of the Old Testament has been given an extreme expression by Wilhelm Vischer.[123] He not only looks for the basis of New Testament revelation in the Old Testament but believes that every word of the Old Testament points to Christ. For him the Old Testament says *what* Christ is, the New Testament says *who* he is. The Old Testament is indeed 'Scripture', but the New Testament is the real content of this Scripture; rather, Christ himself, the Lord who fulfils it, is its content. A few typical statements will illustrate the author's viewpoint. He can maintain that Adam himself was a Christian and that his faith was identical with ours because the time element makes no difference to faith. Like Luther he sees Christ in the 'angel' who wrestled with Jacob. Moses on Sinai was shown an outline of the life of Christ. He sees a clear reference to Christ in the red heifer of Numbers 19:1-10. The taking of Ai by the Israelites teaches that, by faith, we share in the combat of Christ. The capture of Jericho, on the seventh day, is a figure of the last day when, at the sound of a trumpet, the kingdoms of this world will fall into the hands of the Lord and of his Christ. The altar raised by the Transjordan tribes 'not for burnt offering, nor for sacrifice' (*Jos.* 22:26) is the real origin of the synagogue. In short, Old Testament events have no meaning in themselves: they are the prediction in one way or another, of the Christ-event.

Vischer's bizarre interpretation of the Old Testament is a reaction against a desiccated exegesis that had no place for the theological riches of the Bible. His method is superficially historical and recognises modern critical scholarship, but in reality his technique is typological and allegorical. Though he professes to reject 'pneumatic exegesis' and claims to be objective, he strips the Old Testament of its historical value. His purpose is to seek out and present the permanent theological significance of the Old Testament. But he has overlooked the fact that the theological wealth of the Old Testament is to be found, first and foremost, in its literal and historical sense, properly and fully understood. And, by finding as he alleges to find, the New Testament in the Old, Vischer removes any distinction between Old and New and so any real development from one to the other. He makes incarnation and cross pointless and, indeed, makes Christ superfluous.

Pierre Grelot believes it to be timely to take a close look at the Church's experience of the Old Testament as a Christian book, and he has studied in depth the Christian content of the Old Testament.[124] The first part of his work is devoted to a historical introduction in which he examines the place of the Old Testament in Christian theology—first and foremost, in the New Testament. In general, the New Testament writers had two preoccupations in their use of the Old Testament: controversy and apologetics on the one hand, pastoral concern and theology on the other. The new message presented to the world by the witnesses of Jesus was found to be understandable only in terms of its providential background: the Old Testament—its Scriptures, institutions and history. Inversely, these received a new interpretation and took on a deeper significance in the light of the Christian message. A fundamental principle of the New Testament is that of *fulfilment*: history, legal and cultic prescriptions, scripture—these are 'fulfilled', they reach out to the coming of Christ and his economy of salvation. But the New Testament reality *surpasses* all that is imperfect and incomplete in the old regime; there is continuity and yet a movement on to another level. These two principles are reconciled in a third which includes them: the principle of *prefiguration*.

Next Grelot traces the problem of the Old Testament in Christian theology from the patristic era, through the Middle ages and the Counter-Reformation, to modern times. The time seems ripe, he thinks, for a dogmatic treatise on the Old Testament which will, on the one hand, through solid biblical scholarship, establish the literal sense of the text and reconstruct the history of events, institutions and doctrines of the Old Testament and, on the other hand, integrate the theological data which Christian tradition has developed on the basis of the New Testament. 'Biblical criticism should help us to distinguish, in patristic and medieval thought, between the essential doctrinal elements which form part of our faith, and those adventitious elements which modern theology can abandon without loss.'[125]

The second part of the book contains the body of the treatise and deals with the Old Testament in its relation to the divine plan of salvation, and to the mystery of Christ (chs. 2 and 3). The threefold aspect of the Old Testament as law, history, and promise receives a full treatment (chs. 4 to 6). The treatise opens with a consideration of the Old Testament in the plan of salvation; it examines the Christian notion of salvation, the problem of salvation history and the stages of God's saving plan (ch. 2). Profane history and salvation history are not two separate realities; in the concrete there is only one history which unfolds on two planes at once. What happens is that a particular series of events has a deeper significance, perceptible to faith—the events are the acts of God in human history. We might define salvation history as 'the history of the human community called by God to be his people: Israel first, then the Church which emerges at the moment when, through the incarnation, cross and resurrection of Jesus Christ, the *goal* of history is present in its very unfolding. And, at the close of the history of the Church the whole human community will join up with this people of God, so that all profane history will be absorbed in salvation history.'[126] The course of salvation history may be divided into three stages: from Adam to Abraham, from Abraham to Christ, from Christ to the eternal consummation.

Chapter three sets out to show that the Old Testament, which forms the first, provisional stage of the great plan of salvation which culminates in Christ, is linked in an effective manner to that future mystery. The choice of Israel as a people inaugurated a religious regime where the fundamental characteristics of the plan of salvation—Word, people, and covenant—are already revealed and take concrete shape; each of these characteristics already implies the mystery of Christ. For indeed, the mystery of Christ must be present in some fashion in the historical dispensation that prepares for its full flowering. The incarnate Word is somehow present in the Word of God; the people of Israel is in some measure the Church, the Body of Christ; the Sinai covenant reflects the essential mystery of the covenant, the mystery of *God-with-man*. The Word of God is before all ages, and the contemporary of every age. Before his earthly mission he is already at work, and it is *in him and by him* that God speaks to Israel, forms it into his people, and gives it his covenant. The mystery of Israel is thus linked all along the way with the mystery of Christ. Israel, the people of God, has really *lived* in the mystery of Christ; it has received from God a certain *knowledge* of the mystery and it has *participated* in a certain measure in the grace which flows from it.

The faith of the Old Testament (and consequently its hope) was identical in substance with our Christian faith, not only in its existential and psychological aspects, but even in regard to its object. The essential difference lies in the degree of clarity and precision in the revelation. In the New Testament the explicit object of faith is the mystery of God and of salvation, both known in the mystery of Christ already come in history; in the Old Testament it was the mystery of God and of salvation, imperfectly revealed, but implying the mystery of Christ to come. We may make a distinction between 'vital experience', 'notional knowledge' and 'conceptual formulation'. The people of the Old Testament were orientated towards the mystery of faith by a confused vital experience (the mystery of Christ was present and active among them); but they had no notional knowledge of it and so could not formulate it conceptually. But if the mystery of Christ could not be couched in explicit formulas, it could be present 'under the veil of provisional structures'. For, before the event in which the mystery of salvation will find its consummation, there is already a salvation *history*. Before the institutions which will communicate, in its fullness, the grace of salvation, there are sacred *institutions* which, in their fashion, were imperfect sacraments of the faith. And, as a general rule, the *promises* of salvation to come are couched in a veiled language wherein this history and these institutions figure largely. Hence, for a Christian understanding of the Old Testament, it is not enough to affirm, in broad terms, that it prepared the way for Christ or that Christ was present in it. It is necessary to study the different aspects of the preparatory dispensation. And so, the following three chapters are concerned with Israel's laws and institutions, its history, and the promises of the prophets.

The subject of *law* embraces both law properly so called and institutions; in God's saving plan the Law is pedagogy which leads to Christ, while the institutions prefigure him. In its role of educating the people of God, the Law showed itself exacting in its demands, condescending in regard to the actual situation of the people and progressive in its leading them to a higher goal. And the divine pedagogy was efficacious: it raised the people of Israel to the moral and religious level necessary for the preaching of the gospel; by holding up an unattainable ideal, it made the people conscious of its need of redemption. Through fidelity to the divine pedagogy, the just of Israel already entered, in an imperfect but real manner, into the regime of grace.

The religious language of the Old Testament always recognised the existence of an analogy between the divine world and human institutions. At this point, in terms of the institutions, Grelot gives a preliminary definition of prefiguration. It is 'the analogy within the one plan of salvation between two objective orders: on the one hand, the "heavenly realities" (*Heb.* 9:23), made visible in the life and sacrifice of

Christ (cf. 9 : 11), made present under the sign of the Church and its sacraments and destined to be fully revealed at the stage of eternal life.'[127] Prefiguration is to be looked for in an institution taken as a whole, not in its details, and the object prefigured by the institutions of the Old Testament is the mystery of Christ, at once in its profound unity and in its different aspects. The doctrine of prefiguration is of great importance because it alone enables us to understand *how* Christ was present in the Old Testament; or, rather, it helps us to discern which *signs* manifest his presence there, both as object of faith and as principle of justification. The fact is that if one can say, with verisimilitude, that the mystery is the object of Old Testament faith, it is because this mystery was represented by prefiguring signs. Among such signs are the legal institutions of Israel whose figurative significance is indirect in the case of civil institutions and direct in the case of cultic institutions. In such ways Christ was present as an object of faith; and, if so, he was present too as a principle of justification because, thanks to their implicit faith in Christ, the former believers could obtain justification and salvation.

Under the regime of the Law, God directed the history of his people in such a way that it became salvation history. Consequently, this history has played a twofold role in the plan of salvation : pedagogic—to prepare men for the coming of Christ—and figurative—to enable believers, starting with their own historical experience, to gain an anticipated knowledge of the mystery of salvation. In the Old Testament, as in the New, historical experience is the starting-point of faith. God does not make himself accessible to us by means of intellectual reflection or through mystical contemplation, but by the mediation of events where his action becomes almost tangible to us. The absolutely original fact, demanding the most serious attention of exegetes and theologians, is that the historical experience of Israel is the bearer of revelation and the concrete support of a lived faith because Israel's earthly destiny involves the realisation of God's saving plan. The history of Israel is coloured by the people's experience of the gifts, promises, and judgements of God. At the same time, all in the history of Israel, whether it is a question of the history lived by the people of God or of the history related by the inspired writers, is not equally salvation history.

We have noted that the pedagogic role of the Law concerned essentially the moral education of the people. The pedagogic role of history is, in the main, the theological education of the people. The divine Word, speaking in and through history, educates the people in faith, hope and charity—an evident preparation for the time of Christ. History is also prefiguration, and Grelot feels that he can now reply with more precision to the question: what is prefiguration? Prefiguration gives expression, on the level of religious intelligibility, to the essential link between the elements of salvation history at its preparatory stage (events, institutions, persons) and the eschatological consummation of this history. The successive stages of the historical process (which is the concrete stuff of the Old Testament) are marked by this factor. For the God who through these stages educates his people always has the *eschaton* in mind and has inserted the characteristics of his divine plan, in a veiled fashion, into the pattern of facts which led to this term. The basis of prefiguration is, above all else, the relation of the history of Israel to this *eschaton*. 'Prefiguration is thus the analogy established by God between the two successive stages of his saving plan: that of preparation, the stage of divine pedagogy, and that of fulfilment. On the one hand, there are the figures: the *events* which occur in the history of the people of Israel and constitute its experience of faith; the *persons* who, in this setting, take on religious significance; the *institutions* which structure its historical experience and serve as a concrete support to its faith and give it provisional expression.'[128] In studying biblical figures we must always take the literal sense as our point of departure in order to come to know the faith which the figures express. The prefiguration of the mystery of Christ by the history and the institutions of Israel has played a capital role in the theological education of the people of God. It is in this way that the presence of Christ in the Old Testament, both as object of faith and hope and as principle of justification, was given concrete expression throughout the preparatory regime.

The Old Testament possesses an internal dynamism which

gives meaning to its history and which is expressed in a series of promises, renewed from age to age with growing precision. It is necessary to distinguish the promise of eschatological salvation in itself from the literary framework in which the promise is set, and it must be realised, too, that the language of the Old Testament evokes in a concrete manner the mystery of salvation only by dressing it in symbols. In regard to the *eschaton*, the Old Testament has had recourse to a twofold symbolism. On the one hand, the historical experience of Israel, transposed to 'the latter days', furnished a concrete representation of judgement and of salvation. On the other hand, the imagery which described the origin of salvation history could be employed to describe its final perfect state; hence, the salvation to come could appear both as historical and as transcendent. It is hardly surprising that in this matter the eschatological picture presents some ambiguities. Is the salvation to come this-wordly or meta-historical? progressive or instantaneous? does it involve the temporal redemption of Israel or the spiritual redemption of all mankind? Christ is the fulfilment of the promised salvation, which is now a fact of history. The saving event, however, is not limited to the earthly life of Jesus, for there are three stages: the coming of Christ in the flesh, his presence in the Church, his final coming in glory—and it is this whole ensemble which constitutes the fulfilment of the prophecies. The Old Testament principle of fulfilment involves two aspects: the mystery of Christ fulfilled the promises and fulfilled the figures, for it was proclaimed conjointly in promise and figure; secondly, promises and figures are inextricably bound up together. That is why the New Testament writers are little concerned whether the texts which they apply to the mystery of Christ are to be taken in a literal sense, or figuratively.

The third part of Grelot's work, 'The Christian Interpretation of the Old Testament', is the conclusion of his treatise. When we maintain that the Old Testament is the word of God, we mean that in the books of the Old Testament God was not only speaking in time past to the Fathers, but that in these books he is still speaking to us. Because this is so, the interpretation of the Old Testament cannot proceed as an exercise of pure science, abstract and disinterested. It is essential not only to make proper use of critical methods but to keep them in their right place; in other words, it is needful to assimilate criticism, and then to pass beyond it. What gives a vital bearing to the Old Testament texts is not their setting in the past but their essential content, that dimension in which they pass on a message of salvation fundamentally identical with the saving message of the gospel. The discernment of this message certainly goes beyond the results of critical exegesis. Bultmann's demythologisation and existential interpretation of the New Testament has at least served to draw the attention of exegetes and theologians to a capital aspect of their work. For the word of God, by the fact that it is addressed to men, is ordered to life, and the function of its interpreters is to make its vital significance perceptible to men of their age and milieu.

As a first step in the Christian interpretation of the Old Testament, it is necessary to look for a unifying principle in the varied pages of the Old Testament; and it appears that this principle can be found in its formal object, the mystery of salvation. The perspective of the Old Testament is determined by the plan of salvation, as Israel lived it and perceived it, in terms of the religious regime established by the covenant. Because this is so, it follows that the Old Testament is not just a preparation for the mystery of Christ but is already an integral part of that mystery. The mystery of Christ is present in the prophetic *word* which stirred up and gave form to a religious life basically identical with our own; it is present in the *institutions* of the people of God which prepared their hearts to receive Christ; it is present in the *history* of Israel polarised from the beginning by the goal towards which it reached. In short, to say that the mystery of salvation is the unique object of the Old Testament writings is to maintain that their object is the mystery of Christ, progressively revealed to Israel and simultaneously experienced by it, in advance, under the veil of prefiguring events and institutions. The word of God always bears on a mysterious *reality* with which man maintains an existential relationship.

If the object of the Old Testament writings is the mystery

of salvation, the mystery of the living God in his relations with men, we may ask how human language can hope adequately to express this supernatural reality. It is, therefore, a matter of particular importance to study and interpret the biblical language of the Old Testament. We have noticed that, because of its unique destiny, the people of Israel in its historical experience lives the events directed by God, possesses the institutions willed by God, and receives the men sent by God —all in view of the mystery of salvation. This constant reference to the mystery of salvation confers the value of religious experience—whose significance is disclosed by the prophetic word—on the historical experience of Israel. Thus, biblical language refers constantly to the data of this experience; and it can find no better way to give expression to the mystery than in the language of symbols and figures. Hence, biblical figures (events, persons and institutions) belong to the fundamental structure of biblical language. Indeed, Christian authors will continue to feel the need for such language and will express the realities of the New Testament in categories of thought forged by the historical experience of Israel—this has been the first language of Christian theology. For that matter, we need to state quite clearly that 'to translate authentically the divine mesage, without betraying either its eixstential aspect, which gives it its vital value, or its ontological aspect, which assures our authentic knowledge of transcendent realities, there is not, in the last resort, any other language possible except the symbolical language of the Bible in its fully developed New Testament form.'[129]

It is evident that the Christian interpretation of the Old Testament presupposes that the exegete should not be confined within the limits of critical method. It is not enough to seek out only the human ideas of the biblical writers; it is necessary to pay attention to the resonances which the texts may have for us who have been enlightened by Christian revelation. The New Testament, especially the Pauline letters and Hebrews, offers the principles which will help us to pass beyond the results of literary and historical criticism. And so we learn that the Christian understanding of the Old Testament must take cognizance of three 'passages': from the letter to the spirit, from the stage of divine pedagogy to its aim and purpose, from figures to the prefigured Reality. All three are closely associated, are in no way in conflict with the perspectives of critical scholarship, and provide a way of passing from the stage of exegesis to the field of theology.

Grelot accepts the *sensus plenior*. However, his complicated division of the senses of Scripture[130] is not likely to win any further support for a fuller sense. On the other hand, he does point out that the distinction between literal sense and fuller sense is more or less equivalent to Paul's distinction of letter and spirit. The Pauline 'spirit' lies in a *dépassement*, in going beyond the letter to find in the texts the vivifying presence of Christ—and this is what the fuller sense does.

In the same year that saw the appearance of Grelot's book, another French scholar published a work which bore a similar title and covered much the same ground.[131] C. Larcher had set himself the task of finding out whether the New Testament can furnish the key to a real Christian theology of the Old Testament. He therefore proposes to discover at its source, in the New Testament writings, the Christian dimension of the Old Testament. His view is that if we are guided by the reaction of Christ, and of the primitive Church, to the Old Testament writings, we not only avail of an indispensable means towards a higher understanding of the Old Testament, but we agree to read these writings in a Christian environment, in harmony with our faith. Thus, the main body of his work is divided into two parts of equal length: part I considers Jesus' own attitude towards the Old Testament and part II studies that of the early Church. But, first of all, he presents the central problem in a preliminary chapter: 'The Necessity and Difficulties of a Christian Actualisation of the Old Testament'. Difficulties to be faced are the Jewish attitude to the Old Testament, the radical newness of the Christian message, and the fact that Israel's past is not meaningful for us today. It is evident that the words of the Old Testament were not addressed immediately to us. Yet, in the light of Christ, we may now regard them as addressed to us and as helping us to understand our condition of creaturehood; this is at least a possible way of integrating the Old Testament into our faith. But the purpose of the book is to show that there is a more effective way of doing so.

Part I examines Jesus' attitude to and use of the Old Testament; this is a matter of fundamental importance because his attitude determined that of the primitive community. Larcher begins by showing that Jesus had linked the two Testaments indissolubly together in his own self. Jesus used the Old Testament as his book; for him it was Scripture with its own, divine authority. He placed himself at the centre of the former revelation declaring that the Scriptures spoke of him, proclaimed him and gave witness to him. This point is expanded in the second chapter which considers Jesus and the prophetic aspect of the Old Testament. It shows how he deepened its meaning, especially its messianic import; he did so by stressing his mission of Servant and by adopting the title of Son of Man, while he played down royal messianism.

The third chapter takes up, in the Gospels and in Paul, the more complicated problem of the Law. First there is Jesus' attitude to the Law. He had come to give a finality to the Torah in its widest context, the whole of Scripture—to give to the whole and to each detail that fullness of sense and reality demanded by God's purpose and implied dimly in Scripture itself. When he declared that he had not come to abolish the Law and the Prophets but to fulfil them (*Matt.* 5:17), Jesus was not looking to a radical discontinuity between the old and the new economy. It is not enough to say that Jesus has retained the Law only as Scripture, as a sacred book, as a testimony to the ways of God in the past—in other words as a dead letter; he wanted it to continue as a living reality now that it had been fulfilled by him. In fact, the Torah was integrated by him into the definitive revelation of God and so maintains a real, if subordinate, value. Jesus himself continued to be attentive to the whole Old Testament, to respect its values, to put them into practice and to teach them, and the Old Testament continues to play an educative role. Besides, the Torah is also a promise which must receive its fulfilment, and it is a norm of life woven into the very existence of the Jewish people.

If Jesus had thus taken a positive attitude to the Law, raising it to a higher perfection through his fulfilment of it, Paul insists rather that it belongs to a superseded economy. And if he admits that many of its precepts still bind the

Christian, it is because they are subsumed under charity. We must not forget, however, that the Law for Paul is essentially the *Mosaic Law* and that he is taking a stand against the Law considered as an economy of salvation independent of Christ. Indeed, in this respect, Paul makes Christ the antithesis of the Law and stresses that Christians are freed from the Old Law regarded as a system of religious life. However, the moral law, especially the Decalogue, continues in Christian life, but under a different head. If certain precepts of the Law reappear in a Christian climate, it is not because they correspond to the exigencies of the 'natural law' (a later theological justification) but because they are explicitly reassumed in Christian religion and morality or because they are in harmony with it. But it is because they have been taken over and sanctioned by an authority superior to that of the Mosaic Law—the authority of Christ and of the apostles, or the spontaneous instinct of the living Church under the light of the Holy Spirit—that they are binding on Christians. Some concrete precepts reappear in the train of charity and fit into the demands of Christian holiness. Then they are taken over into another context and become more exigent, more pressing. Paul concedes, of course, that the precepts of the Law preserve in their ensemble a teaching value and help to inculcate fundamental lessons. And, in its historical role, the regime of the law contributed to form the conscience of Israel.

Despite the problem constituted by the Mosaic Law, the fact remains that Jesus did fulfil the Old Testament, but in a manner which was unexpected and unforeseeable. He brought out the continuity and the unity of the two Testaments by shedding on them the clear light of his own originality. His example remained living and active in the first Christian generation. The four chapters of part II take up the ways in which the early Church saw the Old Testament: as prophecy, preparation, promise and figure.

The prophetic aspect of the Old Testament is affirmed in a general way in different New Testament texts. Always we find the same basic conviction: Christ is foretold, proclaimed in advance, in the Scriptures. This higher dimension of Scripture, which flows from its divine origin, is recognised by faith.

But it is on this level of faith that the New Testament writers take their stand; and when they read the entire Old Testament with the eyes of faith, they discover in it a single great prophecy. A special charism has played a role in this elaboration of Scripture, but one which operated in terms of the thought-patterns of the apostolic generation. That is why we cannot transfer these procedures into our apologetics; at least we must be careful to distinguish between prophecies which have apologetic value and those texts whose prophetic significance is seen only under the light of faith. Since the New Testament notion of fulfilment was not directed to isolated predictions but was concerned with the historical activity of God in the old economy and with his transcendent plan, Larcher suggests that the scheme prophecy-fulfilment should be replaced by the scheme preparation-fulfilment or promise-accomplishment.

The apostolic exegesis was not content to show that Christ was foretold by or contained in the Old Testament; it found the *preparation* for him in the facts of history, in the economy of the Old Testament rather than in the text of the Bible. And this history is envisaged as the progressive realisation of the plan of God. The Christ-event is the culminating, decisive point of a very complex historical process which unfolds on different levels. For indeed, the preparation has not presented the same intensity nor the same aspects in the course of the history of Israel; its principal phases are situated between the patriarchs and David. The apostolic exegesis, in marking the great stages of preparation in history, has turned deliberately to the oldest periods of Israel's history; thus Paul passes directly from David to Christ. From Exile on, the preparation becomes less evident in the framework of external history. Yet, Israel had the firm conviction that its history was in movement towards a decisive, future goal. Here the prophets have played a decisive role by constantly giving fresh impetus to the sense of expectancy. It is they who inculcated a sense of the dynamism of history, its progress towards a term which is the definitive work of God. The Christ-event has not only confirmed the reality of this dynamism, but has emphasised it retrospectively. It is abundantly clear that 'every attempt to reduce the message of Christ to an atemporal doctrine, to a gnosis, to a residue of eternal truths . . . has resulted in a depreciation of the Old Testament.'[132]

The Old Testament is a book of *promises*; the New Testament view is that the promises have become reality in Christ. In this undreamt-of fulfilment, the absolute gratuity of the divine gift is clearly seen. All who are incorporated into Christ by faith have access to all the goods of the promise— the absolute necessity of faith stands forth. Yet the Old Testament *promises* raise a problem: what is to become of the earthly, temporal, material values and goods that form the burden of the promises, even in the prophetic messianic preaching? Have they been entirely spiritualised? Larcher argues, convincingly, that the promised material goods do find a place in the Christian dispensation. When viewed in the light of the biblical doctrine of creation, it is evident that Christians, the Church on earth, have not withdrawn from this world of ours. They have not the right, even if they had the possibility, of turning their backs on it, of rejecting it: to do so would be a betrayal of the gospel. The Christian condition is characterised by a state of tension between realities already received and lived and those which remain the object of hope. So it is that some Christians do place themselves, as best they can, in an eschatological situation by freely living a poor, frugal, detached life, while others opt for a full presence in the world. In practice, Christian charity transforms the goods of the Old Testament promises and integrates them into Christian life. Love puts God and neighbour in the first place and orders the good things God has made in their proper hierarchy of values.

Larcher is quite brief in his treatment of the Old Testament as 'the Book of Figures'; he is evidently restrained in his approach to typology. He acknowledges that the New Testament makes moderate use of figurative exegesis, as it discovers a mysterious correspondence between Christian realities and realities described in the Old Testament. Thus, persons, events and institutions of the Old Testament prefigure Christ and his work. He would maintain that the New Testament writers have pointed to the authentic types, have indicated the realities of the old economy which, in the divine plan, prefigure Christ and his work. Once we move,

22

in our search of typology, beyond the pages of the New Testament we are no longer on sure ground.

In his 'general conclusions' Larcher summarises the characteristic traits of apostolic exegesis, looks again at the Christ-precedent, and indicates different ways of making the Old Testament actual. A first characteristic of apostolic exegesis of the Old Testament is the manifest conviction of all the New Testament writers that in Christ Jesus God has spoken through his Son and has revealed his plan of salvation. In this light the apostolic generation read the Old Testament to find there the promises, preparation and prefiguration of the Saviour. It is a characteristic reading of the Old Testament which laid bare its deeper meaning; the Spirit thus unveiled the christological sense of the inspired Scripture. Considered in its essential structure, apostolic exegesis is a spiritual exegesis in that it recognises two dimensions in the Old Testament: the letter and the spirit. This marks an opposition between two orders of things, two different economies. But, while stressing the spirit, the New Testament writers keep in close contact with the literal sense of Scripture. So, the most important prophetical texts are brought forward in their literal meaning, but they can then take on a plus-value through the new light under which they are read, the light of fulfilment. Finally, we must not overlook the fact that for the early Christians the Old Testament was 'Bible' *tout court* and had therefore something absolute about it; but, as Christians, they *had* to read it with other than Jewish eyes.

The attitude of the primitive Church is ultimately explained by the attitude of Jesus to the Old Testament; this precedent was decisive. It follows that the presentation of the Old Testament ought to be resolutely Christian since the Old Testament, by itself, does not obviously lead to Christian values. It should be read in its upward movement towards the definitive work of God; so, in fact, one should start with the New Testament. When one comes to speak of a *theology* of the Old Testament, it is necessary that this study should be orientated in depth towards Christ. The literal and historical sense should be prolonged in a fuller sense or, if one prefers to express it so, receive from the revelation of Christ a further clarification of its definitive meaning. While a theology of the New Testament builds on the literal sense, a Christian theology of the Old Testament looks directly to the fuller sense of the whole ensemble of the Old.

In its whole and in its parts, the Old Testament bears a message inspired by the Holy Spirit, and the message speaks 'to us' as Paul expressly affirms (cf. 1 *Cor.* 9:10; 10:11; *Rom.* 4:23-24; 15:4). We must read the Old Testament today in the same way as did the apostles and the New Testament writers—without, however, letting ourselves be cramped by the limits imposed on them by their time and culture. We must profit from the widening of horizons since their time. Larcher would consider the liturgy as a privileged context for a Christian actualisation of the Old Testament. It is in this setting that Scripture regains its sacred dimension and that the saving events of salvation recorded in the Old Testament spring to life again. Christ has brought the two Testaments together; this unity is consecrated by the liturgical celebration of his mystery in the Church's cult. For, in the context of the great mysteries of the life of Christ, Scripture becomes again a living and actual word—but now in the sense in which Jesus fulfilled it, in a total reference to him, to what he did and taught. 'For, in the last analysis' Larcher concludes, 'if the Old Testament can take on life and actuality it is, above all, because it has been integrated, in depth, into the Mystery of Christ.'[133]

Grelot's book is far more precisely planned than Larcher's and is much more readable, and this fact tends rather to bias one in its favour; but, on the whole, one finds a greater measure of agreement with Larcher. It is clear that both authors have much in common. Both stress the importance of the New Testament reading of the Old Testament—Larcher emphasises more the decisive importance of Jesus' attitude to the Old Testament. Both see the Old Testament as promise and preparation and both accept the fuller sense of the Old Testament. Larcher accepts typology, in a restricted sense; he does not share Grelot's broad view of prefiguration. In general, one feels, uneasily, that in Grelot the Old Testament has somehow been stripped of its specific values: it has become a *Christian book*—and not just Christian Scripture. Larcher's most significant contribution is his defence of these specific values when he discusses the Old Testament promises.

## 4. The Values of the Old Testament

Throughout this chapter we have been considering the Christian understanding of the Old Testament. This is surely a valid and important exercise because the Old Testament *is* part of the Bible of the Christian Church, and must have meaning for Christians. But do we too readily look for a Christian meaning there, overlooking the fact that it has its own specific contribution to make? There is some room for misgiving. It has become quite a fashion to refer to a remark of Dietrich Bonhoeffer: 'I don't think it is Christian to want to get to the New Testament too soon and too directly . . . You cannot and must not speak the last word before you have spoken the next to last.'[134] We shall say something, briefly, about the values and relevance of the Old Testament; it is a subject which will find a place, too, in our next chapter.

In the *Concilium* article noted above, John L. McKenzie considers this matter. Even as literature the Old Testament shows, in certain respects, an unequalled breadth of vision. This is particularly true of its sense of man as man, its broad humanitarianism, and of its sense of man in history, of man as a free and responsible agent answerable to the God of history. The Old Testament manifests joy in life while remaining realistically aware of pain and mortality. Joy cannot be bought at the price of moral integrity, and only the acceptance of death may sometimes save the dignity of the person. Such universal values, too often ignored, obviously do not detract from the more specifically religious values of the Old Testament.

Even the limits of the Old Testament may have something to teach us. We can learn that the limits of revelation are not set by God but come from human limitations. Because Israel's experience of God occurred in history and was subject to the contingencies of history, we can see that the response of the people to its God must be the response of which it is capable at each historical moment. Furthermore, and again this is simply the human reality, Israel's experience of God is always conditioned by its culture. It is evident that law is a dominant conception in much of the Old Testament; but law is an imperfect conception of the moral will of God, and the image of God as lawgiver is an imperfect representation of him. Though the Old Testament moved in the direction of the love of enemies, it could not reach the Christian goal because of its adherence to its culture. Nor was Israel ready for the cultural revolution which would establish the full human dignity of woman. Such considerations make us more keenly aware that the human condition in the concrete, and our cultural limitations, do impose limits on man's experience of God and on the effects of that experience. 'If the limits of the Old Testament are so conceived, then the Christian may ask himself about the limits of the Christian revelation; for these limits are also not the limits of God but the limits of man. He will ask himself how the human condition of the Christian has placed limits on the fullness of Jesus Christ living in the Church . . . He may think that Christians have not yet accepted the revolution in the status of the human person which we associate with the Christ event, and that we still define the person in terms of purely secular values. The conclusion may be that Christians have not accepted God totally because they have not accepted man totally; and they cannot say that their sacred books have not revealed this to them.'[135] But this will be evident only if the Old Testament is permitted to speak for itself.

François Dreyfus has looked at the existential value of the Old Testament[136] and maintains that the value of the Old Testament for man today 'does not lie primarily in what it teaches about God, about man, his destiny or his history, but in how it expresses an experience of ever-present value, that of a meeting of God with man, or rather with men.'[137] Since man's true life is the eternal life proclaimed in Scripture, the value of any scriptural text for the man of any age is measured by its aptness in guiding that man's decisions towards the choice of the true life offered him by God. So, in practical terms, the existential value of the Old Testament for the modern Christian is its value for him as one called to life in Jesus Christ. But this means that he must find in the scriptural text a certain resemblance between his situation and that of the original hearers of the word. Thus, the task of the Christian exegete, who knows from his faith that the Old Testament has an existential value for the contemporary

Christian, is to reveal that value. In some cases he will find the task easy—in the case of the wisdom books, by and large, of the psalms, and of many passages in the prophets. But his task is much more difficult when he turns to the historical books and to the legislative material, for the existential significance of these parts of the Old Testament is not obvious to modern man.

The scholar is helped by the fact that the inspired writers, who collected and edited the traditions of Israel, already strove to bring out the existential value of past events by making these events 'present' to their contemporaries. They were not accumulating material on Israel's past, but were inviting their readers to be converted and abide by the covenant— the basic kerygmatic structure of event and commitment is present in the Old Testament as in the New. Thus we find that the Pentateuch, in its final form, places all its legislative section during the sojourn at Sinai; this legislation represents the commitment demanded of Israel, the response of man to the act of God which made Israel his people. The deuteronomists brought out the kerygmatic aspect of the commitment by means of the theological setting of the traditions which indicated the present significance of the events. It is in line with this concern of the inspired writers that we can see the Old Testament's existential value for us.

But, after all, is a search for the existential value of the Old Testament worth the trouble? Do we not find this value, in its final and perfect state, in the New Testament? Have the partial words of the Old Testament lost their value in face of the total Word which is Christ? The New Testament itself does not think so. In the eyes of the New Testament writers, the men and events of the Old Testament have real existential value—as a call to imitation, as conduct to be shunned, as a summons to personal decision. The Old Testament was needed because of the historical reality and restrictions of the incarnation; and so, episodes of the Old Testament can show us, in an existentially clearer way, certain aspects of the mystery of Christ whose claim on us might not otherwise be obvious. For instance, the New Testament writers emphasise the importance of faith for salvation; and, though the attitude of Jesus to his Father perfectly expresses the attitude of faith, it is not he but great figures of the Old Testament, like Abraham and Moses, who are presented as models of faith. We can point, too, to the educational value of the Old Testament. It is a traditional approach, and one which is entirely valid, to see in the events of salvation history a divine education reproduced in the life of every man. Finally, the Old Testament helps to balance an impression that the New Testament can give of lack of concern with temporal values—with the temporal implications of Christian salvation, for instance. It is when we consider the whole development of the idea of salvation in the Bible that we recognise in the New Testament not an indifference towards political oppression nor a lack of interest in the temporal liberation of the oppressed, but a change in the centre of gravity: Jesus placed the accent on the basic freedom, liberation from the slavery of sin. 'The episodes of the Exodus and of the Maccabees, read in the light of Christ, prompt us to evaluate the demands for liberation comprised in the Christian message (Exodus), the lawfulness of struggle and war where human and religious values were flouted (Maccabees) . . . The Old Testament is there to invite us to take very seriously a human history which goes on (even if we are already at the end of the ages, cf. *Heb.* 1 : 2), and which is to culminate in a total liberation of man, in all the dimensions of his humanity.'[138]

The Dogmatic Constitution on Divine Revelation (*Dei Verbum*) of the Second Vatican Council has stated clearly the relevance of the Old Testament for Christians: 'The economy of the Old Testament was deliberately so orientated that it should prepare for and declare in prophecy the coming of Christ, redeemer of all men, and of the messianic kingdom (cf. *Luke* 24 : 44; *John* 5 : 39; 1 *Pet.* 1 : 10), and should indicate it by means of different types (cf. 1 *Cor.* 10 : 11)'[139] It underlines the unity of the two Testaments: 'God, the inspirer and author of the books of both Testaments, in his wisdom has so brought it about that the New should be hidden in the Old and that the Old should be made manifest in the New. For, although Christ founded the New Covenant in his blood (cf. *Luke* 22:20; 1 *Cor.* 11:25), still the books of the Old Testament, all of them caught up into the gospel message, attain and show forth their full meaning in the New Testament (cf. *Matt.* 5:17; *Luke* 24:27; *Rom.* 16:25-26; 2 *Cor.* 3:14-16) and in their turn shed light upon it and explain it.'[140] It is evident that in all this we have nothing more than a restatement of the traditional view on the Christ-orientation of the Old Testament and on the harmony of the two Testaments. What is significant is the Constitution's emphasis, throughout its fourth chapter, on the abiding values of the Old Testament. Thus, we are told that 'the economy of salvation, foretold, recounted, and explained by the sacred authors, appears as the true word of God in the books of the Old Testament; that is why these books, divinely inspired, preserve a lasting value'; and we are reminded of Paul's assurance (*Rom.* 15:4) that in the pages of the Old Testament we Christians will find instruction and encouragement and hope.[141] The following article stresses the abiding worth of the Scriptures of Israel. In the era of preparation, before the coming of Christ, the inspired writers of the Old Testament brought to men a unique understanding of God and man. That is why the Constitution, while admitting the imperfect and the provisional, inseparable from a preparatory dispensation, yet stresses that the books contain 'authentic divine teaching'. Of course that pedagogy can turn to advantage even the imperfect factors; but we should never underestimate the theological wealth of the Old Testament. The closing exhortation, in this context, is certainly not a conventional nod to a venerable but irrelvant body of religious literature: 'Christians should accept with veneration these writings which give expression to a lively sense of God, which are a storehouse of sublime teaching on God and of sound wisdom on human life, as well as a wonderful treasury of prayers; in them, too, the mystery of our salvation is present in a hidden way.'[142] We have more to learn from the Hebrews than, perhaps, we are willing to admit, and we should school ourselves to approach the Old Testament not only with the reverence that befits the word of God but with the intellectual humility that recognises in it a singular achievement of the human spirit.[143]

## Personal Viewpoint

Obviously, there is a widely-shared concern to find a link between the Testaments, and to fit the Old Testament in a meaningful way into a Christian context. My own views may be expressed in the following terms. It seems to me that the category promise/fulfilment is valid, indeed inescapable: the Old Testament holds promises which are fulfilled in the New, the Old Testament as a whole looks to a future, and the Christian does find this future in the New Testament. However, that which unites the Testaments is a situation, a fact, rather than a method of expressing that unity or of bringing out the Christian relevance of the Old Testament. Typology is a valid exegetical method—but in the restricted sense of Eichrodt and Brown. I am of the opinion that, in practice, the only types we can be sure of are those clearly indicated in the New Testament; the 'types' discovered by patristic, liturgical, and later exegetical tradition are too uncertain to command our acceptance. I am much less sure than formerly of the validity of the fuller sense—largely because I am no longer quite happy with the scholastic theory of scriptural inspiration. In the measure that I do acknowledge a fuller sense, I believe that the consciousness of the human writer is not a vital factor; in the hypothesis of a true *fuller* sense, his awareness would be so vague as to be nonexistent. I am still impressed by Benoit's position that the fuller sense is to be found exclusively in the Old Testament texts in the light of the New Testament; the 'fuller sense' due to the development of doctrine is not a scriptural sense. Finally, we do need to take seriously the specific values of the Old Testament. The fact that it forms the necessary background to the New Testament, that it is necessary for an understanding of the New Testament, indicates that it has a real value of its own. It would be a mistake to absorb it into a Christian system, to seek to divert its whole meaning in a Christian direction.

The Old Testament is the word of God, but it is incomplete; the New Testament is its necessary complement and its goal. The saving plan of God unfolds from the Old Testament to the New; the Testaments represent, respectively, the first and the final act of the divine drama. The Christian will read the Old Testament under two aspects: he will see it, in its own historical context, as a record of God's dealing with men and of men's response to God; and he will see it as the

first act of a drama whose *dénouement* he knows. He will find
Christ in it—but in promise, in type, and beneath the surface
of the text. The Old Testament is meaningful for him as
God's word, where God has spoken 'in many and various
ways'; he will hear that older word more clearly because he
has heard the word that God has spoken in his Son. The
Bible is the word of the one God; Christ is the link between
the two parts of this word, the preparation and the fulfilment.
He it is who opens the eyes of men to find God's deeper
meaning in the earlier word—but that earlier word, because
it is God's word, has a profound meaning of its own.

### 5. Biblical Dictionaries

If our reference to biblical dictionaries at this point has all
the appearance of a post-script, that is not because we had overlooked their contribution in the field of biblical theology.
The reason is entirely practical: it is simply not possible to
evaluate so complex a work as a dictionary of biblical theology in the same fashion that we have tried to present other
important works. We have decided not even to attempt this;
we shall indicate some common features of these works and
list the outstanding dictionaries. In line with our concern in
this chapter, the most interesting feature of dictionaries of
the Bible is the tracing of the development of ideas and
themes from the Old Testament on to the New and, indeed,
within the Testaments also. It is assumed, by and large, that
distinctive theological views are found in books or in groups
of books in the Bible. Some of the works listed below are
encyclopedias, but even these have a strong theological
emphasis; others leave encyclopedic matters out of count
altogether and concentrate on theological issues.

A classic work in the field is Hasting's *Dictionary of the
Bible* published in five volumes between 1898 and 1904; it
has been revised and re-edited.[144] The result of the revision is
a none too happy marriage of old and new; nevertheless,
much of the new theological contribution is worthwhile. Comparison with the earlier edition of more than half a century
ago highlights the astonishing advance in biblical scholarship
in the meantime. Another older dictionary has been not so

much revised as replaced. F. Vigouroux published his *Dictionnaire de la Bible* in five volumes;[145] the *Supplément* begun by L. Pirot in 1928 and continued by others (and not yet complete) is a new work.[146] Some of its important articles are virtually book-length monographs. A dictionary published by A. van den Born between 1941 and 1950 has proved very successful.[147] Apart from having a second, thoroughly revised edition, it has been translated into French and Italian and has appeared in adapted form in German[148] and English.[149] The dictionary of J. J. von Allmen is described as 'a popular manual of biblical theology'.[150] Its method is that of the famous Kittel (the emphasis is on the New Testament) but stripped of technical erudition and opened to a wider public. A very fine presentation of biblical theology is given by J. B. Bauer;[151] the third revised edition of the work has been translated into English.[152] The English title is misleading—it is not an encyclopedia in the accepted sense, but gives a comprehensive coverage of the theological themes of the Bible; it has been commended for the bibliography supplied at the end of each article. The absence of a similar bibliography is one of the few complaints voiced against a comparable (but not so extensive) French work: the *Dictionary of Biblical Theology* of X. Léon-Dufour.[153] The 1970 edition of this book is a thorough-going revision; many of the articles have been rewritten, much new material has been added, and the book is longer by 130 pages. Pastoral in approach, it is a conspectus of sound biblical theology. The earlier edition has been translated into English.[154] In the United States, the *Interpreters' Dictionary of the Bible*—a vast work of nearly 4,000 pages— was published in 1962.[155] An important feature is that it includes the Apocrypha in its scope. As the subtitle indicates it is both encyclopedia and dictionary. Many European scholars are among the contributors and some of the studies are by men whose names have become associated with the specific subject. The major themes of biblical theology receive full treatment. Not surprisingly, all the works we have listed represent, each of them, the collaboration of many scholars; a one-man Bible dictionary would seem to be, nowadays, an impossible task. Yet J. L. McKenzie has faced this challenge and his work, a veritable *tour-de-force*, is remarkably good.[156] His book is predominantly encyclopedic in character but includes excellent articles on major biblical themes and concepts.

Lastly, we mention what is acknowledged to be the most outstanding work of all, initiated by Gerhard Kittel in 1933.[157] The work is a noble monument to German Protestant New Testament scholarship. This is a lexical and theological study of all the doctrinally significant Greek words in the New Testament. Since it gives the Old Testament background of the word or its counterpart (as well as its usage in inter-testamental and rabbinical literature), it shows, consistently, that the Old Testament setting is necessary for a proper understanding of the New Testament. This great work is being translated into English—a full and excellent translation of the original;[158] six of the eight volumes have appeared. The place that Kittel has assumed in New Testament scholarship means that we must take account of severe criticism aimed at it, especially by James Barr.[159] He finds fault with its 'great and sweeping linguistic misconceptions'[160] the fundamental misconception being that theological structures can be reflected in linguistic structures. He denies that words have a special religious significance apart from that given by their context—the semantic value of a word as such cannot be religious. He claims that Kittel is a dictionary of concepts rather than a dictionary of words. His concern is to draw attention to a danger of theology which lies in a mistaken use of lexical methods; but his vindication of linguistic precision has carried him too far. Barr's criticism is excessively harsh and his own positions are not unassailable; it may be said that he leans towards nominalism. But we have been warned, and will read Kittel more judiciously. However, it will remain an indispensable tool for a theological study of the New Testament.

We have had occasion, especially in regard to the Old Testament, to lament a lack of important works in the field of biblical theology by Roman Catholic scholars. It would seem that the biblical dictionaries have done somthing to restore the balance. Vigouroux (and the *Supplément*), Van den Born (Haag, Hartman), Bauer, Léon-Dufour and McKenzie are Catholic works—it is quite an imposing list.

## 6. Theological Commentaries

The growing interest in biblical theology finds expression in the more recent scriptural commentaries; more and more the emphasis is on theological content. It will become clear in our next chapter that such exegetical work is, in fact, imperative; it is the only acceptable basis for a fruitful biblical theology. It is sufficient here to draw attention to the tendency, one which is becoming more marked; it can be taken for granted that every important commentary of the last decade has had this theological concern. However, we may mention two outstanding projects which quite explicitly aim at a rigidly scientific exegetical-theological study of the writings of each Testament. The *Biblischer Kommentar Altes Testament*[161] edited by H. W. Wolff and M. Noth already includes several Old Testament books. The pattern of exposition is uniform throughout the work. The text, passage by passage, is analysed under four viewpoints: literary criticism (*Form*), setting (*Ort*), exegesis (*Wort*) and theological significance in the context of the author's thought (*Ziel*).[162]

Then there is *Herder's Theological Commentary on the New Testament* initiated in 1953 with the publication of Rudolf Schnackenburg's commentary on the Johannine epistles.[163] Appropriately, the English translation of the series has begun with the first volume of Schnackenburg's great Commentary on the Fourth Gospel.[164] Characteristic of the series are the valuable excursus—while, of course, the exegesis is consistently exegetical. All this is an excellent preparation for the biblical theology of the future.

### In Summary

*For whatever was written in former days was written for our instruction, that by steadfastness and by the encouragement of the scriptures we might have hope (Rom. 15:4).*

*In many and various ways God spoke of old to our fathers by the prophets; but in these last days he has spoken to us by a Son . . . (Heb. 1:1f.)*

Yes, in 'many and various ways' God has spoken—whether we apply this to the Old Testament, or whether we borrow the words as a simple phrase to describe the various theologies of the Bible discussed in this chapter. On the one hand, the Old Testament spoke of old, or in former days to our fathers; on the other hand, our authors have spoken in more recent days to point out precisely that this early covenant of God's word applies not only to times past but is engraved on the hearts of 'all of us here alive this day' (*Deut.* 5:3). It is related to us not only through the focal event of the new covenant, but even more through what Rowley has called the 'thread of the revelation of the one God'. We shall now try to summarise in a small way what we have said, keeping in mind that our theologians as well as the biblical writers have written for our instruction and encouragement. And we shall see how all these have written, and we have pondered their words on God's word, that we 'might have hope'.

What precisely is this 'hope' which sustained men of old, which has quickened our hearts, and which shall be the central point of this summary—this hope which is as 'a lamp shining in a dark place until the day dawns and the morning star rises in your hearts' (2 *Pet.* 1:19)? Taking it, perhaps, as some vague notion derived from the Bible's unity, we could convey it in Burrows' interesting concept of the Trinity: one, personal God revealed in nature, history and man's experience grounded in faith. Or we could turn to Rowley again and his finding the signature of God uniting both Testaments in a common pattern of revelation. Or we could find this 'hope' in what Vriezen finds so comforting—that, in turning to the Bible, we meet men very like ourselves who know God has spoken to them and came to know him as a friend.

But our 'hope' is more personal than that! No longer, in Burrows' words, are man and God two distinct beings— child and Father, servant and Master. The New Testament has given the new dimension of a perfect communion with God to biblical unity, communion through the One who has called us no longer servants but friends (cf. *John* 15:15). Yes, we shall now turn to see how all the streams of the one God's revelation, and all the channels of our biblical theologies here, flow towards this Jesus, this living Word who is source and 'heir of all things' (*Rom.* 15:4). For, God has indeed spoken to men of both Testaments, to our authors, and to us: 'in these last days, he has spoken to us by a *Son.*'

## 'IN MANY AND VARIOUS WAYS'

As we work towards this Light upon all our biblical theologies, this Son, let us look at the manifold ways in which our authors have written 'for our instruction'—and with the educational value of the Old Testament mind. For Dreyfus, this is primarily the ever-present value of God's meeting with men, guiding them through the events in salvation history to choose true or eternal life—which ultimately means life in the author of salvation, Jesus. This history is a very real and human history, rooted in a concern for temporal values and ending in man's total liberation. As inspired writers made past events present, so too must exegetes actualise Old Testament texts by finding their existential value. Others too have taken their stand on this very real history—from Bultmann's negative 'miscarriage' or 'failure' of history to Pannenburg's consciousness that the incarnation can be understood *only* because *one* history binds the Testaments. Grelot has descibed this salvation history as that of the human community chosen by God, a history containing in seed the mystery of Jesus and preparing for its flowering. Because the incarnate Word was 'in the beginning with God' before all ages (cf. *John* 1 : 1f.), he was also present in God's word to Israel—a word spoken through real events where its action becomes tangible. Not mystical contemplation, but rather this historical experience is the starting point of faith. It is this faith which, through prefiguration, relates history to the *eschaton* and finds in it the deeper significance of the covenant God-with-man: the Emmanuel himself.

And so, another thread our authors have worked with variously is that of the very fabric of this history: human life. For Rowley, it is man who creates the diversity within the Bible's unity; for Wolff, the value of Old Testament typology is that it keeps the Christian message in the midst of a *real* world and real *persons* through whom God acted just as he was to do through Jesus. For Benoit the 'fuller sense' is found because a common religious value links two *concrete* realities of human living, the 'old' and the 'new' (such as manna and the Eucharist). For Vawter, on the other hand, it is the very humanness of the scriptural writers which precludes a fuller sense. Burrows finds a source of the Bible's unity in *all* the good things which God has made and which are to be received with thanksgiving, a thought echoed in *Dei Verbum*'s recognising the Old Testament's 'sound wisdom' on human life. Finally, we have McKenzie's word that the great universal value of the Old Testament, strengthening its religious value, is its vision of man as *man*—this human reality embracing the pain as well as the joy of living.

It follows that this human element in the instructional value of the Old Testament hinges upon human *language*; hence, our authors have consistently noted the role of the biblical idiom. The foundations of Christianity are in both Testaments because faith reshaped old terms and concepts, once used for the 'secrets' of Yahweh's person or his relation with men, in terms of Jesus; indeed, Jesus himself claimed the ancient writings (von Rad). He himself began their 'christological' interpretation (Stauffer). The whole Bible is a documentary history of material bearing witness to Jesus (Vriezen); because Jesus *had* to be proclaimed as Israel's Messiah, Christianity inherited this language (McKenzie). 'Reproduction', one of the conditions Benoit requires for a 'secondary sense', means that *God* has brought about the homogeneous development of the biblical language by using figures and words of the Old Testament preparation in the New Testament fulfilment. For Grelot, the divine message can be transmitted or translated authentically only through the symbolic, figurative biblical language fully developed in the New Testament. For Brown, it is *words* which bring out the religious correpondence between type and antitype.

But whether it be its historical, human, or linguistic aspects, over and over we find biblical thought defined as something *living* rather than a system. Thus, for Burrows, the authority of the Bible lies in the truth of what is revealed when the witness of the Spirit unites with the believer's own spirit. Openness to this same spirit, who will guide us 'into all the truth' (*John* 16:13), makes an absolute norm of biblical interpretation impossible for von Rad, in the same way that for him typology is confined to Israel's *credenda* and takes place only in that Spirit's freedom. Because Israel's knowledge of God is alive, it is not so much 'changed' throughout the Testaments as deepened and purified (Vriezen). And the 'fuller sense' really consists not of something in Scripture itself, but in a living, maturing 'fuller understanding' on the part of the author or exegete (Brown), a 'supernatural depth' called forth from the literal meaning of the text by the Spirit (Coppens). And Grelot, too, having advocated the actual language of the Bible, sees that the Christian understanding of the Old Testament consists in passing beyond the 'letter' to find the 'spirit', the 'vivifying presence of Jesus in the texts'.

Alongside, then, the 'instruction' found in Scripture what are its grounds for 'steadfastness' and 'encouragement'? Surely, one of these must be a factor many of the authors mention: that of human *limitation*—the weaknesses of that human reality which, nevertheless, are made to serve God's purpose. For Swain, it is the human element which makes the *sensus plenior* simply a subjective addition of meaning repeatedly applied to historical circumstances. Grelot speaks of how the difference between the Testaments lies in the *degree* of revelation, though their faith and hope are identical: the 'veil of provisional structures' shrouds a mystery of Jesus present but unable to be formulated. We have McKenzie's wise perception that the 'limitations' in Old Testament revelation come from *human* limitations, conditioned by history and culture. Likewise, not only are the limits of Christian revelation those of man, but also the limits we know in *living* to the full the 'life in more abundance' (*John* 10:10) which Jesus brought, come from our failure to accept totally man—hence the incarnation—our failure to take the Word at his word. Then, we have *Dei Verbum*'s teaching that God turns even the 'imperfect factors' of the Old Testament to advantage. Finally, in this respect, we may mention one of Barr's major reservations regarding the interpretation of the Old Testament: the realness of its *original* setting must be kept in mind. For him, it should be understood frankly as pre-Christian, written at a time when Jesus has not yet come and hence cannot be used as a criterion of what God had 'done before him'.

But even Barr concedes that the Old Testament situations

23

of actual contact with God work toward what happened in Jesus—thus implying an implicit *faith*. It is this biblical faith which, together with our very humanness, creates the firmest steadfastness and provides the warmest encouragement. Almost all our authors include this faith in their discussions—doubtless because they themselves have had to enter this realm of personal decision. For Coppens it is an act of faith which, besides the prophetic charism, can deepen an author's awareness of supernatural depth in the literal meaning of the text. Benoit clearly says that the Christian quite normally understands the Old Testament in its 'fuller sense' because of the light of faith by which he reads it. Grelot's understanding of prefiguration holds that, through prefiguring signs, Jesus is present throughout the Old Testament as an object of faith: he links two objective orders in one plan of salvation, and the figures which relate the history of Israel to the *eschaton* must be taken literally in order then to understand the faith they contain. And if Larcher can proclaim that the New Testament writers discover in the Old Testament one great prophecy, he does so realising they have taken their whole stand upon the eyes of sheer *faith*. So, we are led once again into Eichrodt's realm of 'personal decision'. To *really* accept Jesus as uniting all the strands of Judaism and fulfilling all Old Testament prediction calls for believing without seeing. For, the constant 'postponement' in the fulfilment of Old Testament promises still continues: the only way to leap beyond the appearances contradicting the fact of Jesus' having overcome the world is to make a personal answer as to whether or not he is the Son of God.

Answering 'Yes', we come to see that this Son was given to the world because God *so loved* it (cf. *John* 3:16). For Larcher, the material goods of that world under the old promise *do* find place in the Christian dispensation because they are transformed by love. For Burrows, love is the unifying strand in every situation of the Bible: faith in God's loving goodness and this love as revealed in Jesus, a love from which (from Whom) nothing can separate us (cf. *Rom.* 8:35-39). Having seen 'many and various ways' within the Bible and our theologies let us now turn to *the* Way: this Son by whom God has finally spoken. As the Man who can 'sympathise with our weaknesses because he has been tried in every respect as we are' (*Heb.* 4 : 15), as the Word which is 'very near' to us in our mouths and our hearts (cf. *Deut.* 30 : 14), and as the God who has made his dwelling with men (cf. *Apoc.* 21 : 3), *he* is our *true* steadfastness, encouragement, and hope.

## THE WAY: A SON

Could we find any more fitting start to our entering this Way—to our seeing how our authors converge in Jesus—than by walking beside him on the way to Emmaus? For there, he personally 'interpreted in the scriptures all the things concerning himself' (*Luke* 24 : 27). And we can ask ourselves ever anew, 'Does not our heart burn within us while he talks with us on the road and opens to us the scriptures?' (*Luke* 24 : 32). The living Word's understanding of himself must be our starting point for understanding all words written about him. This 'burning' in our hearts, this intimate sense of knowing the person of Jesus, is beautifully expressed by Burrows. Rather than anything abstract, it was the disciples' actually knowing Jesus personally as their friend which gave them the experience that somehow, in him, they had found God himself. Thus, Burrows could also find that Jesus himself is the 'glad tidings' published of old (cf. *Is.* 52 : 7)—that he is indeed the Good News, the gospel. Barr, in a different approach, asks the same question, that which led the apostles to turn to the Old Testament to 'explain' Jesus afterwards rather than finding him its implicit 'key': 'Do we really *know* Christ?' Vischer, by contrast, by making *every* word of the Old Testament point to Jesus, would make the incarnation pointless. But this incarnation *must* be. It is 'the hint half guessed, the gift half understood' (T. S. Eliot). Do we really *know* Christ? Do we really know the Way beside whom we walk on the way to Emmaus? 'Do you not yet understand?' (*Mark* 7 : 21). The whole kernel of God's having spoken his final word by a Son is this: 'the Word became flesh and pitched his tent among us' (*John* 1 : 14).

Let us look at some of the ways in which the theologians have heard this one decisive Word. As in the preceding chapters, we find that which Vriezen calls the 'golden thread' of all biblical thought: that of the *kingdom* of God. This includes the 'eschatological awareness' and one hope that God is to live with his people and they with him. This one certainty sustained Israel of the old covenant and the Church of the new. For Burrows, Jesus summarises in 'the kingdom' all of individual salvation and cosmic redemption. For Eichrodt, the unitative fact of biblical theology is the action of a single God with a single purpose of establishing his kingdom. Throughout, the perfect fulfilment of God's covenant with man rests on the hope of this kingdom's consummation.

This living *hope* is a thread running throughout the pattern of 'promise—fulfilment' among methods of Old Testament interpretation. Zimmerli speaks of how such a hope, such a flow of promise to fulfilment, is needful because of the historical tension between 'yesterday' and 'tomorrow', a perpetual season when God's purpose veiled and waiting can be distressful. Indeed, von Rad says, the New Testament adds a new dimension of urgency to this flow because the hope was fulfilled in such an unsurpassed way—really beyond any hopes or even dreams. And, for Grelot, this hope sustained the hearts of God's people during all the ages when they could only wait, wait for God's same fundamental promises to be renewed from age to age with growing precision.

Both the themes of the kingdom and of hope look towards something *new—the* newness brought by the One who said, 'Behold, I make all things new!' (*Apoc.* 21 : 5). To von Rad, Jesus is the final, perfect 'reinterpretation' of old material, of the old proclamation. 'Remember not the former things . . . behold, I am doing a new thing' (*Is.* 43 : 19). Yahwism had already been characterised by repeated breaks and fresh beginnings. Now, the light of the new saving-event shone a sense of wonder into the evangelists' and disciples' hearts: they stood on a threshold, the new kingdom *had* come, the whole Old Testament could be reinterpreted in terms of the new Christ-event. Benoit roots the 'fuller sense' of Scripture in a general typology which considers the whole old economy as one complex 'type' issuing in the one antitype who *has* made all things new and ushered in a new order: Jesus himself. Robinson holds that the literal sense of Scripture must be translated into a *new* meaning to be relevant today. Grelot speaks similarly in his view that the Christian interpreter must assimilate Old Testament criticism, then pass beyond it: his task is to make the vital meaning of the Bible perceptible to men of his own milieu since God's word is ordered to *living* situations. The Old Testament can be seen to hold the same saving message as the Gospel; in this sense, the old too becomes the 'new' covenant.

And so, there comes a point when, to use Larcher's term, the New Testament—more precisely, the saving event in Jesus—assumes the nature of *accomplishment* of a promise, of an historical activity moving to a goal in the future, rather than merely the 'fulfilment of a prophecy'. Jesus is the pure gift answering the Old Testament promises and transforming even the material goods of those promises. As the 'Book of Promises', he has made the Old Testament *his* book and linked the Testaments in himself. Even the liturgy can express the actualisation of the old law as it is woven into the mystery of Jesus. Murphy has summed up strikingly this idea of accomplishment: it is simply 'wholeness, the flowering of what was set in motion by the word (or event).'

We find that the 'accomplishment' is ultimately interpreted by the various authors as simply the gift of *salvation* through this Saviour. Since Jesus is the supreme saving event, the chief connection between the Testaments is saving or salvation history (von Rad). The Christian, so grasped and saved by Jesus that he cries out to him, 'My Lord and my God!' (*John* 20: 28), can from this conviction then recognise the Old Testament's 'I am the Lord your God' as a saving event (Baumgärtel). Whether through history, institutions, or men, the unique object of Old Testament writings is the mystery of salvation. Hence, this object must be in the end the mystery of *Jesus* gradually revealed to Israel (Grelot). Dreyfus has expressed the meaning of this saving event in 'existential' terms: the Old Testament is valuable to the Christian in guiding him to choose *life* in Jesus—that true life, that peace which the world cannot give. And this life, this true life, is none other than eternal life—here and now—in Christ. And is not *this* the very 'accomplishment' of all 'promises', salvation itself?

This brings us to our final words in our summary, our pausing to look at *the* unifying bond of all we have said. McKenzie has expressed it in one way by saying that any 'fuller sense' simply means that the meaning of the *whole* Bible is greater than any single passage. To bring in an 'outsider' (who was, in reality, not that at all, but deeply rooted in the Bible), Dante has put it in another way in his profoundly simple image of God as being all the 'leaves' or pages of the universe 'bound into *one* volume by love (*legato con amore in un volume, ciò che per l'universo si squaderna*)' (*Paradiso* 33:85)—a 'book' which could, in one sense, be taken as the Bible itself. And Eichrodt has expressed it in still another way—perhaps the one most in keeping with all we have said here. The abundance of the Old Testament concept of God's word or words needed 'containment' in *one* Word—the *person* of a Redeemer, the 'Word made flesh'. As Sirach puts it, 'the sum of all our words is, "He is the all"' (*Sir.* 43:27). All the words of Scripture have been inspired by God that the man who hears their teachings may be 'complete, equipped for every good work' (2 *Tim.* 3:16f.). But, a man can really receive these words *only* because the one Word 'had to be made like his brethren in every respect' (*Heb.* 2:17)—the Word which God has finally 'spoken to us by a Son', our Lord and Brother and Friend.

## CHAPTER IV

# The Methods and Scope of Biblical Theology

OUR survey has highlighted the major works in the fields of Old Testament theology and New Testament theology and has drawn attention to what has been done in regard to the theology of the Bible as a whole. In this final chapter we look to the theorists, to those who have expressed views as to what biblical theology really is, or who have suggested what it ought to be. Our plan here is, in part, the same as before: after a brief methodological comparison of exegesis and biblical theology, we take up Old Testament theology, New Testament theology, and the theology of the Bible. But then we move on to the vital question of the place of biblical theology in the wider area of theology in general. It would be impractical, and in any case it is beyond our competence, to take into account the sweep of Christian theology in all its confessional variety. We shall be content with an outline of the views of some prominent contemporary theologians and exegetes on the relation of biblical theology to Roman Catholic dogmatic theology.

## 1. Exegesis and Biblical Theology

It is evident that there must be a close relationship between exegesis and biblical theology; here we must specify that relationship. The purpose of exegesis is to establish the intention of the inspired writer, to determine what it is he wishes to say to us. Its object is the (primary) literary sense, as this is perceived by the human writer and given expression in his text. Exegesis proceeds under the light of human reason and employs the usual methods of establishing the meaning of a text: textual, literary, and historical criticism. On the other hand, the purpose of biblical theology is to establish the thought of the divine Author as it is manifested in the human word of the inspired writer. Its object is not only the sense established by exegesis but that deeper level of meaning which follows from the divine authorship of Scripture. It proceeds under the light of faith, which alone assures us that this is indeed the word of God. Its method is to survey and correlate the manifestations of divine thought in the Bible and to work them into a synthesis. Thus understood, biblical theology presupposes and needs exegesis. It takes the conclusions of exegesis as the basis of its own research; it simply cannot do without a solid exegetical foundation if it is to be truly scientific.

While it is thus possible to distinguish between exegesis and biblical theology, in practice the former ought to lead naturally to the other. For, if the biblical theologian moves in the light of faith, the believing exegete, too, is enlightened by his faith. Indeed, we may say that a believing exegete, conscious of his task, will be a theologian from the first, and none better than he can accomplish the first task of theological procedure: to discern, delimit and arrange in proper hierarchy the truths revealed in the Bible. Exegesis will necessarily take on a theological and existential dimension if it is to do justice to the text which it interprets. In fact, exegesis is incomplete when it stops short of biblical theology, and biblical theology demands that exegetical scholarship should be ever conscious of the theological dimension of its task.

If an exegete submits to faith, he does so as to an external rule which enables him to avoid conclusions contrary to faith—that is to say, contrary to the intention of the inspired text. In exegesis, critical method (textual, literary and historical) must have a free hand since the Word of God has taken on, in Scripture, an authentically human form. Yet the biblical theologian needs faith because he must meet with the inspired writer, one who has lived a spiritual reality; the theologian must share the faith of the writer if he is to understand his language and his message, if he is to enter into his thought. But ultimately, the object of biblical theology is not the words, nor even the thoughts of the inspired writers, but the very reality to which they witness; biblical theology is necessarily theocentric.[1]

## 2. Old Testament Theology

### TYPES OF OLD TESTAMENT THEOLOGY

In a survey of work in this field M.-L. Ramlot[2] has, in empirical fashion but conveniently, distinguished four kinds of contemporary research on the biblical theology of the Old Testament:

1. Theologies of a structural type. These are theologies of a descriptive kind which study the architecture of Old Testament religion or Old Testament thought, and determine the fundamental structures on the basis of which other, more secondary, concepts may be explained. Examples are the *Theologies* of Eichrodt, Vriezen and van Imschoot.

2. Diachronic theology. This rather esoteric term describes a theology of the successive traditions and stratifications of Israelite religion. A name and a model emerge with G. von Rad who attempts to discover the developments of the faith and of the traditions of Israel.

3. Lexicographic theology—a fruit of semantic studies. One thinks immediately (despite the criticisms of J. Barr) of Kittel's monumental *Dictionary*. Whereas in diachronic theology one seeks to trace the development of the religion and the organic evolution of the community, here the pre-occupation is with the involvement of language in the successive experiences of the community. The concern is not only with the community but also with the experiences of groups within it. Thus the priestly vocabulary and that of the sages represent what one may call, in each case, a group-language, quite in the manner of any professional language.

4. Biblical themes. In 'biblical themes' semantic research continues beyond the vocabulary to themes and often takes into account a whole constellation of words. In another way, also, this process is distinct from the foregoing: it can happen that for themes as important as *promise, obedience, history* and so on, Hebrew has no specific word. Yet no one can fail to recognise the importance of these conceptions.

In practice these methods of research tend to blend somewhat. However, until recently, the structural type of theology has been the most fully represented.

## NATURE AND METHOD

At the close of his survey of Old Testament theology[3] Robert C. Dentan gives an outline of the nature and method of Old Testament theology, ending with a definition of the discipline. At the outset he maintains that the only description of biblical theology which does justice to the history of the discipline is 'the study of the religious ideas of the Bible in their historical context'.[4] Because Old Testament theology is a Christian theological discipline it has some concern for the relation of the Old Testament to the New. In the context of theological studies as a whole the function of Old Testament theology may be specified in a number of ways. In the first place, because it presupposes other studies, it is the crown of the Old Testament sciences; and it is a preparation for the study of the New Testament. In relation to systematic theology it has a normative role as part of biblical theology. Finally, it can make an important contribution to pastoral theology.

In its scope Old Testament theology should be limited to the canonical books and its primary concern should be with ideas, not with history or institutions. Its proper subject is the normative religion of the Old Testament. The persistence or pervasiveness of particular views or, on the other hand, the distinctiveness of certain ideas, mark the characteristics of normative religion. This Old Testament theology should include all major tendencies of normative Hebrew religion. Likewise it should include a general discussion of ethical principles and of the nature of Hebrew piety.

Because of the historical character of biblical religion and of the Christian faith, biblical theology should use historical and critical methods only and leave allegorical and typical exegesis alone. The primary function of the Old Testament theologian is to declare what the religious concepts of the Old Testament meant to men of Old Testament times. There is need for the sympathy and insight achieved through faith, through sharing the Old Testament faith.

The organisation of Old Testament theology is made

difficult by the fact that there is no system and logic in the Old Testament itself. Nor is it, on the basis of the Old Testament, easy to make choice of any unifying principle. Ultimately, we must turn to the doctrine of God and find that the centrality of the idea of God gives to the Old Testament its structural and organic unity. In the last resort any method of organisation must be imposed from without; so, for practical purposes, the outline presented by systematic theology cannot easily be bettered: theology—anthropology—soteriology.

Dentan then gives his final definition of Old Testament theology:

> Old Testament theology is that Christian theological discipline which treats of the religious ideas of the Old Testament *systematically*, i.e. not from the point of view of the historical development, but from that of the structural unity of Old Testament religion, and which gives due regard to the historical and ideological relationship of that religion to the religion of the New Testament. . . . Its scope should be, not the sum-total of religious phenomena in Israel, but rather the ideas and concepts of the normative or distinctive religion taught or assumed by the canonical books of the Old Testament all of which have their centre in a distinctive doctrine of God (theo-logy); that it should include broadly the subjects of ethics and cultus so far as these are expressions of distinctive religious ideas, but should specifically exclude mere antiquarian information about laws and religious customs; that it should aim, not merely to give a description of the religious ideas of Israel, but to communicate in a vivid and moving way the piety which clothed those ideas with life and colour. We should also add that its method is historical and critical, but like all other historical studies, demands sympathy, insight, and inner participation from the student, and that an invaluable precondition for such inner participation is that the student of Old Testament theology should in some sense share the Old Testament faith—to the extent that that faith continues to form a part of the Christian religious consciousness. Finally we should observe that it is the

function of Old Testament theology to act as the culminating discipline of the Old Testament sciences and to constitute a bridge over which the most significant conclusions of technical studies in Old Testament Introduction, History, and Exegesis pass to become useful materials for the biblical theology of the New Testament and for Historical, Systematic, and Practical Theology.[5]

It would appear that Dentan does not sufficiently distinguish between Old Testament theology and the history of the religion of Israel. In his view, the essential difference between them is that the history of religion approach treats of Israel's religious development in its chronological sequence, in a 'lengthwise section', while the theology describes the persistent and distinctive principles of the Old Testament religion in 'theological' order and in 'cross-section'. This would reduce diachronic-type theology to a history of religion. Though, as we have seen in the case of von Rad, some would agree with this, it does not seem to be a valid assessment. Old Testament theology may, and indeed should, consider the chronological sequence and there is a place for the history of the religion of Israel. But one feels that a satisfactory theology of the Old Testament will combine the diachronic and the structural methods.

### PRESENT STATE AND PROSPECTS

Edmond Jacob has given a helpful outline of the present state and prospects of Old Testament theology.[6] He shows that the method evolved by Eichrodt has been followed by the majority of Old Testament theologies (including Jacob's own *Theology*). It has seemed possible to reconcile the approaches of the history of religion and of theology by cutting a cross-section through the material and bringing to light the common fundamental structure beneath a variety of expression. Eichrodt believed that it was possible to discover the essence of Old Testament theological thought by the historical method alone, with faith intervening in order to pronounce on the truth of what emerges.

The structural theologies show a tendency to reduce the theological element to a common denominator, to what is *semper, ubique ab omnibus creditum.* It may be asked whether the living reality found in the individual and particular is thereby lost to sight—indeed, whether there is a discernible unity and a centre in the Old Testament at all. In contrast to the preceding approach, G. von Rad puts forward his diachronic theology. Instead of looking for a unifying element in certain facts, themes or ideas, he brings out the particular theology of the various traditions whose grouping has shaped the Old Testament. And, indeed he has admirably described the theological motives which have guided the formation of the Old Testament. Jacob, however, has definite reservations in regard to the achievement. In his eyes, von Rad's work is a theology of the Old Testament only in the sense that it describes the theology which the Old Testament has developed; it is not a theology based on or flowing from the Old Testament. Jacob acknowledges the force of the kerygmatic character of von Rad's theology but points to its inherent weakness—the minimising of the historical. However, von Rad has certainly reminded us that our reading of the Old Testament must be theological.

Experience has shown that it is very difficult to group the matter of the Old Testament around a key idea. For the present, it may be as well to settle for the division long regarded as classic: theology—anthropology—soteriology. What theology must do is to bring out the primordial element in the faith of Israel: the living God. Because the revelation of the personal God of Israel has been made to *persons*, we may never neglect the fundamental and unique role played by individuals like Moses and the prophets. This factor must be kept in mind even while we give due weight to traditions and to literary and liturgical processes; and the institutional aspect of Israel's religious life must be taken seriously. Jacob regrets that the history of the formation of the Canon is a neglected basis for Old Testament theology. The progressive formation of a canon might be regarded as the first attempt by the Old Testament itself at a theology.[7] And here, too, we might find a valid unifying principle: the word, the prophetic motive.

Jacob feels that a biblical theology covering both Testaments is a more or less utopian ideal. In so far as it is feasible it must follow the course of history and move from the Old Testament to the New Testament; the inverse order would lead inevitably either to making the Old Testament a collection of *dicta probantia* or would over-emphasise its inferior and preparatory role. He thinks, too, that biblical theology should be content to be a descriptive science and should leave to dogmatic theology the task of tracing the norm. The presentation of biblical data will give theology precisely that awareness of a God at once transcendent and present in the world, thus providing it with a solid basis which will prevent it from slipping into *gnosis* or from being reduced to an anthropology.

Norman W. Porteous reminds us[8] that the religious fact with which the Bible deals is that a word is spoken and received. The reception of the word is a form of religious experience, the regularly partial and imperfect nature of the response serves to emphasise the sovereignty of the Word which can bring into being a new community with a new relationship to God. 'It is in my view the business of a Theology of the Old Testament to illumine the Old Testament primarily from this point of view, because it was through this relationship between God and his people that revelation chiefly came to Israel.'[9] Besides, the unity of the Old Testament is to be found in the reality of a community, based on fellowship with God. It is Eichrodt's merit to have devoted the first part of his work to the relation between God and people.

A constant awareness of this factor may help us to avoid a hazard of biblical theology: the loss of the concrete and personal when what is essentially a living experience is cast into a series of propositions. It is indeed the business of a theology of the Old Testament to keep us aware of God's activity in Israel's history, an activity which consisted in the creation and maintenance of a community. Theology must keep us close to the stuff of real life, the material of history. Beyond the importance of life and history, a theology of the Old Testament can be written only within the context of *faith*. The knowledge of God, so needful for the theologian, is not given to him apart from the religious life, which is realised supremely in community.

Since theology is a critique of our knowledge of God, a

biblical theology must respect the biblical view of the nature of such knowledge of God; and the biblical 'knowledge of God' involves the will and emotions as well as the intellect. The Old Testament theologian must share this knowledge and so operate from inside the biblical faith. Nor is this to be less than scientific for 'it is not scientific to adopt a method which turns into something else the proper object of a particular science.'[10] It is only through personal involvement that he can keep words, ideas and images in vital relationship to the transcendent reality which they symbolise.

God's revelation of himself is the proper object of theology; the *manner* of the revelation is of supreme importance. Hence, to seek to demythologise the Old Testament by getting rid of its images, in which revelation has clothed itself, would be to reject the means by which we may hope to apprehend the reality of God. And it is the business of the biblical theologian to ensure that the Bible should be seen as man's witness to God; for Old Testament man took God more seriously than himself. The Old Testament is not foreign territory to the Christian; he may enter there as of right and even with a fuller understanding of God's continuing purpose. Hence, the images of the Old Testament are transformed as they pass from the Old Testament to the New Testament, and the meaning which they thereby take on is a clue to their meaning in the Old Testament context. While one must be judicious, it is not scientific to refuse such insight. 'The subject, standpoint and method of biblical theology are all determined by the fact that God has given himself to be known by those who live in the fellowship of faith and obedience; for the Biblical theologian neutrality would be unscientific.'[11]

There is a growing consensus of opinion that a fundamental unity underlies the characteristic variety and change of the Old Testament. The newer method of approach concentrates on the thought-content of the different parts of the Old Testament regarded as parts of an integrated whole. And the emphasis is being laid increasingly on the institutions and rituals in which the ideas take concrete form. In other words, we are being pointed back into the actual religious life of the Hebrew community. A careless use of the word 'theology' has not helped the situation; and systematic treatment of the religious-historical material furnished by the Old Testament does not constitute theology.

A theology of the Old Testament can only be written by one who takes the God of the Old Testament seriously as God, one for whom the Old Testament is sacred Scripture, and one who belongs to a religious community for which the Old Testament is sacred Scripture. The Bible, a book of life, will not disclose its meaning to the cold eye of intellectual scrutiny alone. The function of the Old Testament is to bring man into the presence of the living God; a biblical theology can be written as a result of such an encounter and in face of the written witness. Another important factor is that the individual judgements of the theologian are controlled and corrected by the religious community to which he belongs. Under the ultimate authority of God, biblical theology can play a normative role and become a critique of the life which the religious community today is seeking to live. This contact with life—the life of the Bible and the life of the Christian community to-day—is something essential, and is fittingly stressed in Porteous' concluding remark: 'To me nothing is entitled to the name of theology which is not continuously under the control of living religious faith and experience, that faith and experience for their part seeking the correction which a vital biblical theology can supply.'[12]

John Bright[13] can maintain that, after all, the question of the authority of the Old Testament does not end in an impasse but demands instead a retracing of steps, a reversal of direction. For him, the reversal is that we must begin with the Old Testament itself and progress with its line of history and structure of faith ahead to the New Testament. From there, we can then look backwards and understand the Old. The pivotal point of his thesis can be seen to be of immediate relevance to the subject of our study. 'It is here submitted that the key to the solution of the problem is to be found in the theological structure of both Testaments in their mutual relationships—that is to say, through the study of biblical theology.'[14]

Bright enquires into the nature of the theological structure underpinning the Old Testament. He speaks of common themes—the uniqueness of Israel's belief, its distinctive God and singular understanding of history as the theatre of his activity, its concepts of election, covenant, and promise-fulfilment. Behind all these manifold expressions lies a commonly held structure of believing: 'nowhere can Israel's normative faith be said to be really absent, for in one way or another it underlies all parts of the Old Testament.'[15] However, the Old Testament *is* incomplete, and the fulfilment of the promise must always be spoken of in the future tense. As Bright poignantly remarks, 'it is a strange *Heilsgeschichte*, a *Heilsgeschichte* that does not arrive at *Heil*, a broken *Heilsgeschichte*, a truncated *Heilsgeschichte*.'[16] Hence, the entire Old Testament makes this assertion: Jesus Christ fulfils the redemptive purposes of God which began with Abraham and the Exodus, and 'this is the whole meaning of God's history with his people, nay, of history altogether.'[17]

He repeats that the key to Old Testament authority lies in its underlying theology. But, it must be the *whole* Old Testament that is considered valid or authoritative, just as is the New Testament, in order that biblical theology can then delineate this structure of faith and distinguish what is normative and central. Yes, Bright points out, there are degrees of value, and not all parts of the Old Testament are equally important. But, all is valid. Since it is through their theology that passages speak to us, it is not a matter of designating certain passages as valid and disregarding others, but of 'a laying hold in each passage of that theological concern that informs it'.[18] At this point, Bright includes an extremely helpful section which vividly discusses the problem posed by the canon, involving the whole question of exactly what the limits are of authoritative scripture. He answers sagely that, once again, if the underlying theology is established in these writings which are universally accepted, we then have enough evidence to determine what is generally normative to the faith of both Testaments. Hence, the great problem of the deuterocanonical books is less pressing. 'Add a book or two—and nothing essential is added; leave them off—and nothing essential is lost.'[19] He also adds helpful comments as to why the canon must be 'closed': the theology

24

of the Bible does not consist in timeless, abstract teachings, but is grounded in a particular history, and to this particular history there could never again be another primary witness. All later Christian classics somehow derive from it.

Thus, affirms Bright, the Bible speaks to us through its *theology*—and therein lies its authority (even though, since it is no rule book and follows no organised system, it may not be the authority we might want). His conclusion to this chapter of his work can well be our own: the answers which the Bible gives concern ancient problems which cannot always be applied to ours. 'It becomes, therefore, our task to examine its ancient answers and to discern the theology that expresses itself through them, so that we, praying at every step for the Holy Spirit's guidance, may give that theology a new expression in the answers we seek to give.'[20]

### THEOLOGY AND FAITH

Faith is the starting-point, the light and guide of biblical theology as of all theology. A 'theology of the Old Testament' is possible only to the extent that we understand the Old Testament in the sense which it had for its human writers, and find in it the truths which they have sought to express. If he is to accomplish his task, the theologian must enter into the spirit of the Old Testament authors and rediscover the faith to which they bear witness. But normative faith in Israel was not expressed in the articles of a creed. Of course, certain convictions—which we might term 'articles of faith' —were universally held, but it was not thought necessary to formulate them in any precise way. Israel was more interested in formulas for action (laws) because the covenant carried with it the obligation to obey and fulfil the will of God.

Old Testament theology looks to the revelation imparted by God in the historical economy of Israel as it is given expression in the canonical books of the Old Testament; it tries to understand the revelation organically. This theology must bring out the essentially historical character of biblical revelation. The Christian theologian can never forget that, of necessity, the Old Testament must signify something more for him than it did for Israel. In the light of his own faith he will appreciate more fully the destiny towards which God has willed to lead his chosen people. He must recognise that the revelation moves towards Christ as towards its goal; thus a complete theology of the Old Testament must have a Christ-directed dynamism. In all this, certain factors will need to be kept in mind. In the first place, the Old Testament theologian will work directly only on the text of the Old Testament; he will refer to the New Testament only when he wishes to indicate the concrete goal towards which God guided his people. Again, this relationship to the New Testament does not absorb the specific value of the Old Testament, and Old Testament theology remains a qualitative part of biblical theology. The Old Testament is not only God's revelation, but contains an abundance of human theological reflection upon that revelation. The biblical writers show theological concern and one finds true theological activity within the Old Testament—an activity which is given expression in individual statements and in some partial syntheses. A total synthesis of the whole will be the work of the Old Testament theologian. Some sort of systematic arrangement is demanded, but care should be taken that the system is not an alien one, artificially imposed from without on the Old Testament, but rather one which should, in some sense, flow from it.[21]

## CHRISTIAN UNDERSTANDING OF THE OLD TESTAMENT

Traditionally, the idea of a Christian understanding of the Old Testament has been taken in a one-sided fashion—as though the Old Testament had to be justified, and as though somehow Christ must be the 'key'. Roland E. Murphy observes that the Old Testament is something which we *have* in the Church and he goes on to ask how, from an existential point of view, it can function in Christian life as it should.[22] He gives a six-point answer. 1. The idea that the Old Testament is 'fulfilled' in the New Testament has to be treated in a manner that will not, in any sense, suggest a dismissal of the Old Testament; herein lies a theological task that still remains to be worked out. 2. The tension between Old Testament and New Testament should not be glossed over. Otherwise the specific values of the Old Testament may be lost to sight. 3. The Christian needs to find these values in the biblical tradition which is his heritage; he needs to be sure about the Old Testament foundation of his own Christian self-understanding. More importantly, he must realise that in the Old Testament he is dealing with the inspired word of God. 4. The Church needs the Old Testament as a norm against which it is to measure itself. The various elements of the spiritual history of Israel, as they come through with great effect in the wide sweep of the Old Testament, are important for the Church. 5. 'In a world where it is now a distinct minority, Christianity must return to ponder its roots in the Old Testament, simply as a matter of understanding itself *vis-à-vis* the great world religions . . . The problem is that one cannot simply dilute the concrete historical dress in which Christianity appeared in the Fertile Crescent. But it is the task of theology to determine more specifically the OT/ NT roots of the Christian message, and even to delimit it where possible, and certainly to transmute it for other cultures where necessary.'[23] 6. Finally, one should sound a note of warning: let us not underestimate the role of the Spirit. Spiritual understanding, the recognition of spiritual meaning, cannot be something purely technical. The Spirit of Christ cannot be left out of count; thus we must not too easily decide that the time-honoured christological interpretation of the Old Testament has no place in the Church today.

### THE LATEST TREND

During the golden age of Old Testament theology there has been an effort to concentrate on what is permanent and normative in revelation. The works of this period, characterised by the application of the notion of the cross-section, belong to the structural type of theology. Julien Harvey[24] maintains that today priority should be given to diachronic theology. What had seemed to be Von Rad's personal opinion is now seen to have anticipated the crisis of present-day theology: the problem of experiencing God as a living reality and the problem of communicating this experience in language and symbol. Von Rad can find no synthesis of theological thought in the text of the Old Testament; at most, he acknowledges the tendency towards concrete unity found in the continuity of the faith of the Israelite people. Nor can he find in the Old Testament a central axis or sure lines of development, and he is content to narrate what the Old Testament says about its own contents. 'This amounts in practice to making Old Testament biblical theology *the history of Israel's faith lived and proclaimed.*'[25] Von Rad's presentation of the different theologies to be found in the Old Testament is admirable. And by his refusal to seek after a cross-section synthesis and by the priority he has given to religious history as against history as event, he has encouraged the monographic study of the theology of the different biblical writers.[26]

One result of the debate following on the publication of von Rad's *Theology* is that the notion of *Heilsgeschichte* now seems less distinctive of biblical thought than had been presumed. Also, the notion of divine interventions in history must be seen less as *magnalia Dei* than as 'revelatory situation'. It has become clear that von Rad does not posit a duality between factual history and interpretation; rather, both together constitute the real history. What this can mean is that the word of God runs abreast of the accent formerly laid on the acts of God. This allows a better integration of *sapiential* thought into biblical theology.

### 3. New Testament Theology

MEANING AND FUNCTION

Heinrich Schlier[27] declares that the procedures, methods and basic structure of New Testament theology must be derived from its object and from nowhere else. He is quite specific in this regard and lays down certain principles:

1. As it studies the theological content of the New Testament books or groups of books, New Testament theology must allow its concepts to be formed for it by the New Testament.

2. The themes must be suggested by the New Testament itself, and reflect both its variety and its limitations. They should not be imposed on it by dogmatic theology.

3. A New Testament theology will handle the themes in the way indicated by the New Testament books, paying attention to the basic movement of thought in each book or group of books.

New Testament theology will first emerge as a collection of different and fragmentary theologies. Nevertheless, the theologian must penetrate through this variety to a central unity— for the unity of the New Testament is a previous theological conviction. The question is: how is this achieved? The theologian must be involved in the reality which confronts him in the texts of the New Testament, an involvement which takes place in the act of faith. New Testament theology is not only a historical science but demands the involvement of the person in history; and faith is the self-surrender to the history which addresses us from the New Testament.

In seeking the starting-point of New Testament theology, Schlier maintains that the history of Jesus is the presupposition and not merely a part, of New Testament theology. In his view, neither an account of the preaching and life of Jesus (of the kind historical research seeks to draw from the Gospels) nor the historical reconstruction of the events concerning Jesus, belong to a theology of the New Testament. The New Testament contains certain primitive enunciations and formulas which carry the primary explanation of the saving act of God in Jesus Christ. It would seem that a theology of the New Testament should try first of all to present the archaic theology of these authoritative primary forms of the message. This is not an easy task but it would enable us to establish theological principles which form the effective basis of the theology of the New Testament writings.

It is quite certain that we must treat the theology of each of the Synoptic Gospels, for these Gospels are the interpretation and expression of a common tradition of faith and preaching. One must then decide whether the theology of the individual Synoptics (and of Acts) should be succeeded by the Pauline or by the Johannine theology. From the theological point of view Paul is close to the Synoptic Gospels and the theology of the Pauline writings should follow after that of the Synoptics. Paul, as he engages in conscious theological argument, thinks over theologically the traditions of faith handed on by the primitive community. The theology of the other New Testament writings (apart from the Johannine) will follow next; here, of course, Hebrews and 1 Peter are the most weighty. The study of these writings will heighten our awareness that New Testament theology is composed primarily of a number of fragments of theology. The Fourth Gospel is an interpretation of the well-worked out gospel tradition, independent of the Synoptic tradition. And the scope of Johannine theology is broad enough to include the Apocalypse.

The work of New Testament theology is still not complete when the theology of the individual books or groups of writings is presented. The task is done only when we have succeeded in showing the unity of the different 'theologies'; and this underlying theological unity must be brought out as explicitly as possible. Schlier suggests that the best way to do this is to take some major themes and use them to indicate how the various theologies are intrinsically related to one another. In this, two dangers must be avoided. One is that the individuality of the theological conception of a given book may be lost again when the unity of New Testament theology is put too much in the foreground. Another danger is that the theology of a book or group of books could be made the norm of New Testament theology and other theological concepts made to fit it. Again, while the unity of New Testament theology cannot be reduced to the unity of a single theme it must not be left too much to generalities. New Testament theology, like every real theology, must be concrete if it is to be authentic. Finally, for an integral New Testament theology, we should demonstrate its basic unity with the theology of the Old Testament or show its relation to Old Testament theology. Thus only a *biblical* theology can bring into the full light of day the fullness of a New Testament theology.

New Testament theology presupposes a particular concept of the New Testament. In the first place, the New Testament is a collection of varied religious writings from the age of primitive Christianity, writings concerned with the one fact of God's self-revelation in Jesus Christ. Another feature of the New Testament especially noteworthy for biblical theology is that the testimony of revelation is presented in a faith which is already engaged in reflection on itself. Thus the revelation kindled faith and prompted reflection in faith. The Event came to light in and through the believing interpretation of those who declared and transmitted it. Another characteristic of the New Testament, also of importance for its relation to dogmatic theology, is the essentially open character of its statements. This openness is based on a peculiar plenitude 'which consists in the fact that what is said contains things unsaid and the statement flows from what is unsaid.'[28] This open character justifies the elaboration of a theology of the New Testament.

New Testament theology questions the New Testament about its theological subject-matter and statements. It seeks to grasp the revelation-reality in the light of the thoughtful belief of the New Testament and to make it intelligible as the New Testament understood it. It may seem a platitude to maintain that the theology of the New Testament will only enquire into the thought which expresses the belief of the New Testament, but this assertion implies: 1. that it does not enquire into the theology of the supposed sources of the New Testament and, 2. that it accepts the exclusive character of the Canon as an essential presupposition of its work.

'The theology of the New Testament endeavours to elucidate and exhibit in their interconnections the data of revelation as these are understood by that New Testament understanding of the faith. By doing this, the fundamental step is taken towards their interpretation.'[29] Because this theology directs its attention to the theological data as they appear in the light of the New Testament, what will first emerge will be a series of different and fragmentary theologies. This gives rise to a number of questions. How is the pluralistic and fragmentary character of the New Testament theologies to be interpreted? Must we see an invitation to extend the broken lines and to relate the divergent lines? If the one revelation-event is projected in manifold forms of believing thought, is not this thought ultimately aiming at a single theology? And are not the various theological tendencies to be developed with reference to this unified theology? The venture towards one theology must be made, at the cost of trial and error. The tendency towards unity in relation to the 'truth of the gospel' (*Gal.* 2:5), whose growth can be traced in the New Testament, implies an orientation towards a unified theology.

NATURE AND CONTENT

Rudolf Schnackenburg[30] points out that theology did not begin when revelation was explained and systematised with the help of Greek philosophy—it was there, already, in the Bible itself. New Testament theology is genuine theology even when it is content to array the biblical writers' theological statements in a 'biblical' way and to show how they have been synthesised, without probing into them in a speculative way. 'So we may not call into question either the possibility or the legitimacy of New Testament theology, which today is justified in claiming a major role in the general field of theology.'[31]

Looking at the New Testament we find in it, from the beginning, mingled with the handing down of revelation, statements which throw light on that revelation and explain it. Therefore, these statements are the first Christian theology, or rather, the basis of all theology. We find that the 'kerygma' and the 'confession of faith' were the first forms in which faith was expressed and theology took shape. Schnackenburg uses the term the 'theology of the early Church' to designate the commonly held theological ideas which were based on the testimony of the apostles and adopted by the whole body of the early Church. He distinguishes this 'theology of the early Church' in its apostolic form from Jesus' message which constituted the immediate revelation. At any rate, the New Testament is the privileged source of all Christian theology.

Despite the number of 'theologies' within the New Testament we can and we must talk about *a* New Testament theology precisely because the New Testament is a unity. The formal principle of the unity of New Testament theology is the common faith of the early Church. It is not easy to discover its material unity and it is still more difficult to decide what practical starting-point we should adopt to express the unity. Should we keep to the language and ideas proper to each New Testament author, or should we rather seek to grasp that content of revelation which is common to them all, and then express it in our way? The New Testament theologian cannot help introducing new and more universal concepts which are not to be found in the New

Testament but which express New Testament thought—for example, 'salvation history', 'eschatology', and 'christo-centrism'. What we must avoid is the forcing of living forms into the strait-jacket of scholastic terminology, thereby destroying their vitality

We have to decide about the place of the teaching of Jesus: can it be taken as part of New Testament theology, or does it rather provide the basis for this theology? Schnackenburg admits that, from a theological point of view, Schlier is justified in regarding the history of Jesus not as a part of New Testament theology but as its assumed basis. However, this is not the whole of it, because in the Synoptic Gospels and especially in the Fourth Gospel, Jesus' life and deeds have as such been made a part of the evangelists' own theology. It is now generally recognised that Jesus' message, and his revelation of himself, are presented in terms of the theological outlook of each evangelist. But at the same time, the message of Jesus and the account of the saving events of his life, as received by the Synoptists, should be regarded as a stage of the common primitive preaching and theology; this 'primitive theology' would be prefixed to the theology of the individual Synoptic Gospels. Thus, Jesus' message takes its place in any New Testament theology not only as revelation but also as a theology. In view of this it would seem advisable to begin any exposition of New Testament theology with the tradition of the apostles and the primitive community and follow up with the theology of the Synoptic Gospels. Only then would one present the theology of Paul, John and the other New Testament theologians. An exposition along these lines, or at least one which incorporates all these factors, has not yet been achieved.

COMPLEXITY

Anton Vögtle[32] takes the view that while theories as to how a New Testament theology should be constructed continue to differ widely, the programme outlined by H. Schlier would meet with a wide measure of agreement. He himself would see it as our primary task to isolate and describe in appropriate terms the theological contents of the particular writings or groups of writings. Formerly, scholars were content to distinguish three main branches—Pauline theology, Johannine theology and the theology of Hebrews—today a richer and more nuanced picture is presented as the theological dimension of the other New Testament writings is more fully appreciated. However, we are still far from having established *the* theology of the New Testament when we have merely surveyed the contents of the various New Testament writings; we must look to the content and structure of a comprehensive New Testament theology. It undoubtedly falls within the compass of New Testament theology to trace the primitive apostolic preaching and its possible developments; this would show the earliest stage of the theology of the primitive Church. It is a disputed question whether or not the history, or at least the preaching, of Jesus as such is part of New Testament theology—we have noted the views of Schlier and Schnackenburg. The unquestionable multiplicity of theologies within the New Testament raises the methodological question as to how their unity and, above all, their material uniformity, might be brought out. The most practical method would seem to be to use some major theological themes or some more systematic sub-divisions. It should be a recognised principle, however, that the peculiarities of the various theologies should not be blurred for the sake of a superficial harmony. Nor should a theology of one book or group of writings be made the norm according to which the theological views of the other writings are measured. In fact, it should be recognised that the historically conditioned theological assertions of the New Testament may not be reduced over-hastily to a system.

Vögtle points out that the Catholic exegete has two starting-points: 1. the faith and teaching of the Church of today, and 2. the 'essential and fundamental' starting-point—the New Testament itself as a document which must be explained according to strict methods of linguistic and historical research. As for the scope of the New Testament, no single book, nor even the New Testament as a whole, claims to present exhaustively the primitive Church's understanding of revelation. This is a further reason why it is so difficult to reduce the assertions of the New Testament writers to the harmony of a system. For that matter, New Testament theology will always remain something more than theorising or systematising, since it is nothing else than the gospel itself. It is an address to hearts, it is the preaching of a great newness. In this respect F. M. Braun[33] reminds us that the New Testament presents an *inspired theology* and suggests that the role of the theologian, in face of this inspired theology, is not to systematise it but to assimilate it—it already has been elaborated/in its own way. Besides, as a theology inspired by God in its ensemble and in its parts it represents a transcendent norm of all theology.

Werner Georg Kümmel[34] is the latest to give expression to the prevailing view that the primary task of New Testament theology consists in this: to listen first to the single writings or groups of writings and only then to seek out any underlying unity. In other words, the New Testament proclamation of Jesus Christ must first be presented according to its different forms before these can be examined for their common content. Thus, the presentation and arrangement of a theology of the New Testament can only be the *result* of a preoccupation with the different forms of the New Testament proclamation. Karl Rahner puts this theological variety of the New Testament in proper perspective.[35] In all ages, including the apostolic period, the Church has been a unity of churches, differing in time, place, culture and theology. Belonging to the very nature of the Church, these features necessarily appear in the New Testament writings; hence the variety of theologies in the New Testament is not fortuitous, nor even a mark of 'primitiveness'. Rather, the variety already represents what in the later history of the Church became 'schools of theology' and the very nature of such schools consists in the difference of their general perspectives which cannot be replaced by a higher synthesis. The biblical theologian, then, must perceive and work out the plurality of theologies in the New Testament; he must first expound the biblical theologies before *a* biblical theology becomes possible. Nor can he ever hope completely to replace the plurality of theologies in the New Testament by fitting them into a single higher system.

## 4. Biblical Theology

SCRIPTURE

Karl Rahner finds it needful to establish the theological basis of a theology of Scripture; he begins by describing the nature of Scripture.[36] The entire self-disclosure of God is given in Jesus Christ in the form of the final eschatological victorious salvation of the whole human race. Anything that happens from the time of Jesus Christ must be referred back to this all-opening and already all-embracing beginning of the end which is given in Jesus Christ. 'The pure objectivation of this eschatological beginning of the end, i.e. the "primitive Church"—an objectivation therefore which forms an absolutely normative *norma non normata*—is called 'scripture' . . . By inspiration Scripture became the work of God precisely in its role of the objectivation of the faith of the primitive Church understood as the permanent norm of the faith of all later ages, and this is a pure norm.'[37] The primitive Church held the history of the Old Testament to be its own pre-history, and knowledge about the authentic pre-history is a factor of the primitive Church. The pure objectivation of this knowledge is the Old Testament understood as an inspired book and this is also part of the normative elements of the later ages of the Church.

Elsewhere[38] Rahner outlines the theological basis of biblical theology:

1. For Christians the fundamental basis must be a specifically Christian one; only so can the Old Testament be seen as part of *our* Scripture.

2. The theological conception of Scripture has its sole root in the faith, and that under two of its aspects: a) God communicates himself by turning, through his grace, to mankind throughout the whole history of salvation; b) the history of God's self-communication attains its final form in Jesus Christ. The historical manifestation of God's grace-giving will involves the abiding existence of the community of those who believe in Jesus Christ—the Church. The Church can only remain true to its own nature if it understands itself to be the Church of the apostolic age; it is only through the apostolic Church and its testimony to the faith that the Church attains Jesus Christ.

3. The perpetual recourse to the first age requires the Church to be able, truly and unmistakably, to distinguish the activity and faith of the primitive Church. That need is met if written testimony of a normative kind concerning the activity and belief of the primitive Church is available—and it *is* available, as Scripture. Thus, reference to the activity and faith of the primitive Church has to serve as a critical standard of the Church's activity and teaching.

4. We can therefore provisionally say that Scripture is the verbal, written objectivation of the apostolic Church in its activity and confession of faith. 'If the "beginning" of the Church is envisaged not just as its first phase in time but as laying the permanent foundation for its continued existence, that beginning must be permanently present. It must remain present in the Church's historical dimension (though not only in this) in the explicit profession of faith (even when this faith is given conceptual formulation), in the norm of faith binding on all, in the possibility of a humanly verifiable recourse to this enduring normative beginning of the Last Days. Consequently, there exists a pure and therefore absolutely normative objective expression of the permanence of that beginning, *a norma non normata*. This is what we call Scripture.'[39]

The statements of Scripture may in many respects be historically conditioned; but unlike any other possible or actual literature of the apostolic age, Scripture is a pure expression of divine truth in a human embodiment. It has no starting-point from which a definite human element would have to be eliminated if we were not to miss the truth from the start. 'Consequently, for theology, Scripture is a reality which has to be interpreted in the spirit and under the guidance and guarantees of the Church and its magisterium. Yet such interpretation is not really a criticism of Scripture but of its reader. Even the magisterium which interprets Scripture under the guidance of the Spirit, does not thereby place itself above Scripture but under it; it knows that Scripture brought into existence by the Spirit and read by the Church with the assistance of the Spirit conveys its true meaning. In that way Scripture remains the *norma non normata* of theology and the Church.'[40]

## BIBLICAL THEOLOGY

When we turn directly to biblical theology, we are reminded by Hans-Joachim Kraus[41] that the term 'biblical theology' expresses no clear-cut idea. It can mean: either, the theology contained in the Bible or, theology in accordance with, in conformity with, the Bible. When it is taken in the sense of the theology of the Bible, we are then left with the problem: what binds together the many theologies in the Bible into biblical theology?

The exegetical method, with its form-critical emphasis, tends towards isolation, to the marking off of small text-units in order to study form, origin, theme and intention; there is no adequate concern to study a passage in relation to the context, including the broadest context. What is needed is a new orientation of exegesis in the direction of open-context enquiry and towards the seeking out of biblical-theological perspectives—otherwise the undertaking of a 'biblical theology' is unthinkable. For how can a 'biblical theology' be constructed if the basis of exegetical preparatory work is missing? Biblical theology offers a challenge to exegesis, urging it to become conscious of its biblical theological task, only from below may biblical theology be built up. It is desirable that biblical commentaries should work up to and present the theological fruit of exegesis, so providing important preparatory work.

Kraus notes the sober warning of H. Schlier that a satisfactory 'biblical theology' is not in the immediate offing; every attempt to develop biblical theology must become aware of the enormous difficulties involved. A biblical-theology-orientated exegesis is the only way, in the field of Old Testament and New Testament studies, that a first step can be taken, and a first thrust ventured. Thus, we will *not only* ask for a 'theology of the Old Testament' or a 'Pauline theology', but also, in these limited areas, keep the wider context constantly in sight. Besides, key-themes should be sought out and their development followed through both Testaments. This must not be taken to mean that biblical theology should be regarded as a single-line process, with all biblical statements developed along the same *one* line. Of course, under the guidance of the one God, there is one way which leads from the Old Testament to the New Testament, but this *one* way must ever and again be travelled in order that the biblical proclamation can be freshly applied and presented in its proper manifold accents.

In the process of working out the theological aspect of the Bible, the variety of the biblical witness will stand out sharply; what, then, of the unity of the Bible in the context of its undoubted variety? To Kraus it is not helpful to look for a centre (*Mitte*), not even in one Testament or the other; he finds the geometrical metaphor a questionable one. What, then, about the unity? First of all, we must look to the 'self-identity' or 'self-ness' of God in Jesus Christ—that is to say, his fidelity to his promise in respect of Israel; and we must see the multiplicity and differences of the New Testament texts in the context of the Old Testament. The perspective is transformed if Jesus Christ himself is proclaimed as witness, guarantor and revelation of God's faithfulness 'from the beginning'. Yet, one must be on one's guard against presenting a specific picture of Christ as a unifying principle, as the *scopus scripturae*.

THE SCOPE OF BIBLICAL THEOLOGY

Pierre Benoit[42] raises the question whether or not biblical theology can bear on a particular text or a particular book, or whether it must always look to the whole Bible. He maintains that an exegete who seeks the full understanding of a particular text becomes a theologian by that very fact—on condition that he has heard what the divine Author has said in other areas of his revelation, and that he does bring out, by the 'analogy of faith' the aspect of divine faith which God has set in a particular text. This is why it is best that a biblical theologian should study a writer's whole book, and not just a part or parts of it. It is, of course, quite correct and helpful to work out a theology of Isaiah or Jeremiah, of Paul or of John, because each has been a theologian who had himself arrived at an understanding of the divine word received by faith and had sought to give it expression. At the same time, biblical theology can never be limited to one writer alone if it is to discern the full breadth of the divine word. It will broaden its scope, grouping and studying together, the various books which pertain to a certain stage of revelation. Thus we get a theology of the prophets, or of the Old Testament, or a theology of the New Testament.

But it is necessary to go further, beyond one or other Testament—which are really two parts of one and the same revelation. The only complete and perfect biblical theology would be one which, embracing the whole of canonical Scripture, seeks to perceive the whole Truth which God has revealed to men throughout his entire book. It will take up the divine words spoken from the beginning to the end of revelation, comparing, ordering and synthesising them, so as to arrive at a total understanding of the revealed faith.

Roland de Vaux[43] makes a similar observation. He prefaces his remarks by pointing out that theology is the science of faith. It is such not only because of its material aspect but also through its formal object, the light under which it works —*fides quaerens intellectum*. The theologian seeks an understanding of *his* faith, guided by the data of *his* faith. As a Christian theologian I received the Old Testament as the word of God, the word of *my* God addressed to his chosen people but destined also for *me* who am its spiritual descendant. The Old Testament contains the revelation of *my* God.

While the unity of the two Testaments is a datum of faith, the theologian who accepts it cannot any longer consider one Testament to the exclusion of the other. This means that there ought not to be a theology of the Old Testament and a theology of the New Testament: there ought to be only one biblical theology based on all the data of revelation. However, it is quite legitimate to apply this theological method in a limited field—to the parts or to the stages of revelation. In this sense, one may have a theology of Ezekiel, or of the Prophets, or of the whole Old Testament, on condition that none of these partial theologies should be regarded as autonomous. So, for instance, such a theology of Ezekiel could not be maintained in separation from the theology of the Prophets, nor from that of the Old Testament in general. Similarly, a theology of the Old Testament cannot stand aloof from a theology of the New Testament. All these are interdependent parts of an edifice which can have its full impact and significance only when it is seen fully

25

constructed in all its dimensions. For if the books of the Old Testament and of the New Testament are inspired by the same God, if they are witnesses to the activity of the same God in the world, if they contain the teaching of the same God addressed to men, they surely ought to display a unity which is that of God's plan, that of the divine revelation. It is the task of the theologian to find this unity.

Of course, the Bible already contains particular theological syntheses (those, for example, of the Yahwist, of the Chronicler, of John, of Paul), all situated within the development of revelation, and all guaranteed by inspiration. But this work continues in the Church through that search for an understanding of faith which has led to different theological systems that differ, even as the 'theologies' of the Old Testament and of the New Testament differ. This fact follows naturally from man's inability to comprehend God, from the distance which separates the one infinite Truth from its expression for man's sake and geared to man's understanding. But the attempt must be perpetually repeated and the task of biblical theology, of theology *tout court*, is to study the word of God in order to draw closer to the truth of God.

### THE NATURE OF BIBLICAL THEOLOGY

It is the opinion of Pierre Grelot[44] that our picture of biblical theology would be much clearer if exegesis, dogmatic theology and pastoral theology were considered more in their relationship to the word of God, for all three are in the service of that word. Scripture gives authentic expression to the word of God as it has been historically transmitted through the centuries from the prophets to the apostles. The books which make up the Bible have taken shape in a determined place in the living tradition of the people of God, at a time when revelation was still in process of growth: in Israel first, then in the primitive Church. The writings of the New Testament put us in direct contact with the 'apostolic tradition' which is the unique source of the life of the Church. Hence, they have a unique, irreplaceable role in the very structure of the Church, where the word of God actually manifests its presence and its action here below.

The word of God, which is the object of Christian faith,

is that which God has spoken to us in Christ. In Christ all the words formerly spoken and all the books of the Old Law have received their fulfilment and their definite orientation. The texts of the Old Testament must be re-read in this setting if one is to find in them what God continues to say through them to his Church. Besides, if God, in Christ, has spoken to us all that he has willed to speak, it was necessary that this message should be cast in the form of gospel by the apostolic preaching, so that its content should appear in an express manner: it is the object of the apostolic tradition, in which Christian revelation took shape. We owe to this tradition not only the New Testament texts, but also the authentic interpretation of the Old Testament, given to the Church as fulfilled Scripture. We owe too the fundamental structures which actually determine the manner of life of the people of God: the sacraments of the Church and the prayer-life which gravitates around them, the ministers of the Church and the social life which is organised by or attached to them.

Finally, Julien Harvey[45] observes that, from the outset, biblical theology has had to face a fundamental option, without, however, taking a definite decision: should biblical theology be *descriptive*, not normative for the faith, in line with the original programme delineated by Gabler; or, on the contrary, is it to be a 'reading' based on belief, and *normative* for the faith, although adopting the thought categories and the formulations of the biblical authors themselves? Both these lines of thought have in fact been followed; the term 'biblical theology' applies to two disciplines. One, descriptive and historical, leaves to systematic theology the elaboration of a theology normative for the faith. The other claims to be also normative while it carefully and distinctively avoids wandering away from the specific thought pattern of the Bible. This leads us on to a consideration of the place of biblical theology in the field of theology at large.

## 5. Biblical Theology and Dogmatic Theology

### I. THE THEOLOGIANS

Hans-Joachim Kraus has devoted a lengthy section of his survey of biblical theology[46] to the place of biblical theology in Reformed theology; he has paid special attention to the work of Barth and of Tillich. We attempt, on a more modest scale, to discern the place of biblical theology in the field of Roman Catholic theology—or, to be more precise, in Roman Catholic dogmatics.

## Theology

Karl Rahner[47] maintains that dogmatic theology cannot, in fact, avoid engaging in biblical theology. Because systematic theology is the reflective listening to God's revelation in Jesus Christ, it must, with particular earnestness, listen to Scripture, the most direct and the ultimate source of Christian revelation. Besides, one should not overlook the fact that the Church itself, in every age, reads and officially proclaims the Scripture. The Church, too, assigns Scripture to the dogmatic theologian as the direct object of his dogmatic studies. Therefore, he may not regard Scripture only as a *fons romotus* (the ultimate source to which the dogmatic theologian traces back the Church's teaching) but must see it as the precise object of his concern; he cannot set it apart as another 'source' distinct from the actual teaching of the Church. In fact that present-day teaching demands a renewed return to the ultimate source from which it springs, a return to the original teaching whose exposition and actualisation it is meant to be, a return to the Scriptures; again the dogmatic theologian must look to Scripture.

Theology is an intrinsic element of the Church's consciousness of faith. But the Church's consciousness of faith cannot be something purely abstract and unhistorical; it must be something historical. For a Catholic understanding of faith, theology is not merely the non-binding human reflection on an unchangeable phenomenon, but it is the way in which an absolute history of faith takes place, one always open to the future. This history of faith remains bound to its beginning, to the revelation of Jesus Christ in the apostolic age, as it has been objectified in Scripture. We might, indeed, go so far as to say that theology is referred to Scripture as to its only *material* source, absolutely original and (*quoad nos*) underived. 'We may therefore state quite confidently that for theology, Scripture is in practice the only material source of faith to which it has to turn as being the absolutely original, underived source and *norma non normata*. . . . Scripture, then, is in practice the only material source of the Church's consciousness of faith, one which no longer requires any further norm but is in fact the norm of everything else.'[48] Biblical theology, therefore, is an intrinsic element of dogmatic theology itself, and an absolutely outstanding and even unique element at that. However, it does not follow that biblical theology may not and cannot establish itself as a proper science in the complex of theology. Such autonomous development is desirable and, for practical reasons, necessary.

## The Norm of Theology

Edward H. Schillebeeckx[49] observes that we may not regard sacred Scripture as the whole of the revealed religion of Christianity. 'But it is still an essential, fundamental, constitutive and irreplaceable element.'[50] Scripture belongs to the constitution of the Church as an essential part of the fundamental structure of the apostolic Church, as part of the *depositum fidei* by which the apostolic Church is always guided. From this point of view, the Church, and therefore the magisterium, the teaching office, are given their norms by Scripture. While the teaching office is the immediate norm for our faith, this teaching office itself is guided by the primitive apostolic Church, and so by the Scriptures. This amounts to saying, in effect, that without exegesis and biblical theology, no dogmatics is possible. And this is because 'in every instance, Scripture remains, in its quality of special primary archive of the consciousness of the Church, an inviolable norm for all theological activity, even though reading of the Scripture must take place in and with the Church, of which it is the Sacred Scripture.'[51]

For all that, dogmatics is more than exegesis, more than the theology of the Bible; the content of faith includes all that is contained in the salvific call of God to man, a call that is directed to the men of the present day. It is the task of the dogmatic theologian to determine how the word of God, formerly addressed to Israel and to the apostolic Church, may be heard aright by us in our day. Such an investigation will start with a clear idea of how God spoke to

Israel and to the primitive Church—again we are reminded of the dependence of dogmatics on exegesis and biblical theology. We may not forget, however, that there is more to it than that: 'What was heard in Old Testament and apostolic times belongs in fact to the constitutive phase of revelation. Hence it is a once-for-all, an unrepeatable event, which will remain the norm for the obedient ear of the post-apostolic Church. For this reason, exegesis has the place of honour in all theological thinking of the faith.'[52]

The faith of the Church has as its norm the scriptural witness to the historical event of Israel and of Christ, while, at the same time, this faith is the result of the actual, present, self-revelation of the heavenly Christ through his Spirit in the Church. Thus, while the dogmatic theologian must first study Scripture, he is conscious that the word of God is still being addressed to us and so will put questions to the Scriptures which the exegete would not. The dogmatic theologian will take as his norm what Israel and the apostolic Church have heard of the word of God. Then, in his role as a present-day believer, he will listen, too, to the word of God as it addresses his contemporary situation.

The difference between the Christian exegete and the dogmatic theologian is not a difference of standpoint. Both of them listen to Scripture as believing enquirers; both of them submit their critical reason to the light of faith. The difference lies in the particular aspect of their study of the word. The biblical theologian investigates the word of God in its exact biblical setting, as it was heard by Israel and by the apostolic Church. His primary concern is to establish a given manner of thinking out the faith—as for instance, the theology of St. Paul; his interest does not lie in speculative reasoning or structure (*ratio*). The dogmatic theologian studies the same word of God, but as it must be listened to here and now and is addressed to the men of our time. 'Hence the theologian's appeal to "reason" is rather an appeal to speculative reason, while the exegete rather relies on the application of the critical faculty to the factual.'[53]

Significant and essential though Scripture is we must see it in its proper perspective. For, through the life of faith we stand in direct contact with the reality of Christ and of the mystery of salvation and not merely with a biblical account of this reality. Truth is vital, not enclosed in a book or comprised in a word—the truth is the Spirit who speaks in the writer and lives in the hearer. And, inevitably, the biblical utterance of the Holy Spirit will have an intrinsic relationship to the later word which the Spirit brings to utterance in dogmas. Hence the dogmatic theologian has the continuing task of reading Scripture again and again, and of presupposing the findings of Christian exegesis as he does so. For him, Scripture can never be one document among the many he must study. It must maintain a primary and unique significance. In spite of the difference in the immediate viewpoints of each, biblical theology and dogmatics cannot be in conflict. The Church can only present to us, under the guidance of the Spirit, what Christ did, said and was—the Christ-event to which the apostolic message bears direct testimony, a message which reaches us directly in Scripture. The post-apostolic Church rests on the apostolic authority, on the sacraments, on the preaching of the faith; it rests in a special way on the Scriptures read, under the light of the Spirit, in a 'Christian' way.

The biblical theologian has a critical role in relation to dogmatics. It is his task to study the first beginnings, which are guaranteed by God, and to discern the trends to which those beginnings gave rise. 'And these original trends, because they are so thoroughly directed by their beginnings, remain always a critical court of appeal with regard to the further course of the movement then set on foot. It is in this sense that we can make our own the dictum of Karl Rahner concerning Scripture: "It is the ruling principle of dogmatic theology".'[54]

*Biblical Theology and Dogmatic Theology*

Rudolf Schnackenburg[55] acknowledges that while the meeting point of the dogmatic theologian and the biblical theologian is the actual words of Scripture, their procedures differ. The biblical theologian uses the views of the primitive Church as the broad basis from which he studies the literal sense of Scripture. He has a *sensus fidei*, the mind of a believer, and this fact enables him to draw out the deeper theological meaning of the text and directs the particular line of his study. These presuppositions, which constitute both a negative and a positive norm, should not stand in the way of the fullest use of critical method; on the contrary, the presuppositions may be called into question by the text. The dogmatic theologian starts with the doctrine of the Church and looks back to Scripture to recognise there the starting-points of the later more developed doctrines, and indeed to find there the very foundations of the faith. He may take up the doctrinal content of a biblical text worked out by the exegete, and place it in the whole context of the Catholic faith. He is not confined to biblical theology, but makes the fullest use of the doctrine of the Church as it has been developed over the centuries. Of the two disciplines, we may say that 'biblical theology is, in comparison with the doctrines proposed by dogmatic theology, "poorer" in many instances where its utterances have since been deepened and clarified. On the other hand, it is "richer" since it has not yet been so fully exploited, and since it is in fact an inexhaustible treasure.'[56]

Besides, the dogmatic theologian must take pains to understand the biblical way of speaking and of thought, and he may not be false to them. The biblical theologian will take the thoughts clothed in biblical language and, grasping their meaning, will render them clearly for the present day. The dogmatic theologian may show how much more meaningful a text becomes when viewed in the whole context of Catholic teaching, and will show how deeply it has been drawn upon by tradition and by the development of doctrine. The exegete, on the other hand, may call attention to certain limits of speculation which are set by Scripture. A theological system may seek support in the text of the New Testament, but it will lack its only real support if it either ignores the literal sense of Scripture or goes against it.

Heinrich Schlier[57] explains that biblical theology takes the theological data which it has drawn from Scripture, elucidates it and presents it for the Church's further meditation in faith. This meditation takes place expressly in dogmatic theology. When biblical theology thus presents its own exposition of the belief and reflection of Scripture to dogmatic theology, it places the latter in contact with the words which express the data of revelation and in relation to the reality with which they deal. Thus there is in fact a much closer relation between the two theologies than scholastic theology (or, at least, later scholasticism) will in practice admit, or than the present complicated organisation of biblical studies will permit. Biblical theology and dogmatic theology are meant to work together at the great task of expounding revelation.

'There is no question of a conflict between biblical and dogmatic theology. Both share in promoting the great process of interpreting revelation. Biblical theology interprets it as it has expressed itself in Scripture, expounds the biblical belief and reflection in itself and presents it thus expounded to dogmatic theology. The latter thinks out on the matter assigned to it, in certain cases thinks it out to a conclusion. But it does so within the domain and the limits of the open language of Scripture, in perpetual discussion with the whole of tradition. The more carefully each partner here, intent on its own task, listens to the other, the more fruitful will be the theological knowledge obtained. For ultimately the two are interrelated by the character of revelation itself.'[58]

In the view of Anton Vögtle[59] the relationship between the New Testament and systematic, especially dogmatic theology, must be characterised by mutual interrogation, mutual stimulation and critical examination. Biblical theology may find itself impelled by dogmatics to put its questions to the texts in a more nuanced way, while dogmatic theology may hope for many benefits from a source-theology which is a norm for further development of the faith. So, dogmatics may be led to reflect on basic biblical concepts and truths which may have been left in the shade, or even forgotten. Ceslas Spicq[60] is even more specific and maintains that speculative theology and biblical theology should be seen as integral parts of the same specific whole. Both the one and the other are true, authentic theology, though they exercise different functions. The one seeks to understand revelation with the aid of philosophy, while the other studies the sacred documents in the light of literary critical methods. These media are different—philosophical reasoning and historical reasoning—but their inspiration and their basic method are identical because the dogmatic theologian and the biblical theologian alike are guided in their task by the light of faith.[61]

## II. TRADITION AND MAGISTERIUM

Hitherto, in our presentation of the relationship between biblical and dogmatic theology, we have looked at Scripture alone, practically without reference to tradition and the teaching office of the Church. We shall proceed to set biblical theology in its natural setting.

### Tradition

Liam Walsh[62] makes the point that apostolic tradition is essentially active and living; its content has no static existence apart from the living act in which it is being communicated. The function of tradition is to transmit the 'apostolic preaching' which includes everything needed for living the Christian life, as well as for the growth of the Christian faith. 'What is handed on, then, is not merely a doctrine but an entire way of life. Hence it is the Church itself in everything that it is as well as in everything that it believes—in its teaching, life and liturgy—which is the full embodiment of Tradition. What the process of Tradition perpetuates is the Church herself.'[63]

Tradition makes the word of God progressively pervade the total life of the Church; it gives the Church a living understanding of the Scriptures. The words of the Bible must become living and effective in the Church; when tradition is brought to bear on the written word it becomes alive and relevant. Tradition serves Scripture. It is firm in sustaining the essential understanding of Scripture which the Church has held from the time of the apostles. And tradition is free and flexible enough in its expression to be able to draw out, with divine authority, contemporary answers from the letter of Scripture. Through the joint action of tradition and Scripture God speaks here and now to his Church, and the gospel becomes a living voice rather than a historical record.

Karl-Heinz Weger[64] asserts that Vatican II has freed tradition from its narrow post-Tridentine limits.[65] It has established that tradition is not an objectified datum but the faith of the Church in action; and for this reason the living faith of the Church is the ultimate norm for the criterion of tradition within the Church. It is natural that there should be progress and growth in the understanding of the matters and words of tradition, an understanding guided by the promised Holy Spirit. It is reasonable to suppose that this would take the form of the Church as a whole recognising that a given truth of faith is obligatory for the whole time of the Church. Thus, in the matter of doctrine, we arrive at tradition in the strict sense: the doctrines of the faith defined in post-apostolic times by the Church and its teaching office. Nor is there any danger of arbitrariness here, for nothing can be defined which the Church has not long believed and which is not recognised as belonging to the substance of the faith. 'The Catholic Christian knows that his faith in the traditions of his Church does not leave him at the mercy of an arbitrary human magisterium, just as he is not at the mercy of the state of exegetical science at any given moment, or of his own intellectual powers. He knows on the contrary that even in post-biblical times he remains—not indeed as an individual, but as sharing the fellowship of all who believe along with him—under the assistance of the Holy Spirit in the ultimate and decisive matters of faith.'[66]

Two further points should be noted. In the first place, the New Testament, composed in large part of occasional writings, does not claim to represent the total content of the faith of the primitive Church. 'Nonetheless, there is no compelling reason to assume that the writings of the New Testament, being the permanent and divinely-willed norm for all times in the Church of later days, do not contain materially all the essential truths of the Christian faith.'[67] In the second place, dogmatically binding declarations of the Church are obligatory only because they are connected with truths which have been revealed by God *for our salvation*. This means that the whole ministry of the word is *under* Scripture. Hence the infallible utterances of the post-apostolic tradition of the Church must be investigated both to discover their historically-conditioned elements, and to demarcate the *salutary* affirmations they have made. But how can this be done without an objective norm? The teaching office of the Church, which can make these dogmatically binding declarations, must know that Scripture, read by it with the assistance of the Spirit, tells it what is right—and Scripture remains the *norma non normata* for theology and for the Church.

## The Teaching Office

Karl Rahner[68] states that, in practice, Scripture is always, at least implicitly, read together with tradition; there is no question of tradition being replaced by Scripture. Nor, he maintains, is the Church's teaching office in the least excluded or hampered in its function by our description of Scripture as in fact the only material source of the Church's consciousness of faith, and the ultimate norm of faith. 'The Church's magisterium after all is in no way a source of the content of faith since it receives no new revelation but simply has to safeguard and expound the *depositum fidei*. It has, therefore, a conserving, distinguishing and binding function with regard to the property transmitted by Scripture and Tradition (Tradition understood as the expounding transmission of Scripture) to the belief of the later Church and presented to the individual believer with a demand for his faith, but it does not create any new contents. As far as these contents are concerned, the Church of a particular age—just like the individual believer—is dependent on scripture and the tradition which continues to attest it.'[69]

This assessment of the role of the teaching office is borne out by the discussion which led to the choice of a particular phrase in art. 23 of *Dei Verbum*: 'under the watchful eye of the sacred Magisterium' (*sub vigilantia Sacri Magisterii*). In the course of the debates *vigilantia* was introduced to replace the previous term *sub ductu,* in order to make clear that the function of the teaching office is not to lead the way—progress is the concern of scholarship; the teaching office has the basically negative function of setting limits and of marking off impenetrable terrain. We might note, too, that the juxtaposition of the phrases *aptis subsidiis* ('and using appropriate techniques') and *sub vigilantia S. Magisterii* directs our attention not only to two aspects of Church exegesis, the ecclesial and the scientific, but points to an inner tension which cannot be removed but which should be radically accepted as tension.[70]

The fact remains, however, that when it comes to decisive judgement about the meaning of the word of God, the teaching office of the Church is the sole authority, an authority not man-made but God-given. We must be sure about the scope and function of this teaching office and the quality of its exercise of authority; Liam Walsh[71] has described these with clarity and precision (he is commenting on the statement of *Dei Verbum*, art. 10—'This Magisterium is not superior to the word of God, but is its servant'): 'Since it is a Christian authority, Magisterium will take the form of service rather than dominance. It has to serve the Word of God rather than "lord it over" it. This theme of Christian service is prominent in many of the Council's documents. The ideal is rooted in Christ's own example of humble service. It is very appropriate for our own age, with its strong aversion to authoritarianism in any form. It has a particular value for ecumenism. Those outside her tradition have long suspected the Roman Catholic Church of claiming an absolute and arbitrary authority, especially in matters of teaching. This clear statement that the Magisterium, while carrying divine authority is not above the word of God, but its servant, could give new honesty to ecumenical discussion. The Magisterium can only teach what it has received through Scripture and Tradition. It must first listen to the word, and then preserve and expound what it hears, and nothing more. It can only bind the faithful to believe on divine faith what it has itself heard in the deposit of faith. Thus, a truth is already believed by the Church at large before the Magisterium makes it a dogma that must be believed by everyone. It is divine revelation, not dogma, which motivates our faith. Dogma gives precision to the understanding, expression and communication of the faith within the Christian community. As such it is imposed under obligation by those who hold authority within the community. But they can only oblige us to believe what they have already heard of the word of God from Scripture and Tradition.'[72]

*Dei Verbum*

The final chapter of the Constitution on Divine Revelation takes up the place of Scripture in the life of the Church. We shall look only at article 24, which is devoted to the function of Scripture in theology. This article starts by describing the function as that of the foundation of theology, with the emphasis on the element of constancy. The opening sentence of the article specifies that theology relies on the written word of God 'taken together with sacred Tradition' (*una cum sacra Traditione*). Though the phrase was added at a late stage, it corresponds to the facts of the case. For, evn in the Reformed Churches, in practice, the principle of *sola Scriptura* includes the understanding of Scripture in the light of confessional writings. Scripture exists only 'together with tradition' not alone in the sense that Scripture is related to tradition but also that tradition is based upon Scripture. Scripture is described as the permanent *foundation* of theology, on which theology is based. A foundation is the starting-point of a building and its support; in plain terms the work of theology must begin with Scripture and must always come back to it. The second half of the opening sentence qualifies the static character of the image of foundation: theology is 'most firmly strengthened and constantly rejuvenated' (*in eoque ipsa firmissime roboratur semperque iuvenescit*) by the word of God. The 'edifice' of theology is not something constructed once for all, because theologising must go on as a living activity. The image has been transferred into the organic sphere, and Scripture is described as the constant renewing force of theology.

'Thus theology is told to draw its strength, that is its reality and its faith, from its closeness to Scripture. It will also be renewed and restored to youth by constant return to the Bible. It is the business of theology to answer the questions which the human mind puts to the Word of God. But the human mind is always moving on to new questions. A theology which asked and answered the right questions for one generation will not always have ready-made answers to the problems of a later age. It will seek new answers to new questions by returning again to the Word of God. There it will discover new facets of revealed reality, new shades of truth. Theology itself will become richer as a result, and will have more to say to the contemporary generation.'[73] Thus from Scripture theology draws fresh inspiration and new themes for theological reflection. Whereas the precise definitions of former Councils have had the effect of restricting the vision of theologians, Vatican II has not only urged a return to the biblical foundations and to the wide horizon of God's word, but has also given an example of sober reticence in the formulation of doctrine.

The teaching of the Constitution on the relationship of theology and Scripture is clinched by a third image that goes back to Leo XIII: the study of Scripture is 'the soul of theology'. This certainly is not meant to imply that theological research should henceforth bear on Scripture alone and leave later developments aside. What it means to do is to establish the pre-eminence of Scripture, in so far as Scripture not only contains the word of God but is, as inspired word, the authentic word of God. What is in mind here, of course, is Scripture read in and with the faith of the Church. Each generation of theologians has the right and the duty to bring out the understanding which the Church has had of Scripture in the different epochs of its history and to envisage the theological task as a fresh reading of Scripture in their day.

The full force of the statement that Scripture is the soul of theology may be seen when we compare the use of the same term in *Optatam Totius* (Decree on Priestly Formation): the study of sacred Scripture 'ought to be the soul of all theology'. The Decree goes on to state quite directly: 'Dogmatic theology should be so arranged that the biblical themes are presented first (*ut ipsa themata biblica primum proponantur*).'[74] This, in effect, means that in future the Bible must be seen and studied on its own terms and that only then can dogmatic analysis and development take place. It is clear that this conception gives concrete expression and content to the formula that Scripture is the soul of theology. To the extent that this programme is put into practice the systematic shape of Catholic theology will be changed in a radical way. To some extent, this has taken place; the vigorous development of biblical theology is the best—indeed the only —way of ensuring that it will become universal.[75]

III. THE ROLE OF BIBLICAL THEOLOGY

It is fitting to round off this investigation of the role of biblical theology by turning again to Karl Rahner.[76] He maintains that dogmatic theology is not merely a theology of conclusion drawn from the premises of faith; it is a systematic, deliberate attention to God's revelation in Jesus Christ. Consequently, dogmatic theology must listen most attentively to the direct and ultimate source of Christian revelation; it must read Scripture and listen to it. It will read Scripture always in the context of living tradition and under the guidance of the teaching office because it reads Scripture in the Church and studies it as the basis of the Church's present awareness of its faith. Its function in regard to Scripture goes beyond the process of finding *dicta probantia* for the Church's teaching of the faith.

The dogmatic theologian has the task of expounding the Church's present teaching of the faith. The actual teaching of the magisterium is not only what is given in Council documents, encyclicals, catechisms and so on: Scripture itself is always officially proclaimed in the Church and it remains an essential part of the Church's message in all ages.

> Furthermore, theological concern with God's revelation in the actual teaching of the Church's magisterium and in the mind of the Church of one's own time, inevitably leads back to Scripture. The full understanding of present doctrine demands a perpetual return to the source from which, on its own admission, this doctrine is derived. There has to be a return to the doctrine which the Church's teaching itself is intended to expound and actualise here and now. In other words, there has to be recourse to Scripture.[77]
>
> Biblical theology is therefore an intrinsic element in dogmatic theology itself. And it is so not merely as one element side by side with the elements of 'historical theology'. It is an absolutely pre-eminent and unique part of dogmatic theology itself. This does not mean, of course, that biblical theology should not for various reasons establish itself as an independent branch of study within theology as a whole. That is quite appropriate, even on practical grounds. . . . The pre-eminent position which

belongs to biblical theology within dogmatics, in comparison with its other concerns (patristic theology, medieval scholasticism, modern scholastic theology) is therefore better provided for if biblical theology is not pursued solely as part of dogmatics.[78]

## In Summary

This last chapter has helped us to glimpse the enormously difficult undertakings met by each of our authors, whether in works on Old Testament or New Testament theology or on the methods of biblical theology in general. Reviewing these our last pages, we can be guided by another of Paul's warmest biddings: 'whatever is true, whatever is honourable, whatever is pure, whatever is lovely or gracious . . . think on these things' (*Phil.* 4 : 8). And so, let us look back to certain 'things' which are to be 'honoured' and deemed 'just' in approaches to biblical theology. The importance of *history* is frequently noted: for Dentan, biblical theology treats the religious ideas of the Bible in historical context; for Porteous, God's activity in history—in the 'real stuff' of community life—must be kept in mind; and for Rahner, theology must turn to Scripture as its only material source because it must be historical, not abstract. The *variety* of biblical writings must be respected: a New Testament theology can be born only from a concern with the different forms in which the proclamation of Jesus was presented (Kümmel). Different perspectives correspond to different 'schools of theology' and the cluster of communities within the Church (Rahner), and their combination offers all, materially, of the essential Christian teaching of apostolic times (Weger). Correspondingly to be respected is the Bible's *unity*. At the cost of trial and error, the venture must be made towards *one* biblical theology by relating different themes (Schlier). The *one* way leading from the Old Testament to the New Testament must be traversed over and over (Kraus); the theologian's task comes down to finding the unity which *must* underlie the Bible because it has been inspired by *one* God—whose 'plan' *is* that unity (de Vaux).

'Honourable and just', too, is the very *discipline* of biblical theology: Harvey sees two branches of this, the 'descriptive'

26

and the 'normative for faith'. Weger feels that the entire 'ministry of the word', dogmas, theologies—'disciplines' of various kinds—have value at all only because they are connected with the truths, normative in Scripture, which God has revealed for our *salvation*. Indeed, this objective 'pure norm', this *norma non normata*, must be revered as the voice of the apostolic Church—the standard for the Church today (Rahner). These first beginnings guaranteed by God and their ensuing trends ever remain a critical court of appeal for further movement (Schillebeeckx). Finally, the Church's teaching office is to be 'honoured' as authoritative regarding the meaning of God's word; but it functions not as leader, but as a follower and conserver of the Scripture it serves (Rahner).

What, then, of 'gracious things' for us to think about in what we have considered? Somehow, there is a quality of graciousness in the need, voiced by Dentan, Schnackenburg, and others, for us to have a *sympathy* with men of Old Testament times, to realise what the concepts and ideas of the Bible meant to them and to share their faith with the *sensus fidei*, the mind of a believer. And many of our authors in their works have expressed another kind of sympathy— that for man's limitations. Different theologies, whether in the Bible or in the Church, stem from man's inability to comprehend God, the gap between Truth and its human expression (de Vaux). How does one communicate the *living* experience of *God* (Harvey)? Yes, the awareness of our own littleness has a certain quality of 'graciousness'.

So, too, does the recurrent idea of 'service': all theologies are in the service of God's word (Grelot). Tradition serves Scripture by making its words alive and relevant; and the magisterium of the Church, which can teach only what it has heard in faith and received, must 'serve' rather than 'lord it over', as Walsh says. He finds the kernel of this ideal in Jesus' being among us as 'one who serves' (*Luke* 22:27). Then, surely, *the* most grace-filled recurrent theme—rather, reality—of all is that of the guiding role of the Spirit. For Murphy, the Spirit of Jesus has always guided Old Testament interpretations and shall continue to do so. Rahner's definition of Scripture as the 'pure norm' hinges upon its being divine truth forever guided by the Spirit. 'Truth' is, verily, the 'Spirit of Truth'—he who has spoken in the biblical writer and lives on in the hearer, and thus whose utterances in the Bible are inseparable from the later decrees he has inspired (Schillebeeckx). Because 'tradition' is not static data but the faith of the Church in *action*, there is a natural growth in the understanding of its matter and words. One need not hesitate to place faith in this tradition and its 'doctrine', for it is (as we have seen in our first paragraph of this summary) simply the Spirit himself teaching, guiding, 'leading into all the truth' (*John* 16 : 13) (Weger).

What, then, of 'things lovely'? First to come to mind is the familiar, but beautifully ever-green concept of the *word* itself. For Porteous, the religious fact of the Bible is that 'a word is spoken and received'—even though, in the nature of human community, that reception is imperfect. For von Rad, God's acts and word run abreast in history—both facts and interpretation must be included in biblical theology. A 'perfect' theology would be one taking up *all* God's words in his Book and arriving at an understanding of his whole revealed truth, his 'word' (Benoit). This word is, of course, that which God has spoken in Jesus, the living Word in whom all former 'words' are fulfilled (Grelot). And, as the theologian must consider, this 'word of God'—in Scripture, in the person of Jesus— is *still* being addressed to us (Schillebeeckx). Connected with the Word is the thought of the Bible as the Book of *Life*. As such, it will not share the secrets of a *living* God with merely intellectual analysts; there must be contact with the real life in the Bible and in the world today. As Schillebeeckx says, it is the living reality of Jesus here and now, and not merely a past written account, to which biblical and dogmatic theologies must witness: the Truth is beyond the Book itself. In the helpful image of Walsh, tradition hands on not a mere doctrine but a whole way of life. The Gospel is not just a historical record but a living voice.

We can include here too Schlier's hint that this Book of Life provides incentive not only for dynamic activity in today's world, but also for a more quite 'folding of the hands' —the Church's meditation in faith. Indeed, as we have noted in our preceding chapter summaries, the emphasis on *faith* in its different aspects is one of the 'loveliest' threads shared by our authors. Benoit sets down the requirement of faith for both the biblical theologian and the exegete, and we have mentioned how Dentan bids the student share the faith of the Old Testament. Schlier observes sagely that, in the New Testament, it is the *believing interpretation* of the 'Christ-event' which brought it to light; the testimony is presented in a faith already reflecting upon itself. For de Vaux, theology *is* the science of faith: the theologian comes to understand the chosen people's faith in the Word through his own faith as their spiritual heir. Finally, as Spicq says, even though the functions of biblical and dogmatic theology may differ, their inspiration and basic methods are the same because both are guided by faith.

And finally, 'things that are *pure* . . .' How can we not think primarily, once again, of Rahner's picture of Scripture as the *norma non normata*, the 'pure norm' which requires none further but is itself the source of all else? There must be, he says, a continual recourse to this pure norm, a return to Scripture, to gain a full understanding of all 'theological' doctrines in the Church. For Schillebeeckx, while Scripture is not the whole of revealed Christianity, it does remain the 'inviolable norm' for all theological study and teaching because it springs directly from the apostolic Church. *Dei Verbum* is expressing the same truth in entitling scriptural study the 'soul of theology', its strong and vitalising foundation. Part of this 'pureness' is reflected in Vögtle's understanding of the New Testament as the very gospel itself. Far from a 'system', it is a call to hearts, a proclaiming of a great 'newness'. And Grelot sees that this gospel was the necessary form into which the apostolic preaching had to be cast to contain all God's former words now fulfilled in Jesus.

And so we are led to the 'purest' of thoughts which have recurred at all points in all our works studied: those concerning this God and this Jesus, indeed the 'Alpha and the Omega'. We recall de Vaux's understanding of the Old Testament as the revelation of *my* God—the same God who has inspired all the books of the Bible, and hence whose whole 'plan' must be revealed in their unity. For Dentan, the Bible's unifying principle is the 'doctrine of God', even as the *living* God and his revelation to *persons* must be the prime concern of theology for Jacob. The theologian must himself have *seen* this living God since his work is meant to bring men into that living presence: the Bible is man's witness to *God*, not to himself (Porteous). As a theology inspired by *God*, the New Testament is the peak of all theology (Braun). Tradition and Scripture together disclose God's speaking to and guiding his Church here and now (Walsh). We come, then, to the heart, 'pure and simple', of all Christianity and its 'theology', of the Church, of our Bible itself: Jesus. The unity of the Bible is found in God's fidelity to his promise to Israel through his self-identity in Jesus (Kraus); a complete Old Testament theology must be 'Christ-directed' (Alonso-Schökel). God becomes fully disclosed in his Son and the final salvation victory he brings to all mankind (Rahner). As we have already mentioned and Walsh brings out so clearly, it is the Jesus who is 'gentle and humble of heart'—the 'lowly king'—who provides the example for all branches of theology working together—indeed the example for *any* study, teaching, or search for knowledge at all.

'Thinking on these things', as Paul has asked, let us then gather together the final fruits of this final chapter. We may recollect certain small points which are helpfully inspiring in our view of the whole: Schnackenburg's description of Scripture as an 'inexhaustible treasure', or Walsh's awareness that it and tradition are an entire 'way of life'. After all our efforts to try to 'say' things about the Bible or books concerning it where often there have seemed no words, we can be comforted by Schlier's sage reminder of the 'plenitude' of the New Testament—or the Bible itself: it is the *unsaid* from which the *said* flows and to which it always returns. Likewise, we have all experienced finding those new shades of meaning in Scripture noted in *Dei Verbum*.

But there is, perhaps, one special thought which may help us to understand all we have said; we turn to Genesis and to Jeremias' New Testament Theology to guide us. In Genesis 9, we read of how God sets his rainbow in the clouds as a covenant of his peace with the world, a sign of his loving care until the end of time. Such a story of the rainbow has come from an author who has understood, and received, these things with the profoundly simple wisdom of a child—one who, childlike, has seen the rainbow and felt in its sheer beauty all the goodness and tender mercy of its Creator. And as it is with the visible 'sign' of the rainbow, so it is with the verbal 'sign' of one word in the New Testament which sums up (as Jeremias points out) the mission and gift of Jesus: ABBA. This word—the speaking it simply and humbly like a child, as Jesus has taught us to do—embraces all the words of our Bible and all the loving care of the Father and the Son. Jeremias has written of how the one word *Abba* is stronger than all questionings, riddles and anxieties. So too, stronger than all our questions, data, material and discussions in biblical theology or any theology—beyond all our strivings to know, to teach, to study—is simply *our* one word Abba. Yes, 'the Father knows' . . . and he has given us all we need to know in *his* one Word, his Son.

# Conclusion

AT the close of a survey which may reasonably claim to be representative, while not pretending to be exhaustive, certain clear impressions do emerge. In the first place, there can be no doubt about the importance of scientific study of the theological message of the Bible. It cannot be otherwise since the message of the Bible is essentially religious and is altogether concerned with what is pertinent to salvation; it truly reveals all the elements of God's saving plan. Exegetical study has tended more and more to stress the theological content of the biblical writings; we have moved beyond philological and archaeological studies (which still, of course, have their essential place and value). Biblical theology becomes all the more necessary when one takes seriously the assertion that the study of Scripture should be 'the very soul of sacred theology'. The fact remains that biblical theology, as a distinctive theological discipline, is still finding its way. Much has been achieved, much has become clear, but very much remains to be done. It may be helpful to outline our impression of the procedure and shape of biblical theology in the years to come.

## Old Testament Theology

We have suggested that the most rewarding treatment of the Old Testament is likely to be a theology that combines the characteristics of the diachronic and structural approaches. The question is, of course, whether these methods can be combined. In theory, at least, it does not seem inconsistent that a study of the theology of the successive traditions and stratifications of Israelite religion (diachronic theology) should be followed by an arrangement of themes and structures. A more delicate task is a preservation of the specific values of the Old Testament while keeping in view its standing as Christian Scripture. It would appear that we have become more conscious of both these aspects and are more fully determined to do them justice. The basis is that 'open-context' exegesis that looks to a horizon beyond the Old Testament itself. Typology, taken in a restricted sense, can be our headline; the very existence of types shows that this openness is a reality; and we find that only in the light of the New Testament antitypes do the types emerge with full significance. We can look then to the wider category of promise-fulfilment. If we take that terminology seriously we will not lightly undervalue the Old Testament. For a promise, *a fortiori* a divine promise, is a reality; in the historical religion of Israel, the promises are concrete. And the promise abides, for it is the dynamic word of God.

It does not help to seek a single unifying principle and then attempt to arrange the material around it. This method might seem to have certain advantages, but it must inevitably lead to a blurring of perspective. The Old Testament, with its variety of life and history, cannot readily be reduced, or cannot be reduced at all, to a system. Of course, in a presentation of Old Testament theology, there must be a plan of some sort. Now a logically conceived plan is not going to emerge from the Old Testament material. If we want a system it must, to an extent, come from without. But this is not at all the same as *imposing* a system on the Old Testament or forcing the material into an imported system. The approach in mind here *fully* respects the values and the genius of the Old Testament. But, at the same time, it candidly recognises that the Old Testament does not readily lend itself to systematic treatment. In this respect a plan becomes a practical need and is seen as something secondary and, in the nature of the case, never quite satisfactory. In these circumstances, there will be no real danger of distorting the biblical message. The necessary synthesis will be sufficiently elastic and the plan will serve and not dominate. It will be recognised that any plan must be to some extent artificial and can be bettered; it will be accepted that the theological message of the Old Testament is what really matters.

We should not forget that revelation chiefly came to Israel through the relationship between God and his people. It is the business of a theology of the Old Testament to keep us aware of God's activity in Israel's history; this is all the more necessary because theology should keep us close to the stuff of real life, the material of history. Yet, within the context of the community, the revelation of the personal God has been made to persons; we may not neglect the fundamental and unique role played by individuals like Moses and the prophets. The Old Testament theologian must share the biblical 'knowledge of God' and so operate within the biblical faith. The function of Old Testament theology is to bring man into the presence of the living God. A biblical theology can be written as a result of such an encounter and in face of the written witness of Scripture.

The Christian theologian can never forget that, of necessity, the Old Testament must have a Christ-directed dynamism. The images of the Old Testament are transformed as they pass from the Old Testament to the New Testament, and the meaning which they thereby take on is a clue to their meaning in the Old Testament context.

## New Testament Theology

One result of recent theological research is an awareness of the theological pluralism of the New Testament. An obvious and necessary consequence is that the various theologies must be carefully elaborated before there can be any attempt at synthesis. It is no longer sufficient to follow a threefold division: the Synoptic Gospels, the Pauline writings, the Johannine writings—with the rest of the New Testament literature regarded as offering a secondary contribution. Instead, we must study each of the synoptists separately. Then, in the Pauline corpus, we must take the authentic Pauline letters with careful attention to the evolution of Paul's thought, followed by the deutero-Pauline literature: Ephesians and the Pastorals. Hebrews stands apart, of course, as a work of major theological importance. The Johannine writings have tended to fall into second place, after Paul (and Apocalypse has scarcely figured at all). This is understandable in view of the obvious theologising of Paul and the far more subtle methodology of John. Recent outstanding exegetical work on John will restore the balance. There is no rivalry here; rather the two giants continue to grow in stature. The first epistle of Peter is a significant writing, and so is James; and 2 Peter also makes its contribution, notably on eschatology and Christian hope.

It is a matter of major concern to preserve the distinctive contribution of each author, because this is a feature of the very richness of New Testament thought. Not only is this the only satisfactory way to present New Testament thought, given the simple fact that this is how the New Testament has been structured, but also, the resultant emphasis on so many different viewpoints will remind us that our confessional theologies have tended to be selective. They have followed certain lines of New Testament theology but have neglected other aspects. Indeed, the more the individual New Testament writers are understood, the more obvious this selectivity appears. Familiarity with the living and variegated theology of the New Testament makes one more and more impatient of the manual theology of the recent past, more critical of its aridity and its poverty. It will take us some time yet to recover from our practical neglect of the word of God; our 'Denzinger theology' had only served to sustain the legalism that had stifled the Word.

### Theology of the Bible

The fact that we live in an age of increasing specialisation is not necessarily a bad thing for biblical theology. There is the indispensable need of theological exegesis, the need of theological commentaries on each biblical writing; sound exegesis is the only basis on which any acceptable structure can be raised. But, already, the theological process should look beyond isolated writings in two ways. Firstly, the place of the writing in question in the over-all plan of the Bible must be kept in mind, its place in the dynamic process of revelation. Secondly, where a writing has a distinct affinity with others, the theological message of the group should be presented in synthesis. What will emerge, unmistakably, is the presence of several 'theologies'.

When we have worked out, as well as we may, the theologies within the Old Testament and the New Testament, what is the next procedure? The theorists have consistently advocated a synthesis of the whole: a *biblical theology*. Significantly, the practical task has scarcely been attempted. One cannot avoid the impression that the call for a synthesis is bound up with an idea that theology is somehow monolithic, an impressive and coherent system. Today, in theology as in religion, we no longer shrink from the idea, or the reality, of pluralism; and we can see more clearly that different theological 'schools' witness to the reality of this pluralism. It is interesting, too, that those who advocate a biblical synthesis tend, more and more, to stress that the variety must not thereby be sacrificed.

One feels that the 'unity' of the Bible must be understood in a realistic and elastic manner. It will not do, for instance, merely to acknowledge that the Old Testament is a 'torso' without its completion and fulfilment in the New Testament: the lines of that tension towards the future must be drawn. It will not do to presuppose that the New Testament was shaped to some extent in the matrix of the Old Testament: the formative influence of the Old Testament must be shown. These links and this inter-relationship must be worked out at the level of theological exegesis—we constantly come back to this. It is more important to bring out the richness of the Bible's theological thought than to be concerned with a neat and systematic presentation of it. One cannot help feeling that we have been too preoccupied with 'system' in any case. Are we really the gainers if we sacrifice the vitality of the Bible, the dynamism of its message, to our passion for systematic presentation? Does this mean that we must be less scientific? One can answer, reasonably, that it is not scientific to turn the Bible into something it is not. It is abundantly clear that scientific exegesis can alone bring before us the meaning and the message of the Bible. We simply must accept that this message is many-faceted. It is not possible to cast the word of God in any human word, or system of words.

The task of biblical theology will have been made feasible

and easier if the theological commentaries are developed in the way we have suggested. This means that from the basic level of theological exegesis the broader biblical context is never lost to sight. The lines that will stretch out, forward and backward, tenuous though they be at this first stage, will become more clearly defined in the partial syntheses. In other words, the connecting links will be there from the beginning and can be strung together. Perhaps it is not too fanciful to use the image of a jig-saw puzzle. We start with the presupposition that there is a single picture; the Bible is our guide, our pattern to which we can constantly refer. Indeed, it is only by this constant reference to the pattern that one can see where the pieces fit in at all. Theological exegesis shapes the various pieces; until this task is effectively done they will not interlock. Again, the Bible is our pattern. but only in a general sense, because the *theological* picture does not stand out sharply. It is only when the pieces have been shaped and then fitted together that the theological picture will become clear.

Is there a practical way in which this might be achieved? It is obvious that a biblical theology of this nature must be a work of collaboration—no one man can do all the basic exegetical work. We are reminded, then, of some recent examples of successful collaboration in biblical studies: the three one-volume commentaries of *Peake,* the *Jerome Biblical Commentary* and the *New Catholic Commentary*—as well as several *Dictionaries* of biblical theology. Would it be feasible to get a large group of scholars to work together on this other venture? This time we would have not a commentary on each writing, but a presentation of the theology of each writing. It would be the task of a select group to build this material into a 'synthesis'. We need not expect that the result would be entirely satisfactory, but it does seem a worthwhile venture. At least, it would give us a means of judging, in the concrete, whether a biblical theology structured in this fashion matches up to its theoretical promise. The scholars are there; the existing Commentaries and Dictionaries show that they can be organised. Dare we hope that the growing interest in biblical theology and the evident importance of the discipline for theology as a whole, will inspire such a task?

## Biblical Theology

Biblical theology—the theological content of the biblical writings—is a fact, whatever may be said about the methods and methodology. There can be no questioning the importance of it: *Dei Verbum* has made that abundantly clear—it is the foundation of all theology, the living soul of theological study and development. There is no doubt, either, of its place in the wider setting of Christian theology. Scripture, the word of God, is the *norma non normata* for theology and for the Church. This remains so despite the manifestly unsystematic character of the theological content of the Bible. It remains so despite the incomplete and fragmentary character of the biblical theologies (that is, the theologies of the biblical writings themselves). It is obvious that systematic theology, down the centuries, has developed much that is found in the Bible in an inchoative manner, or implicitly. But it is also true that the same systematic theology has, for different reasons, neglected or undervalued, or has even lost sight of, not a few biblical ideas and intuitions. The word of God is richer than we know; we are the poorer if we do not leave ourselves open to its manifold accents. We do this by according biblical theology its proper place. It will not help us to pay lip-service only to the admonition of *Dei Verbum*. 'Word and speech' is not enough; biblical theology must be foundation and soul 'in deed and in truth' (cf. 1 *John* 3 : 18). Nor is this a forced application of the Johannine text: theology is a *diakonia,* in the service not only of the Word but of men. It is a form of *agapē.*

# Bibliography

## I. A Survey of the Biblical Theology of the Old Testament

BAAB, O. J., *The Theology of the Old Testament*, Nashville: Abingdon Press 1949.

BARR, J., 'Gerhard von Rad's *Theologie des Alten Testaments*', *Expos Times* 73 (1962), 146.

—— *The Semantics of Biblical Language*, London: Oxford University Press 1961.

BAUER, B., *Die Religion des Alten Testaments in der geschlichtlichen Entwickelung ihrer Principien*, Berlin 1838-39.

BAUER, G. L., *Beilagen zur Theologie des Alten Testaments enthaltend die Begriffe von Gott und Vorsehung, nach den vershiedenen Büchern und Zeitperioden entwickelt*, Leipzig 1802.

—— *Theologie des Alten Testaments oder Abriss der religiösen Begriffe der alten Hebräer von den ältesten Zeiten bis auf den Aufgang der christlichen Epoche*, Leipzig 1796.

BRIGHT, J., 'Edmond Jacob's *Theology of the Old Testament*' *Expos Times* 73 (1962), 307.

CEUPPENS, F., O.P., *Theologica Biblica*, I, *De Uno Deo*, Rome: Marietti 1948.

CÖLLN, D. C., VON, *Biblische Theologie*, Leipzig 1836.

DAVIDSON, A. B., *The Theology of the Old Testament*, Salmond, S. D. F., ed., Edinburgh: T. and T. Clark 1904.

DAVIDSON, R., 'The Religion of Israel', 114-37; *id.*, 'The Theology of the Old Testament', 138-65; both in R. Davidson and A. R. C. Leaney, *Biblical Criticism*. The Pelican Guide to Modern Theology, vol. 3, Harmondsworth, Middlesex: Penguin Books 1970.

DILLMAN, A., *Handbuch der alttestamentlichen Theologie*, Kittel, R., ed., Leipzig: S. Hirzel Verlag 1895.

DODD, C. H., *The Bible Today*, London: Cambridge University Press 1946.

EICHRODT, W., 'Hat die alttestamentliche Theologie noch selbständige Bedeutung innerhalb der alttestamentlichen Wissenschaft?' *ZATWiss* 47 (1929), 83-91.

—— *Theologie des Alten Testaments* I, *Gott und Volk*, Leipzig: J. C. Hinrichs Verlag 1933.

—— *Theologie des Alten Testaments* 2 vols., 5th rev. ed. Stuttgart: Ehrenfried Klotz Verlag 1957 and 1964; Eng. trans. *Theology of the Old Testament* 2 vols., London: SCM Press 1961 and 1967.

EISSFELDT, O., 'Israelitisch-judische Religionsgeschichte und alttestamentliche Theologie' *ZATWiss 44* (1926), 1-12.

EWALD, H., *Die Lehre der Bibel von Gott oder Theologie des Alten und Neuen Bundes* 2 vols., Leipzig 1871-76; Eng. trans. 2 vols., *Revelation, its Nature and Record: Old and New Testament Theology*, Edinburgh 1884, 1888.

FRUCHON, P., 'Sur l'herméneutique de G. von Rad', *RSPT* 55 (1971), 4-32.

GABLER, J. P., *Opuscula Academica* II, Ulm, 1831, 179-98.

GELIN, A., P.S.S., *L'Ame d'Israel dans le Livre*, Paris: Fayard 1960; Eng. trans. *The Religion of Israel*, New York: 1959; London: Burns and Oates 1959.

—— *Les Idées Maîtresses de l'Ancien Testament*, Paris: Cerf 1947; Eng. trans. *The Key Concepts of the Old Testament*, New York: Sheed and Ward 1955.

—— *Les Pauvres de Yahvé*, Paris: Cerf 1953; Eng. trans. *The Poor of Yahweh*, Collegeville: The Liturgical Press 1964.

HARVEY, J., S.J., 'The New Diachronic Biblical Theology of the Old Testament', *Biblical Theology Bulletin I* (1970), 5-29.

HÄVERNICK, H. A., *Vorlesungen über die Theologie des Alten Testaments*, Hahn, E., ed., Erlangen 1848.

HEINISCH, P., *Theologie des Alten Testaments*, Bonn: P. Hanstein 1940; Eng. trans. *Theology of the Old Testament*, Collegeville: The Liturgical Press 1955.

HETZENAUER, M., *Theologia Biblica* sive Scientia Historiae et Religionis utriusque Testamenti Catholica. Tomus I, Vetus Testamentum, Freiburg I.B.: Herder 1908.

HOFMANN, J. C., *Weissagung und Erfüllung im Alten und Neuen Testaments*, Nördlingen 1841-44.

IMSCHOOT, P., VAN, *Théologie de l'Ancien Testament* 2 vols., Tournai: Desclée 1954, 1956; Eng. trans. *Theology of the Old Testament*, I, *God*, New York: Desclée 1965.

JACOB, E., *Théologie de l'Ancien Testament*, Neuchâtel: Delachaux et Niestlé 1955; Eng. trans. *Theology of the Old Testament*, London: Hodder and Stoughton 1958.

KAUFMANN, Y., *The Religion of Israel*, University of Chicago Press 1960; London: Allen and Unwin 1961.

KAYSER, A., *Die Theologie des Alten Testaments in ihrer geschichtlichen Entwickelung dargestellt*, Reuss, E., ed., Strassbourg 1886.

KNIGHT, G. A. F., *A Christian Theology of the Old Testament*, London: SCM 1959, 2nd rev. ed. 1964.

KÖHLER, L., *Theologie des Alten Testaments,* Tübingen: J. C. B. Mohr 1936; Eng. trans. *Old Testament Theology,* Philadelphia 1957.

KÖNIG, E., *Theologie des Alten Testaments kritisch und vergleichend dargestellt,* Stuttgart 1922.

MCKENZIE, J. L., 'Aspects of Old Testament Thought', *The Jerome Biblical Commentary,* Brown, R. E., Fitzmyer, J. A., Murphy, R. E., eds. Englewood Cliffs, New Jersey: Prentice-Hall 1968; London-Dublin: Chapman 1968, 756-67.

—— *Dictionary of the Bible,* Milwaukee: Bruce 1965; London-Dublin: Chapman 1965.

—— *Myths and Realities,* Milwaukee: Bruce 1963; London-Dublin: Chapman 1963.

—— *The Two-edged Sword,* Milwaukee: Bruce 1956; London: Chapman 1960.

MOWINCKEL, S., *Psalmenstudien II,* Amsterdam: Schippers 1961; Eng. trans. *The Psalms in Israel's Worship II,* Oxford: Blackwell 1962.

PEDERSEN, J., *Israel* I-II; III-IV, 2 vols., Copenhagen: Branner and Korch 1920, 1934; 2nd rev. ed. 1958, 1960; Eng. trans. *Israel: Its Life and Culture,* 2 vols., London: Oxford University Press 1926, 1940; 2nd ed. 1959.

PIEPENBRING, C., *Théologie de l'Ancien Testament,* Paris 1886; Eng. trans. New York 1893.

PORTEOUS, N. W., 'The Theology of the Old Testament', *Peake's Commentary on the Bible,* Black, M., and Rowley, H. H., eds., 2nd rev. ed. London: Nelson 1962, 151-9.

PROCKSCH, O., *Theologie des Alten Testaments,* Gütersloh: G. Bertelsmann Verlag 1949.

OEHLER, G. F., *Old Testament Theology,* Edinburgh 1874-75, New York 1883.

—— *Prolegomena zur Theologie des Alten Testaments,* Stuttgart 1845.

—— *Theologie des Alten Testaments,* Tübingen 1873.

RAMLOT, M.-L., O.P., 'Une Décade de Théologie Biblique', *Revue Thomiste* 64 (1964), 82.

RENCKENS, H., *De Godsdienst van Israël,* Ruremonde: Romen 1962; Eng. trans. *The Religion of Israel,* New York: Sheed and Ward 1966.

RINGGREN, H., *Israelitische Religion,* Stuttgart: W. Kohlhammer 1963; Eng. trans. *Israelite Religion,* London: S.P.C.K. 1966.

ROBINSON, H. WHEELER, *Inspiration and Revelation in the Old Testament,* London: Oxford University Press 1946.

—— ed., 'The Theology of the Old Testament', *Record and Revelation,* London: Oxford University Press, 303-48.

ROWLEY, H. H., ed., *The Old Testament and Modern Study,* London: Oxford University Press 1951.

SCHULTZ, H., *Alttestamentliche Theologie*. Die Offenbarungs-religions auf ihrer vorchristlichen Entwickelungsstufe, Braunschweig 1869; 5th rev. ed. Göttingen 1896; Eng. trans. *Old Testament Theology*, Edinburgh 1892.

SELLIN, E., *Alttestamentliche Theologie auf Religionsgeschichtlicher Grundlage*, I, Israelitisch-jüdische Religionsgeschichte; II, Theologie des Alten Testaments, Leipzig 1933.

SMEND, R., *Lehrbuch der Alttestamentlichen Religionsgeschichte*, Freiburg and Leipzig, 1893.

STEUDEL, J. C. F., *Vorlesungen über die Theologie des Alten Testaments*, Oehler, G. F., ed., Berlin 1840.

STEUERNAGEL, C., 'Alttestamentliche Theologie und alttestamentliche Religionsgeschichte' *ZATWiss* Beiheft 41 (Martifestschrift) (1925), 266-73.

VATKE, W., *Die biblischen Theologie* I, Die Religion des Alten Testaments nach dem kanonishen Büchern entwickelt, Berlin 1835.

VAUX, R. DE, O.P., *Bible et Orient*, 'Peut-on écrire une "Théologie de l'Ancien Testament"?', Paris: Cerf 1957, 59-71.

—— *Les Institutions de l'Ancient Testament*, 2 vols., Paris: Cerf 1958, 1960; Eng. trans. *Ancient Israel. Its Life and Institutions*, London: Darton, Longman and Todd 1961.

—— *Les Sacrifices de l'Ancien Testament*, Paris: Gabalda 1964; Eng. trans. *Studies in Old Testament Sacrifice*, Cardiff: University of Wales Press 1964.

VON RAD, G., *Das Formgeschichtliche Problem des Hexateuchs*, Stuttgart: 1938.

—— *Theologie des Alten Testaments*, 2 vols., Munich: Chr. Kaiser Verlag 1957 and 1960; Eng. trans. *Old Testament Theology*, 2 vols., Edinburgh: Oliver and Boyd 1962, 1965.

VRIEZEN, T. C., *De Godsdienst van Israël*, Arnheim: de Haan 1963; Eng. trans. *The Religion of Ancient Israel*, London: Lutterworth Press 1967.

—— *Hoofdlijnen der Theologie van het Oude Testament*, 2nd rev. ed. Wageningen: H. Veenman & Zoen 1954; Eng. trans. *Outline of Old Testament Theology*, Oxford: B. Blackwell 1958.

WEISER, A., *The Psalms*, Philadelphia: Westminster Press 1962.

WELLHAUSEN, J., *Geschichte Isräels*, Berlin 1878, retitled *Prolegomena zur Geschichte Isräels*, 2nd ed. Berlin 1883.

DE WETTE, W., *Biblische Dogmatik des Alten und Neuen Testaments*, oder kritische Darstellung der Religionslehre des Hebräismus, des Judentums, und des Urchristentums, Berlin 1813.

WRIGHT, G. E., *God Who Acts*. Biblical Theology as Recital, London: SCM 1952.

—— *The Old Testament and Theology*, New York: Harper and Row 1969.

## II. A Survey of the Biblical Theology of the New Testament

ALBERTZ, M., *Die Botschaft des Neuen Testaments*, Zollikon-Zürich: Evangelischer Verlag 1947, 1952, 1954, 1957.

BLACK, M., ed., *The Scrolls and Christianity*. Historical and Theological Significance, London: SPCK 1969.

BONSIRVEN, J., S.J., *L'Évangile de Paul*, Paris: Aubier 1948.

—— *Les Enseignements de Jésus-Christ*, Paris: Beauschesne, 4th ed. 1946.

—— *Théologie du Nouveau Testament*, Paris: Aubier 1951; Eng. trans. *Theology of the New Testament*, London: Burns and Oates 1963.

BOUSSET, W., *Kyrios Christos*. Geschichte des Christusglaubens von Anfängen des Christentums bis Irenaeus, Göttingen: Vandenhoeck & Ruprecht 1913, 4th ed. 1935.

BÜCHSEL, F., *Theologie des Neuen Testaments*. Geschichte des Wortes im Neuen Testament, Gutersloh: Bertelsmann 1935.

BULTMANN, R., *Theologie des Neuen Testaments*. 3 Lieferungen, Tübingen: J. C. B. Mohr (Paul Siebeck) 1948, 1951, 1953, 3rd ed. 1958.

—— *Theology of the New Testament*, 2 vols., London: SCM 1952, 1955.

CONZELMANN, H., *Die Mitte der Zeit*. Studien zur Theologie des Lukas, Tübingen: J. C. B. Mohr (Paul Siebeck) 1953, 2nd ed. 1957 Eng. trans. *The Theology of St Luke*, New York: Harper and Brothers 1960; London: Faber and Faber 1960.

—— *Grundriss der Theologie des Neuen Testaments*, Munich: Christian Kaiser 1968; Eng. trans. *An Outline of the Theology of the New Testament*, London: SCM 1969.

CULLMANN, O., *Christus und die Zeit*. Die urchristliche Zeit-und-Geschichtsauffassung, Zollikon-Zürich: Evangelischer Verlag 3rd ed. 1962; Eng. trans. *Christ and Time*. The Primitive Christian Conception of Time and History, London: SCM 1959. 2nd rev. ed. 1962.

—— *Die Christologie des Neuen Testaments*, Tübingen: J. C. B. Mohr (Paul Siebeck 1957); Eng. trans. *The Christology of the New Testament*, London: SCM 1959, 2nd rev. ed. 1963.

—— *Heil als Geschichte*. Heilsgeschichtliche Existenz im Neuen Testament, Tübingen: J. C. B. Mohr (Paul Siebeck) 1965; Eng. trans. *Salvation in History*, London: SCM 1967.

DAVIES, W. D., *Christian Origins and Judaism*, London: Darton, Longman and Todd 1962.

—— 'Contemporary Jewish Religion', *Peake's Commentary on the Bible*, Black, M., and Rowley, H. H., eds. 2nd rev. ed. London: Nelson 1962, 705-11.

DODD, C. H., *The Apostolic Preaching and its Developments*, London: Hodder and Stoughton 1944; 3rd ed. 1963.

—— *The Parables of the Kingdom,* London: Nisbet 1935, rev. ed. 1961.

FEINE, P., *Theologie des Neuen Testaments,* Leipzig: Hinrichs 1910, 8th ed. 1951.

FITZMYER, J. A., S.J., 'Pauline Theology', *The Jerome Biblical Commentary,* Brown, R. E., Fitzmyer, J. A., Murphy, R. E., eds. Englewood Cliffs, New Jersey: Prentice-Hall 1968; London-Dublin: Chapman 1968, 800-27.

FULLER, R. H., *The Foundations of New Testament Christology,* New York: Charles Scribner's Sons 1965.

GRANT, F. C., *An Introduction to New Testament Thought,* New York: Abingdon Press 1950.

GRECH, P., O.S.A., 'Tradition and Theology in Apostolic Times', *A New Catholic Commentary on Holy Scripture,* Fuller, R. C., ed., London: Nelson 1969, 844-89.

HOLTZMANN, H. J., *Lehrbuch der neutestamentlichen Theologie,* 2 vols., Tübingen: Mohr 1896-97, 2nd rev. ed. 1911.

HUNTER, A. M., *Introducing New Testament Theology,* London: SCM 1957.

JEREMIAS, J., *Die Gleichnisse Jesu,* Göttingen: Vandenhoeck and Ruprecht 1947, 6th rev. ed., 1962; Eng. trans. *The Parables of Jesus,* London: SCM Press 1954, 2nd rev. ed. 1963.

—— *New Testament Theology,* I, The Proclamation of Jesus, London: SCM 1971.

—— 'Qumran et la Théologie', *NRT* 85 (1963), 675-90.

KÜMMEL, W. G., *Die Theologie des Neuen Testaments nach seinen Hauptzeugen Jesus-Paulus-Johannes,* Göttingen: Vandenhoeck & Ruprecht 1969.

KÜSS, O., *Die Theologie des Neuen Testaments.* Eine Einführung, Regensburg: Pustet 1936.

LEMONNYER, A., O.P., *La Théologie du Nouveau Testament,* Paris: Bloud & Gay, 1928; Eng. trans. *The Theology of the New Testament,* London: 1930.

—— and CERFAUX, L., *Théologie du Nouveau Testament,* Paris: Bloud & Gay, 2nd rev. ed. 1963.

MANSON, T. W., *Ethics and the Gospel,* London: SCM 1965.

MARSH, J., 'The Theology of the New Testament', *Peake's Commentary on the Bible,* Black, M., and Rowley, H. H., eds., London: Nelson 2nd rev. ed. 1962, 756-68.

MCKENZIE, J. L., 'The Jewish World in New Testament Times', IV, Beliefs and Morality, *A New Catholic Commentary on Holy Scripture,* Fuller, R. C., ed., London: Nelson 1969, 777-83.

MEINERTZ, M., *Theologie des Neuen Testaments,* 2 vols., Bonn: P. Hanstein 1950.

MURPHY-O'CONNOR, J., O.P., ed., *Paul and Qumran.* Studies in New Testament Exegesis, Chicago: The Priory Press 1968; London-Dublin: Chapman 1968.

NEIL, S., *The Interpretation of the New Testament*, London: Oxford University Press 1964.

RICHARDSON, A., *An Introduction to the Theology of the New Testament*, New York: Harper 1958; London: SCM 1958.

SABOURIN, L., S.J., *Les Noms et les Titres de Jésus: Thèmes de Théologie Biblique*, Paris: Editions de Brouwer 1963; Eng. trans. *The Names and Titles of Jesus: Themes of Biblical Theology*, New York: Macmillan 1967.

SCHLATTER, A., *Die Theologie des Neuen Testaments, 2* vols., Stuttgart: Vereinsbuchhandlung 1909, 1910, 2nd ed. 1922, 1923.

SCHNACKENBURG, R., *Die Sittliche Botschaft des Neuen Testaments*, Munich: Max Huber 1954, 2nd rev. ed. 1962; Eng. trans. *The Moral Teaching of the New Testament*, New York: Herder and Herder 1955; London: Herder/Burns and Oates 1965.

—— *New Testament Theology Today*, London: Chapman 1963, 24-5.

SPICQ, C., O.P., *Agapē*. Prolégomènes a une étude de Théologie Néo-testamentaire, Louvain: Nauwelaerts 1955.

—— *Agapē dans le Nouveau Testament, 3* vols., Paris: 1958, 1959; Eng. trans. (abridged) *Agapē in the New Testament*, 3 vols., St Louis: B. Herder 1963, 1965, 1966.

—— *Théologie morale du Nouveau Testament, 2* vols., Paris: Gabalda 1965.

STANLEY, D. M., S.J., and BROWN, R. E., S.S., 'Aspects of New Testament Thought', *The Jerome Biblical Commentary*, Brown, R. E., Fitzmyer, J. A., Murphy, R. E., eds., Englewood Cliffs, New Jersey: Prentice-Hall 1968; London-Dublin: Chapman 1968, 768-99.

STAUFFER, E., *Die Theologie des Neuen Testaments*, Stuttgart: W. Kohlhammer 1941.

—— *New Testament Theology*, London: SCM 1955.

STENDAHL, K., ed., *The Scrolls and the New Testament*. An Introduction and a Perspective, New York: Harper 1957.

STEVENS, G. B., *The Theology of the New Testament*, Edinburgh: T. and T. Clark 1899, 2nd rev. ed. 1918; reprinted 1968.

TAYLOR, V., *The Person of Jesus in New Testament Teaching*, London: Macmillan 1959.

VAWTER, B., C.M., 'Johannine Theology', *The Jerome Biblical Commentary*, Brown, R. E., Fitzmyer, J. A., and Murphy, R. E., eds., Englewood Cliffs, New Jersey: Prentice Hall 1968; London-Dublin: Chapman 1968, 825-39.

WEINEL, H., *Biblische Theologie des Neuen Testaments*. Die Religion Jesu und des Urchristentums, Tübingen: Mohr 1911, 4th ed. 1928.

WREDE, W., *Über Aufgabe und Methode der sogenannten neutestamentlichen Theologie*, Göttingen 1897.

### III. The Theology of the Bible

ALLMEN, J. J. VON, *Vocabulaire Biblique,* Neuchatel: Delachoux et Niestlé 1954, 2nd ed., 1956.

ANDERSON, B. W., *The Old Testament and Christian Faith,* New York: Harper and Row 1963.

BARR, J., *Old and New in Interpretation.* A Study of the Two Testaments, London: SCM 1966.

—— *The Semantics of Biblical Language,* New York: Oxford University Press 1961.

BAUER, J. B., *Bibeltheologisches Wörterbuch* 2 vols., Graz-Vienna-Cologne: Styria 1959, 3rd ed. 1967; Eng. trans. *Encyclopedia of Biblical Theology,* 3 vols., London: Sheed and Ward 1970.

BENOIT, P., O.P., 'La Plenitude de Sens des Livres Saints', *RB* 67 (1960), 161-96.

—— 'Le Sensus Plenior de l'Écriture', *RB* (1956), 287.

BIERBERG, R., 'Does Sacred Scripture Have a Sensus Plenior?' *CBQ* 10 (1948), 182-95.

BONHOEFFER, D., *Letters and Papers from Prison,* New York: Macmillan 1962.

BRIGHT, J., *The Authority of the Old Testament,* London: SCM 1967.

BROWN, R. E., S.S., 'Hermeneutics', *The Jerome Biblical Commentary;* Brown, R. E., Fitzmyer, J. A., Murphy, R. E., eds., Englewood Cliffs, New Jersey: Prentice-Hall 1968; London-Dublin: Chapman 1968.

—— 'The History and Development of the Theory of a *Sensus Plenior*', *CBQ* 15 (1953), 141-62.

—— 'The Problem of the *Sensus Plenior*', *ETL* 53 (1967), 460-69.

—— 'The *Sensus Plenior* in the Last Ten Years', *CBQ* 25 (1963), 262-85.

—— *The* Sensus Plenior *of Sacred Scripture,* Baltimore: St Mary's University 1955.

BULTMANN, R., *Theology of the New Testament,* 2 vols., London: SCM 1952, 1955.

BURROWS, M., *An Outline of Biblical Theology,* Philadelphia: The Westminister Press 1946.

BUTTRICK, G. A., ed., *The Interpreter's Dictionary of the Bible.* An Illustrated Encyclopedia in Four Volumes, Nashville: Abingdon 1962.

COPPENS, J., *Les Harmonies des Deux Testaments.* Essai sur les Divers Sens de l'Écriture et sur l'Unité de la Révélation, Tournai-Paris: Castermann 1948, 2nd ed. 1949.

—— 'Nouvelles Refléxions sur les Divers Sens des Saintes Écritures', *NRT* 74 (1952), 3-20.

—— 'Levels of Meaning in the Bible', *Concilium,* 10 no. 3 (December 1967), 62-9.

COURTADE, G., 'Les Écritures, ont-elles un Sens Plénier?', *RSR* 37 (1950), 48-9.

DANIÉLOU, J., S.J., *Bible et Liturgie*, Paris: Cerf 1951; Eng. trans. *The Bible and the Liturgy*, University of Notre Dame Press: 1956; London: D.L.T. 1960.

—— *Origène*, Paris: Editions de la Table Ronde 1948; Eng. trans. *Origen*, London: Sheed and Ward 1955.

—— *Sacramentum Futuri*. Études sur les Origines de la Typologie Biblique, Paris: Beauchesne 1950; Eng. trans. *From Shadow to Reality*, London: Burns and Oates 1960.

—— *Dei Verbum*, Dogmatic Constitution on Divine Revelation of the Second Vatican Council.

DREYFUS, F., O.P., 'The Existential Value of the Old Testament', *Concilium* 10 (December 1967), 18-23.

EICHRODT, W., *Theology of the Old Testament*, 2 vols., London: SCM 1961 and 1967.

FERNÁNDEZ, A., S.J., 'Hermeneutica', *Institutiones Biblicae*, Rome: Biblical Institute 1925, 2nd ed. 1927.

GRELOT, P., *Sens Chrétien de l'Ancien Testament*, Tournai: Desclée 1962.

HAAG, H., *Bibellexikon*, Einsiedeln: Benziger 1951.

HARRINGTON, W. J., O.P., *Record of Revelation: The Bible*, Chicago: The Priory Press; Dublin: Helicon 1969, 55-60.

—— and WALSH, L., *Vatican II on Revelation*, Dublin: Scepter 1967.

HARTMANN, L. F., *Encyclopedic Dictionary of the Bible*, New York: McGraw Hill 1963.

HASTINGS, J., *Dictionary of the Bible*, 5 vols. (Edinburgh: Clark 1898-1904; rev. ed: Grant, C., and Rowley, H. H., eds., New York: Scribner's 1963.

KITTEL, G., and FRIEDRICH, G., *Theologisches Wörterbuch zum Neuen Testament*, 8 vols., Stuttgart: W. Kohlhammer 1933-1969.

—— *Theological Dictionary of the Bible*, 8 vols., translated and edited by G. W. Bromiley, Grand Rapids, Michigan: Eerdmans 1969—.

KNIGHT, G. A., *A Christian Theology of the Old Testament*, London: SCM 1959, 2nd rev. ed. 1964.

LARCHER, C., O.P., *'L'Actualité Chrétienne de l'Ancien Testament*, Paris: Cerf 1963.

LÉON-DUFOUR, X., S.J., *Vocabulaire de Théologie Biblique*, Paris: Cerf 1962; 2nd rev. ed. 1970.

—— *Dictionary of Biblical Theology*, New York: Desclée 1967; London-Dublin: Chapman 1968.

DE LUBAC, H., S.J., *Histoire et Esprit*. L'Intelligence de l'Écriture d'après Origène, Paris: Aubier 1950.

MCKENZIE, J. L., *Dictionary of the Bible*, Milwaukee: Bruce 1965; London-Dublin: Chapman 1965.

—— 'Problems of Hermeneutics in Roman Catholic Exegesis', *JBL* 77 (1958), 197-204.

—— 'The Values of the Old Testament', *Concilium* 10, December 1967, 4-17.

MURPHY, R. E., O.CARM., 'The Relationship Between the Testaments', *CBQ* 26 (1964), 349-59.

MURPHY, R. E., 'Christian understanding of the Old Testament', *Theology Digest* 18 (1970), 321-32.

PIROT, L., ROBERT, A., CAZELLES, H., FEUILLET, A., *Dictionnaire de la Bible* (Supplément), Paris: Letouzey 1928—.

ROBINSON, J. M., 'Scripture and Theological Method: A Protestant Study in *Sensus Plenior*'. *CBQ* 27 (1965), 6-27.

ROWLEY, H. H., *The Unity of the Bible*, London: Carey Kingsgate Press: 1953.

SANSEGUNDO, P., O.P., *Exposicion Historico-Critica del hoy llamado 'Sensus Plenior' de la Sagrada Escritura*, Avila: Revista Studium 1963.

SCHNACKENBURG, R., *Die Johannesbriefe*, Freiburg: Herder 1953. *The Gospel according to St. John*, London: Burns and Oates/Herder and Herder 1968.

STAUFFER, E., *New Testament Theology*, London: SCM 1955.

SWAIN, L., 'The Interpretation of the Bible', *A New Catholic Commentary on Holy Scripture*, Fuller, R. C., ed., London: Nelson 1969.

SYNAVE, P., O.P., and BENOIT, P., O.P., *La Prophétie*, Tournai: Desclee 1947; Eng. trans. *Prophecy and Inspiration*, New York: Desclée, 1961, 149-51.

VAN DEN BORN, A., *Bijbels Woordenboek*, Roermond: Romen 1941-1950; 2nd rev. ed. 1954-57.

VAWTER, B., C.M., 'The Fuller Sense: Some Considerations', *CBQ* 26 (1964), 85-96.

VIGOUROUX, F., *Dictionnaire de la Bible*, 5 vols., Paris: Letouzey, 2nd rev. ed. 1912.

VISCHER, W., *Das Christuszeugnis des Alten Testaments* 1, Das Gesetz, Munich: Kaiser 1936; Eng. trans. *The Witness of the Old Testament to Christ*, London: 1949; 11, Die Propheten, Zollikon-Zurich: Evangelischer Verlag 1942.

VON RAD, G., *Theologie des Alten Testaments*, 2 vols., Munich: Chr. Kaiser Verlag 1957 and 1960; Eng. trans. *Old Testament Theology*, 2 vols., Edinburgh: Oliver and Boyd, 1962 and 1965.

VRIEZEN, T. C., *An Outline of Old Testament Theology*, Oxford: B. Blackwell 1958.

WESTERMANN, C., ed., *Probleme alttestamentliches Hermeneutik*, Munich: C. Kaiser 1960; Eng. trans. *Essays on Old Testament Interpretation*, London: SCM, 1964.

WRIGHT, G. E., *The Old Testament and Theology*, New York: Harper and Row 1969.

## IV. The Methods and Scope of Biblical Theology

ALONSO-SCHÖKEL, L., S.J., 'Old Testament Theology', *Sacramentum Mundi*. An Encyclopedia of Theology, IV, Rahner, K., London: Burns and Oates 1969, 286-90.

—— 'Is Exegesis Necessary?', *Concilium* 10, no. 7 (December 1971), 30-38.

BENOIT, P., O.P., 'Exégèse et Théologie Biblique' *Exégèse et Théologie*, III, Paris: Cerf 1968, 1-13.

BLACK, M., 'The Christological Use of the Old Testament in the New Testament', *New Testament Studies* 18 (1971), 1-14.

BRAATEN, C. E., 'Heilsgeschichte and the Old Testament', *New Directions in Theology Today*, II, History and Hermeneutics, London: Lutterworth Press 1968, 103-29.

BRAUN, F. M., O.P., 'La théologie biblique: qu'entendre par là?', *RT* 53 (1953), 22-53.

CARREZ, M., 'La Méthode de G. von Rad appliquée à quelques textes pauliniens', *RSPT* 55 (1971), 4-32.

CHILDS, B. S., *Biblical Theology in Crisis*, Philadelphia: Westminister Press 1970.

DENTAN, R. C., *Preface to Old Testament Theology*, New York: Seabury Press, 2nd ed. 1963.

FRUCHON, P., 'Sur l'herméneutique de Gerhard von Rad', *RSPT* 55 (1971), 4-32.

GRELOT, P., 'Exégèse, théologie et pastorale', *NRT* 88 (1966), 3-13, 132-48.

GRILLMEIER, A., in Dupuy, B. D., *La Révèlation Divine*, Tome II, Constitution dogmatique 'Dei Verbum', Paris: Cerf 1968, 453-6.

GUZIE, T. W., S.J., 'Patristic Hermeneutics and Tradition', *Theological Studies*, 32 (1971), 647-58.

HARRINGTON, W., O.P., and WALSH, LIAM, O.P., *Vatican II on Revelation*, Dublin: Scepter 1967.

HARVEY, J., S.J., 'The New Diachronic Biblical Theology of the Old Testament (1960-1970)', *BibTB* 1, (1971), 5-29.

HASENHÜTTL, G., 'Dialogue between the Dogmatic Theologian and the Exegete', *Concilium* 10, no. 7 (December 1971), 39-46.

JACOB, E., 'La Théologie de l'Ancien Testament. État present et perspectives d'avenir', *ETL* 44 (1968), 420-32.

KRAUS, H.-J., *Die Biblische Theologie*. Ihre Geschichte und Problematik, Neukirchen Vluyn: Neukirchener Verlag 1970.

KÜMMEL, W. G., *Die Theologie des Neuen Testaments*, see p. 410 above.

LOHFINK, N., S.J., *The Christian Meaning of the Old Testament*, London: Burns and Oates 1968.

LORETZ, O., 'The Church and Biblical Exegesis', *Concilium* 10, no. 7 (December 1971), 67-79.

LYONNET, S., S.J., 'De notione et momento theologicae biblicae', *Sacra Pagina*, 1, 132-57.

MURPHY, R. E., O.CARM., 'Christian Understanding of the Old Testament', *Theology Digest* 18 (1970), 330-32.

—— 'The Role of the Bible in Roman Catholic Theology', *Interpretation* 25 (1971) 79-89.

PANNENBERG, W., *Basic Questions in Theology*, London: SCM 1970

PORTEOUS, N. W., 'Semantics and Old Testament Theology', *Living the Mystery*, Oxford: B. Blackwell 1967, 24. 'The Old Testament and Some Theological Thought Forms', 31-46. 'Towards a Theology of the Old Testament', 7-19.

RAHNER, K., S.J., *Sacramentum Mundi*, 1, London: Burns and Oates 1968.

—— *Theological Investigations*, VI, Baltimore: Helicon 1969; London: Darton Longman and Todd 1969.

—— and VORGRIMLER, H., *Concise Theological Dictionary*, London: Herder/Burns and Oates 1965.

RAMLOT, M.-L., O.P., 'Une Décade de Théologie Biblique', *RT* 72 (1964).

SCHELKLE, KARL HERMANN, *Theologie des Neuen Testaments*, I: Schöpfung. Welt—Zeit—Mensch, Düsseldorf: Patmos 1968. Eng. trans. Theology of the New Testament, vol. I: Creation: World—Time—Man, Collegeville, Minn.: The Liturgical Press 1971.

SCHILLEBEECKX, E., O.P., 'Exegesis, Dogmatics, and the Development of Dogma', *Dogmatic versus Biblical Theology*, 115-72. 'The Dogmatic Evaluation of the New Testament', 147-72.

SCHLIER, H., 'The Meaning and Function of a theology of the New Testament', *The Relevance of the New Testament*, New York: Herder and Herder, 1968, 1-25.

SCHNACKENBURG, R., *New Testament Theology Today*, London: Chapman 1963.

SCHOONENBERG, P., 'Notes of a Systematic Theologian', *Concilium* 10, no. 7 (December 1971), 90-97.

SPICQ, C., O.P., 'L'avènement de la Théologie Biblique', *RSPT* 35 (1951), 561-74.

STENDAHL, K., 'Method in the Study of Biblical Theology' in *The Bible in Modern Scholarship*, Nashville 1965, 196-216.

VAN DER PLOEG, J., O.P., ' "Une Théologie de l'Ancien Testament", est-elle possible?' *ETL* 38 (1962), 417-34.

VAN IERSEL, B., 'Theology and Detailed Exegesis', *Concilium* 10, no. 7 (December 1971), 90-89.

VESCO, J.-L., O.P., 'Abraham: actualisation et relectures. Les traditions vétéro-testentaires', *RSPT* 55 (1971), 33-80.

VÖGTLE, A., 'New Testament Theology', *Sacramentum Mundi*, IV, 216-20.

—— 'Progress and Problems in New Testament Exegesis' in H. Vorgrimler, *Dogmatic versus Biblical Theology*, London: Burns and Oates 1964, 67-86.

VON RAD, G., *Weisheit in Israel*, Neukirchener Verlag: Neukirchen-Vluyn 1970.

VORGRIMLER, H., *Dogmatic versus Biblical Theology*, London: Burns and Oates 1964.

—— ed., Commentary on the Documents of Vatican II, London: Burns and Oates/Herder and Herder 1969.

VOSS, G., 'The Relationship between Exegesis and Dogmatic Theology', *Concilium* 10, no. 7 (December 1971), 20-29.

WARE, R., 'The Use of Scripture in Current Theology', *Concilium* 10, no. 7 (December 1971), 115-28.

WATSON, P. S., 'The Nature and Function of Biblical Theology', *Expos Times* 73 (1962), 195-200.

WEGER, K.-H., *Sacramentum Mundi*, VI, 269-74.

WRIGHT, G. ERNEST, *The Old Testament and Theology*, New York: Harper and Row 1969.

# Notes

## CHAPTER I

[1]J. F. Gabler, *Opuscula Academica, II,* Ulm 1831, 179-98.
[2]G. L. Bauer, *Theologie des Alten Testaments oder Abriss der religiösen Begriffe der alten Hebräer von den ältesten Zeiten bis auf den Aufgang der christlichen Epoche,* Leipzig 1796.
[3]G. L. Bauer, *Beilagen zur Theologie des Alten Testaments enthaltend die Begriffe von Gott und Vorsehung, nach den vershiedenen Büchern und Zeitperioden entwickelt,* Leipzig 1802.
[4]W. De Wette, *Biblische Dogmatik des Alten und Neuen Testaments,* oder kritische Darstellung der Religionslehre des Hebräismus, des Judenthums und des Urchristenthums, Berlin 1813.
[5]D. G. C. von Cölln, *Biblische Theologie,* Leipzig 1836.
[6]W. Vatke, *Die biblischen Theologie I,* Die Religion des Alten Testaments nach dem kanonischen Büchern entwickelt, Berlin 1835.
[7]B. Bauer, *Die Religion des Alten Testaments in der geschichtlichen Entwickelung ihrer Principien,* Berlin 1838-39.
[8]J. C. Hofmann, *Weissagung und Erfüllung im Alten und Neuen Testaments,* Nördlingen 1841-44.
[9]J. C. F. Steudel, *Vorlesungen über die Theologie des Alten Testaments,* edited by G. F. Oehler, Berlin 1840.
[10]H. A. Hävernick, *Vorlesungen über die Theologie des Alten Testaments,* edited by E. Hahn, Erlangen 1848.
[11]G. F. Oehler, *Prolegomena zur Theologie des Alten Testaments,* Stuttgart 1845.
[12]G. F. Oehler, *Theologie des Alten Testaments,* Tübingen 1873.
[13]G. F. Oehler, *Old Testament Theology,* Edinburgh 1874-75; New York 1883.
[14]H. Ewald, *Die Lehre der Bibel von Gott oder Theologie des Alten und Neuen Bundes* 2 vols. Leipzig 1871-76; Eng. tr. 2 vols. *Revelation, Its Nature and Record; Old and New Testament Theology,* Edinburgh 1884, 1888.
[15]J. Wellhausen, *Geschichte Isräels,* Berlin 1878; 2nd ed. retitled *Prolegomena zur Geschichte Isräels,* Berlin 1883.

[16]A. Kayser, *Die Theologie des Alten Testaments in ihrer geschichtlichen Entwickelung dargestellt*, edited by E. Reuss, Strasbourg 1886.

[17]R. Smend, *Lehrbuch der alttestamentlichen Religionsgeschichte*, Freiburg and Leipzig, 1893.

[18]A. Dillmann, *Handbuch der alttestamentlichen Theologie*, edited by R. Kittel, Leipzig 1895.

[19]C. Piepenbring, *Théologie de l'Ancien Testament*, Paris 1886; E. tr. New York 1893.

[20]H. Schultz, *Alttestamentliche Theologie. Die Offenbarungsreligion auf ihrer vorchristlichen Entwickelungsstufe*, Braunschweig 1869; 5th rev. ed. Göttingen 1896; E. tr. *Old Testament Theology*, Edinburgh 1892.

[21]A. B. Davidson, *The Theology of the Old Testament*, edited by S. D. F. Salmond, Edinburgh 1904.

[22]*Ibid.*, 13.

[23]*Ibid.*, 11.

[24]E. König, *Theologie des Alten Testaments kritisch und vergleichend dargestellt*, Stuttgart 1922.

[25]C. Steuernagel, 'Alttestamentliche Theologie und alttestamentliche Religionsgeschichte', *ZATWiss* Beiheft 41 (Martifestschrift) 1925, 266-273.

[26]O. Eissfeldt, 'Israelitisch-jüdische Religionsgeschichte und alttestamentliche Theologie', *ZATWiss* 44, 1926, 1-12.

[27]N. W. Porteous, 'Old Testament Theology', *The Old Testament and Modern Study*, edited by H. H. Rowley, London 1951, 321.

[28]W. Eichrodt, 'Hat die alttestamentliche Theologie noch selbständige Bedeutung innerhalb der alttestamentlichen Wissenschaft?' *ZATWiss* 47, 1929, 83-91.

[29]W. Eichrodt, *Theologie des Alten Testaments*, I *Gott und Volk*, Leipzig 1933.

[30]E. Sellin, *Alttestamentliche Theologie auf religionsgeschichtlicher Grundlage*, I *Israelitisch-jüdische Religionsgeschichte;* II *Theologie des Alten Testaments*, Leipzig 1933.

[31]L. Köhler, *Theologie des Alten Testaments*, Tübingen 1936; E. tr. *Old Testament Theology*, Philadelphia 1957.

[32]*Ibid.*, v.

[33]H. Wheeler Robinson, *Inspiration and Revelation in the Old Testament*, Oxford 1946.

[34]'The Theology of the Old Testament', *Record and Revelation*, edited by H. Wheeler Robinson, London, 303-48.

[35]N. W. Porteous, *op. cit.*, 336.

[36]C. H. Dodd, *The Bible Today*, London 1946.

[37]*Ibid.*, 98-9.

[38]O. Procksch, *Theologie des Alten Testaments*, Gütersloh 1949.

[39]*Ibid.*, 1.

420 *The Path of Biblical Theology*

[40]O. J. Baab, *The Theology of the Old Testament*, Nashville 1949.
[41]*Ibid.*, 269.
[42]G. E. Wright, *God Who Acts*. Biblical Theology as Recital, London 1952.
[43]*Ibid.*, 13.
[44]*Ibid.*, 38.
[45]N. W. Porteous, 'The Theology of the Old Testament', *Peake's Commentary on the Bible*, eds., M. Black and H. H. Rowley, 2nd rev. ed. London 1962, 151-9.
[46]*Ibid.*, 152.
[47]G. A. F. Knight, *A Christian Theology of the Old Testament*, London 1959, 2nd rev. ed. 1964.
[48]*Ibid.*, 9f.
[49]*Ibid.*, 81.
[50]*Ibid.*, 109.
[51]*Ibid.*, 148.
[52]*Ibid.*, 153.
[53]*Ibid.*, 239.
[54]*Ibid.*, 213.
[55]*Ibid.*, 343.
[56]W. Eichrodt, *Theologie des Alten Testaments*, 2 vols. 5th rev. ed. Stuttgart 1957 and 1964; E. tr. *Theology of the Old Testament*, 2 vols., London 1961 and 1967.
[57]*Ibid.*, Vol. I, 11.
[58]*Ibid.*, 502-3.
[59]*Ibid.*, 15.
[60]*Ibid.*, 12.
[61]*Ibid.*, 14.
[62]*Ibid.*, 206.
[63]*Ibid.*, 239.
[64]*Ibid.*, 249.
[65]*Ibid.*, 343.
[66]*Ibid.*, 455.
[67]*Ibid.*, II, 63.
[68]*Ibid.*, 109.
[69]*Ibid.*, 267.
[70]T. C. Vriezen, *Hoofdlijnen der Theologie van het Oude Testament*, 2nd rev. ed. Wageningen 1954; E. tr. *Outline of Old Testament Theology*, Oxford 1958.
[71]*Ibid.*, 371.
[72]*Ibid.*, 90.
[73]*Ibid.*, 125.
[74]*Ibid.*, 76.
[75]*Ibid.*, 77.
[76]*Ibid.*, 78.
[77]*Ibid.*, 131.
[78]*Ibid.*, 141.

[79]*Ibid.*, 204.
[80]*Ibid.*, 253.
[81]*Ibid.*, 263.
[82]*Ibid.*, 302.
[83]*Ibid.*, 314.
[84]*Ibid.*, 315.
[85]*Ibid.*, 336.
[86]*Ibid.*, 333.
[87]*Ibid.*, 372.
[88]*Ibid.*, 355.
[89]*Ibid.*, 370.
[90]E. Jacob, *Théologie de l'Ancien Testament*, Neuchâtel 1955; E. tr. *Theology of the Old Testament*, London 1958.
[91]*Ibid.*, 11.
[92]*Ibid.*, 53.
[93]*Ibid.*, 86.
[94]*Ibid.*, 104.
[95]*Ibid.*, 107.
[96]*Ibid.*, 121.
[97]*Ibid.*, 149.
[98]*Ibid.*, 169.
[99]*Ibid.*, 263.
[100]*Ibid.*, 317.
[101]*Ibid.*, 342.
[102]G. von Rad, *Theologie des Alten Testaments*, 2 vols., Munich 1957 and 1960; E. tr. *Old Testament Theology*, 2 vols. Edinburgh 1962 and 1965.
[103]*Old Testament Theology*, II, viii.
[104]*Ibid.*, I, 111.
[105]*Ibid.*, I, 113.
[106]*Ibid.*, I, 135.
[107]*Ibid.*, I, 164.
[108]*Ibid.*, I, 229.
[109]*Ibid.*, I, 303.
[110]*Ibid.*, I, 304.
[111]2 *Sam.* 9-20; 1 *Kings* 1-2.
[112]Von Rad, *op. cit.*, I, 344.
[113]*Ibid.*, I, 355.
[114]*Ibid.*, I, 365.
[115]*Ibid.*, I, 403.
[116]*Ibid.*, I, 428.
[117]*Ibid.*, II, 299.
[118]*Ibid.*, II, 76.
[119]*Ibid.*, II, 130.
[120]*Ibid.*, II, 177.
[121]*Ibid.*, II, 186.
[122]*Ibid.*, II, 203.
[123]*Ibid.*, II, 205.

[124]*Ibid.*, II, 213.

[125]*Ibid.*, II, 250.

[126]*Ibid.*, II, 269.

[127]*Ibid.*, II, 303-4.

[128]J. Bright, 'Edmond Jacob's "Theology of the Old Testament"', *Expos. Times* 73 (1962), 307.

[129]See J. Barr, *The Semantics of Biblical Language*, London 1961, 144-7.

[130]See W. Eichrodt, *Theology of the Old Testament* I, 512-520; R. de Vaux, *Bible et Orient*, 'Peut-on écrire une "Théologie de l'Ancien Testament"?' Paris 1957, 59-71; J. Barr, 'Gerhard von Rad's "Theologie des Alten Testaments"' *Expos. Times* 73 (1962), 146.

[131]'When this great work is closely examined through the eyes of certain of his critics, however, it becomes very clear that each person, von Rad and each of his critics, is operating with a different conception in his mind as to just what theology is. No wonder, then, that theologies differ so radically!' G. Ernest Wright, *The Old Testament and Theology*, New York 1969, 68.

[132]*Old Testament Theology*, II, 'Postcript', 410-29.

[133]See J. Harvey, 'The New Diachronic Biblical Theology of the Old Testament', *Biblical Theology Bulletin* 1 (1970), 5-29.

[134]R. de Vaux, *art. cit.*

[135]For an important study of the hermeneutical method underlying von Rad's *Theology* see P. Fruchon, 'Sur l'herméneutique de G. von Rad', *RSPT* 55 (1971), 4-32.

[136]These have been described, respectively, as 'structural' and 'diachronic' type theologies. Diachronic biblical theology means 'a biblical theology which, opting for a *longitudinal* section of the Bible, pays attention to the chronological sequence of its books rather than to the arrangement of their themes, as is predominantly done in the traditional cross-section treatment'. J. Harvey, *art. cit.*; see M.-L. Ramlot, 'Une Décade de Théologie Biblique', *Revue Thomiste* 64 (1964), 82.

[137]J. Barr, *art. cit.*, 146.

[138]M. Hetzenauer, *Theologia Biblica sive Scientia Historiae et Religionis utriusque Testamenti Catholica, Tomus I Vetus Testamentum*, Freiburg i. B. 1908.

[139]See *ibid.*, 49.

[140]P. Heinisch, *Theologie des Alten Testaments*, Bonn 1940; E. tr. *Theology of the Old Testament*, Collegeville 1955.

[141]*Ibid.*, 55.

[142]*Ibid.*, 171.

[143]*Ibid.*, 296.

[144]F. Ceuppens, *Theologia Biblica*, I, *De Deo Uno*, Rome 1948.

[145]P. van Imschoot, *Théologie de l'Ancien Testament* 2 vols. Tournai 1954, 1956; E. tr. *Theology of the Old Testament*, I, *God*, New York 1965.

146A. Gelin, *Les Idées Maîtresses de l'Ancien Testament*, Paris 1947; E. tr. *The Key Concepts of the Old Testament*, New York 1955.

147A. Gelin, *L'Ame d'Israël dans le Livre*, Paris 1960; E. tr. *The Religion of Israel*, New York 1949.

148A. Gelin, *Les Pauvres de Yahvé*, Paris 1953; E. tr. *The Poor of Yahweh*, Collegeville 1964.

149J. L. McKenzie, *The Two-Edged Sword*, Milwaukee 1956.

150J. L. McKenzie, *Myths and Realities*, Milwaukee, 1963.

151J. L. McKenzie *Dictionary of the Bible*, Milwaukee 1965.

152J. L. McKenzie 'Aspects of Old Testament Thought', *The Jerome Biblical Commentary*, eds. R. E. Brown, J. A. Fitzmyer, R. E. Murphy, Englewood Cliffs N.J. 1968, 736-67.

153H. Renckens, *De Godsienst van Israël*, 1962; E. tr. *The Religion of Israel*, New York 1966.

154Y. Kaufmann, *The Religion of Israel*, Chicago 1960; London 1961.

155*Ibid.*, 22.

156*Ibid.*, 60.

157*Ibid.*, 260.

158*Ibid.*, 402.

159*Ibid.*, 450.

160In his review of the work *RB* 70 (1963), 266-9, R. de Vaux exposes the serious shortcomings of Kaufmann's critical positions.

161H. Ringgren, *Israelitische Religion*, Stuttgart 1963; E. tr. *Israelite Religion*, London 1966.

162*Ibid.*, 153.

163S. Mowinckel, *Psalmenstudien*, II, Amsterdam 1961; E. tr. *The Psalms in Israel's Worship*, II, Oxford 1962.

164G. von Rad, *Das formgeschichtliche Problem des Hexateuchs*, Stuttgart 1938.

165A. Weiser, *The Psalms*, Philadelphia, 1962.

166H. Ringgren, *op. cit.*, 195.

167T. C. Vriezen, *De godsdienst van Israël*, Arnheim 1963; E. tr. *The Religion of Ancient Israel*, London 1967.

168*Ibid.*, 129.

169*Ibid.*, 147.

170*Ibid.*, 195.

171*Ibid.*, 215.

172*Ibid.*, 259.

173*Ibid.*, 268.

174*Ibid.*, 275.

175J. Pedersen, *Israel* I-II; III-IV, 2 vols., Copenhagen 1920, 1934; 2nd rev. ed. 1958, 1960; E. tr. *Israel: Its Life and Culture*, 2 vols., London 1926, 1940; 2nd ed. 1959.

176*Ibid.*, II, 264.

177*Ibid.*, 267.

178R. de Vaux, *Les Institutions de l'Ancien Testament*, 2 vols.,

28

Paris 1958, 1960; E. tr. *Ancient Israel. Its Life and Institutions,* London 1961.
[179]*Ibid.,* 273.
[180]See further R. de Vaux, *Les Sacrifices de l'Ancien Testament,* Paris 1964; E. tr. *Studies in Old Testament Sacrifice,* Cardiff 1964.

## CHAPTER II

[1]H. J. Holtzmann, *Lehrbuch der neutestamentlichen Theologie,* 2 vols., Tübingen 1896-97; 2nd rev. ed. 1911.
[2]W. Wrede, *Uber Aufgabe und Methode der so-genannten neutestamentlichen Theologie,* Göttingen 1897.
[3]H. Weinel, *Biblische Theologie des Neuen Testaments.* Die Religion Jesu und des Urchristentums, Tübingen 1911, 4th ed. 1928.
[4]W. Bousset, *Kyrios Christos.* Geschichte des Christusglaubens von Anfängen des Christentums bis Irenaeus, Göttingen, 1913, 4th ed. 1935.
[5]P. Feine, *Theologie des Neuen Testaments,* Leipzig 1910, 8th ed. 1951.
[6]G. B. Stevens, *The Theology of the New Testament,* Edinburgh 1899; 2nd rev. ed. 1918; reprinted 1968.
[7]*Ibid.,* ix.
[8]A. Schlatter, *Die Theologie des Neuen Testaments,* 2 vols., Stuttgart 1909, 1910, 2nd ed. 1922, 1923.
[9]F. Büchsel, *Theologie des Neuen Testaments.* Geschichte des Wortes im Neuen Testament, Gütersloh 1935.
[10]M. Albertz, *Die Botschaft des Neuen Testamentes* (published in four parts): *vol. I Die Entstehung der Botschaft.* 1. Die Entstehung des Evangeliums; 2. Die Entstehung des apostolischen Schriftenkanons; *vol. II Die Entfaltung der Botschaft.* 1. Die Voraussetzungen der Botschaft; 2. Der Inhalt der Botschaft, Zollikon-Zürich 1947, 1952, 1954, 1957.
[11]A. Lemonnyer, *La Théologie du Nouveau Testament,* Paris 1928; E. tr., *The Theology of the New Testament,* London 1930.
[12]A. Lemonnyer and L. Cerfaux, *Théologie du Nouveau Testament,* 2nd rev. ed. Paris 1963.
[13]O. Küss, *Die Theologie des Neuen Testaments. Eine Einführung,* Regensburg 1936.
[14]F. C. Grant, *An Introduction to New Testament Thought,* New York 1950.
[15]*Ibid.,* 175.
[16]*Ibid.,* 192.
[17]*Ibid.,* 299.
[18]*Ibid.,* 302.
[19]See pp. 178-84 above.

[20]J. Bonsirven, *Théologie du Nouveau Testament*, Paris 1951; E. tr., *Theology of the New Testament*, London 1963.

[21]J. Bonsirven, *Les enseignements de Jésus-Christ*, Paris 4th ed. 1946; *L'Évangile de Paul*, Paris 1948.

[22]*Ibid.*, 43.

[23]A. M. Hunter, *Introducing New Testament Theology*, London 1957.

[24]*Ibid.*, 22.

[25]C. H. Dodd, *The Apostolic Preaching and its Developments*, London 1944, 3rd ed. 1963.

[26]*Ibid.*, 90.

[27]*Ibid.*, 139.

[28]W. G. Kümmel, *Die Theologie des Neuen Testaments nach seinen Hauptzeugen Jesus-Paulus-Johannes*, Göttingen 1969.

[29]*Ibid.*, 294f.

[29a]Karl Hermann Schelke, *Theologie des Neuen Testaments*, I: Schöpfung. Welt—Zeit—Mensch, Düsseldorf: Patmos 1968. E. trs. *Theology of the New Testament*, Vol. I: Creation: World —Time—Man, Collegeville, Minn.: The Liturgical Press, 1971.

[30]T. W. Manson, *Ethics and the Gospel*, London 1960.

[31]*Pirke Aboth*, 1, 2.

[32]*Ibid.*, 52.

[33]C. H. Dodd, *The Parables of the Kingdom*, London 1935, rev. ed. 1961.

[34]J. Jeremias, *Die Gleichnisse Jesu*, Göttingen 1947, 6th rev. ed. 1962; E. tr. *The Parables of Jesus*, London 1954, 2nd rev. ed. 1963.

[35]*Ibid.*, 102.

[36]R. Schnackenburg, *Die sittliche Botschaft des Neuen Testamentes*, Munich 1954, 2nd rev. ed. 1962; E. tr. *The Moral Teaching of the New Testament*, New York 1965.

[37]*Ibid.*, 358.

[38]*Ibid.*, 387f.

[39]C. Spicq, *Théologie morale du Nouveau Testament*, 2 vols., Paris 1965.

[40]*Ibid.*, 15.

[41]Indeed, his own exhaustive study of Agapē in the New Testament had laid the foundations for such an approach. See C. Spicq. *Agapé*. Prolégomènes à une étude de Théologie Néotestamentaire, Louvain 1955; *Agapé dans le Nouveau Testament* 3 vols., Paris 1958, 1959; E. tr. abridged, *Agapē in the New Testament* 3 vols., St Louis 1963, 1965, 1966.

[42]*Théologie morale du nouveau Testament*, I, 10.

[43]See F. Dreyfus, *RB* 75 (1968), 593-5; *RSPT* 53 (1969), 334-6.

[44]R. Bultmann, *Theologie des Neuen Testaments*, 3, Lieferungen, Tübingen 1948, 1951, 1953, 3rd ed. 1958.

[45]R. Bultmann, *Theology of the New Testament*, 2 vols., London 1952, 1955.

[46]*Ibid.*, 1, 3.

[47]*Ibid.*, I, 25.
[48]*Ibid.*, I, 26.
[49]*Ibid.*, I, 43.
[50]*Ibid.*, I, 191.
[51]*Ibid.*, I, 196.
[52]*Ibid.*, I, 264.
[53]*Ibid.*, I, 289.
[54]*Ibid.*, I, 302.
[55]*Ibid.*, I, 303.
[56]*Ibid.*, I, 305.
[57]*Ibid.*, I, 305.
[58]*Ibid.*, I, 335.
[59]*Ibid.*, I, 352.
[60]*Ibid.*, II, 21.
[61]*Ibid.*, II, 46.
[62]*Ibid.*, II, 62.
[63]*Ibid.*, II, 92.
[64]See P. Benoit, *RB* 61 (1954), 433.
[65]*Ibid.*, II, 202.
[66]A. Richardson, *An Introduction to the Theology of the New Testament,* New York 1958.
[67]*Ibid.*, 12.
[68]*Ibid.*, 79.
[69]*Ibid.*, 89.
[70]*Ibid.*, 103.
[71]*Ibid.*, 124.
[72]*Ibid.*, 200.
[73]*Ibid.*, 222.
[74]*Ibid.*, 237.
[75]*Ibid.*, 249.
[76]*Ibid.*, 254.
[77]*Ibid.*, 283.
[78]*Ibid.*, 310.
[79]*Ibid.*, 336.
[80]*Ibid.*, 387.
[81]E. Stauffer, *Die Theologie des Neuen Testaments,* Stuttgart 1941.
[82]E. Stauffer, *New Testament Theology,* London 1955.
[83]See R. Schnackenburg, *New Testament Theology Today,* London 1963, 24-5.
[84]E. Stauffer, *New Testament Theology,* London 1955, 19.
[85]*Ibid.*, 21.
[86]*Ibid.*, 28.
[87]*Ibid.*, 38.
[88]*Ibid.*, 42.
[89]*Ibid.*, 67.
[90]*Ibid.*, 95.
[91]*Ibid.*, 114.

[92]*Ibid.*, 120.
[93]*Ibid.*, 131.
[94]*Ibid.*, 142.
[95]*Ibid.*, 145.
[96]*Ibid.*, 152.
[97]*Ibid.*, 168-9.
[98]*Ibid.*, 175.
[99]*Ibid.*, 204.
[100]*Ibid.*, 229.
[101]*Ibid.*, 257.
[102]M. Meinertz, *Theologie des Neuen Testamentes*, 2 vols., Bonn 1950.
[103]*Ibid.*, II, 268.
[104]*Ibid.*, I, 3.
[105]*Ibid.*, I, viii.
[106]*Ibid.*, II, 338.
[107]*Ibid.*, II, 339.
[108]*Ibid.*, II, 346.
[169]S. Neil, *The Interpretation of the New Testament*, London 1964, 235.
[110]A. Richardson, *op. cit.*, 14; 261 n. 3.
[111]L. E. Keck, 'Problems of New Testament Theology. A Critique of Alan Richardson's "An Introduction to New Testament Theology"' NovTest 7 (1964/65), 237.
[112]H. Conzelmann, *Grundriss der Theologie des Neuen Testaments*, Munich 1968; E. tr. *An Outline of the Theology of the New Testament*, London 1969.
[113]*Ibid.*, 62.
[114]*Ibid.*, 126-7.
[115]*Ibid.*, 198.
[116]*Ibid.*, 227.
[117]*Ibid.*, 265.
[118]*Ibid.*, 267.
[119]*Ibid.*, 274.
[120]*Ibid.*, 277.
[121]*Ibid.*, 282.
[122]*Ibid.*, 340.
[123]*Ibid.*, 348.
[124]*Ibid.*, 350f.
[125]*Ibid.*, 358.
[126]Conzelmann, *op. cit.*, xiv.
[127]O. Cullmann, *Heil als Geschichte*. Heilsgeschichtliche Existenz im Neuen Testament, Tübingen 1965; E. tr. *Salvation in History*, London 1967.
[128]O. Cullmann, *Christus und die Zeit*. Die urchristliche Zeit- und Geschichtsauffassung, Zollikon-Zurich 1946, 3rd ed. 1962; E. tr. *Christ and Time*. The Primitive Christian Conception of Time and History, London 1959, 2nd rev. ed. 1962.

[129]O. Cullmann, *Die Christologie des Neuen Testaments,* Tübingen 1957; E. tr. *The Christology of the New Testament,* London 1959, 2nd rev. ed. 1963.

[130]*Ibid.,* 230.

[131]H. Conzelmann, *Die Mitte der Zeit.* Studien sur Theologie des Lukas, Tübingen 1953, 2nd ed. 1957; E. tr. *The Theology of St Luke,* New York and London 1960.

[132]*Ibid.,* 246.

[133]J. Jeremias, *Neutestamentliche Theologie,* I Teil: *Die Verkündigung Jesu,* Gütersloh 1971; E. tr. *New Testament Theology,* Part One: *The Proclamation of Jesus,* London 1971.

[134]*Ibid.,* 37.

[135]*Ibid.,* 74.

[136]*Ibid.,* 116.

[137]*Ibid.,* 139.

[138]*Ibid.,* 151.

[139]*Ibid.,* 184.

[140]*Ibid.,* 217.

[141]*Ibid.,* 227.

[142]*Ibid.,* 250.

[143]*Ibid.,* 266.

[144]*Ibid.,* 276.

[145]*Ibid.,* 286.

[146]*Ibid.,* 310.

[147]P. Grech, 'Tradition and Theology in Apostolic Times', in R. C. Fuller (ed.), *A New Catholic Commentary on Holy Scripture,* London 1969, 844-89.

[148]*Ibid.,* 853.

[149]*Ibid.,* 853.

[150]*Ibid.,* 876.

[151]D. M. Stanley and R. E. Brown, 'Aspects of New Testament Thought' in R. E. Brown, J. A. Fitzmyer and R. E. Murphy (eds.), *The Jerome Biblical Commentary,* Englewood Cliffs N.J. 1968, 768-99.

[152]*Ibid.,* 782.

[153]*Ibid.,* 788-90.

[154]J. Marsh, 'The Theology of the New Testament', in M. Black and H. H. Rowley (eds.) *Peake's Commentary on the Bible,* London 2nd rev. ed. 1962, 756-68.

[155]*Ibid.,* 762.

[156]*Ibid.,* 763.

[157]*Ibid.,* 767.

[158]J. A. Fitzmyer, 'Pauline Theology', *Jerome Biblical Commentary,* 800-827.

[159]*Ibid.,* 821.

[160]*Ibid.,* 826.

[161]B. Vawter, 'Johannine Theology', *Jerome Biblical Commentary,* 828-39.

[162]*Ibid.*, 832.

[163]*Ibid.*, 835.

[164]O. Cullmann, *Die Christologie des Neuen Testaments,*
Tübingen; E. tr. *The Christology of the New Testament,* London
1959.

[165]*Ibid.*, 3-4.

[166]*Ibid.*, 266f.

[167]*Ibid.*, 293.

[168]*Ibid.*, 326.

[169]V. Taylor, *The Person of Christ in New Testament Teaching,*
London 1959.

[170]*Ibid.*, 60.

[171]*Ibid.*, 294.

[172]*Ibid.*, 304.

[173]R. H. Fuller, *The Foundations of New Testament Christology,*
New York 1965.

[174]*Ibid.*, 232-3.

[175]L. Sabourin, *Les Noms et les Titres de Jésus*: Thèmes de
Théologie Biblique, Paris 1963; E. tr. *The Names and Titles of
Jesus*: Themes of Biblical Theology, New York 1967.

[176]*Ibid.*, xiiif.

[177]*Ibid.*, xvii.

[178]See W. D. Davies, 'Contemporary Jewish Religion', *Peake's
Commentary* 705-11; J. L. McKenzie, 'The Jewish World in New
Testament Times', IV, Beliefs and Morality, *New Catholic
Commentary* 777-83.

[179]J. L. McKenzie, *op. cit.,* 183.

[180]W. D. Davies, *op. cit.,* 710; see his *Christian Origins and
Judaism,* London 1962.

[181]K. Stendahl (ed.), *The Scrolls and the New Testament.* An
Introduction and a Perspective, New York 1957; J. Murphy-
O'Connor (ed.), *Paul and Qumran.* Studies in New Testament
Exegesis, Chicago 1968.

[182]The contributors are: P. Benoit, J. A. Fitzmyer, J. Gnilka,
M. Delcor, J. Murphy-O'Connor, K. G. Kuhn, J. Coppens, F.
Mussner and W. Grundmann.

[183]P. Benoit, 'Qumran and the New Testament', *Paul and
Qumran,* ed. O'Connor, 1-30.

[184]*Ibid.*, 1.

[185]*Ibid.*, 6.

[186]*Ibid.*, 18.

[187]See J. Jeremias, 'Qumran et la théologie', *NRT* 85 (1963)
675-690; M. Black (ed.), *The Scrolls and Christianity.* Historical
and Theological Significance, London 1969.

## CHAPTER III

[1]H. H. Rowley, *The Unity of the Bible,* London 1953.

[2]J. D. Smart warns that 'if we so state this unity that we conceal

in any degree the discontinuity between Old and New Testaments, dealing with Scripture as though there were only one Testament instead of two, we prepare the way again for a reaction that will attempt to subordinate or to exclude the Old Testament'. *The Interpretation of Scripture*, London 1961, 92.

[3]Rowley, *op. cit.*, 96.

[4]*Ibid.*, 106.

[5]*Ibid.*, 108.

[6]*Ibid.*, 121.

[7]M. Burrows, *An Outline of Biblical Theology*, Philadelphia 1946.

[8]*Ibid.*, 5.

[9]*Ibid.*, 50.

[10]*Ibid.*, 82.

[11]*Ibid.*, 106.

[12]*Ibid.*, 115.

[13]*Ibid.*, 128.

[14]*Ibid.*, 153.

[15]*Ibid.*, 170.

[16]*Ibid.*, 327f.

[17]G. von Rad, *Old Testament Theology* II, Part III, 319-429.

[18]*Ibid.*, 428f.

[19]*Ibid.*, 321.

[20]*Ibid.*, 338.

[21]*Ibid.*, 355.

[22]*Ibid.*, 374.

[23]*Ibid.*, 408.

[24]*Ibid.*, 409.

[25]Theodore C. Vriezen, *An Outline of Old Testament Theology*.

[26]*Ibid.*, 10.

[27]*Ibid.*, 34.

[28]*Ibid.*, 85.

[29]*Ibid.*, 92.

[30]Eichrodt, *Theology of the Old Testament* I, 520.

[31]*Ibid.*, 390.

[32]*Ibid.*, 511.

[33]Stauffer, *Theology of the New Testament*, 94-7.

[34]J. L. McKenzie, 'The Values of the Old Testament', *Concilium* 10, December 1967, 4-17.

[35]*Ibid.*, 9.

[36]*Ibid.*, 10.

[37]See also G. A. T. Knight, *A Christian Theology of the Old Testament*.

[38]C. Westermann (ed.), *Probleme alttestamentlicher Hermeneutik*, Munich 1960; E. tr. *Essays on Old Testament Interpretation*, London 1963.

[39]*Ibid.*, 73.

[40]*Ibid.*, 119.

[41]*Ibid.*, 127.

[42]*Ibid.*, 134-59.

[43]*Ibid.*, 323.

[44]*Ibid.*, 331.

[45]*Ibid.*, 97.

[46]*Ibid.*, 115.

[47]See J. Barr, *Old and New in Interpretation. A Study of the Two Testaments*, London 1966, 124.

[48]Von Rad, *Old Testament Theology*, II, viii.

[49]R. E. Murphy, 'The Relationship between the Testaments', *CBQ* 26 (1964), 349-359.

[50]*Ibid.*, 359.

[51]See p. 262 above.

[52]J. D. Smart, *The Interpretation of Scripture*, London 1961.

[53]*Ibid.*, 82.

[54]*Ibid.*, 84.

[55]C. Westermann, *Essays on Old Testament Interpretation*, 17-39.

[56]Von Rad, *Old Testament Theology* II, 371.

[57]Westermann, *op. cit.*, 38.

[58]Westermann, *op. cit.*, 160-99.

[59]*Ibid.*, 189.

[60]*Ibid.*, 199.

[61]Westermann, *op. cit.*, 224-45.

[62]*Ibid.*, 225.

[63]*Ibid.*

[64]*Ibid.*, 226f.

[65]*Ibid.*, 229.

[66]*Ibid.*, 241.

[67]J. D. Smart observes that Old Testament scholars, like von Rad and Wolff, give no encouragement to a typological exegesis that reads New Testament meanings into the text of the Old Testament, even though they use the term 'typology'. Their use of the term 'would seem to be both unnecessary and unfortunate, unnecessary because the term "correspondences" is quite adequate to describe the phenomena with which they are concerned, and unfortunate because in the minds of their readers the very use of the term lends encouragement to the revival of typological interpretation of the patristic and Reformation order.' *Ibid.*, 123.

[68]See pp. 295-9 above.

[69]Melchizedek (*Gen.* 14: 17-20; *Ps.* 110: 4; *Heb.* 7: 1-3); crossing of the Red Sea (*Exod.* 14: 22, 29-31; 1 *Cor.* 10: 1-2); brazen serpent (*Num.* 21: 8-9; *John* 3: 14-15).

[70]R. E. Brown, 'Hermeneutics', *Jerome Biblical Commentary*, 618.

[71]R. E. Murphy, *art. cit.*, 357, shares this conviction. For practical purposes, indication of the typical sense has to be sought in the New Testament; otherwise, the door is open to arbitrary analogies.

[72]A. Fernández, 'Hermeneutica', *Institutiones Biblicae*, Rome 1925, 2nd ed. 1927.

[73]R. E. Brown, *The* Sensus Plenior *of Sacred Scripture*, Baltimore 1955; 'The History and Development of the Theory of a *Sensus Plenior*', *CBQ* 15 (1953), 141-62; 'The *Sensus Plenior* in the Last Ten Years', *CBQ* 25 (1963), 262-85; 'The Problem of the *Sensus Plenior*', *ETL* 53 (1967), 460-69.

[74]J. Coppens, *Les Harmonies des Deux Testaments. Essai sur les Divers Sens de l'Écriture et sur l'Unité de la Révélation*. Tournai-Paris 1948, 2nd ed. 1949.

[75]J. Coppens, 'Nouvelles refléxions sur les divers sens des Saintes Ecritures', *NRT* 74 (1952), 3-20; 'Levels of Meaning in the Bible' *Concilium* 10, no. 3 (December 1967), 62-9.

[76]*Art. cit.*, 64.

[77]P. Synave and P. Benoit, *La Prophétie*, Tournai 1947, 356-9; E. tr. *Prophecy and Inspiration*, New York 1961, 149-51.

[78]P. Benoit, 'La Plenitude de Sens des Livres Saints', *RB* 67 (1960), 161-96; reprinted in *Exégèse et Théologie* III, Paris 1968, 31-68.

[79]W. J., Harrington, *Record of Revelation: The Bible*, Chicago and Dublin 1965, 55-60.

[80]Benoit, *Art. cit.*, *RB*, 1960, 162-3.

[81]*Ibid.*

[82]*Ibid.*, 178.

[83]*Ibid.*, 185.

[84]*Ibid.*, 190.

[85]See note 73 above.

[86]R. E. Brown, 'Hermeneutics', *Jerome Biblical Commentary*, 610-9.

[87]H. De Lubac, *Histoire et Esprit. L'Intelligence de l'Écriture d'après Origène*, Paris 1950; J. Daniélou, *Origène*, Paris 1948; E. tr. *Origen*, London 1955; *Sacramentum Futuri. Études sur les origines de la Typologie biblique*, Paris 1950; E. tr. *From Shadow to Reality*, London 1960; *Bible et Liturgie*, Paris 1951; E. tr. *The Bible and the Liturgy*, University of Notre Dame Press 1956. See also W. Vischer, *op. cit.*

[88]Brown, *art. cit.*, 616.

[89]Brown, 'The Problem of the Sensus Plenior', *ETL* 53 (1967), 467.

[90]See P. Sansegundo, *Exposicion Historico-Critica del hoy llamado 'Sensus Plenior' de la Sagrada Escritura*, Avila 1963.

[91]The principal opponents of the fuller sense are: R. Bierberg, 'Does Sacred Scripture have a Sensus Plenior?' *CBQ* 10 (1948), 182-95; G. Courtade, 'Les Écritures ont-elles un sens plénier?', *RSR* 37 (1950), 48-9; J. L. McKenzie, 'Problems of Hermeneutics in Roman Catholic Exegesis', *JBL* 77 (1958), 197-204.

[92]B. Vawter, 'The Fuller Sense: some considerations', *CBQ* 26 (1964), 85-96.

[93]P. Benoit, 'Le Sensus Plenior de l'Écriture', *RB* (1956), 287.

[94]J. L. McKenzie, *Dictionary of the Bible*, Milwaukee 1965, 393.

[95]L. Swain, 'The Interpretation of the Bible', *New Catholic Commentary* 65.

[96]*Ibid.*

[97]J. M. Robinson, 'Scripture and Theological Method. A Protestant Study in *Sensus Plenior*', *CBQ* 27 (1965), 6-27.

[98]*Ibid.*, 20.

[99]J. Barr, *Old and New in Interpretation. A Study of the Two Testaments*, London 1966.

[100]*Ibid.*, 133.

[101]*Ibid.*, 144.

[102]*Ibid.*, 152.

[103]*Ibid.*, 140.

[104]G. E. Wright, *The Old Testament and Theology*, New York 1969.

[105]R. Bultmann, in B. W. Anderson, *The Old Testament and Christian Faith*, New York 1963, 11.

[106]*Ibid.*, 35.

[107]Wright, *op. cit.*, 37.

[108]*Ibid.*, 39.

[109]R. E. Murphy, 'Christian understanding of the Old Testament', *Theology Digest* 18 (1970), 321-32.

[110]J. Bright, *The Authority of the Old Testament*, London 1967.

[111]*Ibid.*, 143.

[112]*Ibid.*, 236.

[113]*Ibid.*, 75.

[114]*Ibid.*, 71.

[115]*Ibid.*, 72.

[116]*Ibid.*, 77f.

[117]*Ibid.*, 78.

[118]*Ibid.*, 90.

[119]*Ibid.*, 92.

[120]*Ibid.*, 94.

[121]*Ibid.*, 109.

[122]See pp. 358–60 above.

[123]W. Vischer, *Das Christuszeugnis des Alten Testaments*, I. Das Gesetz, Munich 1936; E. tr. *The Witness of the Old Testament to Christ*, London 1949; II. Die Propheten, Zollikon-Zürich 1942.

[124]P. Grelot, *Sens Chrétien de l'Ancien Testament*, Tournai 1962.

[125]*Ibid.*, 88.

[126]*Ibid.*, 112.

[127]*Ibid.*, 214.

[128]*Ibid.*, 299.

[129]*Ibid.*, 431f.

[130]*Ibid.*, 442-99—especially the tables, 457, 496.

[131]C. Larcher, *L'Actualité Chrétienne de l'Ancien Testament*, Paris 1962.

[132]*Ibid.,* 365.

[133]*Ibid.* 530.

[134]D. Bonhoeffer, *Letters and Papers from Prison,* New York 1962, 103f.

[135]*Concilium,* December 1967, 12f.

[136]F. Dreyfus, 'The existential Value of the Old Testament', *Concilium* 10 (December 1967), 18-23.

[137]*Ibid.,* 18.

[138]*Ibid.,* 22.

[139]*Dei Verbum,* Ch. 4, art. 15.

[140]*Ibid.,* art. 16.

[141]*Ibid.,* art. 14.

[142]*Ibid.,* art. 15.

[143]See W. Harrington and L. Walsh, *Vatican II on Revelation,* Dublin 1967, 73-96.

[144]J. Hastings, *Dictionary of the Bible,* 5 vols., Edinburgh 1898-1904; revised ed., C. Grant and H. H. Rowley (eds.), New York 1963.

[145]F. Vigouroux, *Dictionnaire de la Bible,* 5 vols., 2nd rev. ed. Paris 1912.

[146]L. Pirot, A. Robert, H. Cazelles, A. Feuillet, *Dictionnaire de la Bible* (Supplément), Paris 1928.

[147]A. van den Born, *Bijbels Woordenboek, Roermond* 1941-50; 2nd rev. ed. 1954-57.

[148]H. Haag, *Bibellexikon,* Einsiedeln 1951.

[149]L. F. Hartman, *Encyclopedic Dictionary of the Bible,* New York 1963.

[150]J. J. von Allmen, *Vocabulaire Biblique,* Neuchatel 1954; 2nd ed. 1956.

[151]J. B. Bauer, *Bibeltheologisches Wörterbuch,* 2 vols., Graz-Vienna-Cologne 1959; 3rd ed. 1967.

[152]J. B. Bauer, *Encyclopedia of Biblical Theology,* London 1970.

[153]X. Léon-Dufour, *Vocabulaire de Théologie Biblique,* Paris 1962; 2nd rev. ed. 1970.

[154]X. Léon-Dufour, *Dictionary of Biblical Theology,* New York 1967, London-Dublin 1968.

[155]G. A. Buttrick (ed.), *The Interpreter's Dictionary of the Bible.* An Illustrated Encyclopedia in Four Volumes, Nashville 1962.

[156]J. L. McKenzie, *Dictionary of the Bible,* Milwaukee 1965.

[157]G. Kittel and G. Friedrich, *Theologisches Wörterbuch zum Neuen Testament* 8 vols., Stuttgart 1933-1969.

[158]G. Kittel, *Theological Dictionary of the Bible,* 8 vols., translated and edited by G. W. Bromiley, Grand Rapids, Mich. 1964-.

[159]J. Barr, *The Semantics of Biblical Language,* New York 1961.

[160]*Ibid.,* 262.

[161]*Biblischer Kommentar Altes Testament,* Neukirchen.

[162]See J. Harvey, *Biblical Theology Bulletin* 1 (1971), 13f.

[163]R. Schnackenburg, *Die Johannesbriefe,* Freiburg 1953.

[164]R. Schnackenburg, *The Gospel According to St John*, I, London 1968.

## CHAPTER IV

[1]P. Benoit, 'Exégèse et Théologie Biblique', *Exégèse et Théologie*, III, Paris 1968, 1-13; C. Spicq, 'L'Avenèment de la Théologie Biblique', *RSPT* 35 (1951), 561-74; F. M. Braun, 'La théologie biblique: qu'entendre par là?', *RT* 53 (1953), 221-53; P. Grelot, 'Exégèse, théologie et pastorale', *NRT* 88 (1966), 3-13, 132-48; H.-J. Kraus, *Die Biblische Theologie. Ihre Geschichte und Problematik*, Neukirchen-Vluyn 1970.

[2]M.-L. Ramlot, 'Une Décade de Théologie Biblique', *RT* 72 (1964), 65-96.

[3]R. C. Dentan, *Preface to Old Testament Theology*, 2nd ed. New York 1963, 87-125.

[4]*Ibid.*, 90.

[5]*Ibid.*, 122f.

[6]E. Jacob, 'La théologie de l'Ancien Testament. État présent et perspectives d'avenir', *ETL* 44 (1968), 420-32.

[7]See G. Ernest Wright, *The Old Testament and Theology*, Ch. 7 The Canon as Theological Problem, New York 1969, 166-85.

[8]N. W. Porteous, 'Towards a Theology of the Old Testament', *Living the Mystery*, Oxford 1967, 7-19.

[9]*Ibid.*, 15.

[10]'Semantics and Old Testament Theology', *ibid.*, 24.

[11]*Ibid.*, 30.

[12]'The Old Testament and some Theological Thought-Forms', *Ibid.*, 31-46.

[13]J. Bright, *The Authority of the Old Testament*, London 1967.

[14]*Ibid.*, 112.

[15]*Ibid.*, 136.

[16]*Ibid.*, 138.

[17]*Ibid.*, 140.

[18]*Ibid.*, 153.

[19]*Ibid.*, 159.

[20]*Ibid.*, 159f.

[21]L. Alonso-Schökel, 'Old Testament Theology', *Sacramentum Mundi. An Encyclopedia of Theology* IV, edited by K. Rahner, London 1969, 286-90; J. Van der Ploeg, 'Une "Théologie de l'Ancien Testament" est-elle possible?', *ETL* 38 (1962), 417-34.

[22]R. E. Murphy, 'Christian understanding of the Old Testament', *Theology Digest* 18 (1970), 330-32.

[23]*Ibid.*, 332.

[24]J. Harvey, 'The New Diachronic Biblical Theology of the Old Testament (1960-1970)', *BibTB 1* (1971), 5-29.

[25]*Ibid.*, 11.

[26]To mark the seventieth birthday of Gerhard von Rad the

*Revue des Sciences Philosophiques et Théologiques* has published three significant studies of his exegetical and theological methodology: P. Fruchon, 'Sur l'herméneutique de Gerhard von Rad', *RSPT* 55 (1971), 4-32; J.-L. Vesco, 'Abraham: actualisation et relectures. Les traditions vétéro-testamentaires', 33-80; M. Carrez, 'La méthode de G. von Rad appliquée à quelques textes pauliniens', 81-95.

[27]H. Schlier, 'The Meaning and Function of a theology of the New Testament', *The Relevance of the New Testament*, New York 1968, 1-25.
[28]'Biblical and Dogmatic Theology', *Ibid.*, 28.
[29]*Ibid.*, 34.
[30]R. Schnackenburg, *New Testament Theology Today*, London 1963, 15-28.
[31]*Ibid.*, 18f.
[32]A. Vögtle, 'New Testament Theology', *Sacramentum Mundi* IV, 216-20; 'Progress and Problems in New Testament Exegesis' in H. Vorgrimler, *Dogmatic versus Biblical Theology*, London 1964, 67-86.
[33]*Ibid.*, 244f.
[34]W. G. Kümmel, *Die Theologie des Neuen Testaments*, 13-15.
[35]K. Rahner, 'Bible. Biblical Theology', *Sacramentum Mundi* I, 175f.
[36]K. Rahner, *Theological Investigations*, VI, Baltimore 1969, 89-97.
[37]*Ibid.*, 89f.
[38]K. Rahner, *Sacramentum Mundi* I, London 1968, 171-76.
[39]*Ibid.*, 172.
[40]*Ibid.*, 176f.
[41]H.-J. Kraus, *op. cit.*, 367-87.
[42]Benoit, *op. cit.*, 8f.
[43]*Bible et Orient*, Paris 1967, 66.
[44]Grelot, *art. cit.*, 133f.
[45]Harvey, *art. cit.*, 16.
[46]Kraus, *Die Biblische Theologie*, Neukirchen Vluyn, 193-305.
[47]K. Rahner, *Theological Investigations* VI, 89-97.
[48]*Ibid.*, 93.
[49]E. Schillebeeckx, 'Exegesis, Dogmatics and the Development of Dogma', *Dogmatic versus Biblical Theology*, 115-172.
[50]*Ibid.*, 123.
[51]*Ibid.*, 123f.
[52]*Ibid.*, 126.
[53]*Ibid.*, 131f.
[54]*Ibid.*, 144.
[55]R. Schnackenburg, 'The Dogmatic Evaluation of the New Testament', *Dogmatic versus Biblical Theology* edited by H. Vorgrimler, London 1964, 147-72.
[56]*Ibid.*, 155.

[57]H. Schlier, *The Relevance of the New Testament*, 34-8.

[58]*Ibid.*, 38.

[59]A. Vögtle, *Sacramentum Mundi* IV, 185.

[60]Spicq, *art. cit.*, 571.

[61]See F.-M. Braun, *art. cit.*, 237; P. Grelot, *art. cit.*, 137-42.

[62]W. Harrington and L. Walsh, *Vatican II on Revelation*, Dublin 1967, 41-7.

[63]*Ibid.*, 42. Cf. H. Schillebeeckx (*op. cit.*, 125): 'we give the name of Tradition precisely to *the way and manner* in which Scripture and revelation are heard ever anew by man, the maker of history.' T. W. Guzie proposes a definition of the word 'tradition' formulated in the light of patristic hermeneutics: 'Tradition is *continuity with the intentions of the biblical writers*. This formulation of the concept "tradition" has a number of advantages. First, it recognises the Scriptures as normative writings and avoids any suggestion that tradition involves a deposit of revealed truth separate from Scripture. Second, it leaves room for the critical study needed for the intention of the biblical writers to be uncovered, and allows for the fact that the literal meaning intended by these writers can be spiritual as well as historical. Third, it recognises that the Scriptures contain the only formulation of the mystery of Christ which is finally normative; but it also allows for a development in the Church's understanding of the mystery.'—'Patristic Hermeneutics and the Meaning of Tradition', *Theological Studies* 32 (1971), 653.

[64]K.-H. Weger, *Sacramentum Mundi* VI, 269-74.

[65]See *Dei Verbum*, art. 8.

[66]Weger, *op. cit.*, 272.

[67]*Ibid.*, 271. 'Since the believing mind of the later Church, and therefore "Tradition", is always bound as regards its content to the preaching (tradition) of the apostolic age, of which Scripture contains at least the substance, and since it is not possible at least for us to prove with certainty that explicit matters of faith (apart from the scope of the. canon) were held in apostolic times which have not been recorded in Scripture, Scripture alone remains for all practical purposes the sole material source of the faith drawn upon by later Tradition.' K. Rahner and H. Vorgrimler, *Concise Theological Dictionary*, London 1965, 463f.

[68]K. Rahner, *Theological Investigations* VI, 93.

[69]*Ibid.*, 93.

[70]J. Ratzinger, in H. Vorgrimler (ed.), *Commentary on the Documents of Vatican II*, Vol. 3, Dogmatic Constitution on Divine Revelation, London 1969, 268f.

[71]*Ibid.*, 46f.

[72]Compare, *mutatis mutandis,* the parallel statement of a Presbyterian scholar: 'A confessional view of Scripture, rather than a doctrinal, is the only theological stance in which its authority

can be discerned. The Church has never meant that revelation simply means Scripture. It is rather a Scripture which becomes our history, read in a community in which men listen for the Word of God when it is read. Its truth is truth-for-us, or saving truth, heard by a community exhibiting a common trust in the Spirit, the Spirit of Truth, which alone can confirm it.' G. Ernest Wright, *The Old Testament and Theology*, New York 1969, 184.

[73] L. Walsh, *op. cit.*, 122f.

[74] *Optatam Totius*, art. 16.

[75] See A. Grillmeier, in B. D. Dupuy, *La Révèlation Divine*, Tome II. Constitution dogmatique 'Dei Verbum', Paris 1968, 453-6; L. Walsh, *op. cit.*, 114-25.

[76] K. Rahner, *Sacramentum Mundi* I, 177.

[77] Cf. *Optatam totius*, 16.

[78] K. Rahner, *op. cit.*, 177.